Floriography Today

The Symbolic Meanings & The Possible Powers
of
Trees, Plants and Flowers

ISBN-13: 978-1479216550

ISBN-10: 1479216550

Floriography Today

The Symbolic Meanings & The Possible Powers
of
Trees, Plants and Flowers

S. Theresa Dietz

FAYSHONESHIRE
2012

Flora
by
Louise Abbéma
1853 — 1927

Dedication

To: God

To: The Fairies

To: My dear friend, Robert

To: My grandsons, Dakota & Noah

To: My daughter, Melanie and son-in-law, Jason

To: My sister and brothers, Sharon, Steve and Scott

To: My Dad, who loved zinnias and my Mom, who loved pansies

To: My nephews and nieces, Nick, Nolan, Kyler, Ashlee and Courtney

To: All the interesting interested people in the world who are all naturally curious about all things mystical, and who truly love trees, plants and flowers...just like me.

I wish Peace & Love to you and yours, forever and ever.

Table of Contents

Acknowledgments

For nearly a decade prior to starting this project, I was persistently coaxed to begin it by my friend, Robert, who shares my interest in this subject. It was he who offered constant encouragement for me to stay on task during the grinding years of tedious research that was required. And it was he who produced the completely unexpected surprise of the most beautiful roses I have ever seen; with them arriving with great fanfare as if sent from a fantastic grand reoccurring dream of colored lights and beautiful music. Again, I say "Thank you."

Introduction

The Symbolic Meanings for *Filipendula ulmaria* are both *usefulness* and *uselessness*!

It is because of diametrically conflicting meanings such as those noted above that this project commenced. I had been wondering about how many convoluted messages derailed potential Victorian romances that never made it past the tussie-mussie's fractured translation. How many long ago lovers broke up over poorly decoded posies?

Flowers have power. To one recipient, a particular nosegay might send her over the moon with joy. The exact same nosegay in the hands of another recipient might bring her to tears. This would be because of misinterpretations between the floriography books of that time. I find that confusion to be quite sad. And, as it turned out, a fairly common occurrence back in those days. Personal flowers were sent as a go-between. The flowers' decoding manuals were mangling the sensitivity of the intimate floral messages. When sending complex, or even simple, floral messages it was vital for both the sender and the recipient to possess the same book. However, that was not often the case.

It genuinely bothered me that trees, plants, and flowers...which I so dearly love...would be the vehicle for sending messages that might have ended a relationship; or may have given false hope to someone in an otherwise genuinely hopeless situation. I turned to the internet seeking wisdom and knowledge. What I discovered *there* were endless web sites of copy/pasted information that was just repeatedly compounding the problem of miscommunication. There were even flowers listed in a great many of the lists that were extinct, had botanical name changes ages ago, were mythological, and even a few that were completely fictional.

As my exasperation with the confusing language of flowers grew I became increasing curious as to what the truth might actually be. I began by making a short list, that incessantly grew longer. This made for extensive deepening research until four years later, a consolidation of the available data on the subject of *Floriograpy* had been exhausted, clarified and, to the best of my ability, brought up-to-date. This massive endeavor resulted in over 900 plants with over 7,600 plant names, with over 2,000 symbolic meanings, and with over 600 possible powers. In the years it took to accomplish this feat, I came to realize...with absolute certainty...that *the very best way* to send *any* type of message with flowers is to kindly include your intent in your message. Write it down in your note or speak it to the recipient. The symbolic meanings are too often quite extensive and quite often conflicting and therefore prone to gross misinterpretation, misunderstanding, and overall confusion.

However, magical thinking is at it's most potent when there are as many relative elements included to empower any magical effort. So, for something as meaningful as a bridal bouquet, flowers that resonate with the bride, herself, would make the bouquet even more meaningful...not just beautiful. The same would be for any event. If you want powerful flowers, choose flowers relative to the exact power or powers that you seek.

I have not indicated what part or parts of the plant are toxic, nor when they are toxic or if their toxicity is eliminated with ripening, etcetera. *Please be acutely aware that some plants are so extremely poisonous that simply touching them or breathing in smoke where they may be burning can be fatal.* I have in no way, whatsoever, suggested anywhere in this book that any plant represented should be ingested, inhaled, or put on the skin. Please do take the time to do further research of your own with regard to what you are going to touch before you dare to touch it. The internet is a wonderful source for that kind of scientific information. Please do be aware (and wary) that plants that have any toxic element whatsoever have this symbol beside the scientific name listed:

Be informed, stay safe, feel free to tap into the innate powers of trees, plants and flowers, always let the recipients of your floral gifts know what significant thoughts and feelings are in your heart...and please, whatever you do and whenever you do it: *do not* even dare to vex the fairies.

HOW TO USE THIS EASY-TO-READ CROSS-REFERENCED BOOK:

000 << this cross-reference number is used when searching *from* any index
Primary Scientific name is italicized ☠ << Toxicity symbol
| *Other Known Scientific Names* | *Common Names* |
★ **SYMBOLIC MEANINGS:**
I love you; Come to me; I am shy; My heart is aching for you; etc.; etc.;
★ **POTENTIAL POWERS:**
Love; Healing; Protection; etc.; etc.;
★ **FOLKLORE AND FACTS:**
Tidbits of factual or fictional information when applicable.
⊚ **SPECIFIC COLOR MEANING > When applicable for a particular color:**
I love you; Come to me; I am shy; My heart is aching for you; etc.; etc.;
▶ *Spray, Seed, Branch, etc,:*
I love you; Come to me; I am shy; My heart is aching for you; etc.; etc.;

The Flowers

All the names I know from nurse:
Gardener's garters, Shepherd's purse,
Bachelor's buttons, Lady's smock,
And the Lady Hollyhock.

Fairy places, fairy things,
Fairy woods where the wild bee wings,
Tiny trees for tiny dames —
These must all be fairy names!

Tiny woods below whose boughs
Shady fairies weave a house;
Tiny tree-tops, rose or thyme,
Where the braver fairies climb!

Fair are grown-up people's trees,
But the fairest woods are these;
Where, if I were not so tall,
I should live for good and all.

Robert Louis Stevenson
1850 – 1894

Speak My Language

Peace rose to me sure not to fail to soothe the arguments we fret;

Myrtle to me when you think of where we were when we first met;

Violets picked when seen first Spring to vow you wished for us True Love;

For my pocket you have plucked the highest almond reached above;

Affection for me shown by
When you hand to me a perfect pear;

In peace you'd give an olive sprig
For me to tuck into my hair;

Angelica to grow nearby
For broad protection that I need;

Your faith in us,
Most precious thing,
Immense...
....proved with one mustard seed.

S.Theresa Dietz

inspire me

001
Abies

| Fir | Fir Tree |

★ SYMBOLIC MEANINGS:
Elevation; Friendship; Height; Honesty; Longevity; Manifestation; Perceptiveness; Progress; Remembrance; Resilience; Time;

002
Abutilon

| *Abortopetalum* | Abu Tilon | Chinese Bell Flower | Chinese Lantern Mallow | Flowering Maple | Indian Mallow |

★ SYMBOLIC MEANINGS:
Meditation; Enlightenment;

003
Acacia

| Mimosa | Thorn Tree | Thorntree | Umbrella Acacia | Umbrella Acacia | Wattle | Whistling Thorn | Yellow Acacia | Yellow-Fever Acacia |

★ SYMBOLIC MEANINGS:
Chaste love; Concealed love; Elegance; Endurance of the soul; Friendship; Immortality; Platonic love; Purity; Resurrection; Secret love; Sensitiveness;

★ POTENTIAL POWERS:
Abundance; Advancement; Banishing; Conscious will; Divination; Energy; Exorcism; Friendship; Growth; Healing; Joy; Leadership; Life; Light; Love; Money; Natural power; Prophetic dreams; Protection; Purification; Repel demons; Repel ghosts; Success;

★ FOLKLORE AND FACTS:
Legend tells that the *Acacia* tree could have been the "burning bush" that Moses encountered in Exodus 3:2 of The Holy Bible.

004
Acacia senegal

| Arabic Gum | Cape Gum | Egyptian Thorn | Gum Arabic Tree | Gum Arcacia

| Gum Senegal Tree | Hashab Gum | Mgunga | Mokala | Kikwata | Mkwatia | Rfaudraksh |

★ **SYMBOLIC MEANINGS:**
Platonic love;

★ **POTENTIAL POWERS:**
Money; Platonic love; Protection; Psychic Powers; Purify evil; Purify negativity; Purification; Spirituality; Wards off evil;

★ **FOLKLORE AND FACTS:**
A sprig of *Acacia senegal* over a bed on a hat will supposedly ward off evil. • *Acacia senegal* will purify an area of evil and negativity.

005
Acanthus mollis

| Bear's Breach | Bear's Breeches | Oyster Plant |

★ **SYMBOLIC MEANINGS:**
Art; Artifice; Fine Arts; Misery; The Arts;

★ **FOLKLORE AND FACTS:**
Acanthus mollis leaves are reasonably believed to be the artistic inspiration for the elaborate leafy carvings used on the capitals of Corinthian columns which are liberally present in Greco-Roman architecture.

006
Acer

| Maple | Maple Tree |

★ **SYMBOLIC MEANINGS:**
Reserve;

★ **POTENTIAL POWERS:**
Longevity; Love; Money;

007
Achillea filipendulina

| Cloth-Of-Gold | Cloth of Gold Yarrow | Fernleaf Yarrow |

★ **POTENTIAL POWERS:**
Animal communications;

008
Achillea millefolium

| *Achillea* | Achi Uea | Arrowroot | Bad Man's Plaything | Carpenter's Weed | Common Yarrow | Death Flower | Devil's Nettle | Eerie | Field Hops | Gearwe | Gordaldo | Hundred Leaved Grass | Knight's Milfoil | Knight's Milefoil | Knyghten | Milefolium | Milfoil | Millefoil | Militaris | Military Herb | Millefolium | Noble Yarrow | Nosebleed | Nosebleed Plant | Old Man's Mustard | Old Man's Pepper | Plumajillo | Sanguinary | Seven Year's Love | Snake's Grass | Soldier | Soldier's Woundwort | Stanch Griss | Stanch Weed | Staunch Weed | Tansy | Thousand Leaf | Thousand Seal | Wound Wort | Woundwort | Yarrow | Yarroway | Yerw |

★ **SYMBOLIC MEANINGS:**
Courage; Healing; Heartache; Love; Psychic powers; War;

★ **POTENTIAL POWERS:**
Attraction; Beauty; Courage; Cure for heartache; Exorcism; Friendship; Gifts; Harmony; Healing; Health; Joy; Love; Love; Pleasure; Protection; Psychic powers; Sensuality; The Arts;

★ **FOLKLORE AND FACTS:**
In traditional Yi Jing (I Ching), dried *Achillea millefolium* stalks are tossed to create the shape that is used to divine the future. • It was also thought that if *Achillea millefolium* were once used in a wedding decoration and it was then hung over a marriage bed, seven years of true love would be insured. • Wear *Achillea millefolium* for courage and protection. • Carry *Achillea millefolium* to attract friends. • *Achillea millefolium* is used to banish evil from any place, any thing, and anybody.

009
Achimenes

| *Achimenes cupreata* | Cupid's Bower | Hot Water Plant | Magic Flowers | Widow's Tears |

★ **SYMBOLIC MEANINGS:**
Such worth is rare;

010
Aconitum napellus ☠

| Aconite | Bear's Foot | Common Monkshood | Cupid's Car | English Monkshood | Friar's Cap | Fuzi | Hecates | Helmet Flower | Leopard's Bane | Monkshood | Monk's Blood | Official Aconite | Soldier's Cap | Storm Hat | Thor's Hat | Witch Flower | Wolfsbane | Wolf's Bane | Wolf's Hat |

15

★**SYMBOLIC MEANINGS:**
A deadly foe is near; A foe is near; Beware; Chivalry; Danger is near; Deceit; Fraternal love; Gallantry; Knight; Knight-errantry; Misanthropy; Poisonous words; Temperance; Treachery;

★**POTENTIAL POWERS:**
Balance; Cure for werewolves; Invisibility; Neutralization; Protection from vampires; Protection from werewolves;

★**FOLKLORE AND FACTS:**
Near the end of the ancient Roman period of European history *Aconitum napellus* was banned. Anyone discovered to be growing it could have been legally sentenced to death. • In Medieval times, *Aconitum napellus* was associated with witches. • For healing, string *Aconitum napellus* seeds like beads and wear them around the neck or wrist. • Carry *Aconitum napellus* seeds in a dried lizard's skin to become invisible whenever you want to.

011
Acorus calamus ☠

| Bajai | Bhutanashini | Calamus | Gladdon | Gora-bac | Jatil | Haimavati | Lubigan | Myrtle Flag | Myrtle Grass | Myrtle Sedge | Sweet Cane | Sweet Flag | Sweet Grass | Sweet Root | Sweet Rush | Sweet Sedge | Vacha | Vadaja | Vasa | Vasa Bach | Vashambu | Vayambu | Vekhand |

★**SYMBOLIC MEANINGS:**
Affection; Aflutter; Aphrodisiac; Delusion; Fitness; Lamentation; Love; Lust;

★**POTENTIAL POWERS:**
Emotions; Fertility; Generation; Healing; Inspiration; Intuition; Love; Luck; Lust; Money; Protection; Psychic ability; Sea; Subconscious mind; Tides; Travel by water;

★**FOLKLORE AND FACTS:**
Acorus calamus was a favorite plant of Henry David Thoreau. • Walt Whitman, wrote a section of poems inspired by *Acorus calamus* that were devoted to affection, love and lust as an addendum to the third printing of *Leaves Of Grass*, titled "Calamus". • *Acorus calamus* seeds can be strung on thread as beads and worn for healing purposes. • Place a small piece of *Acorus calamus* in each corner of the kitchen to guard against poverty and hunger.

012
Actaea racemosa ☠

| *Actaea* | Black Bugbane | Black Cohosh | Black Snakeroot | Bugbane | *Cimicifuga racemosa* | Fairy Candle | Squaw Root |

★POTENTIAL POWERS:
Courage; Love; Lust; Money; Potency; Protection;

★FOLKLORE AND FACTS:
Sprinkle *Actaea racemosa* around the perimeter of your house or on door thresholds to protect your home against evil entering into it. • In the case of impotency, make a pouch of *Actaea racemosa* and carry it on you. • In the case of meekness, make a pouch of *Actaea racemosa* and carry it on you for strength.

013
Adenium obesum ☠

| *Adenium* | *Adenium coetaneum* | *Adenium honghel* | **Desert-Rose** | **Kudu** | *Nerium obesum* | **Sabi Star** |

★SYMBOLIC MEANINGS:
Death; Delusion; Fictional; Illusion;

014
Adiantum

| **Maidenhair Fern** |

★SYMBOLIC MEANINGS:
Discretion; Secrecy; Secret bond of love;

★POTENTIAL POWERS:
Beauty; Love;

★FOLKLORE AND FACTS:
The Druids believed *Adiantum* could provide invisibility.

015
Adonis

| *Adonis flos* | **Blooddrops** | **Blood Drops** | *Flos Adonis* | **Pheasant's Eye** | **Pheasant's-eye** |

★SYMBOLIC MEANINGS:
Painful recollections; Recollection of Life's Pleasure; Sad memories; Sorrowful recollections;

★FOLKLORE AND FACTS:
Legend tells that the goddess Venus cried so much for Adonis, who was suddenly killed by a wild boar while out hunting, that she was utterly inconsolable. The story is that wherever her fallen tears mingled with his blood, the *Adonis* plant is said to

have emerged as a symbol of her sorrowful remembrance of her love for him and the fragile transience of life.

016
Adoxa moschatellina

| *Adoxa* | **Five-Faced Bishop** | **Hollowroot** | **Moschatel** | **Muskroot** | **Townhall Clock** | **Tuberous Crowfoot** |

★**SYMBOLIC MEANINGS:**
Weakness;

017
Aesculus

| **Buckeye Tree** | **Red Chestnut** | **White Chestnut** |

★**POTENTIAL POWERS:**
Divination; Luck; Money; Prosperity; Wealth;

018
Aesculus hippocastanum ☠

| **Buckeye** | **Common Horse Chestnut** | **Conker Tree** |

★**SYMBOLIC MEANINGS:**
Luxury;

★**POTENTIAL POWERS:**
Healing; Money;

★**FOLKLORE AND FACTS:**
Aesculus hippocastanum seeds, or "conkers" as they are known, are believed to keep away moths and spiders if placed in household furniture.

019
Aethusa cynapium

| **Fool's Cicely** | **Fool's Parsley** | **Poison Parsley** |

★**SYMBOLIC MEANINGS:**
Foolishness; Gullibility; Silliness;

020
Aframomum melegueta

| African Pepper | Alligator Pepper | Grains of Paradise | Guinea Grains | Guinea Pepper | Melegueta Pepper |

★POTENTIAL POWERS:
Divination; Determining guilt; Love; Luck; Lust; Money; Wishes;

★FOLKLORE AND FACTS:
Aframomum melegueta wishes are made by holding some of the herb in your hands, make your wish, then toss a little in each of the four directions beginning with North and ending with West.

021
Agapanthus ☠

| African Lily | Blue African Lily | Lily of the Nile |

★SYMBOLIC MEANINGS:
Love; Love letters;

★POTENTIAL POWERS:
Love;

★FOLKLORE AND FACTS:
Woman of the Xhosa tribe make necklaces of dried *Agapanthus* roots to wear as fertility talismans and assure strong, healthy babies will be born to them. • *Agapanthus* is believed to offer protection against the fear of storms and thunder.

022
Agathosma

| Buchu | Boegoe | Bookoo | Bucoo | Bucco | Buku | Diosma |Sab | Pinkaou|

★POTENTIAL POWERS:
Psychic powers; Prophetic dreams;

023
Agave ☠

| Aloe | American Agave | American Aloe | American Century | Century Plant | False Aloe | Flowering Aloe | Maguey | Mexican Tree of Life and Abundance | Miracle of Nature | Rattlesnake-Master | Spiked Aloe | West Indian Dagger-log |

★SYMBOLIC MEANINGS:
Security;

★POTENTIAL POWERS:

19

Abundance; Healing; Lust;

024
Ageratum ☠

| Flossflower | Floss Flower | Whiteweed |

★SYMBOLIC MEANINGS:
Delay;

025
Agrimonia eupatoria

| *Agrimonia* | Church Steeples | Cocklebur | Common Agrimony | Garclive | Ntola | Odermenning | Philanthropos | Sticklewort | Stickwort | Umakhuthula |

★SYMBOLIC MEANINGS:
Gratitude; Thankfulness;

★POTENTIAL POWERS:
Banish negative energy; Banish entities; Barrier against negative energies; Breaks hexes; Enhances psychic healing; Protection; Protection against evil; Protection against goblins; Protection against poison; Protection against psychic attack; Reverse spells; Sends spells back to the hexer; Sleep; Wards off witchcraft;

★FOLKLORE AND FACTS:
It is believed that if *Agrimonia eupatoria* is placed under the head a sleeper, it must removed for the sleeper to fully awaken. • It was believed that scattering *Agrimonia eupatoria* seeds would fend off witchcraft; or if they were scattered around the perimeter of one's home, carried in one's pockets or in a pouch around the neck or waist. • *Agrimonia eupatoria* is believed to determine if a witch is present or nearby. • *Agrimonia eupatoria* is believed to be able to offer protection against evil, poison, and goblins as well as banish negative energies and negative spirits.

026
Agrostemma githago ☠

| Common Corn Cockle | Common Corncockle | Corn Cockle | Corncockle | Old-Maid's-Pink |

★SYMBOLIC MEANINGS:
Gentility;

★FOLKLORE AND FACTS:
Poisonous *Agrostemma githago* was once such a common deadly scourge in grains

fields that, in the Middle Ages it was once written *"What hurt it doth among Corne, the spoile of bread, as well as in colour, taste, and unwholesomenesse, is better knowne than desired."* Since then agricultural advances in seed sorting has made strides in keeping *Agrostemma githago* seeds out of all cereal crop seeds. Even so, regular attention to field monitoring is a conscious duty of grain farming.

❧━❧

027
Ajuga

| *Abiga* | **Bugle** | **Bugleweed** | *Bugula* | **Carpet Bugle** | *Chamaepitys* | **Ground Pine** |

★**SYMBOLIC MEANINGS:**
Cheers the heart; Lovable;

❧━❧

028
Alcea rosea

| **Common Hollyhock** | **Hollyhock** |

★**SYMBOLIC MEANINGS:**
Ambition; Ambition of a scholar; Fecundity; Fruitfulness; Liberality;

❧━❧

029
Alchemilla

| *Alchimilla* | **Bear's Foot** | **Dewcup** | **Dew-cup** | *Lachemilla* | **Lady's Mantle** | **Leontopodium** | **Lion's Foot** | **Nine Hooks** | **Stellaria** | *Zygalchemilla* |

★**POTENTIAL POWERS:**
Attract love; Femininity; Love;

★**FOLKLORE AND FACTS:**
In the Middle Ages, drops of dew that were on the *Alchemilla* leaves were collected as they were considered sacred. These dew drops were used in magical potions, giving the *Alchemilla* the name "Dew-cup". • *Alchemilla* is believed to have the ability to attract fairies. • A pillow containing *Alchemilla* or placing *Alchemilla* under a pillow supposedly promotes a good night's sleep. • In the Middle Ages it was seriously believed that *Alchemilla* could actually restore a girl's lost virginity.

❧━❧

030
Aletris farinosa ☠

| **Ague Grass** | **Ague Weed** | **Aletris** | **Aloeroot** | **Backache Root** | **Bettie Grass** |

21

Bitter Grass | Black Root | Blazing Star | Colic Root | Colicroot | Colicweed | Crow Corn | Devil's Bit | Mealy Starwort | Rheumatism Root | Star Root | Star-grass | Starwort | True Unicorn Root | Unicorn Plant | Unicorn Root |

★POTENTIAL POWERS:

Breaks hexes; Gain protection from good spirits; Keeps evil away; Protection; Reversing negative spells; Turns away evil; Reversing negative spells; Turns away evil;

★FOLKLORE AND FACTS:

Form crosses using *Aletris farinosa* roots and place them outside each entry to your house if evil is plaguing your home.• *Aletris farinosa* has been carried to fend off evil. • *Aletris farinosa* is a useful in uncrossing rituals and is believed to be an effective hex breaker.

031
Aleurites moluccana ☠

| *Aleurites javanicus* | *Aleurites pentaphyllus* | *Aleurites remyi* | *Aleurites trilobus* | Buah Keras | Candlenut | Candleberry | Indian Walnut | *Jatropha moluccana* | Kemiri | Kuki | Kukui Nut Tree | Nuez del la India | Varnish Tree |

★SYMBOLIC MEANINGS:

Enlightenment;

★POTENTIAL POWERS:

Enlightenment;

★FOLKLORE AND FACTS:

The ancient Hawaiians would open the *Aleurites moluccana*, skewer the oily nutmeats (which are smaller than walnuts) then set them afire. These primitive "candles" burned for close to 45 minutes. • Native Hawaiians may still use *Aleurites moluccana* oil for lighting stone lamps. • All parts of the *Aleurites moluccana* Tree have been deemed very useful in the day to day life of all Polynesian people. • The polished nuts (unpainted or painted), then strung as a beautiful lei is a highly prized necklace.

032
Allamanda ☠

| Buttercup Flower | Golden Allamanda | Golden Cup | Golden Trumpet | Yellow Allamanda | Yellow Bell | Yellow Trumpet Vine |

★SYMBOLIC MEANINGS:

Heavenly chief;

033
Allium

★**SYMBOLIC MEANINGS:**
Strength; You're elegant; You're perfect; You're perfect and elegant;

034
Allium ampeloprasum

| Ail à Grosse Tête Alho Porro | Alho Bravo | Alho Inglês | *Allium porrum* | Broadleaf | Cebolla Puerro | Elephant Garlic | Great-headed Garlic | Iraakuuccittam | Kurrat | Pearl Onion | Petit Poireau Antillais Poireau | Perpétuel | Poireau | Leek | Wild Leek |

★**POTENTIAL POWERS:**
Exorcism; Love; Protection;

035
Allium cepa

| Bulb Onion | Common Onion | Oingnum | Onion | Onyoun | Unyoun | Yn-Leac |

★**POTENTIAL POWERS:**
Exorcism; Healing; Lust; Money; Prophetic Dreams; Protection; Purification; Spiritual Cleansing; Spirituality;

★**FOLKLORE AND FACTS:**
The ancient Egyptians worshipped *Allium cepa* as the round shape, the layers, and the concentric rings when sliced symbolized eternal life and were included in burials. • In the Middle Ages *Allium cepa* was so valuable that people gave them as gifts and could even pay their rents with them. • *Allium cepa* is commonly used as an antidote for psychic attack or for sensing and then removing negative energy in the house. This is done by cutting one into quarters and placing the pieces where negativity seems evident, which is most often in the sleeping areas. Remove the *Allium cepa* quarters twelve hours later by taking the pieces all the way out of the house to throw them away. Use fresh *Allium cepa* every night. • Early American settlers would hang strings of *Allium cepa* over the doors to protect the inhabitants of the home from infections. • A interesting divination when you have a decision to make is using *Allium cepa* to make the decision for you. Using a separate *Allium cepa* for each option, carve a possibility on each one. Put them all into a dark place, checking them one time each day. The first one that sprouts will provide the answer.

036
Allium oschaninii

| *Allium ascalonicum* | Eschalot | French Gray Shallot | Griselle | Shallot |
True Shallot |

★ **POTENTIAL POWERS:**
Purification;

037
Allium sativum

| Ajo | Artichoke Garlic | Creole Garlic | Crow Garlic | Field Garlic | Garlic |
Hard Necked Garlic | Meadow Garlic | *Ophioscorodon* | Porcelain Garlic | Purple Stripe Garlic | Rocambole Garlic | *Sativum* | Silverskin Garlic | Soft Necked
Garlic | Wild Garlic | Wild Onion |

★ **SYMBOLIC MEANINGS:**
Courage; Get well; Strength;

★ **POTENTIAL POWERS:**
Anti-theft; Aphrodisiac; Exorcism; Healing; Lust; Protection; Protection against evil spirits; Protection against vampires; Protection against werewolves; Unrequited love; Wards off evil; Wards off illness; Wards off The Evil Eye; Wards off vampires; Wards off werewolves;

★ **FOLKLORE AND FACTS:**
The earliest Sanskrit writings and also the Shih Ching (The Book of Songs), written by Confucius, mention *Allium sativum*. • A superstitious matador will wear a clove of *Allium sativum*on on a string around his neck as protection prior to a bullfight. • To dream of *Allium sativum* is good fortune. • To dream of giving away *Allium sativum* is bad luck. • *Allium sativum* wreaths outside a house's door is to ward off witches and psychic vampires. • A clove of *Allium sativum* worn on a string around the neck protects a traveler. • *Allium sativum* supposedly grew during a waning moon. • Sailors should carry *Allium sativum* on board to protect the against shipwreck.

038
Allium schoenoprasum

| Chives | Civet | Rush Leek | Sweth |

★ **SYMBOLIC MEANINGS:**
Usefulness; Why are you crying?

★ **POTENTIAL POWERS:**
Healing; Promotes psychic powers; Protection from evil; Protection from negativity;

★**FOLKLORE AND FACTS:**
At one time, bunches of *Allium schoenoprasum* were hung in homes to repel evil spirits. • Early American Dutch settlers deliberately planted *Allium schoenoprasum* in the fields used for grazing their cattle so they could enjoy milk naturally flavored with the distinctive taste.

039
Allium tuberosum

| Chinese Chives | Chinese Leek | Garlic Chives | Jeongguji | Jiu Cai | Ku Chai | Nira | Oriental Garlic Chives | Sol |

★**SYMBOLIC MEANINGS:**
Courage; Strength;

★**POTENTIAL POWERS:**
Prophetic dreams; Protection; Psychic powers;

040
Alnus

| Alder |

★**SYMBOLIC MEANINGS:**
Giving; Nurturing;

★**FOLKLORE AND FACTS:**
Appreciated for its bright tone, *Alnus* wood has been used for the bodies of Fender Stratocaster and Telecaster electric guitars since the 1950's.

041
Aloe vera

| *Aloe* | *Aloe barbadensis* | Barbados | Barbados Aloe | Burn Plant | Crocodile's Tail | Crocodile's Tongue | Curacao Aloe | First-aid Plant | Gheekvar | Ghiu Kumari | Ghrtakumari | Guar Patha | GwarPatha | Immortality Plant | Ka-traazhai | Kattar vazha | Korphad | Kumari | Lidah Buaya | Lidah Buaya | Lily of The Desert | Lu hui | Medicinal Aloe | Medicine Plant | Miracle Plant | Plant of Immortality | Quargandal | Quinine Leaf | Sabila | Saqal | Savia | Savila | Single Bible | True Aloe | Zabila |

★**SYMBOLIC MEANINGS:**
Bitterness; Dejection; Grief; Integrity; Luck; Most effective healer; Religious superstition; Sorrow; Superstition; Small talk; Wisdom;

★**POTENTIAL POWERS:**

Brings good luck; Guards against evil influences; Healing; Luck; Prevents feelings of loneliness; Prevents household accidents; Protection; Repel evil; Security; Shelter from harm; Worldly success;

★**FOLKLORE AND FACTS:**

Aloe vera has been planted on graves to help promote pre-reincarnation peacefulness. • Drawings of *Aloe vera* have been discovered on the walls of the tombs of Egyptian Pharaohs. • There are ongoing studies into the extensive benefits of the *Aloe vera* plant. • Growing *Aloe vera* as a houseplant will protect against household accidents and evil. • *Aloe vera* hung over doors and windows will both keep out evil and bring in luck.

042
Alopecurus pratensis

| *Alopecurus* | **Foxtail Grass** |

★**SYMBOLIC MEANINGS:**

Fun; Sport; Sporting;

043
Aloysia citrodora

| *Aloysia citriodora* | **Cedron** | **Hierba Luisa** | **Lemon Beebrush** | **Lemon Verbena** | *Lippia citriodora* | *Lippia triphylla* | **Louisa** | **Louiza** | *Verbena citriodora* | *Verbena triphylla* | **Yerba Luisa** |

★**SYMBOLIC MEANINGS:**

Attraction; Attracts the opposite sex; Love; Sexual attraction; Sexual attractiveness;

★**SYMBOLIC POWERS:**

Arts; Attraction; Beauty; Friendship; Gifts; Harmony; Joy; Love; Love; Pleasure; Protection; Purification; Sensuality; The Arts;

★**FOLKLORE AND FACTS:**

Aloysia citrodora can be added to your bath water to purify yourself of negative energies.

044
Alpinia

| **Ginger** |

★**SYMBOLIC MEANINGS:**

Comforting; Diversity; Pleasant; Safe; Strength; Unlimited wealth; Warming; Wealth;

★POTENTIAL POWERS:
Abundance; Accidents; Advancement; Aggression; Anger; Carnal desires; Conflict; Conscious will; Energy; Friendship; Growth; Healing; Joy; Leadership; Life; Light; Love; Lust; Machinery; Money; Natural power; Power; Rock music; Strength; Struggle; Success; War;

045
Alpinia galanga

| Blue Ginger | Chewing John | China Root | Chittarattai | Colic Root | Court Case Root | East India Catarrh Root | Galangal | Galingal | Galingale | Galanga | Galanga Root | Gargaut | India Root | Kaempferia Galanga | Kha | Laos | Langkwas | *Languas galanga* | Little John To Chew | Low John The Conqueror | *Maranta galanaga* | Rhizoma Galangae | Thai galangal | Thai Ginger |

★POTENTIAL POWERS:
Break hexes; Health; Legal matters; Lust; Protection; Psychic powers;

★FOLKLORE AND FACTS:
Carry or wear *Alpinia galanga* to foster your psychic abilities. • Carry or wear *Alpinia galanga* to pull in good luck to you. • Put *Alpinia galanga* into a leather pouch with silver coins to bring money. • To promote lust sprinkle *Alpinia galanga* around the home.

046
Alstroemeria

| Inca Lily | Lily of the Incas | Peruvian Lily | Peruvian Princess | Petite Alstroemeria | Ulster Mary |

★SYMBOLIC MEANINGS:
Powerful bond;

★POTENTIAL POWERS:
Fortune; Longevity; Powerful bond with another; Prosperity; Wealth;

047
Althaea officinalis

| *Althaea* | Althea | Common Marshmallow | Heemst | Marshmallow | Marsh Mallow | Marshmellow | Mortification Root | Slaz | Sweet Weed | Wymote |

★SYMBOLIC MEANINGS:
Dying for love; Unmarried;

★POTENTIAL POWERS:

Applying knowledge; Astral plane; Attract Good spirits; Beneficence; Controlling lower principles; Finding lost objects; Overcoming evil; Persuasion; Protection; Psychic powers; Regeneration; Removing depression; Sensuality; Uncovering secrets; Victory;

★**FOLKLORE AND FACTS:**
Carry *Althaea officinalis* as a sachet to stimulate psychic power. • *Althaea officinalis* is believed that it will draw in good spirits.• A vase of *Althaea officinalis* in the window will attract a lover who is straying.

048
Alyssum

|Alison | *Aurinia saxatilis*| *Lobularia maritima*| Sweet Alyssum|

★**SYMBOLIC MEANINGS:**
Worth beyond beauty;

★**POTENTIAL POWERS:**
Calm anger; Moderating anger; Protection;

★**FOLKLORE AND FACTS:**
Alyssum will expel negative charms if worn as an amulet. • *Alyssum* can calm an angry person if it is placed in their hand or on their body. • When *Alyssum* is hung in the house it supposedly can protect those in it against magically imposed illusions and fascinations.

049
Alyxia oliviformis

|*Alyxia stellata* | *Gynopogon stellata* | Maile | Maile Vine |

★**SYMBOLIC MEANINGS:**
Fragrance of Love;

★**POTENTIAL POWERS:**
Binding; Celebration; Healing; Love; Protection;

★**FOLKLORE AND FACTS:**
In ancient Hawaii the only marriage tradition that existed (and continues as one of many new traditions practiced) is for the bride and groom to be brought in front of the Kahuna, who would wrap their joined hands with interlocking leis made of fragrant *Alyxia oliviformis* vines. • It is tradition in Hawaii for the groom and his groomsmen to wear *Alyxia oliviformis* leis. • In Hawaii a lei made of *Alyxia oliviformis* is suitable for all special occasions.

050
Amaranthus

| Amarant | Amaranth | Flower Gentle | Flower Velour | Huautli | Kiwicha | Lady Bleeding | Pilewort | Prince's Feather | Prince's Feathers | Red Cock's Comb | Spleen Amaranth | Velour Flower | Velvet Flower |

★ **SYMBOLIC MEANINGS:**
Endless love; Fidelity; Immortality; Never fading flower; Un-withering;

★ **POTENTIAL POWERS:**
Guards against evil; Healing; Immortality; Invisibility; Protection; Protection against cooking burns; Protection against household accidents;

★ **FOLKLORE AND FACTS:**
If someone were to wear a garland or wreath of this plant, it would facilitate invisibility for the wearer. • Ancient Greeks believed so intensely in the *Amaranthus* being a strong symbol of Immortality, they would commonly spread the *Amaranthus* flowers over graves. • Carry dried *Amaranthus* flowers to heal a broken heart.

051
Amaranthus caudatus

| Foxtail Amaranth | Love Lies A'bleeding | Love Lies Bleeding | Love-lies-a'bleeding | Love-lies-bleeding | Pendant Amaranth | Quilete | Tassel Flower | Velvet Flower |

★ **SYMBOLIC MEANINGS:**
Desertion; Hopeless; Hopelessness; Hopeless not heartless;

★ **POTENTIAL POWERS:**
Magical attack; Magical protection;

052
Amaranthus hypochondriacus

| Blero | Floramon | Flower of Immortality | Huauhtli | Love-Lies Bleeding | Prince-of-Wales-Feather | Prince's Feather | Princess Feather | Red Cockscomb | Quelite | Quintonil | Velvet Flower |

★ **SYMBOLIC MEANINGS:**
In waiting; Love;

★ **POTENTIAL POWERS:**
Healing; Invisibility; Protection;

★ **FOLKLORE AND FACTS:**
Amaranthus hypochondriacus was once outlawed in Mexico by the colonial Spanish

because it was used in Aztec rituals. • A circlet of *Amaranthus hypochondriacus* flowers worn on top of the head is believed to accelerate healing. • *Amaranthus hypochondriacus* is believed to be able to cure a broken heart. • Wearing a *Amaranthus hypochondriacus* wreath will supposedly give the wearer the power of invisibility.

❧

053
Amaryllis ☠

| Amarillo | Amaryllis belladona | Belladonna Lily | Dutch Amaryllis | Naked Lady | Oxblood Lily | South African Amaryllis |

★SYMBOLIC MEANINGS:
Artistic endeavors; Beautiful but timid; Horseman's star; Innocence; Pastoral poetry; Pride; Radiant beauty; Scholastic achievement; Shy; Shyness; Sparkling; Splendid beauty; Success won after a struggle; Timidity; True beauty; Writing;

★POTENTIAL POWERS:
Adventurousness; Enthusiasm; Passion;

❧

054
Ambrosia artemisiifolia

| Ragweed | Bitterweed | Bloodweed |

★SYMBOLIC MEANINGS:
Courage; Immortal; Love is reciprocated; Love returned; Mutual love; Your love is given back; Your love is reciprocated; Your love is returned to you;

★POTENTIAL POWERS:
Banish negative spirits; Courage;

❧

055
Amorphophallus titanum

| Bunga Bangkai | Cadavar Plant | Corpse Flower| Corpse Plant | Titan Arum |

★SYMBOLIC MEANINGS:
Decomposition;

★FOLKLORE AND FACTS:
Amorphophallus titanum roughly translated from Greek means "Giant Misshapen Penis". • *Amorphophallus titanum* Flower is the largest unbranched flower blossom in the world and will bloom only one day per year. • The corm of the *Amorphophallus titanum* flower weighs approximately 110 pounds. • The fragrance of the open *Amorphophallus titanum* blossom smells like rotting mammal meat.

056

Anacamptis papilionacea

| Butterfly Orchid |

★SYMBOLIC MEANINGS:
Domestic quiet; Gaiety;

057

Anacardium occidentale

| Acajú | *Anacardium curatellifolium* | Bibo Tree | Caju | Cashew Tree | Cashew Apple Tree | Cashew Nut Tree | Jambu Monyet | Kasui | Marañón Tree | Mbiba | Mente Tree | Mkanju |

★POTENTIAL POWERS:
Money; Prosperity;

058

Anagallis arvensis

| *Anagallis phoenicea* | Poorman's Barometer | Poor Man's Weather Glass | Red Chickweed | Red Pimpernel | Scarlet Pimpernel | Shepherd's Clock | Shepherd's Weather Glass |

★SYMBOLIC MEANINGS:
Appointment; Assignation; Change; Faithlessness; Rendezvous;

★POTENTIAL POWERS:
Health; Protection;

★FOLKLORE AND FACTS:
Anagallis arvensis only opens when the sun is shining.

059

Ananas comosus

| Abacaxi | Alanaasi | Anaasa | Ananá | Ananas | Anarosh | Annachi Pazham | Kaitha Chakka | Nanas | Nanasi | Nenas | Piña | Pineapple | Pine Apple | Sapuri-PaNasa |

★SYMBOLIC MEANINGS:
Chastity; Joy; Perfection; You are perfect;

★POTENTIAL POWERS:
Luck; Money;

▶ *Ananas comosus Flower:*
You are perfect;

060
Anastatica hierochuntica

| *Anastatica* | **Dinosaur Plant** | **Jericho Rose** | **Mary's Flower** | **Mary's Hand** | **Palestinian Tumbleweed** | **Resurrection Plant** | **Rose of Jericho** | **Saint Mary's Flower** | **St. Mary's Flower** | **True Rose of Jericho** | **Wheel** |

★**POTENTIAL POWERS:**
Abundance; Peace; Power;

★**FOLKLORE AND FACTS:**
Anastatica hierochuntica is both a tumbleweed and a resurrection plant. The process of curling and uncurling is completely reversible and can be repeated many times.

061
Anchusa officinalis

| **Alkanet** | **Common Bugloss** |

★**SYMBOLIC MEANINGS:**
Falsehood;

★**POTENTIAL POWERS:**
Attract prosperity; Healing; Prosperity; Protection; Purification; Repel negativity;

★**FOLKLORE AND FACTS:**
Anchusa officinalis attracts all kinds of prosperity.

062
Anemone

| **Garden Anemone** |

★**SYMBOLIC MEANINGS:**
Abandonment; Abiding love; Anticipation; Being forsaken; Expectation; Estrangement; Every gardener's pride; Fading youth; Forsaken; Healing; Health; Illness; Love; Refusal; Sickness; Sincere; Sincerity; Suffering and death; Staunch love; Withered hopes;

★**POTENTIAL POWERS:**
Healing; Love; Protection; Protection against Sickness;

063

Anemone coronaria

| Anemone | Calanit | Calanit Metzouya | Crown Anemone | Dag Lalesi | Kalanit | Poppy Anemone | Shaqa'iq An-Nu'man | Spanish Marigold |

★SYMBOLIC MEANINGS:
Forsaken; Sickness; Immortal love; Withered hopes;

★POTENTIAL POWERS:
Healing; Health; Protection;

064

Anemone nemorosa ☠

| Smell Fox | Thimbleweed | Windflower | Wood Anemone |

★SYMBOLIC MEANINGS:
Abandonment; Desertion; Forsaken; Love; Sickness; Sincerity;

★POTENTIAL POWERS:
Healing; Health; Protection;

★FOLKLORE AND FACTS:
The *Anemone nemorosa* has a long history of superstition behind it. In ancient times the *Anemone nemorosa* was thought to be the cause of all forms of pestilence, bringing diseases so deadly that people would run through a field in bloom, holding their breaths, because they believed even the air around them would bring death. • The Chinese call the *Anemone nemorosa* "The Flower of Death". • The early Egyptians considered *Anemone nemorosa* to be an emblem of sickness. • Long ago, the English once believed that the first *Anemone nemorosa* that one would set eyes upon should be picked then wrapped in a piece of clean white silk then carried as an amulet against pestilence.

065

Anethum graveolens

| Aneton | *Anethum* | Buzzalchippet | Chathakuppa | Chebbit | Dill | Dill Weed | Dilly | Endro | Garden Dill | Hariz | Hulwa | Keper | Lao Cilantro | Laotian Coriander | Mirodjija | Phak Chee Lao | Phak See | Sada Kuppi | Sapsige Soppu | Sathakuppa | Savaa | Shevid | Soa | Sowa | Soya | Soya-kura |

★SYMBOLIC MEANINGS:
Good cheer; Luck;

★POTENTIAL POWERS:
Love; Lust; Money; Protection; Soothing; Survival; Wards off evil;

★FOLKLORE AND FACTS:

In the Middle Ages, *Anethum graveolens* was frequently used in magic spells and witchcraft . • Hanging *Anethum graveolens* at a door offers protections against harm and will keep out anyone who is envious of you or unpleasant in nature. • A sprig of *Anethum graveolens* tucked on the cradle is supposedly able to protect the child in it.

066
Angelica archangelica

| Amara Aromatica | Angel Plant | *Angelica* | *Angelica officinalis* | *Angelica officinalis himalaica* | Archangel | Archangelica | Arznei-engelwurz | Bellyache Root | Boska | Dead Nettle | European Wild Angelica | Fádnu | Garden Angelica | Goutweed | Grote engelwortel | Herb of The Angels | Herb of The Holy Ghost | High Angelica | Holy Ghost | Holy Ghost Root | Holy Herb | Hvonn | Hvönn | Kuanneq | Kvan | Kvanne | Kvanne | Masterwort | Norwegian Angelica | Purple Angelica | Purplestem Angelica | Rássi | Sonbol-e Khatayi | Väinönputki | Wild Angelica | Wild Celery |

★SYMBOLIC MEANINGS:
Inspiration; Inspire me; Symbol of Good Magic; Symbol of Poetic Inspiration;

★POTENTIAL POWERS:
Courage; Exorcism; Eliminates the effects of intoxication; Healing; Magic; Remove curses; Removes enchantments; Removes hexes; Removes lust; Renders witchcraft and The Evil Eye to be harmless; Protection; Strength; Visions; Wards off lightning strikes; Wards off disasters of all types; Wards off evil spirits;

★FOLKLORE AND FACTS:
Angelica archangelica is said to have protected entire villages during The Plague. • The fragrance of an angel is said to be exactly the same fragrance as that of *Angelica archangelica* leaves. • *Angelica archangelica* plants were planted at each of the four corners of a house or sprinkled as protection against all forms of wickedness and pestilence. • In a bath *Angelica archangelica* will supposedly remove any kind of spell, curse, hex or negativity that has been cast against the bather. • Gamblers have been known to carry *Angelica archangelica* in a pocket for protection against losing their money and luck at winning some.

067
Angraecum sesquipedale

| Angcm | *Angraecum* | Angrek | Christmas Orchid | Comet Orchid | Darwin's Orchid | King of the Angraecums | *Ornithogalum narbonense* | Star of Bethlehem | Star of Bethlehem Orchid |

★**SYMBOLIC MEANINGS:**

Atonement; Guidance; Hope; Idleness; Purity; Reconciliation; Royalty;

★**FOLKLORE AND FACTS:**

The unusually long spur (27- 43 cm) on the extraordinary star shaped flower of the *Angraecum sesquipdedale,* inspired Charles Darwin to predict (in an 1862 publication regarding his study of this flower) that the wild *Angraecum sesquipdedale* would *have to be* pollinated by an then unknown moth with an unprecedentedly long enough proboscis to reach the concentrated nectar at the end of the long spur. Darwin was ridiculed for his prediction. It was not until 21 years *after* Darwin's death, in 1903, that his prediction was finally verified when the very large moth in question was discovered in Madagascar . It was named *Xanthopan morganii praedicta,* and is more commonly known as a the Morgan's Sphinx Moth.

068
Anigozanthos

| Catspaw | Green Kangaroo Paw | Kangaroo Paw | Mangles' Kangaroo Paw |

★**SYMBOLIC MEANINGS:**

Unusual;

069
Anthemis nobilis

| Camomile | Camomyle | *Chamaemelum nobile* | Chamaimelon | Chamomile | English Chamomile | Garden Camomile | Ground Apple | Heermannchen | Lawn Chamomile | Low Chamomile | Manzanilla | Maythen | Perennial Chamomile | Roman Camomile | Roman Chamomile | Whig Plant | Wild Chamomile |

★**SYMBOLIC MEANINGS:**

All who know you will love you; Attracts wealth; Energy in Action; Energy in adversity; Energy in times of adversity; Initiative; Ingenuity; Love in adversity; Patience; Sleep; Sleepiness; Sleepy; Wisdom;

★**POTENTIAL POWERS:**

Abundance; Advancement; Calming; Conscious will; Energy; Friendship; Growth; Healing; Joy; Leadership; Life; Light; Love; Luck; Meditation; Money; Natural power; Purification; Sleep; Success; Tranquility;

★**FOLKLORE AND FACTS:**

Anthemis nobilis was considered as a "plant doctor" and planted near weaker plants to strengthen them. • Some gamblers wash their hands with a *Anthemis nobilis* infusion before gambling with hopes of increasing their chances of winning. • The same

Anthemis nobilis infusion can be used for bathing with hopes of increasing the chances of attracting love. • Sprinkling *Anthemis nobilis* infusion around the perimeter of one's property is believed to have the power to remove curses and spells cast upon the residents who live on that property.

070
Anthoxanthum odoratum

| *Anthoxanthum nitens* | **Bison Grass** | **Buffalo Grass** | *Hierochloe ororata* | **Holy Grass** | **Manna Grass** | **Mary's Grass** | **Seneca Grass** | **Sweetgrass** | **Sweet Grass** | **Sweet Vernal-Grass** | **Vanilla Grass** | **Vernal Grass** |

★**SYMBOLIC MEANINGS:**
Poor but happy;

★**POTENTIAL POWERS:**
Calling in good spirits; Meditation; Purification;

071
Anthriscus cerefolium

| **Chervil** | **French Parsley** | **Garden Chervil** | **Gourmet Parsley** | **Myrrhis** | **Salad Chervil** |

★**SYMBOLIC MEANINGS:**
Serenity; Sincerity;

★**FOLKLORE AND FACTS:**
It was the Romans who spread *Anthriscus cerefolium* by planting it close to all its camps across the entire Roman empire.

072
Antirrhinum

| **Calf's Snout** | **Dog's Mouth** | **Lion's Mouth** | **Toadflax** | **Toad's Mouth** | **Snapdragon** |

★**SYMBOLIC MEANINGS:**
Creativity; Deception; Force of will; Gracious lady; Indiscretion; Never; Presumption;

★**POTENTIAL POWERS:**
Break hexes; Clairaudience; Hex breaking; Protection; Protection against deceit; Protection against negativity; Protection against curses; Strength;

★**FOLKLORE AND FACTS:**

If you sense evil near you, step on or hold an *Antirrhihum* flower in your hand until you feel the evil pass by. • If someone has sent their negative energy to you or cursed you, place a vase of *Antirrhihum* flowers in front of a mirror and the negativity and curses will be sent back to the sender. • Wear *Antirrhihum* seed around your neck to protect yourself from being bewitched. • It was thought that if you hid an *Antirrhihum* on your person, you would appear to be gracious and quite fascinating. • Wear or carry any part of an *Antirrhihum* to protect yourself against deception.

073
Anthurium

| Boy Flower | Flamingo Flower | Heart of Hawaii | Painted Tongue |

★SYMBOLIC MEANINGS:
Abundance; Adoration; Happiness; Hospitality; Love; Lusty love; Romance; Sensuality; Sex; Sexuality;

★POTENTIAL POWERS:
Endurance;

074
Apium graveolens

| Aipo | *Apium* | Celeriac | Celery | Elma | Karafs | Marshwort |

★SYMBOLIC MEANINGS:
Banquet; Entertainment; Feast; Festivity; Lasting pleasures; Merriment; Rejoicing; Useful knowledge;

★POTENTIAL POWERS:
Aphrodisiac; Balance; Concentration; Lust; Male virility; Mental clarity; Mental powers; Psychic powers; Sleep;

★FOLKLORE AND FACTS:
The ancient Greeks regarded *Apium graveolens* with the same esteem as *Laurus nobilis* (Bay Laurel), using it in wreath making for the crowning of champion athletes.

075
Apocynum ☠

| Dogbane | Indian Hemp | Rheumatism Weld | Wild Ipecac |

★SYMBOLIC MEANINGS:
Deceit; Falsehood; Inspiration;

★POTENTIAL POWERS:

Assistance; Fertility; Harmony; Independence; Love; Material gain; Persistence; Stability; Strength; Tenacity;

076
Aptenia cordifolia

| Aptenia | Baby Sunrose | Crystal Ice Plant | Dew Plant | Heartleaf Ice Plant | Heart Leaf Ice Plant | Mesembryanthemum cordifolium |

★SYMBOLIC MEANINGS:
A serenade; Serenade;

077
Aquilaria malaccensis

| Agar | Agarwood | Lignum Aloes | Lolu | Mapou | Oodh | Wood Aloes |

★POTENTIAL POWERS:
Attracts good fortune; Attracts love; Love; Spirituality;

★FOLKLORE AND FACTS:
Aquilaria malaccensis attracts love if carried. • *Aquilaria malaccensis* has been used in magic for centuries to attract good fortune and bring love forward.

078
Aquilegia ☠

| Columbine | Lion's Herb |

★SYMBOLIC MEANINGS:
Courage; Cuckoldry; Deserted Love; Desertion; Folly; Foolishness; Love; Strength; Wisdom;

★POTENTIAL POWERS:
Courage; Love;

★FOLKLORE AND FACTS:
Aquilegia has been a symbol of Foolishness because the flower looks like a jester's cap with bells. • It is bad luck for the giver to give a *Aquilegia* flower to a woman. • *Aquilegia* is considered one of the most beautiful of all the wildflowers of the world. • Wear an *Aquilegia* flower for courage. • Put *Aquilegia* seeds in a small pouch and carry it to attract love.

◉ SPECIFIC COLOR MEANING > Purple:
Resolved to win;

◉ SPECIFIC COLOR MEANING > Red:

Anxious; Anxious and trembling; Trembling;

079
Araucaria heterophylla ☠

| *Araucaria excelsa* | Norfolk Island Pine |

★**POTENTIAL POWERS:**
Anti-hunger; Protection;

★**FOLKLORE AND FACTS:**
If grown near the home or as a potted houseplant within the home *Araucaria heterophylla* is believed to protect against evil spirits and hunger.

080
Arbutus

| **Madrona** | **Madrone** | **Madroño** | **Strawberry Tree** |

★**SYMBOLIC MEANINGS:**
Only love; Thee only do I love; True love; You are the only one I love;

★**POTENTIAL POWERS:**
Exorcism; Fidelity; Protection;

081
Arbutus unedo

| **Apple of Cain** | **Cane Apple** | **Irish Strawberry Tree** | **Killarney Strawberry Tree** | **Strawberry Tree** |

★**SYMBOLIC MEANINGS:**
Esteem and love; Esteemed love;

★**POTENTIAL POWERS:**
Exorcism; Protection;

★**FOLKLORE AND FACTS:**
There have been reported incidences of bears becoming intoxicated from eating fermented *Arbutus unedo* berries that had been left on or under the trees. • The ancient Romans used *Arbutus unedo* to protect small children by chasing off evil around them.

082
Arctotheca calendula

| Cape Dandelion | Cape Marigold | Cape Weed |

★ **SYMBOLIC MEANINGS:**
Omen; Presage; Sign;

083
Arecaceae

| Palm | Palmae | Palm Tree |

★ **SYMBOLIC MEANINGS:**
Fertility; Peace; Spiritual; The Tropics; Victory and Success; Vacations; Victorious;

★ **FOLKLORE AND FACTS:**
Arecaceae is the global iconic image that symbolizes the tropics and a get-away vacation.

084
Arctium lappa

| *Arctium* | Bardana| Beggar's Buttons | Bugloss | Burdock | Burrseed | Clotbur | Cockleburr | Edible Burdock | Great Burdock | Greater Burdock | Happy Major | Hardock | Hurrburr| Lappa Burdock | Niúbàng | Niúpángzi | Personata |

★ **SYMBOLIC MEANINGS:**
Boredom; Falsehood; Importunity; Touch me not;

★ **POTENTIAL POWERS:**
Healing; Protection;

★ **FOLKLORE AND FACTS:**
Velcro was inspired by a Burr.• *Arctium lappa* roots gathered during a waning moon, cut into short lengths, strung on a red thread then dried can be worn like a bead necklace as protection against negativity and evil. • Discreetly stick *Arctium lappa* burrs around the home to fend off negativity.

▸ *Arctium lappa* **Burr:**
Rudeness; You weary me;

085
Arctostaphylos uva-ursi ☠

| Arberry | Common Bearberry | Bearberry | Bear's Grape | Crowberry | Foxberry | Hog Cranberry | Kinnikinnick | Mealberry | Mountain Box | Mountain Cranberry | Mountain Tobacco | Pinemat manzanita | Red Bearberry | Sagack-

homi | Sandberry | Upland Cranberry | Uva Ursa | Uva-ursi |
★**POTENTIAL POWERS:**
Psychic powers; Psychic workings;

086
Arenaria verna

| Golden Moss | Irish Moss |
★**POTENTIAL POWERS:**
Luck; Money; Protection;

087
Argentina anserina

| Common Silverweed | *Potentilla anserina* **| Richette | Silverweed | Silver-weed Cinquefoil |**
★**SYMBOLIC MEANINGS:**
Simplicity; Naiveté;
★**POTENTIAL POWERS:**
Wards off evil spirits; Wards off witchcraft;
★**FOLKLORE AND FACTS:**
Argentina anserina was once put into shoes to absorb perspiration.

088
Arisaema dracontium

| Green Dragon | Dragon Root |
★**SYMBOLIC MEANINGS:**
Ardor;

089
Arisarum

★**SYMBOLIC MEANINGS:**
Ardor; Deceit; Ferocity;

090
Armeria

| Sea Pinks | Thrift |

★**SYMBOLIC MEANINGS:**

Sympathy; Sympathy for the fallen;

091

Armoracia rusticana

| Horseradish | *Cochlearia armoracia* **| Horseradish Root | Horse-Radish | Moolee | Western Wasabi |**

★**POTENTIAL POWERS:**

Exorcism; Purification;

★**FOLKLORE AND FACTS:**

Putting a piece of *Armoracia rusticana* in your purse or pocket during New Year's Eve supposedly promises a year of adequate funds. • In Greek mythology it is written that the Oracle of Delphi once told Apollo that *Armoracia rusticana* was worth it's weight in gold. • To clear all evil powers and dissipate negative spells cast upon your home sprinkle ground dried *Armoracia rusticana* around the home, on the entry steps into the home, on every windowsill, and in every corner.

092

Artemisia abrotanum

| Appleringie | Boy's Love | European Sage | Garden Sagebrush | Garderobe | Garde Robe | Lad's Love | Lemon Plant | Lover's Plant | Maid's Ruin | Old Man | Oldman Wormwood | Our Lord's Wood | Lad's Love | Siltherwood | Southernwood | Southern Wormwood |

★**SYMBOLIC MEANINGS:**

Absence; Aphrodisiac; Bantering; Constancy; Fidelity; Jest; Jesting; Lustful bed partner; Pain; Seduction;

★**POTENTIAL POWERS:**

Antidote for magic potions; Repel moths; Repel snakes; Exorcism; Love; Lust; Male virility; Protection; Purification; Seduction; Sex appeal; Ward off evil spirits;

★**FOLKLORE AND FACTS:**

Artemisia abrotanum is considered to be the most potent antidote for magic potions. • *Artemisia abrotanum* is supposedly used to keep snakes and thieves away. • One of the beliefs about *Artemisia abrotanum* is that it can cause impotence in men. • In Medieval times, a sprig of *Artemisia abrotanum* was very often included in bouquets presented by young men to girls as a secret mode of seducing them. • A sprig of *Artemisia abrotanum* placed under the bed is supposed to arouse lust

093
Artemisia absinthium ☠

| Absinthium | Absinthe | Absinthe Wormwood | Common Wormwood | Crown For A King | Grand Wormwood | Madderwort | Old Woman | Wormwode | Wermode | Wormwood | Wormot |

★SYMBOLIC MEANINGS:
Absence; Adultery; Bitterness; Destruction; Do not be discouraged; Exile; Idolatry; Love; Poverty; Separation; Torment of Love; Unpleasant;

★POTENTIAL POWERS:
Calling Spirits; Dispels anger; Divination; Drawing a lover; Exorcism; Love; Prevents strife; Prevents war; Protection; Protection while traveling; Psychic powers; Scrying;

★FOLKLORE AND FACTS:
It is believed that if *Artemisia absinthium* is burned in a graveyard it will induced the spirits of the dead to arise and they will speak to the conjurer. • There is a legend that *Artemisia absinthium* marked the path that Satan took on his exit from The Garden of Eden. • *Artemisia absinthium* is believed to offer protection against bewitchment.

094
Artemisia dracunculus

| Dragon Herb | Dragon Wort | Dragon's Herb | Dragon's Wort | Dragon's-wort | French Tarragon | Fuzzy Weed | Green Dragon | King of Herbs | Snakesfoot | Tarragon |

★SYMBOLIC MEANINGS:
Horror; Lasting commitment; Lasting interest; Lasting involvement; Permanence; Shocking occurrence; Terror;

★POTENTIAL POWERS:
Hunting; Love; Snake-bite cure;

★FOLKLORE AND FACTS:
Artemisia dracunculus is considered to be a desirable companion plant that protects the other plants near to it because it's taste and scent is disliked by common garden pests. • Carry *Artemisia dracunculus* for good luck when hunting.

095
Artemisia vulgaris ☠

| *Artemisia* | **Artemis Herb** | **Chornobylnik** | **Chrysanthemum Weed** | **Common Wormwood** | **Felon Herb** | **Muggons** | **Mugwort** | **Naughty Man** | **Old Man** | **Old Uncle Henry** | **Sailor's Tobacco** | **Saint John's Herb** | **Saint John's Plant** | **Western Mugwort** | **White Mugwort** | **Wild Wormwood** |

★**SYMBOLIC MEANINGS:**

Awareness of our spiritual path; Dignity; Good luck; Happiness; Tranquility;

★**POTENTIAL POWERS:**

Astral projection; Attraction; Beauty; Friendship; Gifts; Harmony; Healing; Healing; Health; Joy; Longevity; Love; Pleasure; Prophetic dreams; Protection against dark forces; Protection; Psychic powers; Sensuality; Strength; The Arts;

★**FOLKLORE AND FACTS:**

Carried, Artemisia vulgaris brings your journeying loved ones safely home and offers protection along the way from wild animals, sunstroke, and fatigue. • Carried, Artemisia vulgaris will also increase fertility and lust. • Artemisia vulgaris was thought to have magical powers and would be worn as protection from evil powers. • It was believed that if Artemisia vulgaris was collected on the evening before the Feast Day of Saint John the Baptist it would offer protection against evil, misfortune, and diseases. • It is believed that if you place *Artemisia vulgaris* in your shoes for long runs you will get strength from it. • A pillow stuffed with *Artemisia vulgaris* will give you prophetic dreams when you sleep upon it. • Place *Artemisia vulgaris* beneath or around a crystal ball to help with psychic readings while using it. • The ancient Japanese and Chinese once believed that the evil spirits of disease hated the smell of *Artemisia vulgaris.* So they would hang bunches of it over doors to keep illness out. • If put next to the bed *Artemisia vulgaris* is supposed to help achieve astral projection. • Carry *Artemisia vulgaris* to prevent backache and cure madness.

096
Arum maculatum

| **Adam and Eve** | **Bobbins** | **Cows and Bulls** | **Cuckoo-Pint** | **Devils and Angels** | **Indian Turnip** | **Jack in the Pulpit** | **Jack-in-the-Pulpit** | **Lords and Ladies** | **Naked Boys** | **Starch-Root** | **Wake Robin** | **Wild Arum** |

★**SYMBOLIC MEANINGS:**

Ardor; Zeal;

★**POTENTIAL POWERS:**

Attract love; Happiness;

097
Arundo donax

| *Arundo* | **Carrizo** | **Giant Cane** | **Giant Reed** | **Spanish Cane** | **Wild Cane** |

★**SYMBOLIC MEANINGS:**
Chanter; Clarification; Communication; Complaisance; Imprudence; Music; Musical; Pipes; Purpose; Rendezvous; Song; Traveling; Woodwind;

★**POTENTIAL POWERS:**
Fishing; Protection; Purification;

★**FOLKLORE AND FACTS:**
Arundo donax has been use for flute making for over 5,000 years. • *Arundo donax* is the primary material used for constructing reeds for woodwind instruments and bagpipes.

098
Asclepias ☠

| **Milkweed** |

★**SYMBOLIC MEANINGS:**
Hope in misery;

099
Asclepias curassavica ☠

| *Asclepias* | **Bastard Ipecacuanha** | **Bloodflower** | **Blood Flower** | **Blood-flower** | **Bloodroot** | **Blood Root** | **Mexican Butterfly Weed** | **Scarlet Milkweed** | **Tropical Milkweed** |

★**SYMBOLIC MEANINGS:**
An attack against love for love; Leave me;

100
Asclepias tuberosa ☠

| *Asclepias* | **Butterfly Love** | **Butterfly Weed** | **Canada Root** | **Chigger Flower** | **Chiggerflower** | **Fluxroot** | **Indian Paint Brush** | **Indian Paintbrush** | **Indian Posy** | **Orange Milkweed** | **Orange Swallow-wort** | **Pleurisy Root** | **Silky Swallow-wort** | **Tuber Root** | **White-Root** | **Windroot** | **Yellow Milkweed** |

★**SYMBOLIC MEANINGS:**
Heartache cure; Let me go; Love;

★**POTENTIAL POWERS:**
Heartache cure; Love;

101
Asparagus densiflorus

| *Asparagus aethiopicus* | Asparagus Fern | Sprenger's Asparagus |

★SYMBOLIC MEANINGS:
Fascination;

102
Asparagus officinalis

| Ashadhi | Aspar Grass | Asparag | Asparagio | Asparago | *Asparagus* | Aspargo | Asper Grass | Asperge | Espárrago | Grass | Love Tips | Majjigegadde | Mang tây | No mai farang | Points d'Amour | Sipariberuballi | Spar Grass | Spargel | Sparrow Grass | Sparrow Guts | Sperage | Spárga |

★SYMBOLIC MEANINGS:
Fascination;

103
Asphodeline
| King's Spear |

★SYMBOLIC MEANINGS:
Languor; Regret;

104
Asphodelus

| Asphodel |

★SYMBOLIC MEANINGS:
For the dead; I will be faithful unto death; My regrets follow you to the grave; Regret, Regrets beyond the grave; Remembered beyond the tomb; The Underworld; Unending regret;

★POTENTIAL POWERS:
Afterlife; Death; Fend off sorcery; Induce sorcery; Snake-bites; Fend;

105
Asteraceae

| *Acarnaceae* | *Ambrosiaceae* | *Anthemidaceae* | *Aposeridaceae* | *Arctotidaceae* | *Artemisiaceae* | Aster | *Athanasiaceae* | *Calendulaceae* | *Carduaceae* | *Cassiniaceae* | *Cichoriaceae* | *Compositae* | *Coreopsidaceae* | Cosmos | Compositae |

Cynaraceae | **Daisy Echinopaceae** | *Eupatoriaceae* | *Helichrysaceae* | *Inulaceae* | *Lactucaceae* | *Mutisiaceae* | *Partheniaceae* | *Perdiciaceae* | *Senecionaceae* | *Vernoniaceae* |

★SYMBOLIC MEANINGS:
Daintiness; Love; Modesty; Orderly;

106
Aster amellus

| *Amellus officinalis* | *Amellus vulgaris* | *Aster* | *Aster acmellus* | *Aster albus* | *Aster amelloides* | *Aster amellus bessarabicus* | *Aster atticus* | *Aster bessarabicus* | *Aster collinus* | *Aster elegans* | *Aster noeanus* | *Aster ottomanum* | *Aster pseudoamellus* | *Aster purpureus* | *Aster scepusiensis* | *Aster tinctorius* | *Aster trinervius* | *Diplopappus asperrimus* | *Diplopappus laxus* | **European Michaelmas Daisy** | **Eye of Christ** | *Galatella asperrima* | **German Aster** | *Kalimares amellus* | **Michaelmas Daisy** | **Starwort** |

★SYMBOLIC MEANINGS:
Afterthought; Daintiness; Elegance; Faith; Farewell; Fidelity; Hope; I partake your sentiments; Light; Love; Like a star; Power; Symbol of Love; Talisman of Love; Valor; Variety; Wisdom;

★POTENTIAL POWERS:
Drives away serpents; Keeps away evil spirits; A talisman of Love; Magic; Wish that things had turned out differently;

★FOLKLORE AND FACTS:
Carry *Aster amellus* to win love. • Grow *Aster amellus* in the garden as a wish for love.

107
Astilbe

| **False Goat's Beard** | **False Spirea** |

★SYMBOLIC MEANINGS:
I'll still be waiting;

108
Astragalus glycyphyllos

| **Liquorice Milkvetch** | **Wild Licorice** | **Wild Liquorice** |

★SYMBOLIC MEANINGS:
I declare against you;

★POTENTIAL POWERS:
Courage;

<hr />

109
Astragalus

| Milkvetch | Milk-Vetch | Goat's-Thorn |

★SYMBOLIC MEANINGS:
Your presence softens my pain;

<hr />

110
Atropa belladonna ☠

| *Atropa* | Atropa Bella-Donna | Banewort | Belladonna | Black Cherry | Deadly Nightshade | Death Cherries | Death's Herb | Devil's Berries | Devil's Cherries | Divale | Dwale | Dwaleberry | Dwayberry | Dway Berry | Fair Lady | Naughty Man's Cherries | Sorcerer's Berry | Witches' Berry |

★SYMBOLIC MEANINGS:
Falsehood; Hush; Loneliness; Silence; Warning;

★POTENTIAL POWERS:
Astral projection; Hallucinations; Visions; Hallucinatory witch flight;

★FOLKLORE AND FACTS:
All parts of the *Atropa belladonna* are deadly poisonous and should be completely avoided.

<hr />

111
Aurinia saxatilis

| Basket of Gold | Gold Basket | Gold-Dust | Golden Alyssum | Golden-Tuft Alyssum | Golden-Tuft Madwort | Goldentuft Alyssum | Rock Madwort |

★SYMBOLIC MEANINGS:
Tranquility;

<hr />

112
Autumn Leaves

★SYMBOLIC MEANINGS:
Melancholy;

<hr />

113
Avena sativa

| Groats | Oat | Joulaf |

★SYMBOLIC MEANINGS:
Music; Musical; The witching soul of music;

★POTENTIAL POWERS:
Money;

114
Azadirachta indica

| Arya Veppu | Azad Dirakht | Bevu | Divine Tree | Dogon Yaro | Heal All | Indian Lilac | Kohomba | Margosa | Muarubaini | Nature's Drugstore | Neeb | Neem Tree | Nimba |Nimm | Nimtree | Panacea For All Diseases | Tamar | The Cure Tree | The Tree of Good Health | The Tree of Life | Tree of the Forty | Tree of the Forty Cures | Vempu | Vepa | Vepu | Village Pharmacy |

★SYMBOLIC MEANINGS:
Complete; Freedom; Imperishable; Life; Noble; Perfect; The cure; To life; To live;

★POTENTIAL POWERS: Healing;

115
Azalea ☠

| Thinking of Home Bush |

★SYMBOLIC MEANINGS:
Fragile; Fragile Passion; Fragility; Modest; Passion; Patient; Romance; Take care; Take care of yourself for me; Temperance; Temporary Passion; Womanhood;

natural power

116
Bambusa vulgaris

| Aur Beting | Bamboo | Bambou de Chine | Bambu Ampel | Bambu Vulgar | *Bambuseae* | Buddha's Belly Bamboo | Buloh Aur | Buloh Minyak | Buloh Pau | Common Bamboo | Daisan-Chiku | Gemenier Bambus | Golden Bamboo | Kauayan-kiling | Mai-Luang | Murangi | Mwanzi | Ohe | Phai-Luang |

★SYMBOLIC MEANINGS:
Good fortune; Loyalty; Luck; Protection; Steadfastness; Strength; Rendezvous; Wishes;

★POTENTIAL POWERS:
Break hexes; Hex-breaking; Luck; Represents all four elements: Air-Water-Fire-Earth; Protection; Wishes;

★FOLKLORE AND FACTS:
Carve a wish on a piece of *Bambusa vulgaris* then find a quiet place to bury it. • To protect the home and for good fortune carefully carve the symbols of protection and good luck, on a length of viable *Bambusa vulgaris.* Plant it in the ground near the house and then nurture it to grow.

117
Banksia laricina

| Rose Banksia | Rose-Fruited Banksia | Pom-Pom Banksia | Pom-Pom Rose | Pompom Rose |

★SYMBOLIC MEANINGS:
Gentility;

118
Bassia scoparia

| Belvedere | Burningbush | Burning Bush | Fireball | Firebush | *Kochia scoparia* | *Kochia trichophylla* | Mexican Fireweed | Ragweed | Summer Cypress |

★SYMBOLIC MEANINGS:
I declare against you;

★POTENTIAL POWERS:
Courage;

★FOLKLORE AND FACTS:

If wind or water detaches the whole *Bassia scoparia* plant it can become a tumble-weed.

ᐟᐧᐧᐧᐟᐧ

119
Begonia

★SYMBOLIC MEANINGS:

A fanciful nature; Balance; Be cordial; Beware; Deformed; Deformity; Fanciful; Fanciful nature; Forewarn; Goodness; Send a warning;

★POTENTIAL POWERS:

Heightened awareness; Psychic ability;

ᐟᐧᐧᐧᐟᐧ

120
Bellis perennis ☠

| *Aster bellis* | **Baimwort** | *Bellis alpina* | *Bellis armena* | *Bellis croatica* | *Bellis hortensis* | *Bellis hybrida* | *Bellis integrifolia* | *Bellis margaritifolia* | *Bellis minor* | *Bellis perennis caulescens* | *Bellis perennis discoidea* | *Bellis perennis fagetorum* | *Bellis perennis hybrida* | *Bellis perennis margaritifolia* | *Bellis perennis microcephala* | *Bellis perennis plena* | *Bellis perennis pumila* | *Bellis perennis pusilla* | *Bellis perennis rhodoglossa* | *Bellis perennis strobliana* | *Bellis perennis subcaulescens* | *Bellis perennis tubulosa* | *Bellis pumila* | *Bellis pusilla* | *Bellis scaposa* | *Bellis validula* | **Bruisewort** | **Common Daisy** | **Daisy** | **English Daisy** | *Erigeron perennis* | **Eye of the Day** | **Eyes** | **Field Daisy** | **Garden Daisy** | **Lawn Daisy** | **Llygady Dydd** |**Maudlinwort** | **Moon Daisy** | **Wild Daisy** |

★SYMBOLIC MEANINGS:

Beauty; Beauty and innocence; Cheer; Cheer; Childlike playfulness; Contempt for worldly goods; Creativity; Decisions; Do you love me; Faith; Forever-young attitude; Gentleness; Gentleness on behalf of both giver and recipient; Happy-go-lucky; I partake your sentiments; I share your sentiments; I will think of it; I'll Never tell; Innocence; Loyal love; Purity; Simplicity; Simplify; Strength; You have as many virtues as this daisy has petals;

★POTENTIAL POWERS:

Divination; Divination for love; Heightened awareness; Inner strength; Love; Lust;

★FOLKLORE AND FACTS:

Bellis perennis is a sentimental and much loved flower among lovers, poets and children. • It was once believed that if a *Bellis perennis* chain were wrapped around a child, the flower chain would protect the child from being stolen by fairies • If you sleep with a *Bellis perennis* root under your pillow your lost lover may return. •

Wear a *Bellis perennis* flower to bring you love. • It was once believed that whoever it is that picks the very first *Bellis perennis* flower of the season will be uncontrollably flirtatious.

121
Bellis perennis flore plen

| **Double Daisy** |

★**SYMBOLIC MEANINGS:**
Participation; Enjoyment;

122
Berberis

| **Barberry** | **Pepperidge Bush** |

★**SYMBOLIC MEANINGS:**
Ill temper; Petulance; Satire; Sharpness; Sharpness of temper; Sourness; Sourness of temper

★**FOLKLORE AND FACTS:**
Italian legend claims that *Berberis* was used in The Crown of Thorns that Jesus was forced to wear.

123
Bertholletia excelsa

| **Brazil Nut Tree** |

★**POTENTIAL POWERS:**
Love;

★**FOLKLORE AND FACTS:**
Carry a *Bertholletia excelsa* nut as a talisman to have good luck in love.

124
Beta vulgaris

| **Beet** | **Beetroot** | **Blood Turnip** | **Mangel** | **Mangold** | **Sugar Beet** |

★**POTENTIAL POWERS:**
Love;

★**FOLKLORE AND FACTS:**
Use *Beta vulgaris* juice to write words of love to a lover. • If a woman and a man eat

of the same *Beta vulgaris*root, they will fall in love.

❧

125
Betula

| Beithe | Bereza | Berke | Beth | Birch | Birch Tree | Bouleau | Lady of The Woods |

★SYMBOLIC MEANINGS:
Adaptability; Dreams; Elegance; Grace; Gracefulness; Growth; Initiation; Meekness; Pioneer spirit; Renewal; Stability; Transformation;

★POTENTIAL POWERS:
Astral travel; Exorcism; Protection; Purification;

★FOLKLORE AND FACTS:
At one time cradles were made from *Betula* wood to protect the babies who slept in them from evil. • Gently strike a person suspected of being possessed with *Betula* twigs to cleanse and heal them of the affliction. • In Russia it was a practice to tie a red ribbon around a *Betula* tree or branch, or around a twig to wear in order to repel or expel The Evil Eye from themselves. • A traditional witch's broom was known to be made of *Betula* twigs.

❧

126
Billardiera

| *Calopetalon* | *Labillardiera* | *Marianthus* | *Oncosporum* | *Pronaya* | *Sollya* |

★SYMBOLIC MEANINGS:
Hope for better days;

❧

127
Borago officinalis

| Borage | Borak | Bugloss | Burrage | Herb of Gladness | Starflower |

★SYMBOLIC MEANINGS:
Abruptness; Bluntness; Bravery; Rudeness;

★POTENTIAL POWERS:
A sense of well-being; Courage; Psychic powers;

★FOLKLORE AND FACTS:
The simple five-point bright blue *Borago officinalis* blossoms were a common subject carefully stitched into needlework designs.• To fortify your courage, carry *Borago officinalis*. • Wear a *Borago officinalis* flower when walking outdoors for protection.

128
Boswellia sacra

| *Boswellia* | *Boswellia carterii* | *Boswellia thurifera* | **Frankincense Plant** | **Olibans** | **Olibanum** | **Olibanus** | **Sacred Boswellia** |

★**POTENTIAL POWERS:**

Abundance; Advancement; Conscious will; Energy; Exorcism; Friendship; Growth; Healing; Joy; Leadership; Life; Light; Natural power; Protection; Purification; Spirituality; Success;

★**FOLKLORE AND FACTS:**

The earliest known record of the use of Frankincense (which is the aromatic resinous sap obtained from the *Boswellia sacra* tree) is inscribed on ancient Egyptian tombs. • The charred remains of burned Frankincense is known as the eyeliner called kohl. • Incense has been used in the rituals of many different religions since ancient times, since it was believed that the smoke of the *Boswellia sacra* incense carried prayers and petitions directly upward. • Frankincense was discovered within a sealed flask in Pharaoh Tutankhamun's tomb when it was opened in 1922. The incense was still viable, releasing scent after being in the vial for 3,300 years. • The used of Frankincense is vital for magical purposes such as atmospheric tonics, blessings, and initiation rituals. • *Boswellia sacra* has a very high and powerful vibration which makes it one of the best of all herbs used to drive away evil. • Frankincense was written in The Holy Bible to be one of the three gifts offered by The Magi to the infant Jesus at the stable in Bethlehem.

129
Botrychium lunaria

| **Common Moonwort** | **Grapefern Moonwort** | **Moonwort** |

★**SYMBOLIC MEANINGS:**

Forgetfulness; Unfortunate;

★**POTENTIAL POWERS:**

Love; Money;

130
Bougainvillea ☠

| **Paper Flower** | *Tricycla* |

★**SYMBOLIC MEANINGS:**

Correspondence;

131
Bouvardia

★**SYMBOLIC MEANINGS:**
Enthusiasm;

132
Brachyscome decipiens

| Field Daisy | Party-Coloured Daisy | Party-Colored Daisy | Parti-Colored Daisy |

★**SYMBOLIC MEANINGS:**
Beauty;

▶ *Brachyscome decipiens Single Flower:*
I will think of it;

133
Brassica oleracea

| Cabbage | Wild Cabbage |

★**SYMBOLIC MEANINGS:**
Profit; Self-willed;

★**POTENTIAL POWERS:**
Luck; Wealth;

★**FOLKLORE AND FACTS:**
The first thing that newlyweds should do to wish good luck on their marriage and on their garden is to plant *Brassica oleracea.*

134
Brassica rapa

| *Brassica campestris* | Field Mustard | Mustard Plant | Turnip | Turnip Mustard | Turnip Rape | Wild Mustard |

★**SYMBOLIC MEANINGS:**
Charity; Indifference;

★**POTENTIAL POWERS:**
Banish negativity; Endings; Ending relationships; Fertility; Mental clarity; Mental powers; Protection;

★**FOLKLORE AND FACTS:**
Carry *Brassica rapa* seed in a red cloth pouch to increase your mental powers. • Bury *Brassica rapa* seeds under or near your doorstep to keep supernatural beings from coming into your home.

▸ ***Brassica rapa Seed:***
Good luck charm; Indifference; Visible faith;

135
Briza

| Quaking Grass |

★**SYMBOLIC MEANINGS:**
Agitation; Frivolity;

136
Bromeliaceae

| Bromeliad |

★**POTENTIAL POWERS:**
Divination; Money; Protection;

137
Browallia speciosa

| Amethyst Flower | Bush Violet |

★**SYMBOLIC MEANINGS:**
Admiration;

138
Brugmansia ☠

| Angel's Trumpet | Maikoa |

★**SYMBOLIC MEANINGS:**
Fame; Separation;

139
Bryonia ☠

| Bryonie | Briony | Bryony |

★POTENTIAL POWERS:
Money; Protection;

★FOLKLORE AND FACTS:
Hang *Bryonia* root in the garden to protect it against damaging or bad weather.

140
Bryonia alba ☠

| Devil's Turnip | English Mandrake | Kudzu of the Northwest | White Bryony |

★POTENTIAL POWERS:
Image magic; Money;

★FOLKLORE AND FACTS:
To increase money place some near a *Bryonia alba* and leave it there. When the money offering is removed from that location, the increase will cease.

141
Bryophyta

| Moss | Bryophyte |

★SYMBOLIC MEANINGS:
Ennui; Maternal love;

★POTENTIAL POWERS:
Binding; Change; Charity; Courage; Fluctuations; Liberation; Luck; Mercy; Money; Victory;

142
Butomus umbellatus

| *Butomus* | Flowering Reed | Flowering Rush | Grass Rush |

★SYMBOLIC MEANINGS:
Confide in Heaven; Confidence in Heaven; Quietness; Rely on God;

143
Buxus

| Box | Box Tree | Boxwood |

★SYMBOLIC MEANINGS:
Constancy; Constancy in friendship; Indifference; Stoicism;

aphrodisiac

144
Cactaceae

| Cactus |

★SYMBOLIC MEANINGS:

Ardent love; Bravery; Burns with Love; Chastity; Endurance; You left me; Lust; Maternal love; My Heart Dreams come to fruition; Protection; Sex; Warmth;

★POTENTIAL POWERS:

Chastity; Protection;

★FOLKLORE AND FACTS:

Cactaceae grown indoors will protect the home against burglaries and intrusions. • Plant four *Cactaceae* plants outside the home, facing in each of the four directions, to protect it. • *Cactacea* spines have be known to be used by to magically mark wax and soft roots with words and symbols, after which the marked item is either carried or buried.

145
Caladium ☠

| Angel Wings | Elephant Ear | Heart of Jesus |

★SYMBOLIC MEANINGS:

Great joy and delight;

146
Calceolaria

| Lady's Purse | Pocketbook Flower | Shoemaker Flower | Slipper Flower | Slipperwort |

★SYMBOLIC MEANINGS:

I offer you my fortune; I offer you financial assistance; I offer you pecuniary assistance;

147
Calendula officinalis

| *Calendula* | *Calendula officinalis prolifera* | Common Marigold | Drunkard | Garden Marigold | English Marigold | Husbandman's Dial | Marigold | Mary-

bud | Mary's Gold | Pot Marigold | Prophetic Marigold | Prophetic Marygold | Ruddles | Scottish Marigold | Summer's Bride | Throughout-The-Months |

★SYMBOLIC MEANINGS:

Affection; Constructive loss; Cruelty; Despair; Fidelity; Grace; Grief; Health; Jealousy; Joy; Longevity; Pain; Sacred affection; Trouble;

★POTENTIAL POWERS:

Amorousness; Dream magic; Evil thoughts; Helps with Seeing Fairies; Legal matters; Prediction; Protection; Prophetic dreams; Psychic powers; Rebirth; Sleep;

★FOLKLORE AND FACTS:

Carry *Calendula officinalis* petals with a *Laurus nobilis* leaf to quiet gossip being passed around about you. • *Calendula officinalis* flower heads follow the sun like sunflowers do. • Early Christians would place *Calendula officinalis* flowers by statues of The Virgin Mary. • *Calendula officinalis* is considered to be one of the most sacred herbs of ancient India, the flower heads were commonly strung into garlands and used in temples and at weddings.

148

Callistephus chinesis

| Aster | Aster Mini Rainbow | *Callistephus* | China Aster | Chinese Aster | Large-Flowered Aster | Mini Rainbow | Rainbow Aster |

★SYMBOLIC MEANINGS:

Afterthought; Beautiful crown; Daintiness; Differences; Elegance; Fidelity; Gained wisdom and good fortune; I will think of it; I will think of thee; I will think of you; Jealousy; Love; Love of variety; Magical; Patience; Symbol of Love; Talisman of love; True yet; Variety;

★POTENTIAL POWERS:

Love;

★FOLKLORE AND FACTS:

Grow *Callistephus* chinesis to wish for love. • Carry a *Callistephus chinesis* flower to win love.

▶ *Callistephus chinesis Single flower:*
I will think of it;

▶ *Callistephus chinesis Double flower:*
I partake your sentiments;

149
Calluna vulgaris

| Calluna | Common Heather | Erica | Ling | Heath | Heath Heather | Scottish Heather |

★SYMBOLIC MEANINGS:

Admiration; Attraction; Beauty; Good Luck; Healing from within; Increases physical beauty; Luck; Protection from Danger; Purity; Refinement; Romance; Solitude; Reveals the inner self; Wishes will come true;

★POTENTIAL POWERS:

Cleansing; Healing; Immortality; Initiation; Intoxication; Ghost conjuring; Good Luck; Protection; Protection against theft; Protection against rape; Protection against violent crimes; Rainmaking; Weather-working; Warding off inappropriate suitors; Wish magic;

★FOLKLORE AND FACTS:

Wearing an amulet made of *Calluna vulgaris* wood will help facilitate awareness of one's own true immortal soul. • Heather twigs were once used as brooms • One of the two traditional plants used in the making of a Witch's broom was *Calluna vulgaris* (the other being *Broom*). • A sprig of *Calluna vulgaris* is carried as a protection charm against violent crimes, most specifically rape. • A sprig of white *Calluna vulgaris* is carried as a good luck charm

⊙ SPECIFIC COLOR MEANING > Pink:

Good Luck;

⊙ SPECIFIC COLOR MEANING > Purple:

Admiration; Beauty; Solitude;

⊙ SPECIFIC COLOR MEANING > White:

Protection From Danger;

150
Calotropis procera ☠

| *Asclepias procera* | Apple of Sodom | Sodom Apple | Tapuah Sdom |

★SYMBOLIC MEANINGS:

Uneatable; A monstrosity; Purposelessness;

★POTENTIAL POWERS:

Powerlessness; Exposure of one's own vanity; Vivid exposure of one's own pomposity; Methodical removal of one's own magical power;

151
Caltha palustris ☠

| Balfae | Cowslip | Gollins | Horse Blob | Kingcup Buttercup | Kingcups |

King's Cup | Marsh Marigold | Mollyblobs | Mary Gold | May Blobs | May-flower | Pollyblobs | Publican | *Trollius paluster* | Water Blobs | Water Bubbles |

★SYMBOLIC MEANINGS:
Brilliancy; Childishness; Desire of riches; I wish I was rich; Ingratitude; Wishing for wealth;

152
Calycanthus

| Sweetshrub | Sweet Shrub |

★SYMBOLIC MEANINGS:
Benevolence;

153
Calystegia sepium ☠

| Bugle Vine | Great Bindweed | Heavenly Trumpets | Hedge Bindweed | Larger Bindweed | Rutland Beauty |

★SYMBOLIC MEANINGS:
Dead hope; Extinguished hopes; Insinuation;

154
Camassia

| Camas | Indian Hyacinth | *Phalangium* | Quamash | Wild Hyacinth |

★SYMBOLIC MEANINGS:
Play;

155
Camellia

| Cháhua | Dongbaek-kkot | Hoa chè | Hoa trà | Tsubaki |

★SYMBOLIC MEANINGS:
Admiration; Deep longing; Delicate and elegant; Desire; Excellence; Good luck gift to a man; Gratitude; Masculine energy; Passion; Perfection; Perfect loveliness; Pity; Refinement; Riches; Steadfastness; Transience of Life;

★POTENTIAL POWERS:
Luxury; Prosperity; Riches; Wealth;

⊙ SPECIFIC COLOR MEANING > Pink:

Desire; Longing; Longing for you; Persistent desire;

⊙ SPECIFIC COLOR MEANING > Red:

Ardent love; In love; You're a flame in my heart;

⊙ SPECIFIC COLOR MEANING > White:

Adoration; Beauty; Loveliness; Perfection; Waiting; You're adorable;

⊙ SPECIFIC COLOR MEANING > Yellow:

Longing;

156
Camellia japonica

| **Fishtail Camellia** | **Japan Rose** | **Japanese Camellia** | **Kingyo-tsubaki** | **Rose of Winter** | **Unryu** | **Zig-Zag Camellia** |

★ SYMBOLIC MEANINGS:

Admiration; Deep longing; Desire; Excellence; Good Luck gift to a man; Gratitude; Masculine energy; Passion; Perfection; Perfect loveliness; Pity; Refinement; Riches; Unpretending excellence;

★ POTENTIAL POWERS:

Luxury; Prosperity; Riches; Wealth;

⊙ SPECIFIC COLOR MEANING > Pink:

Desire; Longing; Longing for you; Persistent desire;

⊙ SPECIFIC COLOR MEANING > Red:

Ardent love; In love; You're a flame in my heart;

⊙ SPECIFIC COLOR MEANING > White:

Adoration; Beauty; Loveliness; Perfection; Waiting; You're adorable;

⊙ SPECIFIC COLOR MEANING > Yellow:

Longing;

157
Campanula

| **Bellflower** | *Brachycodon* | *Diosphaera* | **Flora's Bellflower** | **Flora's Bell** | **Little Bell** | *Rapuntia* | *Rapuntium* | *Rotantha* | *Symphiandra* | *Tracheliopsis* |

★ SYMBOLIC MEANINGS:

Constancy; Gratitude; Indiscretion; I will be ever constant; Thinking of you; Without pretension;

158
Campanula medium

| Bell Flower | Canterbury Bells |

★SYMBOLIC MEANINGS:

Acknowledgment; Constancy; Constancy in adversity; Gratitude; Obligation; Thinking of you; Warning;

159
Campanula pyramidalis

| Chimney Bellflower |

★SYMBOLIC MEANINGS:

Aspiring; Thinking of you; Gratitude;

160
Campanula rotundifolia

| Bluebell | Harebell |

★SYMBOLIC MEANINGS:

Gratitude; Grief; Humility; Retirement; Submission; Thinking of you;

★POTENTIAL POWERS:

Luck; Truth;

★FOLKLORE AND FACTS:

Whoever wears a *Campanula rotundifolia* flower will feel the need to tell the truth about anything. • The one you love will someday love you in return, if you can turn a *Campanula rotundifolia* blossom inside out without damaging it.

161
Camellia sinensis

| Black Tea | *Camellia angustifolia* | *Camellia arborescens* | *Camellia assamica* | *Camellia dehungensis* | *Camellia dishiensis* | *Camellia longlingensis* | *Camellia multisepala* | *Camellia oleosa* | *Camellia parvisepala* | *Camellia parvisepaloides* | *Camellia polyneura* | *Camellia tea* | *Camellia waldeniae* | Cha | China Tea | Green Tea | Kukicha | Oolong | Pinyin | Puerh Tea | Tea Plant | *Thea assamica* | *Thea bohea* | *Thea cantonensis* | *Thea chinensis* | *Thea cochinchinensis* | *Thea grandifolia* | *Thea olearia* | *Thea oleosa* | *Thea parvifolia* | *Thea sinensis* | *Thea viridis* | *Theaphylla cantonensis* | White Tea |

★POTENTIAL POWERS:

Courage; Healing; Strength; Prosperity; Riches;

★FOLKLORE AND FACTS:

Wear a pouch of *Camellia sinensis* as a talisman to increase your strength and give yourself a boost of courage.

162
Campsis radicans

| Ash-Leaved Trumpet Flower | *Bignonia radicans* | Cow Itch Vine | Hummingbird Vine | Trumpet Creeper | Trumpet Vine |

★SYMBOLIC MEANINGS:

Separation;

163
Cannabis sativa

| Cannibis | Chanvre | Gallowgrass | Gallow Grass | Ganeb | Ganja | Grass | Hanf | Hemp | Hempseed Plant | Industrial Hemp Plant | Kif | Marijuana | Neckweed | Neckweede | Scratch Weed | Tekrouri | Weed |

★SYMBOLIC MEANINGS:

Fate; Hardiness; Roughness;

★POTENTIAL POWERS:

Contemplation; Healing; Love; Meditation; Sleep; Visions;

★FOLKLORE AND FACTS:

Since ancient times in China, ropes made from *Cannabis sativa*, more commonly simply called "hemp rope" were used as proxy snakes to beat sickbeds with to drive out demons that cause illness.

164
Capparis spinosa

| Abiyyonah | Abiyyonot | Caper Bush | Caperberry Bush | Caper Berry Bush | Fakouha | Kápparis | Kypros | Lasafa | Shaffallah | Zalef |

★POTENTIAL POWERS:

Aphrodisiac; Love; Lust; Potency;

▶ *Capparis spinosa Berry:*

Aphrodisiac; Love; Lust; Potency;

165

Header: S.Theresa Dietz

Caprifolium

| *Lonicera* | **Monthly Honeysuckle** |

★**SYMBOLIC MEANINGS:**
Bonds of love; Domestic happiness; Inconstancy; I will not answer hastily; Lasting pleasure; Permanence and steadfastness; Sweet Dispostion;

★**POTENTIAL POWERS:**
Money; Protection; Psychic powers;

166
Capsella bursa-pastoris

| **Shepard's Purse** | **Shepard's-Purse** |

★**SYMBOLIC MEANINGS:**
I offer you my all;

167
Capsicum

| **Aji** | **Bell Chillie** | **Bell Peppers** | **Chile** | **Chili** | **Chili Pepper** | **Chilli** | **Chillie** | **Chilli Pepper** | **Green Pepper** | **Guindilla** | **Hot Capsicum** | **Hot Peppers** | **Paprica** | **Paprika** | **Papryka** | **Papryka Ostra** | **Papryka Piman** | **Piment** | **Slodka** | **Peperoncino** | **Pepper** | **Pimienta** | **Pimiento** | **Poivron** | **Red Pepper** | **Spaanse Pepers** | **Spanish Peppers** | **Sweet Capsicum** | **Sweet Peppers** | **Togarashi** | **Xilli** |

★**POTENTIAL POWERS:**
Break hexes; Fidelity; Hex breaking; Love; Wards off evil spirits; Wards off The Evil Eye;

★**FOLKLORE AND FACTS:**
If you believe that you have had a curse placed upon you, encircle your house to with red *Capsicum* to break the curse.

168
Cardamine

| **Bittercress** | **Bitter-Cress** | **Dentaria** |

★**SYMBOLIC MEANINGS:**
Paternal error;

169
Cardamine pratensis

| **Cuckoo Flower** | **Lady's Smock** |

★**SYMBOLIC MEANINGS:**
Ardor; Sacred to fairies;

★**POTENTIAL POWERS:**
Fertility; Love;

★**FOLKLORE AND FACTS:**
Cardamine pratensis is believed to be unlucky if brought into home; *Cardamine pratensis* is considered to be a sacred fairy flower. Because of that, it is not included in May Day wreaths and garlands, so as not to offend the fairies.

170
Carduus

| **Common Thistle** | **Lady's Thistle** | **Thistle** | **Thrissles** |

★**SYMBOLIC MEANINGS:**
Austerity; Harshness; Independence; Nobility; Retaliation; Sternness;

★**POTENTIAL POWERS:**
Assistance; Break hexes; Exorcism; Fertility; Harmony; Healing; Independence; Material gain; Persistence; Protection; Stability; Strength; Tenacity;

★**FOLKLORE AND FACTS:**
Wear or carry a *Carduus* blossom to rid yourself of feeling melancholy. • A vase of fresh *Carduus* in a room will renew the vitality of all that and all who are within it. • Grow *Carduus* in the garden to fend off thieves. • Carry a *Carduus* blossom for protection against evil. • A man can carry a *Carduus* blossom to improve his lovemaking skills. • There was a time in England when a wizard would select the tallest *Carduus* they could find for use as a magic wand.

▸ *Carduus Seed Head:*
Depart;

171
Carica papaya ☠

| **Papao** | **Papaya** | **Papaw** | **Pawpaw** | **Paw-paw** | **Put** | **Lechoza** | **Mugua** |

★**POTENTIAL POWERS:**
Love; Protection; Wishes;

★**FOLKLORE AND FACTS:**
A piece of *Carica papaya* wood over the door will keep evil from entering the home.

172
Carphephorus odoratissimus

| Deer's Tongue | Vanillaleaf | Vanilla Leaf |

★POTENTIAL POWERS:

Attraction; Beauty; Friendship; Gifts; Harmony; Joy; Love; Pleasures; The Arts; Sensuality;

173
Carpinus

| Hornbeam |

★SYMBOLIC MEANINGS:

A treasure; Extravagance; Ornament;

174
Carum carvi

| Alcaravea | Al-karawYa | Caraway | Caro | *Carum* | Cumino Tedesco | Finocchio Meridionale | Kamoon | Karavi | Karve | Kreuzkümmel | Kümmel | Meridian Fennel | Persian Cumin |

★SYMBOLIC MEANINGS:

Faithfulness;

★POTENTIAL POWERS:

Anti-theft; Business transactions; Caution; Cleverness; Communication; Creativity; Faith; Faithfulness; Health; Health; Illumination; Initiation; Intelligence; Keeps lovers true; Learning; Lust; Memory; Mental powers; Protection; Protection against Lilith; Prudence; Repel negativity; Science; Self-preservation; Sound judgment; Thievery; Wisdom;

★FOLKLORE AND FACTS:

In the Middle Ages, *Carum carvi* was a common ingredient in love potions created to prevent lovers from turning and wandering away from each other. • *Carum carvi* seeds amongst your prized possessions repels burglary. A thief who makes it into a house will be transfixed until arrested. • Wearing an amulet of *Carum carvi* seeds is supposed to improve the memory. • Tuck a small pouch of *Carum carvi* seeds in a hidden place in a child's room as protection against illness.

175

Carya illinoinensis

| *Carya oliviformis* | *Carya pecan* | *Hicorius pecan* | *Juglans illinoinensis* | *Juglans oliviformis* | *Juglans pecan* | **Pecan** |

★**POTENTIAL POWERS:**
Employment; Money;

176
Carya ovata

| **Shagbark Hickory** |

★**POTENTIAL POWERS:**
Legal matters;

★**FOLKLORE AND FACTS:**
A good charm to make to protect your home against trouble with the law is this: burn a piece of *Carya ovata* root until it is reduced to ashes. Mix the ashes with a little bit of *Potentilla* (Cinquefoil). Put the mix into a small box that you then hand over the entrance door(s) to your home.

177
Castanea

| **Castan-wydden** | **Châtaigne** | **Chestnut** | **Chinkapin** | **Chinquapin** | *Fagus castanea* | **Gështenjë** | **Kastanje** | **Kistinen** | **Sweet Chestnut** |

★**SYMBOLIC MEANINGS:**
Do me justice; Independence; Injustice; Justice; Luxury;

★**POTENTIAL POWERS:**
Love;

178
Catalpa

| **Catawba** | **Cigar Tree** | **Indian Bean Tree** |

★**SYMBOLIC MEANINGS:**
Beware of the coquette;

179
Catananche caerulea

| **Blue Cerverina** | **Cupidone** | **Cupid's Dart** | **Cupidone** |

★**SYMBOLIC MEANINGS:**
Spells; Compulsion;

★**POTENTIAL POWERS:**
Induce passion; Inspire love;

★**FOLKLORE AND FACTS:**
In ancient Greece, *Catananche caerulea* was the main ingredient in love spells.

180
Cattleya

| **Cattleya Orchid** |

★**SYMBOLIC MEANINGS:**
Mature charms;

181
Cattleya pumila

| *Bletia pumila* | *Cattleya marginata* | *Cattleya pinelli* | *Cattleya pumila major* | *Cattleya spectabilis* | **Dwarf Sophronitis** | *Hadrolaelia pumila* | *Laelia pumila* | *Laelia pumila mirabilis* | *Laelia spectabilis* |

★**SYMBOLIC MEANINGS:**
Matronly grace;

182
Cedrus

| **Cedar** |

★**SYMBOLIC MEANINGS:**
Goals; I live but for thee; I live for thee; I live for you; Strength; Think of Me;

★**POTENTIAL POWERS:**
Cures the tendency to have bad dreams; Healing; Money; Protection; Purification;

★**FOLKLORE AND FACTS:**
A piece of *Cedrus* kept where your keep your money will draw more money to it.

▶ *Cedrus Leaf:*
I live for thee; I live for you;

▶ *Cedrus Sprig:*
Constancy in love; I live for thee; I live for you;

183
Cedrus libani

| Cedar of Lebanon | Lebanon Cedar | Taurus Cedar | Turkish Cedar |

★ **SYMBOLIC MEANINGS:**
Incorruptible; Incorruptibility;

★ **POTENTIAL POWERS:**
Healing; Money; Protection; Purification;

★ **FOLKLORE AND FACTS:**
A three pronged stick of *Cedrus libani* can be pushed into the ground near the house with the prongs up to protect the home against all forms of evil. • A small piece of *Cedrus libani* placed wherever money is usually kept will draw money to it.

184
Celastgrus scandens ☠

| American Bittersweet | Bittersweet |

★ **POTENTIAL POWERS:**
Death; Healing; Lunar activity; Protection; Rebirth; Truth;

185
Celosia

| Cockscomb | Cockscomb Amaranth | Mfungu | Rooster Comb | Soko Yokoto | Woolflower |

★ **SYMBOLIC MEANINGS:**
Affection; Foppery; Love; Partnerships; Silliness; Singularity;

★ **POTENTIAL POWERS:**
Love; Partnerships;

186
Celtis

| Hackberry | Nettle Tree |

★ **SYMBOLIC MEANINGS:**
Concert;

187
Centaurea cyanus

| Bachelor's Button | Bluebottle | Bluet | Boutonniere Flower | Centaury | Common Cornflower | Cornflower | Cyani Flower | Devil's Flower | Hurtsickle | Red Campion |

★ **SYMBOLIC MEANINGS:**

Celibacy; Delicacy; Elegance; Hope; Hope in love; Love; Patience; Refinement; Single blessedness; Single wretchedness;

★ **POTENTIAL POWERS:**

Love; Snake removing;

★ **FOLKLORE AND FACTS:**

There was a time when *Centaurea cyanus* flowers were worn by men in love. If the flower faded too fast it was a sign that the man's love would not be returned.

188
Centaurea moschata

| Sweet Sultan |

★ **SYMBOLIC MEANINGS:**

Felicity; Happiness; Widowhood;

189
Centaurea scabiosa

| Greater Knapweed | Purple Scabiosa | Purple Scabious |

★ **SYMBOLIC MEANINGS:**

Mourning;

190
Centaurium

| Centaury | Christ's Ladder | *Erythraea* | Feverwort |

★ **SYMBOLIC MEANINGS:**

Delicacy;

★ **POTENTIAL POWERS:**

Snake removing;

191
Centella asiatica

| Antanan | Asiatic Pennywort | Bai Bua Bok | Bemgsag | Brahma Manduki |

Brahmanduki | Brahmi | Brahmi Booti | Bai Bua Bok | Divya | Ekpanni | Gotu Kola | *Hydrocotyle asiatica* | Indian Pennywort | Khulakhudi | Kudakan | Kudangal | Kula Kud | Luei Gong Gen | Maha Aushadhi | Mandookaparni | Manduckaparni | Manduki | Mandukparni | Manimuni | Ondelaga | Pegaga | Pegagan | Rau má | Saraswathi Plant | Takip-Kohol | Thankuni | Thankuni Pata | *Trisanthus cochinchinensis* | Vallarai | Vallaarai | Yahong Yahong |

★POTENTIAL POWERS:
Healing; Meditation; Stamina; Youthful aging;

192
Centranthus ruber

| Jupiter's Beard | Red Valerian | Spur Valerian | Valerian |

★SYMBOLIC MEANINGS:
Facility;

★POTENTIAL POWERS:
Love; Protection; Purification; Sleep;

193
Cerastium

| Mouse-Ear Chickweed |

★SYMBOLIC MEANINGS:
Ingenuous simplicity; Simplicity;

194
Ceratonia siliqua

| Alfarrobeira | Algarrobo | Caaroba | Caroba | Carobinha | Carob Tree | Caroube | Caroubier | Carrubba | Garrofa | Haroupia | Haruv | Johannisbrotbaum | Keçiboynuzu | Kharrub Kharrub | Ksylokeratia | Locust Tree | Rogac | Saint John's Bread |

★SYMBOLIC MEANINGS:
Affection beyond the grave; Elegance; Love after death; Love beyond the grave;

★POTENTIAL POWERS:
Health; Protection;

★FOLKLORE AND FACTS:
During ancient times in the Middle East, weighing gold and gemstones against *Ceratonia siliqua* seeds was common and also the source of the term "carat" • Wear *Cera-*

tonia siliqua to guard against evil and maintain your good health.

❧

195
Cercis siliquastrum

| **Judas Tree** | *Siliquastrum orbicularis* |

★**SYMBOLIC MEANINGS:**
Betrayal; Betrayed; Unbelief;

❧

196
Cestrum nocturnum

| **Da Lai Huong** | **Da Ly Huong** | **Dama de Noche** | **Dok Ratree** | **Hasnuhana** | **Kulunya** | **Lady of The Night** | **Mesk el-leel** | **Night Blooming Cestrum** | **Night Blooming Jasmine** | **Night Blooming Jessamine** | **Queen of The Night** | **Raat ki Rani** | **Raat Rani** | **Yè Lái Xiang** | **Yè Xiang Mù** |

★**SYMBOLIC MEANINGS:**
Gift from God;

★**POTENTIAL POWERS:**
Enchantment; Encourages the magic of the evening; Love; Mystery; Psychic dreams;

❧

197
Cetraria islandica

| **Iceland Moss** |

★**SYMBOLIC MEANINGS:**
Health;

❧

198
Chaenomeles

| **Flowering Quince** | **Japanese Quince** | **Japonica** | *Pyrus japonica* |

★**SYMBOLIC MEANINGS:**
Excellence; Fairies' fire;

❧

199
Chamelaucium

| **Wax Flower** |

★**SYMBOLIC MEANINGS:**
Happiness in marriage;

200
Cheiranthus cheiri

| Aegean Wallflower | *Erysimum cheiri* | Gilliflower | Gillyflower | Gilly-Flower | Giroflée | Goldlack | Revenelle | Violacciocca | Wallflower |

★**SYMBOLIC MEANINGS:**
Adversity; Bonds of affection; Enduring beauty; Faithful in adversity; Fidelity in adversity; Fidelity in misfortune; Friendship; Lasting beauty; Misfortune; Natural beauty; Promptness;

201
Chelidonium ☠

| Celydoyne | *Chelidonium majus* | Devil's Milk | Garden Celandine | Greater Celandine | Kenning Wort | Swallow Herb | Swallow-Wort | Tetterwort |

★**SYMBOLIC MEANINGS:**
Deceptive hopes;

★**POTENTIAL POWERS:**
Escape; Happiness; Joy; Legal matters; Protection;

★**FOLKLORE AND FACTS:**
If worn *Chelidonium* will impart joy, good spirits and cure depression. • .Wear *Chelidonium* against the skin, replacing it every three days to escape any unwarranted imprisonments or entrapments of any kind. Wear *Chelidonium* to a court hearing as protection and to garner the favor of the judge and jury.

202
Chenopodium

| Bluebush | Goosefoot |

★**SYMBOLIC MEANINGS:**
Goodness; Insult;

203
Chenopodium bonus-henricus

| Good King Henry | Lincolnshire Spinach | Markery | Perennial Goosefoot | Poor Man's Asparagus |

★**SYMBOLIC MEANINGS:**
Goodness;

204
Chenopodium botrys

| *Dysphania botrys* | Feathered Geranium | Jerusalem Oak | Jerusalem Oak Goosefoot |

★**SYMBOLIC MEANINGS:**
Your love is reciprocated;

205
Chimaphila umbellata

| False Wintergreen | Ground Holly | Pipsissewa | Price's Pine | Prince's Pine | Princess Pine | Umbellate Wintergreen |

★**POTENTIAL POWERS:**
Calling in good spirits; Money;

★**FOLKLORE AND FACTS:**
Carry or wear a sprig of *Chimphila umbellata* to attract money to you.

206
Chiranthodendron pentadactylon

| Devil's Hand Tree | Hand Flower Tree | Mexican Hand Tree | Monkey's Hand Tree |

★**SYMBOLIC MEANINGS:**
Warning;

207
Chlorophytum comosum

| Airplane Plant | *Anthericum comosum* | *Hartwegia comosa* | Spider Plant |

★**POTENTIAL POWERS:**
Death; Destiny; Initiations; Needlework; Spiritual growth;

208
Chorizema varium

| Limestone Pea |

★SYMBOLIC MEANINGS:
You have my love;

209
Chrysanthemum

| Chrysanth | Mums | Flower of Happiness | Flower of Life | Flower of The East |

★SYMBOLIC MEANINGS:
Abundance; Abundance and Wealth; Abundance and loveliness; A heart left to desolation; Cheerfulness; Cheerfulness and rest; Cheerfulness in adversity; Fidelity; Happiness; Loveliness; Optimism; Promotes mental health; Wealth; You're a wonderful friend;

★POTENTIAL POWERS:
Protection;

★FOLKLORE AND FACTS:
Chinese Feng Shui suggests that *Chrysanthemum* will bring happiness into the home. • During the years of Imperial Reign in China, common people were not permitted to grow *Chrysanthemum*, only Nobility had that privilege. • *Chrysanthemum* is a sacred flower in Asia. • In Malta and in Italy it is considered to be unlucky to have *Chrysanthemum* in the house.

⊙ SPECIFIC COLOR MEANING > Red:
I Love; I Love You; Love; Slighted Love;

⊙ SPECIFIC COLOR MEANING > Rose:
In Love;

⊙ SPECIFIC COLOR MEANING > White:
Truth;

⊙ SPECIFIC COLOR MEANING > Yellow:
Imperial; Scorned in love; Slighted love;

▶ *Chrysanthemum Spray:*
Hope;

210
Chrysanthemum morifolium

| Red Daisy | Red Daisy Chrysanthemum | Red Daisy Mum |

★SYMBOLIC MEANINGS:
Beauty unknown to possessor; Unconscious beauty;

211
Chrysocoma linosyris

| *Aster linosyris* | Flax-Leaved Golden-Locks | Flax-Leaved Golden Locks | Flax-Leaved Goldilocks | Flax-Leaved Goldy-Locks |

★ SYMBOLIC MEANINGS:
Tardiness; You're late;

212
Chrysopogon zizanioides

| Khus | Khus-Khus | Moras | Vetiver | *Vetiveria zizanoides* |

★ POTENTIAL POWERS:
Anti-theft; Attraction; Beauty; Break hexes; Friendship; Gifts; Harmony; Joy; Love; Love; Luck; Money; Pleasure; Sensuality; The Arts;

★ FOLKLORE AND FACTS:
To be more attractive to the opposite sex, add *Chrysopogon zizanioides.* to the bath. • Place a sprig of *Chrysopogon zizanioides* in a cash register for more business. • Carry *Chrysopogon zizanioides* for luck.

213
Cichorium endivia

| Endive |

★ SYMBOLIC MEANINGS:
Frugality;

★ POTENTIAL POWERS:
Love; Lust;

★ FOLKLORE AND FACTS:
If worn as a talisman to attract love then the fresh *Cichorium endivia* needs to be replaced every third day.

214
Cichorium intybus

| Blue Sailors | Chicory | Coffeeweed | Common Chickory | Cornflower | Hendibeh | Intybus | Succory | Wild Cherry | Wild Succory |

★ SYMBOLIC MEANINGS:
Delicacy; Economy; Frigidity;

★ POTENTIAL POWERS:

Favors; Frugality; Invisibility; Luck; Removing obstacles;

★ FOLKLORE AND FACTS:

On Saint James' Day (July 25th), if a lock picker held *Cichorium intybus* leaves and a gold knife against a lock, it would magically open ONLY IF the deed was done in total silence...or else death would be the consequence for even a single word spoken. • Early American settlers would carry *Cichorium intybus* for good luck. • Carry a sprig of *Cichorium intybus* to promote frugality and to also remove the obstacles that stand between you and your goals. • It is said that if you bless yourself with *Cichorium intybus* juice then great people will pay attention to you and offer you favors.

215
Cinchona

| **Bark of Barks Tree** | **Holy Bark Tree** | **Jesuit's Bark Tree** | **Peruvian Bark Tree** | **Quina** | **Quinine Tree** |

★ POTENTIAL POWERS:

Luck; Protection;

★ FOLKLORE AND FACTS:

Homeopathy, a form of alternative medicine, began upon the Dr. Samuel Hahnemann's testing of *Cinchona* bark. • Carry a small piece of *Cinchona* bark to protect yourself from evil and bodily harm.

216
Cineraria

★ SYMBOLIC MEANINGS:

Always delightful;

217
Cinnamomum camphora

| **Camphire** | **Camphor Laurel** | **Camphor Tree** | **Camphorwood** | **Chang Nao** | **Harathi Karpuram** | **Kafrovník Lékarsky** | **Kafoor** | **Kapoor** | **Karpooram** | **Karpuuram** | **Kusu No Ki** | **Nok Na Mu** | **Pacchaik Karpooram** | **Paccha Karpoora** | **Paccha Karpooramu** | **Pachai Karpuram** | **Ravintsara** | **Shajarol-kafoor** | **Trees of Kafoor** | **Zhangshù** | **Zhang Shu** |

★ SYMBOLIC MEANINGS:

Chastity; Divination; Health;

★**POTENTIAL POWERS:**
Chastity; Divination; Emotions; Fertility; Generation; Health; Inspiration; Intuition; Psychic ability; Sea; Subconscious mind; Tides; Travel by water;

218
Cinnamomum verum

| Baker's Cinnamon | Ceylon Cinnamon | Cinnamomum zeylanicum | Cinnamon | Cinnamon Tree | Sri Lanka Cinnamon | Sweet Wood | True Cinnamon |

★**SYMBOLIC MEANINGS:**
Beauty; Business; Forgiveness of injuries; Logic; Love; Lust; Power; Success; Temptress; The Temptress;

★**POTENTIAL POWERS:**
Abundance; Advancement; Conscious will; Energy; Friendship; Growth; Healing; Joy; Leadership; Life; Light; Love; Lust; Natural power; Passion; Power; Protection; Psychic powers; Spirituality; Success;

★**FOLKLORE AND FACTS:**
Ancient Hebrew High Priests used *Cinnamomum verum* oil as a vital ingredient of a holy anointing oil. • The ancient Egyptians used *Cinnamomum verum* oil in mummification. • *Cinnamomum verum* used as incense or in a sachet provides the power to increase spiritual vibrations, help heal, bring in money, stimulate psychic powers, and provide protection. • Ancient Chinese and Egyptians used *Cinnamomum verum* to purify their temples.

219
Circaea lutetiana

| *Circaea* | Enchanter's Nightshade |

★**POTENTIAL POWERS:**
Sorcery; Spell; Witchcraft;

220
Cirsium

| Fuller's Thistle | Plume Thistle |

★**SYMBOLIC MEANINGS:**
Misanthropy;

★**POTENTIAL POWERS:**
Assistance; Fertility; Harmony; Independence; Material gain; Persistence; Stability; Strength; Tenacity;

221
Cistaceae
| Rock Rose | Rock-rose |

★SYMBOLIC MEANINGS:
Popular favor; Security; Surety;

222
Cistus ladanifer
| Brow-eyed Rockrose | Gum Cistus | Gum Ladanum | Gum Rockrose | Jara Pringosa | Ladanum |

★SYMBOLIC MEANINGS:
I shall die tomorrow;

223
Citrullus lanatus
| Watermelon | Water-Melon |

★SYMBOLIC MEANINGS:
Bulkiness; Peace;

224
Citrus bergamia
| Bergamot | Bergamot Orange | Bitter Orange | *Citrus aurantium bergamia* | Orange Bergamot | Orange Mint|

★SYMBOLIC MEANINGS:
Enchantment; Irresistibility;

★POTENTIAL POWERS:
Irresistible; Money; Prosperity; Success;

★FOLKLORE AND FACTS:
Rub *Citrus bergamia* leaves on money before spending it to ensure that it comes back to you. • Put a few *Citrus bergamia* leaves wherever you carry your money to attract money.

225
Citrus medica

| Cederat | Cedro | Cedro | Citron | Cédrat | Cédrat | Etrog | Forbidden Fruit | Median | Persian Apple | Rough Lemon | Sukake | Youzi Cha | Yuzucha |

★SYMBOLIC MEANINGS:
Estrangement; Ill-natured beauty;

★POTENTIAL POWERS:
Healing; Psychic powers;

226
Citrus x aurantium

| Bigarade Orange | Bitter Orange | Marmalade Orange | Seville Orange | Sour Orange |

★POTENTIAL POWERS:
Aphrodisiac;

227
Citrus x latifolia

| Bearss Lime | Persian Lime | Tahiti Lime |

★SYMBOLIC MEANINGS:
Fornication;

★POTENTIAL POWERS:
Healing; Love; Protection;

228
Citrus x limon

| *Citrus limon* | Lemon | Lemon Tree | Ulamula |

★SYMBOLIC MEANINGS:
Long-suffering; Patience; Pleasant thoughts; Zest;

★POTENTIAL POWERS:
Friendship; Love; Longevity; Purification;

★FOLKLORE AND FACTS:
Add *Citrus x limon juice* to your bath water during a full Moon to purify yourself of negative energies.

▸ *Citrus x limon Blossom:*
Discretion; Fidelity; Fidelity in love; I Promise to be true; Prudence;

229
Citrus sinensis

| **Love Fruit** | **Orange** | **Orange Tree** | **Sweet Orange** |

★ **SYMBOLIC MEANINGS:**

Eternal Love; Generosity; Innocence;

★ **POTENTIAL POWERS:**

Divination; Love; Luck; Money;

★ **FOLKLORE AND FACTS:**

During the Victorian times, brides carried fresh *Citrus sinensis* blossoms whenever possible, even wearing wreaths of the flowers or attaching the wreaths to their veils.
• The Chinese considers *Citrus sinensis* a symbol of good luck and good fortune.

▶ *Citrus sinensis Blossom:*

Bridal festivities; Brings wisdom; Chastity; Eternal love; Fruitfulness; Innocence; Marriage; Your purity equals your loveliness;

230
Citrus tangerina

| **Clementine** | **Mandarin Orange** | **Tangerine** |

★ **POTENTIAL POWERS:**

Prosperity;

★ **FOLKLORE AND FACTS:**

Citrus x tangerina has been cultivated in China for over 3,000 years.

231
Clarkia amoena

| **Farewell To Spring** | *Godetia* | *Godetia amoena* | **Satin Flower** | **Silk Flower** |

★ **SYMBOLIC MEANINGS:**

The variety of your conversation delights me;

232
Clematis ☠

| **Leather Flower** | **Old Man's Beard** | **Pepper Vine** | **Traveller's Joy** | **Vase Vine** | **Virgin's Bower** |

★ **SYMBOLIC MEANINGS:**

Artfulness; Artifice; Love; Ingenuity; Mental beauty; Soul mates;

▶ *Clematis Evergreen:*

85

Poverty; Want;

233
Cleome

| Beeplant | Bee Plant | Spiderflower | Spider Flower | Spiderplant | Spider Plant | Spiderweed | Spider Weed |

★ SYMBOLIC MEANINGS:
Elope with me;

234
Clianthus puniceus

| Kakabeak | Kaka Beak | Kowhai Ngutu-kaka | Kowhai ngutukaka | Lobster Claw | Parrot-billed Aloe | Parrot's Beak | Parrot's Bill |

★ SYMBOLIC MEANINGS:
Self-seeking; Small Talk; Worldliness;

235
Clitoria

| Butterfly Pea |

★ SYMBOLIC MEANINGS:
Feminine power;

★ POTENTIAL POWERS:
Feminine powers;

236
Cnicus benedictus

| Blessed Thistle | *Centaurea benedicta* | *Cnicus* | Holy Thistle | Saint Benedict's Thistle | Spotted Thistle |

★ POTENTIAL POWERS:
Animal healing; Assistance; Break hexes; Fertility; Harmony; Independence; Material gain; Persistence; Protection; Purification; Stability; Strength; Tenacity;

★ FOLKLORE AND FACTS:
Wear or carry a piece of *Cnicus benedictus* as protection from evil.

237

Cobaea scandens

| Cathedral Bells | Cup-and-Saucer Vine | Violet Ivy |

★ **SYMBOLIC MEANINGS:**
Knots; Gossip;

238
Cocos nucifera

| Argell Tree | Coco | Côca | Cocoanut | Coconut | Coconut Palm | Indian Nut | Jawz Hindi | Malabars Temga | Narle | Niyog | *Nux indica* | Quoquos | Ranedj | Tenga | Ranedj |

★ **SYMBOLIC MEANINGS:**
Chastity;

★ **POTENTIAL POWERS:**
Chastity; Protection; Purification;

★ **FOLKLORE AND FACTS:**
For protection hang a whole *Cocos nucifera* nut in the home or you can cut a *Cocos nucifera* nut in half, fill it will other appropriate protection leaves, seeds, petals, and such. Close the two halves and reseal it however you can. Then bury it on your property.

239
Codariocalyx motorius

| Aravaattip pachchilai | *Hedysarum gyrans* | Semaphore Plant | Snake Charmer's Root | Telegraph Plant | Thozhukanni |

★ **SYMBOLIC MEANINGS:**
Agitation;

240
Coeloglossum viride

| *Dactylorhiza viridis* | Frog Ophrys | Frog Orchid | Long-Bracted Green Orchid |

★ **SYMBOLIC MEANINGS:**
Disgust;

241

Coffea

| Coffee | Coffee Tree |

★**POTENTIAL POWERS:**
Change; Courage; Fluctuations; Liberation; Mercy; Victory;

242
Coix lacryma-jobi

| Adlai | Adlay | Bali | Bo Bo | Chinese Pearl Barley | Christ's Tears | Chuan Gu | Coix | Coixseed | Coix Seed | *Croix* | *Croix agrestis* | *Croix arundinacea* | *Croix exaltata* | *Croix lacryma* | Croix Seed | Curom Gao | David's Tears | Hanjeli | Hatomugi | Hot Bo Bo | Jali | Job's Tears | Jobs Tears | Juzudama | Lacryma Christi | *Lacryma-jobi* | Luk Dueai | Saint Mary's Tears | Tear Drops | Tear Grass | Y Di | Yì Yi | Vyjanti Beads | Yulmu |

★**POTENTIAL POWERS:**
Healing; Luck; Wishes;

★**FOLKLORE AND FACTS:**
Coix lacryma-jobi is a wild grass with seeds that are perfect beads...with natural holes...so they can be easily strung and worn as jewelry. • *Coix lacryma-jobi* are also used inside hollow dried gourds to create shaker instruments. • To make a wish, concentrate on your wish while counting out seven *Coix lacryma-jobi* seeds, then carry them for seven days.   At the end of seven days, make your wish once more then throw the seven seeds into running water.

243
Colchicum autumnale ☠

| Autumn Crocus | Naked lady | Meadow Saffron |

★**SYMBOLIC MEANINGS:**
Autumn; Growing old; My best days are gone; My best days are past; My best days fled; My happy days are past;

244
Coleonema

| Breath of Heaven | Confetti Bush | Diosma |

★**SYMBOLIC MEANINGS:**
Good for nothing; Usefulness; Your simple elegance charms me;

245
Colutea arborescens

| Bladder Senna | Bladder-Senna | *Colutea* |

★SYMBOLIC MEANINGS:
Frivolous amusement;

246
Commiphora gileadensis

| Balm of Gilead Tree | Balm of Mecca Tree | Balsam of Mecca Tree | Balsam of Gilead Tree | *Commiphora opobalsamum* |

★SYMBOLIC MEANINGS:
Healing perfume;

★POTENTIAL POWERS:
Binding; Building; Death; History; Knowledge; Limitations; Obstacles; Time;

★FOLKLORE AND FACTS:
To heal a broken heart carry *Commiphora gileadensis* buds.

▶ *Commiphora gileadensis Resin:*
Cure; Healing; I am cured; Love; Manifestations; Protection; Relief;

247
Conium ☠

| Beaver Poison | *Conium chaerophylloides* | *Conium maculatum* | Devil's Porridge | Hemlock | Herb Bennet | Keckies | Kex | Musquash Root | Poison Hemlock | Poison Parsley | Spotted Corobane | Spotted Hemlock | Water Parsley |

★SYMBOLIC MEANINGS:
You will be my death; You will cause my death;

★POTENTIAL POWERS:
Induces astral projection; Destroys the libido; Diminishes the libido; Power; Purification;

★FOLKLORE AND FACTS:
Every part of the *Conium* plant is deadly poisonous and for that reason it is too dangerous to use for any reason whatsoever.

248
Consolida ☠

| Larkspur |

★**SYMBOLIC MEANINGS:**
Levity; Lightness; Open Heart; Swiftness;

★**POTENTIAL POWERS:**
Fend off ghosts; Fend off scorpions; Fend off venomous creatures; Health; Protection;

★**FOLKLORE AND FACTS:**
Consolida is believed to keep ghosts away.

⊙ **SPECIFIC COLOR MEANING > Pink:**
Fickleness; Lightness;

⊙ **SPECIFIC COLOR MEANING > Purple:**
Haughtiness;

249
Convallaria majalis ☠

| Convall Lily | Convall-lily | Convallaria | Jacob's Ladder | Jacob's Tears | Ladder To Heaven | Ladder-to-Heaven | Lily Constancy | Lily Constancy | Lily of the Valley | Lily-of-the-Valley | Male Lily | May Bells | May Lily | May Lily | Muguet | Our Lady's Tears |

★**SYMBOLIC MEANINGS:**
Christ's second coming; Fortune in love; Good luck; Happiness and purity of heart; Humility; Joy; Purity of heart; Return of happiness; Returning happiness; Sociability; Sweet; Sweetness; Tears of The Virgin Mary; Trustworthy; Unconscious sweetness; You've made my life complete;

★**POTENTIAL POWERS:**
Happiness; Healing; Making the right choice; Mental clarity; Mental powers; Power of people to visualize a better world;

★**FOLKLORE AND FACTS:**
Put *Convallaria majalis* in a room to uplift and cheer all the people in it.

250
Convolvulus arvensis ☠

| *Convolvulus arvensis linearifolius* | Field Bindweed | Small Bindweed |

★**SYMBOLIC MEANINGS:**
Busybody; Coquette; Humble Perseverance; Humility; Perserverance; Uncertainty;

251
Corchorus

| Jute Plant | Molokhia | Mulukhiyah | *Oceanopapaver* |

★ **SYMBOLIC MEANINGS:**
Impatience of happiness; Impatient of absence;

252
Cordyline fruticosa

| *Asparagus terminalis* | Auti | Cabbage Palm | *Convallaria fruticcosa* | *Cordyline terminalis* | *Dracaena terminalis* | Good Luck Plant | Ki | Ki La'i | Lauti | Palm Lily | Si | *Terminalis fruticosa* | Ti Plant | Ti Pore |

★ **POTENTIAL POWERS:**
Healing; Protection;

★ **FOLKLORE AND FACTS:**
Place a bit of the green variety of *Cordyline* fruticosa leaf under the bed to protect you when you sleep. • The Hawaiian hula skirt and Tongan dance dress is made up of the green variety of *Cordyline fruticosa* leaves. • In ancient Hawaii, the red variety of *Cordyline fruticosa* leaves were believed to have great spiritual power and only the high priests and chiefs were permitted to were permitted to wear the red variety of *Cordyline fruticosa* leaves around their necks during rituals. • Bring the green variety of *Cordyline fruticosa* leaves onboard the ship with you when traveling by water to ensure that you will not drown. • The green variety of *Cordyline fruticosa* was often used in ancient Hawaii to outline property borders. • Plant a *Cordyline fruticosa* boarder around your property as protection against evil...but be sure to only use the green variety and not the red variety for this purpose. The red variety of *Cordyline fruticosa* is sacred to Pele and will give homeowners very bad luck if planted as protection, as they do not have the Divine privilege to use red *Cordyline fruticosa* in this way at all. • To grow the red variety of *Cordyline fruticosa* in a pot in the home is considered to be extremely unlucky.

253
Coreopsis

| *Acispermum* | *Calliopsis* | *Epilepis* | *Leptosyne* | *Pugiopappus* | *Selleophytum* | Tickseed | *Tuckermannia* |

★ **SYMBOLIC MEANINGS:**
Always cheerful; Impatience of happiness; Impatient of absence; Love at first sight;

254
Coreopsis tinctoria

| Arkansas Arkansas Calliopsis | *Coreopsis* | *Coreopsis elegans* | *Calliopsis* | *Calliopsis elegans* | Plains Coreopsis | Prairie Coreopsis |

★SYMBOLIC MEANINGS:
Love at first sight;

255
Coriandrum sativum

| Chinese Parsley | Cilantro | Cilentro | Coreander | Coriander | Coriandre | Coriandrum | Culantro | Dhania | Hu-Sui | Koriadnon | Koriandron | Koriannon | Ko-ri-ja-da-na | Stinkdillsamen | Uan-Suy |

★SYMBOLIC MEANINGS:
Hidden worth; Hidden merit; Peace between those of us who do not get along

★POTENTIAL POWERS:
Aphrodisiac; Healing; Health; Helps to find romance; Intelligence; Immortality; Love; Lust; Virility; Protects gardeners and all those in their households; Protection;

★FOLKLORE AND FACTS:
Hang a small bunch of *Coriandrum sativum* in the home for protection. • In the Middle Ages, *Coriandrum sativum* was used in love potions and spells. • Wear a amulet of *Coriandrum sativum* seeds to ease a headache.

▶ *Coriandrum sativum Seeds:*
Promotes peace between people who do not get along;

256
Coronilla

★SYMBOLIC MEANINGS:
Success to you; Success crowns your wishes; You will succeed;

257
Cornus

| Cornel Tree | Dogwood |

★SYMBOLIC MEANINGS:
Durability; Duration;

★POTENTIAL POWERS:
Protection; Wishes;

★ **FOLKLORE AND FACTS:**
The wood from the *Cornus* tree is so hard it can be used as a splitting wedge to split other woods.

258
Cornus florida

| American Dogwood | Boxwood | Budwood | Cornelian Tree | Dogtree | False Box | False Boxwood | Florida Dogwood | Flowering Cornel | Flowering Dogwood | Green Osier | Indian Arrowwood | Virginia Dogwood | White Cornel |

★ **SYMBOLIC MEANINGS:**
Durability; Indifference;

★ **POTENTIAL POWERS:**
Protection; Wishes;

★ **FOLKLORE AND FACTS:**
It is believed that if you put a small amount of *Cornus florida* sap on a handkerchief on Midsunmmer Eve then carry the handkerchief without fail, then this will grant any wish you may have about anything. • Carry bits of *Cornus florida* wood or some leaves for protection.

259
Cornus mas

| Cornelian Cherry Tree | European Cornel |

★ **SYMBOLIC MEANINGS:**
Durability; Duration;

★ **POTENTIAL POWERS:**
Protection; Wishes;

260
Corylus avellana

| Coll | Common Hazel | Hazelnut Tree | Hazel |

★ • **SYMBOLIC MEANINGS:**
Communication; Creative inspiration; Epiphanies; Reconciliation;

★ **POTENTIAL POWERS:**
Anti-Lightning; Divination; Fertility; Heightened awareness; Luck; Meditation; Protection; Visions; Wishes;

★ **FOLKLORE AND FACTS:**

Give *Corylus avellana* nuts to a bride to wish her good fortune, fertility and wisdom. • Make a wishing crown by weaving *Corylus avellana* together. Wear this crown when making wishes. • A forked *Corylus avellana* branch is the diviners dowsing rod of first choice.

261
Corylus maxima

| Filbert |

★SYMBOLIC MEANINGS:
Reconciliation;

262
Cosmelia rubra

★SYMBOLIC MEANINGS:
Love at first sight;

263
Cotinus coggygria

| Eurasian Smoketree | Purple Smokebush | *Rhus cotinus* | Smoke Bush | Smoketree | Smoke Tree | Venetian Sumac | Venetian Sumach |

★SYMBOLIC MEANINGS:
Intellectual excellence; Splendor;

264
Crassula dichotoma

| *Grammanthes chloriflora* | *Tillaea* |

★SYMBOLIC MEANINGS:
Your temper is too hasty;

265
Crassula ovata

| *Crassula argentea* | Dollar Plant | Friendship Tree | Jade Plant | Lucky Plant | Money Plant | *Crassula obliqua* | *Crassula portulacea* |

★SYMBOLIC MEANINGS:
Affluence; Friendship; Good luck;

266
Crataegus

| Bread and Cheese Tree | English Hawthorn | Gaxels | Glastonbury Thorn | Hagthorn | Halves | Haw | Hawberry Tree | Haweater Tree | Hawthorn Tree | Hazels | Huath | Ladies' Meat | May | Mayblossom | May Blossom | May Bush | May Flower | Mayflower | May Tree | Quick | Quick-Set | Shan-cha | Thorn | Thorn Apple | Thornapple Tree | Tree of Chastity | White Thorn |

★SYMBOLIC MEANINGS:
Duality; Chastity; Contradictions; Hope; Male energy; Union of opposites; Spring;

★POTENTIAL POWERS:
Chastity; Continuity; Death; Fertility; Fishing Magic; Happiness; Hope;

★FOLKLORE AND FACTS:
There is a legend that Joseph of Arimathea went to Britain to carry the message of Christ there. At one point, he pushed his staff in the ground to sleep nearby. When he awoke he discovered the staff had taken root, grew, and blossomed into a Crataegus Tree. It is said that he left the staff there, undisturbed and that it flowered every Christmas and again every spring. Cuttings had since been taken of it, and one of those cuttings were planted near Glastonbury Abbey, and grows there still today as the Glastonbury Thorn. A branch of this particular tree is annually displayed at Christmastime at Buckingham Palace in London, England. • The Romans attached Crataegus leaves to baby cradles to repel evil spirits. • In Medieval Europe if Crataegus branches were brought inside it was an omen of illness and death for one member of the household. • Crataegus is considered one of a witch's favorite plants. In the spring on Walpurgis Night (Walpurgisnacht), when witches supposedly turn themselves into Crataegus Trees, the Crataegus is to be avoided. • Because of it's correspondence with fertility, Crataegus has been added into spring wedding flowers. • Put Crataegus under a mattress and around a bedroom to maintain or even enforce chastity. • Tuck a Crataegus leaf into your hat to promote a good catch when fishing. • Wear a spring of Crataegus if troubled, sad, or depressed to help return you to a state of happiness. • Sprigs or leaves of Crataegus place around the home will protect it against lightning and storm damaged. • Sprigs or leaves of Crataegus place around the home will protect it evil, and malicious ghosts. • Crataegus is sacred to fairies. • It is believed that one will be able to see fairies where these three trees grow together: *Crategus*, *Quercus*, and *Fraxinus excelsior*.

267
Crepis

| Bearded Crepis | Hawksbeard | Hawk's-beard |

★POTENTIAL POWERS:
Protection;

268
Crocus sativus

| **Autumn Crocus** | **Crocus** | **Karcom** | **Kesar** | **Krokos** | **Kunkuma** | **Saffer** | **Saffron** | **Saffron Crocus** | **Spanish Saffron** |

★SYMBOLIC MEANINGS:
Ancient symbol of The Sun; Beware of excess; Cheerfulness; Do not abuse; Excess is dangerous; Happiness; Mirth;

★POTENTIAL POWERS:
Abuse; Aphrodisiac; Happiness; Healing; Laughter; Love; Lust; Magic; Psychic powers; Raise up spirits; Spirituality; Strength; Wind raising;

★FOLKLORE AND FACTS:
In India *Crocus sativus* flowers are often scattered on the marriage bed of newly-weds. • During the Bronze Age, *Crocus sativus* was used in Minoan religious rituals, to later be adopted, over time, by other religions for their own religious rituals. • Once a *Crocus sativus* was smuggled into England (then throughout Europe) from the Middle East inside a walking stick, it's value was considered priceless. Changing it, by adding to it anything of a lesser value, to increase it quantity but lower the quality, was punishable by horrible deaths...including being buried alive! • When *Crocus sativus* reached India, it was discovered, there, that a beautiful golden colored dye could be rendered from it for fabrics, the color of which is used for royal garments in many different countries and cultures. • During the Middle Ages, inks made from *Crocus sativus* were used by the poorer illuminators to replace gold leaf in their religious art renderings. • There was a time in Ireland when the bed linen was rinsed with an infusion of *Crocus sativus* with the belief that the arms and legs would be made stronger while sleeping upon them. • Ancient Persians would toss *Crocus sativus* into the air as an attempt to raise the wind.

269
Crocus vernus

| **Crocus** | **Giant Dutch Crocus** | **Spring Crocus** |

★SYMBOLIC MEANINGS:
Abuse not; Attachment; Cheerfulness; Gladness; Heavenly bliss; I am his; Impatience; Love; Resurrection; Resurrection and Heavenly bliss; Youthful gladness;

★POTENTIAL POWERS:
Love; Visions;

★**FOLKLORE AND FACTS:**
It is believed that you can attract love by growing *Crocus vernus*.

270
Croton ☠

| *Agelandra* | *Aldinia* | *Angelandra* | *Anisepta* | *Anisophyllum* | *Argyra* | *Astraea* | *Astrogyne* | *Aubertia* | *Banalia* | *Barhamia* | *Brachystachys* | *Calypteriopetalon* | *Cascarilla* | *Centrandra* | *Cieca* | *Cleodora* | *Codonocalyx* | *Comatocroton* | *Crotonanthus* | *Crotonopsis* | *Cyclostigma* | *Decarinium* | *Drepadenium* | *Eluteria* | *Engelmannia* | *Eremocarpus* | *Eutrophia* | *Friesia* | *Furcaria* | *Geiseleria* | *Gynamblosis* | *Halecus* | *Hendecandras* | *Heptallon* | *Heterochlamys* | *Heterocroton* | *Julocroton* | *Klotzschiphytum* | *Kurkas* | *Lasiogyne* | *Leptemon* | *Leucadenia* | *Luntia* | *Macrocroton* | *Medea* | *Merleta* | *Monguia* | *Myriogomphus* | *Ocalia* | *Oxydectes* | *Palanostigma* | *Penteca* | *Pilinophyton* | *Piscaria* | *Pleopadium* | *Podostachys* | *Saipania* | *Schradera* | *Semilta* | *Tiglium* | *Timandra* | *Tridesmis* | *Triplandra* | *Vandera* |

★**POTENTIAL POWERS:**
Emotions; Fertility; Generation; Inspiration; Intuition; Psychic ability; Subconscious mind; Travel by water; Sea; Tides;

271
Cryptanthus

| **Chameleon Star** | **Earth Star** |

★**POTENTIAL POWERS:**
Money; Protection;

★**FOLKLORE AND FACTS:**
For household protection, and an increase in money and luxury grow a Cryptanthus plant inside the home.

272
Cucumis sativus

| **Cucumber** |

★**SYMBOLIC MEANINGS:**
Chastity; Criticism;

★**POTENTIAL POWERS:**
Chastity; Fertility; Healing;

★**FOLKLORE AND FACTS:**

Roman midwives would carry *Cucumis sativus*, then throw them away when they delivered a baby. • Roman wives, desiring a baby, would wear *Cucumis sativus* around the waist. • Roman households used *Cucumis sativus* to frighten away mice that would enter into their homes.

273
Cucurbita pepo

| Field Pumpkin | Pompion | Pumpkin | Squash |

★ SYMBOLIC MEANINGS:
Coarseness; Grossness;

274
Cuminum cyminum

| Cumin | Cumino | Cumino Aigro | Cummin | Cymen | Gamun | Geerah | Kammon | Kammun | Kimoon | Ku-mi-no | Kuminon | Sanoot |

★ SYMBOLIC MEANINGS:
Faithfulness; Fidelity;

★ POTENTIAL POWERS:
Anti-theft; Exorcism; Fidelity; Protection;

★ FOLKLORE AND FACTS:
Cuminum cyminum will supposedly prevent the theft of anything that has this spice on or in it. • Mixed with salt and scattered on the floor *Cuminum cyminum* will supposedly drive out evil. • A spring of *Cuminum cyminum* is sometimes worn by a bride to keep any negativity away on her wedding day. • Carry *Cuminum cyminum* for peace of mind.

275
Cupressus

| Cypress | Tree of Death |

★ SYMBOLIC MEANINGS:
Death; Despair; Mourning; Sorrow;

★ POTENTIAL POWERS:
Comfort; Eternity; Healing; Immortality; Longevity; Protection;

★ FOLKLORE AND FACTS:
Wear a sprig of *Cupressus* for comfort to ease the mind of grief upon the death of a friend or relative. • Since it is such a strong symbol of immortality growing *Cupres-*

sus provides blessings and protection.

276
Curcuma longa

| Harldar | Haldi | Haridra | Indian Saffron | Manjal | Tumeric |

★ **POTENTIAL POWERS:**
Luck; Power; Purification;

★ **FOLKLORE AND FACTS:**
In every part of India *Curcuma longa* is considered to be very lucky and used in Indian wedding and religious ceremonies for thousands of years.

277
Cuscuta

| Angel Hair | Beggarweed | Devil's Guts | Devil's Hair | Devil's Ringlet | Dodder | Fireweed | Goldthread | Hailweed | Hairweed | Hellbine | Hellweed | Lady's Laces | Love Vine | Pull-Down | Scaldweed | Strangel Tare | Strangleweed | Witch's Hair |

★ **SYMBOLIC MEANINGS:**
Baseness; Meanness; Parasite;

★ **POTENTIAL POWERS:**
Knot magic; Love Divination;

★ **FOLKLORE AND FACTS:**
A love divination that might work is to pluck a large sprig of *Cuscuta* the throw it over the shoulder at the plant you picked if from while asking if the person you love loves you in return. Leave, then return the next day and examine the sprig. If it has not reattached itself, your answer is *no*. If the sprig has reattached, then the answer is *yes*.

278
Cyclamen

| Groundbread | Pain de Pourceau | Pan Porcino | Sowbread | Swinebread | Varkensbrood |

★ **SYMBOLIC MEANINGS:**
Diffidence; Goodbye; Resignation;

★ **POTENTIAL POWERS:**
Fertility; Happiness; Lust; Protection;

★FOLKLORE AND FACTS:

If grown in a bedroom *Cyclamen* is believed to protect those there sleeping and no negative spells can have any power there.

279
Cymbidium

| Boat Orchid | *Cymbidium* Orchid | *Cyperochis* | *Iridorchis* | *Jensoa* | *Pachyrhizanthe* |

★SYMBOLIC MEANINGS:

Beauty; Love; Refinement;

280
Cydonia oblonga

| Quince |

★SYMBOLIC MEANINGS:

Scornful beauty; Temptation;

★POTENTIAL POWERS:

Happiness; Love; Protection;

★FOLKLORE AND FACTS:

Art seen in the excavated remains of Pompeii have revealed images of bears carrying *Cydonia oblonga* fruit in their paws. • To carry even one *Cydonia oblonga* seed will protect you against accidents, evil, and harm against your body.

281
Cylindropuntia imbricata

| Cane Cholla | Chainlink Cactus | *Opuntia imbricata* | Tree Cholla | Walking Stick Cholla |

★POTENTIAL POWERS:

Uprightness; Sentiments of Honor;

282
Cymbopogon ☠

| Barbed Wire Grass | Cha de Dartigalongue | Citronella Grass | Fever Grass | Gavati Chaha | Hierba Luisa | Lemongrass | Lemon Grass | Silky Heads | Tanglad |

★POTENTIAL POWERS:

Lust; Psychic powers; Repel insects; Repel snakes;

★**FOLKLORE AND FACTS:**
Cymbopogon planted around the home is believed to repel snakes.

283
Cynanchum

| Dog-Strangling Vine | Swallow Wort | Swallow-Wort |

★**SYMBOLIC MEANINGS:**
Cure for headache; Withered hopes;

284
Cyperus papyrus

| Paper Reed | Papyrus Plant | Papyrus Sedge |

★**POTENTIAL POWERS:**
Protection;

★**FOLKLORE AND FACTS:**
The *Cyperus papyrus* plant has great historical fame as it is the plant that the ancient Egyptians used to make papyrus paper. • It was believed that *Cyperus papyrus* inside a boat will protect it from attack by crocodiles.

285
Cypridedium

| Adam's Grass | Adam's Head | *Arietinum* | *Calceolaria* | *Calceolus* | Camel's Foot | *Ciripedium* | *Criogenes* | *Criosanthes* | Cuckoo's Slippers | *Cypripedioideae* | *Cypripedium* | *Fissipes* | *Hypodema* | Lady Slipper Orchid | Lady's Slipper | Moccasin Flower | *Paphiopedilum* | *Phragmipedium* | *Sacodon* | *Schizopedium* | Slipper Orchid | Squirrel Foot | Steeple Cap | Venus' Shoes | Whippoorwill Shoe |

★**SYMBOLIC MEANINGS:**
Capricious beauty; Fickleness; Win me; Win me and wear me;

★**POTENTIAL POWERS:**
Anti-theft; Drives away evil spirits; Good for every ill; Protection; Protection against curses; Protection against The Evil Eye; Protection against hexes; Protection against spells;

★**FOLKLORE AND FACTS:**
Carry *Cypridedium* within an amulet to provide personal protection.

286
Cytisus scoparius ☠

| Banal | Basam | Besom | Bisom | Bizzon| Breeam | Broom Topos | Brum | Common Broom | English Broom | Genista Green Broom | *Genista scoparius* | Hog Weed | Irish Broom | Irish Tops | Link | *Sarothamnus bourgaei* | *Sarothamnus oxyphyllus* | *Sarothamnus scoparius* | Scotch Broom | Scot's Broom | *Spartium scoparium* |

★POTENTIAL POWERS:

Protection; Purification; Union;

★FOLKLORE AND FACTS:

Hang *Cytisus scoparius* outside the home to keep evil from entering into it.

desire to please

287
Dahlia

| Acoctli | Belia | Bishop of Llandaff | Cocoxochitl | Deri | *Georgina* | Mexican Georgiana | Peony of India | Tenjikubotan |

★SYMBOLIC MEANINGS:
Dignity; Dignity and Elegance; Elegance and dignity; Elegance; Eloquence and dignity; Forever yours; Good taste; Instability; Novelty; Pomp; Refinement; Warning of change;

★POTENTIAL POWERS:
Portent of betrayal; Spiritual evolution;

288
Daphne ☠

★SYMBOLIC MEANINGS:
Glory; Immortality;

289
Daphne cneorum

| Rose Daphne |

★SYMBOLIC MEANINGS:
I desire to please;

290
Daphne mezereum

| Mezereon |

★SYMBOLIC MEANINGS:
A flirt; Coquetry; Desire to please; Flirt;

291
Daphne odora

| Jinchoge | Winter Daphne |

★**SYMBOLIC MEANINGS:**
I would not have you otherwise; Painting the lily; Unnecessarily adorn; Unecessarily make beautiful that which is beautiful; Make beautiful that which is beautiful;

292
Datura ☠

| Angel's Trumpet | Devil's Cucumber | Devil's Trumpet | Devil's Apple | Devil's Weed | Floripondio Tree | Ghost Flower | Hell's Bells | Herb of The Devil | Indian Apple | Indian Whiskey | Jamestown Weed | Jimson Weed | Jiimsonweed | Loco Weed | Locoweed | Love-Will | Mad Apple | Madherb | Mad Herb | Mad Seeds | Malpitte | Manicon | Nana-honua | Prickly Burr | Pricklyburr | Sorcerer's Herb | Stink Weed | Stinkweed | Thornapple | Thorn Apple | Tolache | Tolguacha |Witches' Thimble | Yerbe del Diablo |

★**SYMBOLIC MEANINGS:**
Deceitful charms; Deceitfulness; Disguise; Suspicion;

★**POTENTIAL POWERS:**
Gross mental and physical disturbances; Death;

★**FOLKLORE AND FACTS:**
Datura is extremely poisonous. • *Datura* has the ability to change according to the location where it is growing, the size of plant, leaf, and flowers.

293
Daucus carota

| Bee's-nest | Bee's-nest Plant | Bird's-nest | Bird's-nest Plant | Bird's-nest Root | Bishop's Flower | Crow's-nest | Carota | Carotte | Carrot | Common Carrot | Daucon | Dawke | Devil's-plague | Fiddle | Gallicam | Garden Carrot | Gelbe Rübe | Gingidium | Gizri | Hill-trot | Laceflower | Mirrot | Möhre | Philtron | Queen Anne's Lace | Rantipole | Staphylinos | Wild Carrot | Zanahoria |

★**SYMBOLIC MEANINGS:**
Do not refuse me; Fantasy; Haven; Sanctuary;

★**POTENTIAL POWERS:**
Fertility; Lust;

★**FOLKLORE AND FACTS:**
Daucus carota, known as Queen's Ann'e Lace is named so after England's Queen Anne, who was an renown expert lace maker. • One dreadful superstition is that if someone picks *Daucus carota* then brings it into their home, their mother will die. • Another superstition is that if a woman who is true to herself plants *Daucus carota* in her garden, the plant will thrive.

294
Delonix regia

| **Flamboyant** | **Flame Tree** | **Flower of Pupil** | **Gulmohar** | **Krishnachura** | **Llama del Bosque** | **Malinche** | **Peacock Tree** | **Phoenix's Tail Tree** | **Poinciana** | **Royal Poinciana** | **Tabachine** |

★**POTENTIAL POWERS:**
Protection; Prosperity; Wealth;

★**FOLKLORE AND FACTS:**
In the Caribbean, the seed pods of *Delonix regia* are used as a percussion shaker instrument, which is a type of maraca.

295
Delphinium ☠

| **Elijah's Chariot** | **Lark's Claw** | **Lark's Heel** | **Little Larkspur** | **Low Larkspur** | **Montane Larkspur** |

★**SYMBOLIC MEANINGS:**
Ability to transcend the bounds of space and time; Airy; An open heart; Ardent attachment; Big-Hearted; Fickleness; Fun; Heavenly; Hilarity; Levity; Lightness;

★**POTENTIAL POWERS:**
Lightness; Swiftness; Drive away scorpions;

296
Dendrobium

| *Callista* | *Dendrobium* **Orchid** | *Pierardia* | *Thelychiton* |

★**SYMBOLIC MEANINGS:**
Beauty; Love; Refinement;

★**POTENTIAL POWERS:**
Friendship; Greed; Joy; Longevity; Love; Lust; Wealth;

297
Dendrobium tetragonum

| *Callista tetragona* | **Common Spider Orchid** | *Dendrocoryne tetragonum* | **Rectangular-Bulbed Dendrobium** | **Tree Spider Orchid** | *Tropolis tetragona* | *Tetrabaculum tetragonum* |

★**SYMBOLIC MEANINGS:**

Adroitness;

★POTENTIAL POWERS:
Dexterity; Skill;

298
Dianthus

| Pink |

★SYMBOLIC MEANINGS:
Boldness; Make haste; Pure affection; Pure love;

⊙ SPECIFIC COLOR MEANING > Pink:
Pure love;

⊙ SPECIFIC COLOR MEANING > Red:
Ardent love; Pure love;

⊙ SPECIFIC COLOR MEANING > White:
Ingeniousness; You are fair; Talent;

⊙ SPECIFIC COLOR MEANING > Yellow:
Disdain; Unreasonableness;

⊙ SPECIFIC COLOR MEANING > Varigated::
Refusal;

▸ *Dianthus Double Flower:*
Unchanging love;

299
Dianthus barbatus

| **Sweet William** | **Sweete Williams** |

★SYMBOLIC MEANINGS:
Artifice; Dexterity; Finesse; Gallantry; Grant me one smile; Perfection; Scorn; Treachery; Will you smile;

300
Dianthus caryophyllus

| **Carnation** | **Clove Pink** | **Divine Flower** | **Gillies** | **Gilliflower** | **Jove's Flower** | **Nelka** | **Pinks** | **Scaffold Flower** | **Sops-In-Wine** |

★SYMBOLIC MEANINGS:
Admiration; Bad luck; Bonds of affection; Dignity; Disappointed; Disdain; Distinction; Fascination; Good fortune; Good luck; Gratitude; Health and energy; Heav-

enly; Joy and commitment; Love; Misfortune; Pride; Pride and beauty; Pure and deep love; Pure love; Self-esteem; Strength; True love; Woman's love;

★POTENTIAL POWERS:
Divination; Healing; Luck; Protection; Strength;

★FOLKLORE AND FACTS:
In ancient Greece, *Dianthus caryophyllus* were the most loved of all flowers. • A corsage or nosegay made up of a *Dianthus caryophyllus*, a sprig of *Rosmarinus officinalis*, and a *Geranium* flower means: Love, Fidelity, and Hope. • Fresh red *Dianthus caryophyllus* in the room of a convalescing patient will promote strength and energy. • Wearing a *Dianthus caryophyllus* flower was popular during Elizabethan times because it was believed that the flower helped prevent being put to death on the scaffold.

◉ SPECIFIC COLOR MEANING > Pink:
A woman's love; Deep love; I'll never forget you; Sentimental love; A mother's undying love; Always on my mind; A mother's love; Mother's Day symbol; Woman's love;

◉ SPECIFIC COLOR MEANING > Red:
Admiration; Admiration from afar; Affection; Alas! For my poor heart; Ardent love; Desire; Desires that never come to pass; Forlorn; My heart aches for you; Poor heart; Pure; Pure and ardent love; Deep Romantic Love;

◉ SPECIFIC COLOR MEANING > Light Red:
Admiration;

◉ SPECIFIC COLOR MEANING > Dark Red:
Affection; Alas for my poor heart; Deep love;

◉ SPECIFIC COLOR MEANING > Deep Red:
Affection; Alas for my poor heart; Deep love;

◉ SPECIFIC COLOR MEANING > Mauve:
Dreams of fantasy;

◉ SPECIFIC COLOR MEANING > Purple:
Antipathy; Capriciousness; Changeability; Condolences; Whimsical; Changeable; Unreliability;

◉ SPECIFIC COLOR MEANING > White:
Disdain; Innocence; Pure love; Purity; Sweet and lovely; Sweet Love; Good luck; Faithfulness;

◉ SPECIFIC COLOR MEANING > Yellow:
Disappointment; Disdain; Rejection; You have disappointed me; Unreasonableness;

◉ SPECIFIC COLOR MEANING > Solid:
Yes; Acceptance; I want to be with you; Affirmative;

⊙ SPECIFIC COLOR MEANING > Striped:
No; Refusal; Regret that love cannot be reciprocated; Rejection; Sorry, I can't be with you;

301
Dianthus chinensis

| China Pink |

★**SYMBOLIC MEANINGS:**
Aversion;

302
Dictamnus albus

| Burning-Bush | *Dictamnus* | False Dittany | Fraxinella | Gas Plant |White Dittany | White Ditto |

★**SYMBOLIC MEANINGS:**
Fire; Passion; Perfected loveliness;

★**FOLKLORE AND FACTS:**
The volatile oils in *Dictamnus albus* is such that the plant is easily combustible in hot weather. Because of this natural tendancy, it is a contender for being the "burning-bush" referred to in the Bible.

303
Dierama

| Fairy Bells | Fairy's Fishing Rods | Fairy Wands | Fairy's Wands | Funnel Flower | Hairbells | Harebells | Wandflower | Wand Flowers | Wedding Bells |

★**SYMBOLIC MEANINGS:**
A bell;

304
Digitalis purpurea

| Common Foxglove | Cow Flop | Dead Man's Bells | Digitalis | Dog's Finger | Fairy Fingers | Fairy Petticoats | Fairy Thimbles | Fairy-caps | Fairy Weed | Fingerhut | Floppy-Dock | Floptop | Folk's Gloves | Fox Bells | Foxes Glofa | Fox-Glove | Foxglove | Gant de Notre Dame | Goblin's Gloves | Lady's Glove | Lion's Mouth | Lusmore | Lus Na Mbau Side | Our Lady's Glove | Purpur | Purple Foxglove | The Great Herb | Wiches Bells | Wiches Thimbles | Witch'

Bells | Wiches' Thimbles | Witch's Thimble |

★ **SYMBOLIC MEANINGS:**

A wish; Deception; I am ambitious only for you; Insincerity; Mystery; Occupation; Stateliness; Youth;

★ **POTENTIAL POWERS:**

Magic; Protection;

★ **FOLKLORE AND FACTS:**

There is a legend that fairies wear *Digitalis purpurea* blossoms as mittens. • There is a superstition that if you pick a *Digitalis purpurea*, the fairies will be offended. • Medieval witches kept *Digitalis purpurea* growing in their gardens because they were a regular ingredient in spells. • At one time Welsh housewives would create a black dye using the *Digitalis purpurea* leaves that they would use to paint crossed lines on the outside of their houses to fend off evil.

305

Dionaea muscipula

| Flytrap | Tipitiwitchet | Tippity Twitchet | Venus Flytrap | Venus' Flytrap | Venus's Trap | White Flytrap |

★ **SYMBOLIC MEANINGS:**

Artifice; Caught at last; Confinement; Deceit; Incarceration;

★ **POTENTIAL POWERS:**

Love; Protection;

★ **FOLKLORE AND FACTS:**

Although there are a few naturalized areas of plants growing in some specific USA areas in northern Florida and New Jersey, the carnivorous *Dionaea muscipula* is native *only* within a 60 mile radius surrounding Wilmington, North Carolina.

306

Dioscorea communis

| Black Bryony | Bryony | *Tamus communis* |

★ **SYMBOLIC MEANINGS:**

Support;

307

Diospyros

| Ebony | Lama | Obeah | Persimmon |

★**SYMBOLIC MEANINGS:**
Bury me amid nature's beauties; Lust;

★**POTENTIAL POWERS:**
Changing sex; Healing; Luck; Protection;

★**FOLKLORE AND FACTS:**
A wand made of *Diospyros* will give a magician undiluted pure power. • An amulet made from *Diospyros* will offer protection to the wearer. • It is believed that to be rid of the chills tie one string to a *Diospyros* tree for each chill you've experienced. • Bury a green *Diospyros* fruit for good luck.

308
Diospyros ebenum

| Ceylon Ebony Tree | Ebony | India Ebony |

★**SYMBOLIC MEANINGS:**
Blackness; Hypocrisy;

★**POTENTIAL POWERS:**
Power; Protection;

309
Diospyros lotus

| Caucasian Persimmon | Date-Plum | Dios Pyros | Khormaloo | The Fruit of The Gods |

★**SYMBOLIC MEANINGS:**
Resistance;

★**POTENTIAL POWERS:**
Fertility; Potency;

310
Dipsacus fullonum

| Fuller's Teasel | Wild Teasel |

★**SYMBOLIC MEANINGS:**
Benefit; Jealousy; Misanthropy;

311
Dipteryx odorata ☠

| Coumaria Nut | *Coumarouna* | *Coumarouna odorata* | *Coumarouna tetraphylla* | Cumaru | *Dipteryx tetraphylla*| Kumaru | Kumarú | Tonka | Tonka Bean Plant | Tonqua | Tonquin Bean |

★POTENTIAL POWERS:
Courage; Love; Money; Wishes;

★FOLKLORE AND FACTS:
Some believe that *Dipteryx odorata* beans can grant wishes by holding a bean in the hand while whispering the wish to it, then carrying the bean until the wish comes true...then burying or stomping on the bean afterwards. Another method is that the wished upon bean is buried in a fertile, hospitable location and the wish will come true during the time that the plant is growing. • Radio-carbon dating of large *Dipteryx odorata* stumps left behind by a loggers in the Amazon, proved that *Dipteryx odorata* is definitely a species of tree that could live to a great age...over 1,000 years!

312
Dodecatheon

| American Cowslip | Cowslip | Mad Violets | Mosquito Bills | Sailor-Caps | Shooting Stars |

★SYMBOLIC MEANINGS:
Divine beauty; Divinity; My divinity; Native grace; Pensiveness; Rusticity; Treasure finding; You are my divinity; Winning grace; Youthful beauty;

★POTENTIAL POWERS:
Healing; Youth;

313
Dracaena

| Dragon Plant | *Sanseviera* | Shrubby Dracaena | *Terminalis* |

★SYMBOLIC MEANINGS:
Snare; You are near a snare; I'm going to get you.

314
Dracaena arborea

| Dragon Tree |

★POTENTIAL POWERS:
Inner Power; Power;

315
Dracaena cinnabari

| **Dragon Blood Tree** | **Dragon's Blood Tree** | *Pterocarpus draco* | **Socotra Dragon Tree** |

★**POTENTIAL POWERS:**
Accidents; Aggression; Anger; Carnal desires; Conflict; Exorcism; Love; Lust; Machinery; Potency; Power; Protection; Purification; Rock music; Strength; Struggle; War;

★**FOLKLORE AND FACTS:**
Being that the resinous sap of *Dracaena cinnabari* is crimson red, it was highly prized as being "Dragon's Blood" in the ancient world. Therefore it was, and still is, commonly used in ritual magic and alchemy. • To quiet a boisterous home and impose peace and quiet put equal parts of powered *Dracaena cinnabari,* salt and sugar in a tight fitting jar and then hide it in the house where it cannot be found. • *Dracaena cinnabari* is used for religious purposes in American hoodoo, New Orleans voodoo, and African-American folk magic. • *Dracaena cinnabari* resin is added to ink to create "Dragon's Blood Ink", which is used to inscribe magical talismans and seals.

316
Dracaena reflexa ☠

| **Pleomele** | **Red-edged Dracaena** | **Song of India** |

★**POTENTIAL POWERS:**
Healing;

317
Dracaena sanderiana ☠

| **Belgian Evergreen** | **Lucky Bamboo** | **Ribbon Dracaena** | **Ribbon Plant** |

★**SYMBOLIC MEANINGS:**
Life everlasting;

★**POTENTIAL POWERS:**
Health; Healing; Longevity;

★**FOLKLORE AND FACTS:**
Feng Shui practitioners believe that *Dracaena sanderiana* represents the wood and water elements. A red ribbon tied around the plant's stalks incorporate the element of fire and ignites the positive flow of chi in the room. Take care to use the correct number of *Dracaena sanderiana* stalks as three is for happiness, five is for wealth, six is for health. Do not use four stalks because the word "four" sounds like the word

"death" in Chinese, and therefore it should especially be avoided in this particular circumstance.

318
Dracunculus vulgaris

| Black Arum | Black Dragon | Dragon Arum | Dragonwort | Drakondia | Ragons | Snake Lily | Stink Lily | Voodoo Lily |

★SYMBOLIC MEANINGS:
Astonishment; Dread; Horror; Snare;

319
Drimys winteri

| Canelo | *Drimys* | True Winter's Bark | Wintera | Wintera Aromatics | Winter's Bark | Winter's Cinnamon |

★POTENTIAL POWERS:
Success;

★FOLKLORE AND FACTS:
Carry a piece of *Drimys winteri* for success in whatever you do.

320
Drosera rotundifolia

| Common Sundew | Round-leaved Sundew |

★SYMBOLIC MEANINGS:
Disdain; Manners; Regret; Surprise;

★POTENTIAL POWERS:
Promotes psychic abilities; Wards off The Evil Eye;

★FOLKLORE AND FACTS:
Drosera rotundifolia is a carnivorous plant that feeds on insects that become attracted to then stuck upon sticky hairs that cover the leaves.

321
Dryas

| Avens |

★POTENTIAL POWERS:
Exorcism; Love; Purification;

322
Dryopteris filix-mas

| **Common Male Fern** | **Male Fern** | **Worm Fern** |

★**POTENTIAL POWERS:**
Love; Luck;

★**FOLKLORE AND FACTS:**
Dryopteris filix-mas was often an important addition to the making of a potent love potion.

323
Drypetes deplanchei

| *Drypetes australasica* | **Grey Bark** | **Grey Boxwood** | *Hemecyclia australasica* | **Yellow Tulip Tree** | **Yellow Tulipwood** | **White Myrtle** |

★**SYMBOLIC MEANINGS:**
Sociability;

324
Duranta erecta

| **Aussie Gold** | *Duranta repens* | **Golden Dewdrop** | **Pigeon Berry** | **Skyflower** | **Xcambocoché** |

★**SYMBOLIC MEANINGS:**
Indifference;

325
Durio

| **Durian Tree** | **King of The Fruits Tree** | **Stinky Fruit Tree** |

★**POTENTIAL POWERS:**
Aphrodisiac;

★**FOLKLORE AND FACTS:**
The Javanese people have long believed that the fruit of the *Durio* is a reliable aphrodisiac. • *Durio* flowers are closed during the day and open at night to be pollinated by fruit bats. • In Southeast Asia, it is forbidden to bring the *Durio* fruit (which is known as Stinky Fruit for a good reason) into many hotels, airports, restaurants, subways, and on nearly all public transportation.

stimulation

326
Echinacea

| Black Sampson | *Brauneria* | Coneflower | *Helichroa* | Narrow-leaved Purple Coneflower | Purple Coneflower | Red Sunflower | Sacred Plant | Sampson Root |

★**POTENTIAL POWERS:**
Health; Immunity; Strength; Strengthening spells;

327
Elettaria cardamomum

| Cardamom | Cardamon | Ceylon Cardamom | *Elettaria repens* | Ela | Elachi | Elaichi | Elakkaai | Elam | Green Cardamom | True Cardamom | Truti |

★**SYMBOLIC MEANINGS:**
Will bring peaceful thoughts;

★**POTENTIAL POWERS:**
Love; Lust;

328
Epigaea repens

| Ground Laurel | Mayflower | May Flower | Trailing Arbutus |

★**SYMBOLIC MEANINGS:**
Budding beauty; Perseverance; Welcome;

329
Epilobium

| *Boisduvalia* | *Chamaenerion* | *Chamerion* | French Willow | *Pyrogennema* | Willowherb | *Zauchneria* |

★**SYMBOLIC MEANINGS:**
Bravery; Bravery and humanity; Constancy; Humanity;

330
Epilobium angustifolium

| Boisduvalia | *Chamaenerion angustifolium* | *Chamerion angustifolium* | Fire-weed | French Willow | Rosebay Willowherb | Spiked Willowherb | Spike-Primrose | Willow Herb | Willowherb |

★ **SYMBOLIC MEANINGS:**

Bravery; Humanity; Pretension; Production;

★ **FOLKLORE AND FACTS:**

Because *Epilobium angustifolium* can establish itself rapidly upon burnt ground the abandoned bomb sites, in sharp contrast to their grim reminders, were very quickly covered over with this prolific flowering plant.

331

Epipremnum aureum ☠

| Centipede Tongavine | Devil's Ivy | Golden Pothos | Money Plant | Pothos | Silver Vine | Solomon Islands' Ivy |

★ **POTENTIAL POWERS:**

Endurability;

332

Equisetum hyemale

| Bottle Brush | Dutch Rushes | Horsetail Rush | Paddock Pipes | Pewterwort | Rough Horsetail | Scouring Rush | Shavegrass | Snake Grass |

★ **SYMBOLIC MEANINGS:**

Docility;

★ **POTENTIAL POWERS:**

Fertility; Snake charming;

333

Eremurus

| Desert Candles | Foxtail Lilies |

★ **SYMBOLIC MEANINGS:**

Endurance;

334

Erigeron

| Fleabane | *Stenactis* | Summer Starwort |

★**SYMBOLIC MEANINGS:**
Chastity;

★**POTENTIAL POWERS:**
Chastity; Exorcism; Protection;

★**FOLKLORE AND FACTS:**
Erigeron hung over the doors will keep evil from entering.

335
Eriodictyon californicum

| Bear Weed | Consumptive's Weed | Gum Bush | Holy Herb | Mountain Balm | Sacred Herb | *Wigandia californica* | Yerba Santa |

★**POTENTIAL POWERS:**
Beauty; Business; Expansion; Healing; Honor; Leadership; Politics; Power; Protection; Psychic powers; Public acclaim; Responsibility; Royalty; Success; Wealth;

★**FOLKLORE AND FACTS:**
Carry a sprig of *Eriodictyon californicum* to attain beauty.

336
Eruca sativa

| Arugula | Aruka | Beharki | Borsmustár | Garden Rocket | *Eruca* | Jarjeer | Oruga | Rauke | Rocket | Rocket Leaf | Rocketsalad | Roka | Rokka | Roquette | Ruca | Ruchetta | Rucola | Rúcula | Rughetta | Rugola | Rukola |

★**SYMBOLIC MEANINGS:**
Rivalry;

337
Eryngium

| Sea-holly | Eryngo | Yerba del Sapo |

★**POTENTIAL POWERS:**
Peace; Love; Lust; Traveler's luck;

★**FOLKLORE AND FACTS:**
Carry *Eryngium* when traveling as a charm for luck and safety. • Scatter *Eryngium* wherever people are quarreling to promote peace between the battling parties.

338

Erythronium dens-canis ☠

| Adder's Tongue | Adder's-tongue | American Trout Lily | Dog's-Tooth Violet | Dog's Tooth Violet | Dogtooth Violet | *Erythronium* | Fawn Lily | Fawn-lily | Serpent's Tongue | Trout-lily | Trout Lily | Yellow Adder's Tongue | Yellow Fawn-lily | Yellow Snowdrop |

★**POTENTIAL POWERS:**
Fishing magic; Healing;

339
Erythroxylum coca

| Coca Plant |

★**POTENTIAL POWERS:**
Healing; Pain relief; Stimulation;

★**FOLKLORE AND FACTS:**
Although *Erythroxylum coca* has been outlawed in many countries, its daily use has played a role in South American religious rituals and communal life for thousands of years (particularly in the Andes region).

340
Eschscholzia ☠

★**SYMBOLIC MEANINGS:**
Do not refuse me;

341
Eucalyptus

| Eukkie | Gum Tree |

★**POTENTIAL POWERS:**
Healing; Protection;

★**FOLKLORE AND FACTS:**
Carry *Eucalyptus* leaves to maintain good health. • Hang a piece of *Eucalyptus* over a sick bed to encourage healing.

342
Eucalyptus regnans

| Mountain Ash | Stringy Gum | Swamp Gum | Tasmanian Oak | Victorian Ash

|

★SYMBOLIC MEANINGS:
I watch over you; Loftiness; Prudence; Quiet;

343
Eucharis

| Eucharis Lily |

★SYMBOLIC MEANINGS:
Enchantment; Glamour; Maiden charms;

344
Euonymus

| Spindle | Spindle Tree |

★SYMBOLIC MEANINGS:
Likeness; Your charms are graven on my heart; Your image is engraved on my heart;

345
Euonymus atropurpureus ☠

| Burning-bush| Eastern Wahoo | Hearts Bursting With Love | Indian Arrow Wood | Spindle Tree | Wahoo |

★POTENTIAL POWERS:
Break hexes; Courage; Success;

★FOLKLORE AND FACTS:
Carry *Euonymus atropurpureus* for courage.

346
Eupatorium

| Boneset | Justiceweed | Thoroughwort | Snakeroot | Snake's Root | Yankee-weed |

★SYMBOLIC MEANINGS:
Delay; Horror;

★POTENTIAL POWERS:
Binding; Break hexes; Building; Death; Exorcism; History; Knowledge; Limitations; Luck; Money; Obstacles; Protection; Time; Wards off evil spirits;

★FOLKLORE AND FACTS:

Eupatorium wards off evil spirits if sprinkled around the home.

347
Euphorbia ☠

| Akoko | Catshair | Crown of Thorns | Mziwaziwa | Spurge | Tabaibas | Wolf's Milk |

★SYMBOLIC MEANINGS:
Persistence;

★POTENTIAL POWERS:
Protection; Purification;

★FOLKLORE AND FACTS:
Euphorbia is a very poisonous plant and care should be given to it. • Grown indoors or outside *Euphorbia* is considered to be a protective plant.

348
Euphorbia pulcherrima ☠

| Poinsettia | Noche Buena | Skin Flower | Flor de Pascua | Crown of the Andes | Christmas Flower | Christmas Eve Flower | Cuitlaxochitl | Easter Flower | Bent El Consu | The Consul's Daughter |

★SYMBOLIC MEANINGS:
Be of Good Cheer; Good cheer; Merriment;

349
Euphrasia

| Augentrostkrout | *Euphrasiae herba* | Eyebright | Eye Bright | Herba Euphrasiae | Herbe d'Euphraise |

★POTENTIAL POWERS:
Joy; Mental clarity; Mental powers; Psychic powers;

★FOLKLORE AND FACTS:
Carry *Euphrasia* when it is needed to see the truth in any matter. • Carry *Euphrasia* to increase psychic powers.

350
Eustoma

| Gentian | Lisianthus | Prairie Gentian | Texas Bluebell | Tulip Gentian |

★SYMBOLIC MEANINGS:
Outgoing nature;

★POTENTIAL POWERS:
Luck; Truth;

351
Euthrochium

| Gravelroot | Hempweed | Joe-Pie | Joe-Pye Weed | Jopi Weed | Trumpet Weed |

★POTENTIAL POWERS:
Love; Respect;

★FOLKLORE AND FACTS:
Carry a few *Euthrochium* leaves to encourage those you meet to look upon you favorably and respectfully.

352
Evergreen (any)

★SYMBOLIC MEANINGS:
Poverty; Poverty and worth;

353
Evergreen Thorn (any)

★SYMBOLIC MEANINGS:
Solace in adversity;

pride of birth

354
Fagopyrum esculentum

| **Beechwheat** | **Bitter Buckwheat** | **Common Buckwheat** | *Fagopyrum tataricum* |

★**POTENTIAL POWERS:**
Money; Protection;

★**FOLKLORE AND FACTS:**
Convert *Fagopyrum esculentum* grains into a powder then sprinkle this flour around the entire perimeter of your house to keep evil from it.

355
Fagraea berteriana

| *Fagraea berteroana* | **Perfume Flower Tree** | **Pua-kenikeni** | **Pua Keni Keni** | **Pua-Lulu** | **Ten Cent Flower Tree** |

★**SYMBOLIC MEANINGS:**
From Heaven;

★**FOLKLORE AND FACTS:**
According to Tahitian legend the flowers of the *Fagraea berteriana* Tree's fragrance is heavenly because it originated in The Tenth Heaven. • *Fagraea berteriana* is often used to create beautiful, fragrant Hawaiian leis.

356
Fagus

| **Beech** | **Beech Tree** | **Beechwood** | **Bok** | **Boke** | **Buche** | **Buk** | **Buke** | **Faggio** | **Fagos** | **Faggots** | **Faya** | **Haya** | **Hetre** |

★**SYMBOLIC MEANINGS:**
Lovers' tryst; Personal finances;

★**POTENTIAL POWERS:**
Creativity; Gambling; Money; Prosperity; Wishes;

★**FOLKLORE AND FACTS:**
Carry *Fagus* leaves or a piece of it's wood to promote and increase creativity. • To make a wish, carve it on a *Fagus* stick then bury it. It the wish is meant to be, it will be.

357
Ferula assa-foetida

| Asafetida | Asafoetida | Asant | Assyfetida | Devil's Dung | *Ferula assafoetida* | Food of the Gods | Giant Fennel | Hilteet | Hing | Ingu | Ingua | Kaayam | Perungayam | Stinking Gum | Ting | Ungoozeh |

★POTENTIAL POWERS:
Avoiding spirits; Curses; Exorcism; Evoke demonic forces and bind them; Fish bait; Protection; Protection from demonic forces; Protection from illness; Purification; Repel spirits; Wolf bait;

★FOLKLORE AND FACTS:
Ferula assa-foetida is believed to destroy all manifestations of spirits. • *Ferula assa-foetida* has one of the most horrible odors of all herbs and merely the scent of it is known to induce vomiting.

358
Ferula moschata

| Euryangium *Ferula sumbul* | Muskroot | Musk Root | Jatamansi | Moschuswurzel | Ofnokgi | Ouchi | Racine de Sumbul | Sum'bul | Sumbul | Sumbul Radix | Sumbulwurzel |

★POTENTIAL POWERS:
Health; Love; Luck; Psychic powers;

★FOLKLORE AND FACTS:
Carry a piece of *Ferula moschata* to attract love.

359
Ficus

| Fig Tree |

★SYMBOLIC MEANINGS:
A kiss; Prolific;

360
Ficus benghalensis

| Aalamaram | Arched Fig | Banyan | Bargad | Borh | *Ficus* | Bengal Fig | *Ficus indica* | India Fig | Indian Fig Tree| Indian God Tree | Nyagrodha | Peral | Strangler Fig | Wad | Vada Tree |

★**POTENTIAL POWERS:**
Happiness; Luck;

★**FOLKLORE AND FACTS:**
To be married beneath a *Ficus benghalensis* tree brings happiness and good luck to the couple. • To sit under a *Ficus benghalensis* tree will bring good luck. • To look at a *Ficus benghalensis* tree will bring good luck.

361
Ficus carica

| **Chagareltin** | **Common Fig** | **Doomoor** | **Dumur** | **Fico** | **Mhawa** |

★**SYMBOLIC MEANINGS:**
Argument; Desire; Longevity; Long-lived;

★**POTENTIAL POWERS:**
Divination; Fertility; Love;

★**FOLKLORE AND FACTS:**
Ficus carica leaves were what Adam and Eve supposedly clothed themselves with in the Bible's *Book of Genesis*. As a consequence, *Ficus carica* leaves were often used to modestly cover the genitals of many other nude figures in artworks throughout the ages. • For both men and women to increase fertility and also to overcome any sexual incompetence carry a small phallic carving made using *Ficus carica* wood.

362
Ficus religiosa

| **Bodhi** | **Bo Tree** | **Bo-Tree** | **Peepal** | **Pipul** | **Sacred Fig** | **Sacred Tree** |

★**SYMBOLIC MEANINGS:**
Awakening; Bright energy; Enlightenment; Fertility; Good luck; Happiness; Inspiration; Longevity; Meditation; Peace; Prosperity; Religiousness; Remembrance; Sacredness; Sacred tree; Ultimate potential; Wisdom;

★**POTENTIAL POWERS:**
Enlightenment; Fertility; Meditation; Protection; Wisdom;

★**FOLKLORE AND FACTS:**
Legend tells that Siddhartha Bautama was sitting under a *Ficus religiosa* tree at the time of his enlightening. He sat under it for six years. A direct descendant of this particular tree is enshrined within the Mahabodhi Temple in Bodh Gaya, India and is a frequent destination for Buddhist pilgrims. • It takes approximately 100 to 300 years for a *Ficus religiosa* tree to be fully grown. • The *Ficus religiosa* tree has very distinctive heart shaped leaves. • Religious Buddist art can be found painted on

Ficus religiosa leaves. • *Ficus religiosa* leaves are often possessed as sacred treasures. • Walk around a *Ficus religiosa* tree several times to make evil flee.

363
Ficus sycomorus

| Fig-Mulberry | Sycamore | Sycamore Fig | Sycomore |

★SYMBOLIC MEANINGS:
Curiosity; Grief;

364
Filipendula ulmaria

| Bridewort | Dollof | Lady of the Meadow | Meadow Queen | Meadow Sweet | Meadow-Wort | Meadowsweet | Meadsweet | Pride of the Meadow | Queen of the Meadow | Ulmaria |

★SYMBOLIC MEANINGS:
Usefulness; Uselessness;

★POTENTIAL POWERS:
Divination; Happiness; Love; Peace;

★FOLKLORE AND FACTS:
Filipendula ulmaria was the preferred floor strewing herb of Queen Elizabeth I. • Evidence of *Filipendula ulmaria* was found with cremated remains dating back to the Bronze Age in Wales.

365
Foeniculum

| Fennel | Marathron |Samar | Sheeh | Sweet Fennel | Wild Fennel |

★SYMBOLIC MEANINGS:
Charm ingredient; Courage; Deceit; Endurance; Flattery; Force; Grief; Healing; Long life; Protection; Purification; Strength; Worthy of all praise;

★POTENTIAL POWERS:
Exorcism; Courage; Healing; Immortality; Longevity; Protection; Purification; Repels evil spirits; Strength; Virility;

★FOLKLORE AND FACTS:
Plugging keyholes with *Foeniculum* Seeds is thought to keep ghosts from entering. • Hanging *Foeniculum* at the windows and doors will keep evil spirits from entering. • Carry *Foeniculum* seeds to keep evil spirits away from you.

366
Forsythia

★**SYMBOLIC MEANINGS:**
Anticipation;

367
Fragaria vesca

| Alpine Strawberry | European Strawberry | Fraises des Bois | Fressant | Jordboer | Poziomki | Tchilek | Wild European Strawberry | Wild Strawberry | Woodland Strawberry |

★**SYMBOLIC MEANINGS:**
Perfect excellence;

★**POTENTIAL POWERS:**
Love; Luck;

★**FOLKLORE AND FACTS:**
Carry *Fragaria vesca* leaves for good luck.

368
Fragaria x ananassa

| Common Strawberry | Garden Strawberry | Strawberry |

★**SYMBOLIC MEANINGS:**
Perfect excellence; Perfect goodness; Perfection;

★**POTENTIAL POWERS:**
Love; Luck;

▶ *Fragaria x ananassa Blossom:*
Love; Luck;

369
Franciscea latifolia

| *Brunfelsia latifolia* |

★**SYMBOLIC MEANINGS:**
Beware of a false friend; Beware of false friends; You have a false friend;

370

Fraxinus excelsior

| Ash | Ashe | Ash Tree | Common Ash | European Ash | Fraxinus |

★**SYMBOLIC MEANINGS:**

Expansion; Grandeur; Greatness; Growth; Health; Higher perspective;

★**POTENTIAL POWERS:**

Healing; Love; Protection; Prosperity; Sea Rituals;

★**FOLKLORE AND FACTS:**

In Norse mythology a mythical *Fraxinus excelsior* called "Yggdrasil" is considered to be the center of the world, with it's roots in the underworld to be watered by wisdom and faith; with the trunk supporting the earth and the canopy touching the arch of heaven. • If going out to sea, carry a solar cross carved from *Fraxinus excelsior* wood as protection against drowning. • A *Fraxinus excelsior* staff placed over doors and windows is used as protection against sorcery. • Burn a Yule log of *Fraxinus excelsior* for prosperity. • Carry *Fraxinus excelsior* leaves to gain love from the opposite sex. • Placing *Fraxinus excelsior* leaves under a pillow is believed to promote prophetic dreams. • Scatter *Fraxinus excelsior* leaves in all four directions near the home to protect the house and entire area around it. • Fresh *Fraxinus excelsior* leaves in a bowl of fresh water beside the bed overnight then discarded in the morning is supposedly a preventative against illness.

371
Freesia

★**SYMBOLIC MEANINGS:**

Childish; Faithfulness through the seasons; Fidelity; Immature; Innocence; Love's honorable character; Trust;

372
Fritillaria imperialis

| Crown Imperial | Crown Imperial Lily | Imperial Lily | Kaiser's Crown |

★**SYMBOLIC MEANINGS:**

Arrogance; Majesty; Power; Pride; Pride of birth;

373
Fritillaria meleagris

| Checkered Daffodil | Checkered Fritillary | Chequered Fritillary | Chess Flower | Fritillary | Frog-Cup | Guinea-Hen Flower | Kockavica | Kungsängslilja | Lazarus Bell | Leper Lily | Snake's Head | Snake's Head Frital-

lary |

★SYMBOLIC MEANINGS:
Persecution;

374
Fuchsia

| Fuchia | Fuchias | Fuchsias | Lady's Ear-Drop |

★SYMBOLIC MEANINGS:
Amiability; Confiding love; Faithfulness; Frailty; Frugality; Good taste; Humble love; Love secrets; My ambitious love plagues itself; Taste; The ambition of my love thus plagues itself;

375
Fucus vesiculosus

| Bladder Fucus | Black Tang | Black Tany | Bladderwrack | Bladder Wrack | Cut Weed | Cutweed | Dyers Fucus | Red Fucus | Rockweed | Rock Wrack | Sea Oak | Sea Spirit |

★POTENTIAL POWERS:
Money; Protection; Psychic powers;

★FOLKLORE AND FACTS:
Fucus vesiculosus is a seaweed most commonly found on the shores of the British Isles, *Fucus vesiculosus* is also found beaches of the western Baltic Sea, the North Sea, the Atlantic Ocean, and the Pacific Ocean. • *Fucus vesiculosus* is the original source of therapeutic iodine. • Carry a *Fucus vesiculosus* amulet for when traveling on or over the sea as protection to the traveler.

376
Fumaria

| Fumewort | Fumitory |

★SYMBOLIC MEANINGS:
Gall; Hatred; Ill at ease; Longevity; Spleen;

★POTENTIAL POWERS:
Exorcism; Money;

creativity

377
Galanthus nivalis

| Candlemas Bells | Church Flower | Common Snowdrop | Dingle-Dangle | Fair Maid Of February | February Fairmaids | Maids Of February | Mary's Tapers | Perce-Neige | Snowdrop | Snow Piercers |

★SYMBOLIC MEANINGS:
Consolation; Friend in adversity; Friend in need; Hope; Hope in sorrow; Purity and hope;

★FOLKLORE AND FACTS:
There is a superstition that it is unlucky to bring *Galanthus nivalis* into the home, and that supposedly merely the sight of a single *Galanthus nivalis* growing in the garden foretold a pending disaster.

378
Galega officinalis ☠

| French Honeysuckle | French Lilac | *Galega bicolor* | Goats Rue | Goat's Rue | Italian Fitch | Lavamani | Professor-Weed | Rutwica |

★SYMBOLIC MEANINGS:
Reason;

★POTENTIAL POWERS:
Exorcism; Healing; Health; Protection;

★FOLKLORE AND FACTS:
It is believed by some that putting *Galega officinalis* leaves into your shoes will prevent rheumatism.

◉ SPECIFIC COLOR MEANING > Purple:
First emotions of love; Love at first sight;

379
Galium aparine

| Catchweed | Cleavers | Clivers | Coachweed | Goosegrass | Robin-run-the-hedge | Stickyjack | Stickyleaf | Stickyweed | Stickywilly |

★POTENTIAL POWERS:
Binding; Commitment; Protection; Relationships; Tenacity;

▸ *Galium aparine Burr:*
Cling to me.

380
Galium odoratum ☠

| *Asperula odorata* | Herb Walter | Master of the Woods | Sweet Woodruff |
Waldmeister | Wild Baby's Breath | Wood Rove | Woodruff | Wuderove |

★SYMBOLIC MEANINGS:
Humility;

★POTENTIAL POWERS:
Money; Protection; Victory;

★FOLKLORE AND FACTS:
Carry *Galium odoratum* to attract money. • Carry *Galium odoratum* as protection against harm. • Carry a spring of *Galium odoratum* to be victorious in sports or battle of any kind.

381
Galium triflorum

| Cudweed | Fragrant Bedstraw | Sweet-scented Bedstraw |

★POTENTIAL POWERS:
Love;

★FOLKLORE AND FACTS:
Wear or carry a sprig of *Galium triflorum* to attract love.

382
Galium verum

| Bedstraw | Cheese Rennet | Cheese Renning | Frigg's Grass | Gul Snerre |
Lady's Bedstraw | Maid's Hair | Our Lady's Bedstraw | Petty Mugget | Yellow
Bedstraw |

★SYMBOLIC MEANINGS:
Love; Rejoicing; Rudeness:;

★FOLKLORE AND FACTS:
The legend is that *Galium verum* was the hay used in the Bethlehem manger where Jesus was placed as a newborn. • In days of old, dried *Galium verum* was often used as a mattress stuffing because it was thought to be a fairly effective flea killer as well. • Wear or carry a sprig of *Galium verum* to attract love.

383
Gardenia jasminoides

| Cape Jasmine | Cape Jessamine | Common Gardenia | *Gardenia* |

★SYMBOLIC MEANINGS:

Ecstasy; Emotional support; Exhilarating emotions; Good luck; Healing; I am too happy; I Love You In Secret; Joy; Love; Peace; Purification; Purity; Refinement; Secret love; Spirituality; Sweet love; Transient joy; Transport; Transport of joy; You're lovely; You are lovely;

★POTENTIAL POWERS:

Healing; Love; Peace; Spirituality;

★FOLKLORE AND FACTS:

Due to the extremely high spiritual vibrations of *Gardenia jasminoides,* float a blossom in a bowl of fresh water or scatter dried petals around the room to promote a sense of extreme inner peacefulness and increased spirituality.

384
Gaultheria procumbens

| American Wintergreen | Boxberry | Canada Tea | Checkerberry | Deerberry | Eastern Teaberry | Ground Berry | Groundberry | Hillberry | Hill Berry | Mountain Tea | Partridge Berry | Partridgeberry | Spiceberry | Spice Berry | Spicy Wintergreen | Spring Wintergreen | Teaberry | Wax Custer | Wintergreen |

★SYMBOLIC MEANINGS:

Harmony;

★POTENTIAL POWERS:

Breaking hexes; Healing; Protection;

★FOLKLORE AND FACTS:

It is believed that a sprig of *Gaultheria procumbens* under a child's pillow offers protection and a life of good fortune.

385
Gaultheria shallon

| Gaultheria | Salal | Shallon |

★SYMBOLIC MEANINGS:

Zest;

386
Gelsemium sempervirens

| Carolina Jasmine | Carolina Jessamine | Clinging Woodbine | Evening Trumpetflower | Gelsemium | Jessamine | Woodbine | Yellow Jasmine | Yellow Jessamine |

★ **SYMBOLIC MEANINGS:**
Elegance; Fraternal love; Grace; Grace and elegance; Grace and eloquence; Modesty; Separation;

387
Gentiana

| Bitter Root | Gentian | Hochwurzel |

★ **SYMBOLIC MEANINGS:**
Loveliness;

★ **POTENTIAL POWERS:**
Applying knowledge; Astral plane; Break hexes; Controlling lower principles; Finding lost objects; Love; Overcoming evil; Power; Regeneration; Removing depression; Sensuality; Uncovering secrets; Victory;

388
Gentiana andrewsii

| Bottle Gentian | Closed Bottle Gentian | Closed Gentian |

★ **SYMBOLIC MEANINGS:**
Sweet be thy dreams; I wish you Sweet Dreams; Sweet Dreams;

389
Gentiana crinita

| Blue Gentian | Fringed Gentian |

★ **SYMBOLIC MEANINGS:**
Autumn; I look to Heaven; Intrinsic worth;

★ **POTENTIAL POWERS:**
Breaks hexes; Love; Power;

390

Geranium

| Cranesbill | Hardy Geranium | True Geranium |

★SYMBOLIC MEANINGS:

Availability; Constancy; Deceit; Envy; Fertility; Folly; Friendship; Frustrations passing away; Gentility; Health; Joy; Preference; Protection; Returning joy; Stupidity; True friend;

★POTENTIAL POWERS:

Healing; Love; Peace; Spirituality;

★FOLKLORE AND FACTS:

There is a superstition that snakes and flies will not go near *Geraniums* that are white.

391

Geranium maculatum

| Alum Bloom | Alum Root | Crowbill | Crows-bill | Crowfoot | Crow-foot | Spotted Spotted Cranesbill | Geranium | Old Maid's Nightcap | Wild Cranesbill | Wild Geranium |

SYMBOLIC MEANINGS:

Envy; Steadfast piety; Gentility;

392

Geranium phaeum

| Black Widow | Dark Geranium | Dusky Cranesbill | Mourning Widow |

★SYMBOLIC MEANINGS:

Gentility; Melancholy; Sadness; Sorrow;

393

Geranium versicolor

| Pencilled Crane's-bill | Pencilled Geranium | Veiny Geranium |

★POTENTIAL POWERS:

Gentility; Ingenuity;

394

Gerbera

| African Daisy | Barberton Daisy | Gerbera Daisy | Transvaal Daisy |

★SYMBOLIC MEANINGS:
Innocence; Purity and strength; Purity; Strength;

395
Geum urbanum

| Assaranaccara | Avens | Bennet | Blessed Herb | Cloveroot | Clove Root | Colewort | Golden Star | Goldy Star | Harefoot | Herb Bennet | Minart | Minarta | Pesleporis | Star of The Earth | St. Benedict's Herb | Way Bennet | Wood Avens | Yellow Avens |

★POTENTIAL POWERS:
Drives away evil spirits; Exorcism; Love; Purification;

★FOLKLORE AND FACTS:
If worn as an amulet *Geum urbanum* protects against attacks by beasts, dogs, and venomous snakes.

396
Ginkgo biloba

| Gingko | Ginkgo | Ginnan | In Xìng | Icho | Tree of Life | Maidenhair Tree |

★SYMBOLIC MEANINGS:
Age; Old age; Remembering; Survival; Thoughtfulness; True Tree of Life;

★POTENTIAL POWERS:
Aphrodisiac; Fertility; Healing; Intense concentration; Longevity; Love; Mental acuity;

397
Gladiolus

| Corn Lilies | Glad | Sword Lily |

★SYMBOLIC MEANINGS:
Flower of the gladiators; Generosity; Give me a break; I'm sincere; Infatuation;Integrity; Love at first sight; Moral integrity; Ready armed; Remembrance; Strength; Strong character; Strength Of Character; Vibrancy; You pierce my heart;

★FOLKLORE AND FACTS:
Gladiolus grew wild in the Holy Land and along the coast of Africa so abundantly that they are thought to be the actual "Lilies of The Field" that Jesus spoke of in his Sermon On The Mount.

398
Glechoma hederacea ☠

| Alehoof | Catsfoot | Cat's Foot | Creeping Charlie | Creeping Charley | Creeping Jenny | Field Balm | Gill-Over-The-Ground | Ground Ivy | Ground-Ivy | Haymaids | Hedgemaids | Lizzy-Run-Up-The-Hedge | *Nepeta glechoma* | *Nepeta hederacea* | Robin-Run-In-The-Hedge | Run-Away-Robin | Runnaway Robin | Tunhoof |

★ POTENTIAL POWERS:
Divination;

★ FOLKLORE AND FACTS:
To find out who is working against you using negative magic, starting on a Tuesday encircle a yellow candle with *Glechoma hederacea* and then light the candle. The knowledge of who will come to you.

399
Gleditsia triacanthos

| Green Locust Tree | Honey Locust |

★ SYMBOLIC MEANINGS:
Affection beyond the grave; Elegance; Love after death; Love beyond the grave;

400
Gloxinia

★ SYMBOLIC MEANINGS:
Love at first sight;

401
Glycyrrhiza glabra ☠

| *Glycyrrhiza glandulifera* | Lacris | Licorice | Licourice | Liquorice | Lycorys | Mulaithi | Reglisse | Sweet Root |

★ POTENTIAL POWERS:
Business transactions; Caution; Cleverness; Communication; Creativity; Faith; Fidelity; Illumination; Initiation; Intelligence; Learning; Love; Lust; Memory; Prudence; Science; Self-preservation; Sound judgment; Thievery; Wisdom;

★ FOLKLORE AND FACTS:
Carry a piece of *Glycyrrhiza glabra* root to attract love. • *Glycyrrhiza glabra* is believed to make a good wand.

402
Gnaphalium

| American Cudweed | Cudweed |

★**SYMBOLIC MEANINGS:**
I think of thee;

403
Gnaphalium uliginosum

| Chafe Weed | Everlasting | Field Balsam | Indian Posy | Marsh Everlasting |
Old Field Balsam | Sweet Scented Life-Everlasting | White Balsam |

★**SYMBOLIC MEANINGS:**
Never ceasing memory; Never ceasing remembrance; Perpetual remembrances; Unceasing remembrance;

★**POTENTIAL POWERS:**
Longevity; Health; Healing;

★**FOLKLORE AND FACTS:**
Carry and/or keep *Gnaphalium uliginosum* in the home to help prevent illness.

404
Gomphrena globosa

|Bachelor Button | Bozu | Globe Amaranth | *Globe Amaranthus* | Lehua Pepa |
Lehua Moa Loa | Saam Pii |Sennichisou | Supadi Phool |Vadamalli |

★**SYMBOLIC MEANINGS:**
Endless love; Immortality; Love; Immortal love; Unchangeable;

★**POTENTIAL POWERS:**
Healing; Protection;

★**FOLKLORE AND FACTS:**
Gomphrena globosa flowers are used in long-lasting Hawaiian leis because they hold their shape and color long after the flowers have dried.

405
Gossypium

| Cotton Plant | Lint Plant | Cotton Shrub | *Erioxylum* | *Ingenhouzia* | *Notoxylinon* | *Selera* | *Stutia* | *Thuberia* | *Ultragossypium* |

★**SYMBOLIC MEANINGS:**

I feel my obligations; Obligations;

★**POTENTIAL POWERS:**

Fishing; Healing; Luck; Rain; Protection;

★**FOLKLORE AND FACTS:**

Gossypium that is either scattered or planted on your property will keep ghosts away. • *Gossypium* cloth should be your first choice when you require cloth for magical purposes. • Burning a piece of *Gossypium* supposedly will bring rain. • A piece of *Gossypium* in the sugar bowl brings good luck. • Throw *Gossypium* over your right shoulder when the sun rises and it will bring good luck that day. • Little balls of *Gossypium* that have been soaked in white vinegar and placed on all the windowsills will keep evil from entering.

406
Grain

★**POTENTIAL POWERS:**

Protection;

407
Grevillea ☠

| Silky-Oak | Spider Flower | Toothbrush |

★**SYMBOLIC MEANINGS:**

Elope with me; Impulsive acts of love;

408
Guarianthe skinneri

| *Cattleya deckeri* | *Cattleya laelioides* | *Cattleya pachecoi* | *Cattleya skinneri* | *Epidendrum huegelianum* | **Flor de San Sebastian** |

★**SYMBOLIC MEANINGS:**

Mature charm;

409
Gypsophila ☠

| **Baby's Breath** | **Gyp** | **Happy Festival** | **Love Chalk** | **Soap Wort** |

★**SYMBOLIC MEANINGS:**

Everlasting love; Happiness; Innocence; Modesty; Pure of heart; Purity; Sweet beauty;

constancy

410
Hamamelis

| *Hamamelis virginiana* | Snapping Hazelnut | Spotted Alder | *Ulmus glabra* | Wice Hazel | Winterbloom | Witch-Hazel | Witch Hazel | Wych Elm |

★ **SYMBOLIC MEANINGS:**
A magic spell; A spell; A spell is on me; Changeable; Chastity;

★ **POTENTIAL POWERS:**
Divination; Protection;

★ **FOLKLORE AND FACTS:**
A forked twig of *Hamamelis* wood is what is most commonly used as an effective divining rod. • Carry a sprig of *Hamamelis* to heal a broken heart.

411
Hebe speciosa

| New Zealand Hebe | Showy Hebe | Showy-Speedwell | *Veronica speciosa* |

★ **SYMBOLIC MEANINGS:**
I dare not; Keep this for me; Keep this for my sake;

412
Hedera helix

| Bindwood | Common Ivy | English Ivy | Gort | *Hedera acuta* | *Hedera arborea* | *Hedera baccifera* | *Hedera grandifolia* | Ivy | Ivy Vine | Lovestone | Teardrop | Tree Ivy |

★ **SYMBOLIC MEANINGS:**
Affection; Dependence; Endurance; Fidelity; Friendship; Happy love; Marriage; Matrimony; Wedded love; Friendship and Fidelity in marriage; Wedded Love;

★ **POTENTIAL POWERS:**
Healing; Protection;

★ **FOLKLORE AND FACTS:**
Hedera helix was once carried by women to bring luck. • *Hedera helix* is a symbol of eternal life to both pagans and Christians. • If *Hedera helix* is blended with *Ilex aquifolium* (Holly) at Christmas it is thought to bring peace to husband and wife in their home. • *Hedera helix* can climb up into the canopy of trees and grow so densely that

the trees topple over from the weight of it all. • Although the mental vision of an ivy covered cottage is a romantic one, in actuality *Hedera helix* aerial rootlets forcing into dry stacked stone, weakened mortar, and pushing under and through boards can be extensively destructive. • Where *Hedera helix* grows or is strewn it will guard the area against disasters and negative energies.

▶ *Hedera helix Sprig:*
Longings;

▶ *Hedera helix Sprig of Tendrils:*
Affection; Anxious to please; Assiduous to please;

413
Hedysarum coronarium

| Cock's Head | French Honeysuckle |

★ **SYMBOLIC MEANINGS:**
Rustic beauty;

414
Helenium

| Common Sneezeweed | Helenium autumnale | Large-Flowered Sneezeweed | Sneezeweed |

★ **SYMBOLIC MEANINGS:**
Tears;

★ **POTENTIAL POWERS:**
Expel evil spirits;

★ **FOLKLORE AND FACTS:**
The act of actually sneezing is what gave Helenium the supposed power of being able to rid oneself of evil spirits by sneezing them out.

415
Helianthella parryi

| Parry's Dwarf-Sunflower |

★ **SYMBOLIC MEANINGS:**
Adoration; Your devout admirer;

416

Helianthus

| Corona | Marigold of Peru | Queen of Annuals | Solis | Solo Indianus | Sunflower |

★**SYMBOLIC MEANINGS:**

Ambition; Constancy; Devotion; False appearance; False riches; Flexibility; Good luck; Haughtiness; Healing; Homage; Inspiration; Lofty thoughts; Loyalty; Nourishment; Opportunity; Power; Pride; Pure; Pure and lofty thoughts; Spiritual attainment; Strength; Unhappy love; Vitality; Warmth; Wealth;

★**POTENTIAL POWERS:**

Constancy; Deep loyalty; Fertility; Happiness; Health; Longevity; Loyalty; Nourishment; Power; Sustenance; Warmth; Wisdom; Wishes; Wish magic;

★**FOLKLORE AND FACTS:**

In 1532 Pizarro reported that he had seen those in the Peruvian Incan Empire worshipping giant *Helianthus* flowers, the design of which was also in gold on the robes of the Incan priestesses. • If growing *Helianthus* in the garden the gardener will have very good luck. • It is believed that if you put a *Helianthus* flower under the bed, you will dream about anything you need to know the truth about. • The face of the *Helianthus* flowers follow the sun. • Native American prairie Indians would put bowls of *Helianthus* seeds as a tribute on the graves of their dead loved ones. • An interesting love Divination is that a girl will put three *Helianthus* seeds down her back and she will marry the first boy she happens to meet. • It is believed by some that a necklace of *Helianthus* seed, strung as beads, will protect the wearer against contracting smallpox. • It is believed by some that if you cut a *Helianthus* stalk at sunset while making a wish, the wish will come true before sunset the next day.

417

Helianthus giganteus

| Giant Sunflower | Tall Sunflower |

★**SYMBOLIC MEANINGS:**

Intellectual greatness; Misery; Splendid; Splendor; Pure; Pure and lofty thoughts; Lofty thoughts;

★**POTENTIAL POWERS:**

Fertility; Happiness; Health; Sustenance; Wisdom; Wishes; Wish magic;

418

Helianthus tuberosus

| Earth Apple | Jerusalem Artichoke | Sunchoke | Sunroot | Topinambour |

★**POTENTIAL POWERS:**
Healing;

419
Helichrysum

| **Everlasting | Immortelles | Life Everlasting | Paper Daisy | Strawflower |**

★**SYMBOLIC MEANINGS:**
Agreement; Constancy; Continual happiness; Health; Healing; Longevity;

420
Helichrysum italicum

| **Curry Plant | Helichrysum angustifolium | Immortelle | Scaredy-cat Plant |**

★**POTENTIAL POWERS:**
Exorcism; Protection;

421
Heliconia

| **False Bird-of-Paradise | Lobster-Claws | Wild Plantains |**

★**SYMBOLIC MEANINGS:**
Great returns;

422
Heliotropium ☠

| **Cherry Pie | Garden Heliotrope | God's Herb | Heliotrope |** *Heliotropium arborescens* **| Herb of Love | Hindicum | Marine Heliotrope | Princess Marina | Turnsole |**

★**SYMBOLIC MEANINGS:**
Devoted attachment; Devotion; Eternal Love; I adore you; Intoxication of love; I remain true; Success; The intoxication of love;

★**POTENTIAL POWERS:**
Exorcism; Healing; Invisibility; Prophetic dreams; Wealth;

★**FOLKLORE AND FACTS:**
If you have been the victim of a burglary and want to know who it was that stole from you, put *Heliotropium* flowers and leaves in a small white cotton or white silk pouch to place under your pillow. The thief will appear in a dream.

423
Heliotropium peruvianum ☠

| **Peruvian Heliotrope** |

★**SYMBOLIC MEANINGS:**
Adoration; Devotion; Faithfulness; I love; Infatuation; I turn to thee; I turn to you;

★**POTENTIAL POWERS:**
Exorcism; Healing; Prophetic dreams; Wealth;

424
Helleborus ☠

| **Christmas Aconite** | **Christmas Rose** | **Hellebore** | **Lenton Rose** |

★**SYMBOLIC MEANINGS:**
Anxiety; Calumny; Relief; Relieve my anxiety; Scandal; Tranquilize my anxiety; Wit;

★**POTENTIAL POWERS:**
Protection;

★**FOLKLORE AND FACTS:**
Although every part of the *Helleborus* is deadly poisonous, and for that reason it is too dangerous to use for any reason whatsoever, it was once believed that bringing a vase of *Helleborus* into a room full of dreadful negativity would push out the unpleasantness and replace it with tranquility.

425
Helleborus foetidus ☠

| **Bear's Foot** | **Dungwort** | **Stinking Hellebore** |

★**SYMBOLIC MEANINGS:**
Chivalry; Knight; Misanthropy;

★**FOLKLORE AND FACTS:**
Every part of the *Helleborus foetidus* is deadly poisonous and for that reason it is too dangerous to use for any reason whatsoever.

426
Helleborus niger ☠

| **Black Hellebore** | **Christmas Rose** | **Melampode** | **Winter Rose** |

★**POTENTIAL POWERS:**

Astral projection; Exorcism; Invisibility; Peace; Protection; Tranquility;

★ **FOLKLORE AND FACTS:**

Every part of the *Helleborus niger* is deadly poisonous and for that reason it is too dangerous to use for any reason whatsoever.

427
Hemerocallis

| **Common Daylily** | **Daylily** | **Day Lily** |

★ **SYMBOLIC MEANINGS:**

Coquetry;

428
Hemerocallis fulva

| **Ditch Lily** | **Orange Daylily** | **Outhouse Lily** | **Railroad Daylily** | **Roadside Daylily** | **Tawny Daylily** | **Tiger Daylily** |

★ **SYMBOLIC MEANINGS:**

Coquetry; Diversity; Tenacity;

429
Hemerocallis lilioasphodelus

| **Gum Jum** | *Hemerocallis flava* | **Husan t'sao** | **Lemon Day-Lily** | **Lemon Lily** | **Pinyin** | **Tawny Lily** | **Yellow Day-Lily** | **Yellow Daylily** |

★ **SYMBOLIC MEANINGS:**

Coquetry; Motherhood; Forgetfulness;

★ **POTENTIAL POWERS:**

Diminish sorrow by causing forgetfulness;

430
Hepatica

| **Edellebere** | **Heart Leaf** | **Herb Trinity** | **Liverleaf** | **Liverweed** | **Liverwort** | **Trefoil** |

★ **SYMBOLIC MEANINGS:**

Confidence; Constancy; Trust;

★ **POTENTIAL POWERS:**

Love; Protection;

★FOLKLORE AND FACTS:
For a woman to secure a man's love she should carry *Hepatica* at all times.

431
Hesperis matronalis

| Damask Violet | Dame's Gilliflower | Dame's Rocket | Dame's Violet | Dames-Wort | Julienne des Dames | Mother-of-the-Evening | Night Scented Gilliflower | Queen's Gilliflower | Queen's Rocket | Rogue's Gilliflower | Summer Lilac | Sweet Rocket | Winter Gilliflower |

★SYMBOLIC MEANINGS:
Fashion; Fashionable; You are the queen of coquettes; Watchfulness;

⊙ SPECIFIC COLOR MEANING > White:
Despair not; God is everywhere;

432
Hibiscus rosa-sinensis

| Bunga Raya | Chemparathy | Chijin | Chinese Hibiscus | Erhonghua | Flor de Jamaica | Fosang | Fusang | Graxa | Gumamela | Hibiscus | Hongfusang | Hongmujin | Huohonghua | Jaba | Jaswand | Jiamudan | Kembang Sepatu | Kharkady | Mamdaram | Mondaro | Queen of Tropical Flowers | Rjii | Sangjin | Sembaruthi | Shoe Flower | Shoeflower | Songjin | Tuhonghua | Tulipan | Wada Mal | Zhaodianhong | Zhongguoqiangwei |

★SYMBOLIC MEANINGS:
Beauty; Delicate; Delicate beauty; Peace and Happiness; Rare beauty;

★POTENTIAL POWERS:
Attitude; Ambition; Clear thinking; Divination; Harmony; Higher understanding; Logic; Love; Lust; Manifestation in material form; Spiritual concepts; Thought processes;

★FOLKLORE AND FACTS:
The *Hibiscus rosa-sinensis* is called "Shoe Flower" because the petals can be used to shine shoes. • In the Pacific Islands a red *Hibiscus rosa-sinensis* flower is worn by women as a sign of their interests. If worn behind the left ear it signals that she desires a lover. If behind the right ear, she already has a lover. If a *Hibiscus rosa-sinensis* is worn behind both ears it signals that she has a lover but would like another one. • In the tropical countries, *Hibiscus rosa-sinensis* flowers are tucked into marital wreaths that are used as a marriage ceremony decoration.

433
Hibiscus syriacus

| *Althaea frutex* | Mugunghwa | Rose of Althea | Rose of Sharon | Shrub Althea | Syrian Ketmia | Syrian Mallow |

★**SYMBOLIC MEANINGS:**
Consumed by love; Persistant love; Persuasion;

★**POTENTIAL POWERS:**
Exorcism; Love; Protection;

434
Hibiscus trionum

| Ajannäyttäjä | Bladder Hibiscus | Bladder Ketmia | Bladder Weed | Flower of an Hour | Flower-of-an-Hour | Modesty | Puarangi | Rosemallow | Shoofly | Venetian Mallow | Venice Mallow |

★**SYMBOLIC MEANINGS:**
Delicate beauty; Frailty;

435
Hieracium

| Hawkweed |

★**SYMBOLIC MEANINGS:**
Adhesiveness; Quick sight;

436
Hippomane mancinella ☠

| *Hippomane aucuparia* | *Hippomane biglandulosa* | *Hippomane cerifera* | *Hippomane dioica* | *Hippomane fruticosa* | *Hippomane glandulosa* | *Hippomane horrida* | *Hippomane ilicifolia* | *Hippomane mancanilla* | *Hippomane spinosa* | *Hippomane zeocca* | Machineal Tree | Manchineel Tree | Machioneel | *Mancanilla* | *Mancinella* | Marzanilla | Manzanilla del la muerte | Little Apple of Death |

★**SYMBOLIC MEANINGS:**
Betrayal; Falsehood; Falseness;

★**FOLKLORE AND FACTS:**
Found on or near coastal beaches, the *Hippomane mancinella* tree is one of *the most poisonous trees in the world.* Every part of it is deadly poisonous. • Explorer Juan Ponce de Leon died a few days after being struck from an arrow poisoned with *Hip-*

pomane mancinella sap by Calusa Indians camped near St. Petersburg, Florida. • The ancient Carib and Calusa Indians favored a manner of killing captives by simply tying the victim to the trunk of the *Hippomane mancinella* tree and letting the poisonous bark do the painful dirty deed. • A single drop of the milky sap of the *Hippomane mancinella* tree mixed with even one drop of rainwater or dew merely falling on the skin will cause blistering, so never take cover under it for any reason. • The smoke from a burning *Hippomane mancinella* tree can can cause blindness. • These trees are usually *not* marked as being deadly poisonous in most places, but in some places you might see on the trunk marks such as a red "X", a red band a few feet up from the ground, or a actual warning sign to indicate that this tree is extremely dangerous and to entirely stay away from it.

437
Hordeum vulgare
| Akiti | Barley | Jt | Sma |

★POTENTIAL POWERS:
Love; Healing; Protection;

★FOLKLORE AND FACTS:
Hordeum vulgare was one of the first grains that were actually domesticated in the Near East dating back to approximately 1500 - 850 BD. Evidence of *Hordeum vulgare spontaneum* (Wild Barley) dates back to approximately 8,500 BC. • The important significance of *Hordeum vulgare* is in religious ritual during ancient Middle East, Greece, and Egyptian times. • In Medieval times, a type of divination using cakes made of *Hordeum vulgare* were often used to determine guilt or innocence. This is known as *alphitomancy*, if there was a group of suspected criminals to sort through all of them they were fed cakes or bread made of *Hordeum vulgare.* Supposedly, the person who got ingestion was the guilty party. • Scatter *Hordeum vulgare* on the ground near to your home to keep evil and negativity from approaching it.

438
Hosta
| Corfu Lily | Day Lily | Funkia | *Funkiaceae* | Giboshi | *Hostaceae* | Plantain Lily | Urui |

★SYMBOLIC MEANINGS:
Devotion;

439
Houstonia caerulea

| Azure Bluet | *Houstonia* | Quaker Ladies |

★ **SYMBOLIC MEANINGS:**
Content; Innocence;

440
Hoya

| Pentagram Flowers | Pentagram Plant | Waxflower | Waxplant | Waxvine |

★ **SYMBOLIC MEANINGS:**
Contentment; Sculpture; Susceptibility;

★ **POTENTIAL POWERS:**
Protection; Power;

★ **FOLKLORE AND FACTS:**
When grown in the house, *Hoya* offers protection. • Dry the *Hoya* flowers to wear as an amulet for power and protection.

441
Humulus lupulus

| Beer Flower | Common Hop | Flores de Cerveza | Hop |

★ **SYMBOLIC MEANINGS:**
Injustice; Mirth; Pride and passion;

★ **POTENTIAL POWERS:**
Healing; Sleep;

★ **FOLKLORE AND FACTS:**
Sleep on a pillow that has been stuffed with dried *Humulus lupulus* for improved rest.

442
Hyacinthoides non-scripta

| Bluebell | Common Bluebell | English Bluebell |

★ **SYMBOLIC MEANINGS:**
Constancy; Delicacy; Grateful; Gratitude; Humility; Kindness; Luck; Solitude; Sorrowful regret; Truth;

443
Hyacinthus orientalis

| Common Hyacinth | Dutch Hyacinth | Garden Hyacinth | Hyacinth |

★**SYMBOLIC MEANINGS:**

Benevolence; Constancy; Faith; Game; Games and Sports; Gentleness of nature; Happiness; Impulsiveness; Jealousy; Love; Overcoming grief; Play; Protection; Rashness; Sport;

★**POTENTIAL POWERS:**

Death and Revival; Delays sexual maturity; Happiness; Love; Protection;

★**FOLKLORE AND FACTS:**

Sniffing fresh *Hyacinthus orientalis* flowers will ease depression and grief. • Grown in a pot in the bedroom *Hyacinthus orientalis* will prevent nightmares.

⊙ **SPECIFIC COLOR MEANING > Blue:**

Consistency;

⊙ **SPECIFIC COLOR MEANING > Pink:**

Harmless mischief; Play; Playful Joy;

⊙ **SPECIFIC COLOR MEANING > Purple:**

I'm sorry; Jealousy; Please forgive me; Regret; Sadness; Sorrow; Sorrowful;

⊙ **SPECIFIC COLOR MEANING > Red:**

Harmless mischief; Play; Playful Joy;

⊙ **SPECIFIC COLOR MEANING > White:**

I'll pray for you; Loveliness; Prayers for those in need; Unobtrusive loveliness;

⊙ **SPECIFIC COLOR MEANING > Yellow:**

Jealousy;

444

Hybrides remontants

| Hybrid Perpetual Rose | Perpetual Rose | Rosa Perpetua |

★**SYMBOLIC MEANINGS:**

Immortal beauty;

445

Hybrid Tea

| Hybrid Tea Rose | Tea Rose |

★**SYMBOLIC MEANINGS:**

I'll remember; Always; Enduring desire; Desire; Always lovely;

446

Hydrangea

| Hortensia | Seven Barks |

★**SYMBOLIC MEANINGS:**

A boaster; Carelessness; Devotion; False pride; Frigidness; Frigidity; Gratefulness and price; Heartfelt praise and appreciation; Heartlessness; Pride; Remember; Ruthlessness; Thank you for understanding; Uncrossing; Vain glory; You are cold;

★**POTENTIAL POWERS:**

Break hexes; Hex breaking;

★**FOLKLORE AND FACTS:**

Carry or scatter *Hydrangea* bark around the home to break a hex.

447

Hydrastis canadensis ☠

| Eye Balm | Eye Root | Goldenseal | Ground Raspberry | Indian Dye | Indian Paint | Jaundice Root | Orangeroot | Orange Root | Orange-Root | Tumeric Root | Warnera | Wild Curcurma | Yellow Puccoon | Yellow Root |

★**POTENTIAL POWERS:**

Healing; Money;

448

Hylocereus undatus

| Belle of the Night | Buah Naga | *Cactus triangularis aphyllus* | Cardo-ananaz | Cato-barse | *Cereus triangularis major* | *Cereus undatus* | *Cereus tricostatus* | Cierge-Lézard | Conderella Plant | Distelbirne | Drachenfrucht | Dragonfruit | Flor de Caliz | Fruit du Dragon | Huolóngguo | *Hylocereus tricostatus* | Junco | Junco Tapatio | Kaeo Mangkon | Luna Flower | Lunar Flower | Moon Flower | Night Blooming Cereus | Nightblooming Cereus | Panini-O-Ka-Puna-Hou | Panini o Kapunahou | Pitahaya Orejona | Pitahaya Roja | Pitajava | Poire de Chardon | Princess of The Night | Punahou cactus | Queen of the Night | Rainha da Noite | Red Pitahaya | Red Pitaya | Reina de la Noche | Röd Pitahaya | Skogskaktus | Strawberry Pear | Tasajo | Thanh Long |

★**SYMBOLIC MEANINGS:**

Transient beauty; Beauty under the moon's light; Moonlit beauty;

★**FOLKLORE AND FACTS:**

A enormous hedge of *Hylocereus undatus* that was planted in Honolulu in 1836 at the Punahou School by a woman by the name of "Mrs. Bingham" is supposedly the mother plant of nearly all of *Hylocereus undatus* in Hawaii, started from cuttings taken at the Punahou School for well over a century.

449
Hyoscyamus niger

| Black Nightshade | Cassilago | Cassilata | Deus Caballinus | Devil's Eye | Hebenon | Henbane | Henbells | Hogsbean | Isana | Jupiter's Bean | Jusquiame | Poison Tobacco | Stinking Nightshade | Symphonica |

★**SYMBOLIC MEANINGS:**
Blemish; Defect; Fault; Imperfection;

★**POTENTIAL POWERS:**
Death; Love; Witchcraft;

★**FOLKLORE AND FACTS:**
Every part of the *Hyoscyamus niger* plant is deadly poisonous and for that reason it is too dangerous to use for any reason whatsoever.

450
Hypericum perforatum

| Amber | Chase-devil | Chase Devil | Common Saint John's Wort | Fuga Daemonum | Goat Weed | Herba John | John's Wort | Klamath Weed | Tipton's Weed | Saint John's Wort | Scare Devil | Sol Terrestis | St. John's Wort | Tipton Weed |

★**SYMBOLIC MEANINGS:**
Animosity; Simplicity; Superstition;

★**POTENTIAL POWERS:**
Courage; Divination; Exorcism; Happiness; Health; Love Divination; Money spells; Power; Protection; Strength;

★**FOLKLORE AND FACTS:**
Hypericum perforatum was said to be so offensive to evil spirits that one sniff of it would force them to fly. • *Hypericum perforatum* has the power to drive spirits away. • It was once thought that for girls to sleep with *Hypericum perforatum* under the pillow and it would then chase away evil sprits and they would dream of who their husbands would someday be. • It was once believed that if *Hypericum perforatum* did not bloom that someone would die. • Worn as an amulet *Hypericum perforatum* is supposed to protect against evil. • *Hypericum perforatum* was believed to protect a house against such calamities as fire, lightning, and storms.

451

Hypocalymma angustifolium

| *Leptospermum angustifolium* | **White Myrtle** |

★**SYMBOLIC MEANINGS:**

Love; Love in absence;

452
Hyssopus officinalis

| **Herb Hyssop** | **Holy Herb** | **Hyssop** | **Hyssop Herb** | *Hyssopus* | *Hyssopus decumbens* | **Isopo** | **Ysopo** | **Yssop** |

★**SYMBOLIC MEANINGS:**

Cleanliness; Holiness;

★**POTENTIAL POWERS:**

Healing; Protection; Purification; Spiritual cleansing; Wards away evil spirits;

★**FOLKLORE AND FACTS:**

Having been used since ancient times, *Hyssopus officinalis* is the most often used purification herb. • Hang *Hyssopus officinalis* in the home to force out evil and negativity.

good news

453
Iberis

| Candytuft |

★**SYMBOLIC MEANINGS:**
Architecture; Indifference;

454
Iberis sempervirens

| Evergreen Candytuft | Everlasting Candytuft | Perennial Candytuft |

★**SYMBOLIC MEANINGS:**
Indifference;

455
Ilex aquifolium ☠

| Aquifolius | Bat's Wings | Christmas Holly | Christ's Thorn | English Holly | European Holly | Holly | Holly Bush | Holly Herb | Holly Tree | Holm Chaste | Hulm | Hulver Bush | *Ilex* | Mexican Holly | Tinne |

★**SYMBOLIC MEANINGS:**
Am I forgotten; Courage; Defense; Difficult victory attained; Domestic happiness; Dreams; Enchantment; Forecast; Foresight; Good cheer; Good luck; Goodwill; Looking; Man's symbol; Protection; Questioning; Subconscious; The symbol of a human being; The symbol of Man; Vigilance; Wisdom;

★**POTENTIAL POWERS:**
Anti-Lightning; Attracts and repels energies; Dream Magic; Immortality; Luck; Protection; Protection against harm in dreams; Protection against witchcraft; Protection against The Evil Eye;

★**FOLKLORE AND FACTS:**
Ilex aquifolium is sometimes carried by men to bring luck. • The ancient Druids once believe that *Ilex aquifolium* kept the earth beautiful during the time that *Quercus* (Oak) trees had no leaves. During that period, the Druids wore *Ilex aquifolium* in their hair when it was time to watch their priests cut the *Viscum album* (Mistletoe), which was sacred to them. • In Medieval Europe, *Ilex aquifolium* was planted near homes to protect them from lightning and to bring good fortune. • In England it was thought that a sprig of *Ilex aquifolium* on a bedpost would bring about sweet

dreams. • In Wales it was thought that if *Ilex aquifolium* were brought into the home before it was Christmastime that it would instigate family arguments. • It was also believed that if *Ilex aquifolium* was left to decorate past Twelfth Night that a misfortune would occur numbering for each of the *Ilex aquifolium* leaves and branches remaining within the house. • It is thought that bringing *Ilex aquifolium* into the home of a friend would cause death. • Another belief is that if a piece of *Ilex aquifolium* is kept that was used in a church for a Christmas decoration it will bring about good fortune throughout the year. • If *Ilex aquifolium* is picked on Christmas Day it will be very good protection against evil spirits and witches. • One divination that can be used is to place tiny candles on *Ilex aquifolium* leaves and float them on water. If the *Ilex aquifolium* leaves stay afloat, an endeavor that the seeker has in mind will prosper. However, if any of the leaves sink to extinguish a candle, it is a sign that it is best to not do it. • It is believed that throwing *Ilex aquifolium* at wild animals will make them leave you alone even if they are not actually touched by any part of the plant. • A weather divination that was once frequently taken very seriously is that if the *Ilex aquifolium* bush had an over abundance of berries that it was a sign that winter would be harsh. • The Druids believed that it was an important safety measure to bring *Ilex aquifolium* into their dwellings in the winter to give shelter the elves and fairies who would house with humans to escape the bitter cold.

▸ *Ilex aquifolium Berries:*
Christmas joy;

456
Ilex paraguariensis

| Erva Mate | Erva-Mate | Mate | Paraguay Tea | Yerba | Yerba Mate | Yerba Maté | Yerva Mate |

★**POTENTIAL POWERS:**
Binding; Building; Death; Fidelity; History; Knowledge; Limitations; Love; Lust; Obstacles; Time;

★**FOLKLORE AND FACTS:**
Wear a sprig of *Ilex paraguariensis* to attract the opposite sex. • Spill an infusion of *Ilex paraguariensis* to break off what was once a romantic relationship.

457
Illicium verum

| Badian | Badian Khatai | Badiana | Badiane | Bunga Lawang | Chinese Star Anise | Eight-Horn | Khata |Star Aniseed | Thakolam |

★**SYMBOLIC MEANINGS:**

Good luck; Luck;

★POTENTIAL POWERS:
Good luck charm; Psychic powers;

★FOLKLORE AND FACTS:
Carry *Illicium verum* in a pocket for luck. • Make a using *Illicium verum* necklace and then wear it to increase your psychic powers. • A powerful pendulum can be made using a *Illicium verum* on a string.

458
Impatiens

| Balsam | Balsamine | Bang Seed | Beijo de Frade | Fen Hsien | Garden Balsam | Hosen-ka | *Impatiens balsamina* | Impatient | Jewelweed | Ji Xing | Kina Cicegi | Pop Weed | Rose Balsam | Spotted Snapweed | Snapweed | Touch-Me-Not |

★SYMBOLIC MEANINGS:
Ardent love; Impatience; Impatient resolves; Touch-Me-Not; Touch me not; Waiting is difficult for me to do;

⊙ SPECIFIC COLOR MEANING Red:
Touch me not; Impatience resolves;

⊙ SPECIFIC COLOR MEANING > Yellow:
Impatience;

459
Impatiens walleriana

| Balsam | Busy Lizzy | *Impatiens* | *Impatiens sultanii* | Patient Lucy | Sultana |

★SYMBOLIC MEANINGS:
Impatient;

460
Inula helenium

| Alantwurzel | Alycompaine | Aunee | Elecampane | Elf Dock | Elfwort | Horse-Heal | Marchalan | Nurse Heal | Scabwort | Velvet Dock | Wild Sunflower |

★SYMBOLIC MEANINGS:
Tears;

★**POTENTIAL POWERS:**
Love; Protection; Psychic powers;

★**FOLKLORE AND FACTS:**
Wear *Inula helenium* for protection and to attract love.

461
Ipomoea ☠

| *Acmostemon* | *Batatas* | **Bindweed** | *Bonanox* | *Calonyction* | *Calycantherum* | **Convolvulus** | *Diatremis* | *Dimerodisus* | *Exogonium* | **Flying Saucers** | **Glory Flower** | **Heavenly Blue** | **Homoeos** | **Indian Jasmine** | *Mina* | **Morning Glory** | *Parasitipomoea* | *Pharbitis* | *Quamoclit* | **Wormweed** |

★**SYMBOLIC MEANINGS:**
Affection; Attachment; Bonds; Coquetry; Death; Death and rebirth; Deference; Embrace; Glorious beauty; Humility; I attach myself to you; Love in vain; Night; Obstinacy; Repose; She loves you; Spontaneity; Uncertainty; Willful promises;

★**POTENTIAL POWERS:**
Happiness; Peace;

★**FOLKLORE AND FACTS:**
Blue *Ipomoea* will bring peacefulness and happiness if grown in the garden. • *Ipomoea* seeds under the pillow will supposedly stop all nightmares.

⊙ **SPECIFIC COLOR MEANING > Pink:**
Worth sustained by judicious and tender affection;

462
Ipomoea alba ☠

| **Moonflower** | **Moonflower Vine** | **Moon Vine** | **Night-Blooming Morning Glory** |

★**SYMBOLIC MEANINGS:**
Dreaming of love; Night; Tonight;

463
Ipomoea batatas ☠

| **Canoe Plant** | **Kumara** | **Sweet Potato** | **Tuberous Morning Glory** | **Ubi** | **Uwi** | **Yam** |

★**SYMBOLIC MEANINGS:**
Attachment; Hard times; I attach myself to you;

★FOLKLORE AND FACTS:

According to New Zealand legend, when the *Ipomoea batatas* tuber is in the ground it is so powerful that an enemy can be driven mad and will then simply run away.

464
Ipomoea coccinea

| Mexican Morning Glory | Quamoclit | *Quamoclit coccinea* | Red Morning Glory | Redstar |

★SYMBOLIC MEANINGS:

Busybody;

465
Ipomoea cordatotriloba ☠

| Convolvulus Major | Little Violet Morning Glory | Purple Bindweed |

★SYMBOLIC MEANINGS:

Eminence; Extinguished hopes;

466
Ipomoea jalapa ☠

| High John the Conqueror | John de Conquer | John the Conker | John the Conquer | John the Conquer Root | John the Conqueror | John the Conqueroo |

★POTENTIAL POWERS:

Breaks hexes; Confidence; Happiness; Health; Love; Money; Sex; Strength; Success;

★FOLKLORE AND FACTS:

Carry *Ipomoea jalapa* to stop depression, bring love, protect you against all hexes and curses that you don't have upon you, and to break and drive away all spells, curses, and hexes that you do have you, but then it again protects you from getting them back again.

467
Ipomoea quamoclit ☠

| Cardinal Creeper | Cardinal Vine | Cypress Vine | Cypressvine Morning Glory | Hummingbird Vine | Star Glory |

★SYMBOLIC MEANINGS:

Busybody; Protection;

468
Iris

| Flag | Sword Flag |

★SYMBOLIC MEANINGS:

A message; Courage; Faith; Faith; Fire; Flame; Friendly; Good news; Graceful; Hope; I burn; I am burning with love; Idea; I have a message for you; Message; My compliments; Pleasant message; Promise; Promise in love; Pure heart; Purity; A Rainbow; Travel; Valor; Victory and conquest but also pain; Wisdom; Your Friendship Means So Much To Me.

★POTENTIAL POWERS:

Authority; Faith; Healing; Magic; Magic and energy for pure aims; Power; Protection from evil spirits; Purification; Reincarnation; Wisdom;

★FOLKLORE AND FACTS:

The *Iris* has been a sacred symbol of divine protection and royalty the world over since around the 5th Century. • Place a vase of fresh *Iris* flowers in an area that requires energy cleansing. • The points of the *Iris* flower symbolize faith, wisdom and valor.

469
Iris germanica

| Bearded Iris | Florentine Iris | German Iris | Queen Elizabeth Root Iris |

★SYMBOLIC MEANINGS:

Flame;

★POTENTIAL POWERS:

Purification; Wisdom;

★FOLKLORE AND FACTS:

In Japan the *Iris germanica* root was considered protection against evil spirits and were hung from the eaves of their homes. • An interesting and unusual divination pendulum can be created using a whole *Iris germanica* root suspended by a cord from a *Ipomea batatas* tuber (yam).

▶ *Root (Orris Root):*

Love; Protection; Divination;

470
Iris pseudacorus

| Flame Iris | Flaming Iris | Fleur-de-lis Iris | Yellow Flag | Yellow Iris |

★**SYMBOLIC MEANINGS:**
Flame; Passion;

★**POTENTIAL POWERS:**
Purification; Wisdom;

471

Iris versicolor ☠

| **American Blue Flag** | **Blueflag** | **Blueflag Iris** | **Blue Flag Iris** | **Dagger Flower** | **Flag Lily** | **Harlequin Blueflag** | **Larger Blue Flag** | **Multi-Colored Blue Flag** | **Northern Blue Flag** | **Poison Flag** | **Snake Lily** | **Water Flag** |

★**POTENTIAL POWERS:**
Money; Success in business; Wealth;

★**FOLKLORE AND FACTS:**
Increase business by keeping a piece of *Iris versicolor* root in the cash register.

472

Isatis tinctoria

| **Asp of Jerusalem** | *Isatis indigotica* | **Woad** |

★**SYMBOLIC MEANINGS:**
Modest merit;

473

Ixia

| **Corn Lily** |

★**SYMBOLIC MEANINGS:**
Happiness;

474

Ixora

| **Bunga Jarum** | **Burning Love** | **Chann Tanea** | **Flame of The Wood** | *Ixora coccinea* | **Jarum-Jarum** | **Jungle Flame** | **Jungle Geranium** | **Jungle Geranium** | **Kheme** | **Needle Flower** | **Pan** | **Ponna** | **Rangan** | **Santan** | **Techi** | **West Indian Jasmine** |

★**SYMBOLIC MEANINGS:**
Passion;

amiability

475
Jacaranda mimosifolia

| Blue Jacaranda | Jacaranda | *Jacaranda acutifolia* |

★ **SYMBOLIC MEANINGS:**
Power; Imperial;

476
Jasminum grandiflorum

| Anbar | Catalonian Jasmine | Chameli | Jessamin | Moonlight On The Grove | Royal Jasmine | Spanish Jasmine | Yasmin |

★ **SYMBOLIC MEANINGS:**
Sensuality;

★ **POTENTIAL POWERS:**
Love; Money; Prophetic dreams;

★ **FOLKLORE AND FACTS:**
Jasminum grandiflorum flowers attract spiritual love. • The fragrance of *Jasminum grandiflorum* flowers help to promote sleep.

477
Jasminum officinale

| Common Jasmine | Jasmine | Jessamine | Poet's Jasmine | Yeh Hsi Ming | Yeh-hsi-ming |

★ **SYMBOLIC MEANINGS:**
Amiability; Material wealth; Wealth;

★ **POTENTIAL POWERS:**
Business; Divination; Dream magic; Emotions; Expansion; Fertility; Generation; Honor; Inspiration; Intuition; Leadership; Love; Money; Politics; Power; Prophetic dreams; Psychic ability; Public acclaim; Responsibility; Royalty; Sea; Subconscious mind; Success; Tides; Travel by water; Wealth;

★ **FOLKLORE AND FACTS:**
Jasminum officinale flowers attract spiritual love. • The fragrance of *Jasminum officinale* flowers help to promote sleep.

⊙ **SPECIFIC COLOR MEANING > Red:**

Folly; Glee;

⊙ **SPECIFIC COLOR MEANING > White:**
Cheerfulness; Amiability;

⊙ **SPECIFIC COLOR MEANING > Yellow:**
Modesty; Timidity;

478
Juglans regia ☠

| A Nut Fit for a God | Carya | Carpathian Walnut | Caucasian Walnut | Common Walnut | English Walnut | *Juglans duclouxiana* | *Juglans fallax* | *Juglans orientis* | Persian Walnut | Walnoot | Walnut | Wealhhutu |

★**SYMBOLIC MEANINGS:**
Infertility; Intellect; Presentiment; Stratagem;

★**POTENTIAL POWERS:**
Health; Mental clarity; Mental powers; Strong mental powers; Wishes;

★**FOLKLORE AND FACTS:**
All your wishes will be granted if someone gives you a gift of a bag of *Juglans regia*.

479
Juncus tenuis

| Field Rush | Path Rush | Slender Rush | Slender Yard Rush | Wiregrass | Wire-Grass | Yard Rush |

★**SYMBOLIC MEANINGS:**
Docility;

480
Juniperus

| Enebro | Gemeiner Wachholder | Geneva | Gin Berry | Ginepro | Gin Plant | Juniper |

★**SYMBOLIC MEANINGS:**
Aid; Asylum; Love; Succor;

★**POTENTIAL POWERS:**
Abundance; Advancement; Anti-theft; Binding; Building; Conscious will; Curse breaking; Death; Drive off snakes; Energy; Exorcism; Friendship; Growth; Healing; Health; Hex breaking; History; Joy; Knowledge; Leadership; Life; Light; Limitations; Natural power; Obstacles; Protection; Psychic powers; Purification; Success; Time;

★FOLKLORE AND FACTS:

Juniperus hung at a door will protect the home from both evil forces and evil people.
• Wear a sprig of *Juniperus* as protection against accidents, attacks by wild animals, ghosts, and sicknesses. • Men can carry *Juniperus* berries to increase their potency..

481
Justicia

| *Acelica* | *Adhatoda* | *Amphiscopia* | *Anisostachya* | *Aulojusticia* | *Averia* | *Beloperone* | *Calliaspidia* | *Calymmostachya* | *Chaetothylopsis* | *Chiloglossa* | *Cyphisia* | *Cyrtanthera* | *Cyrtantherella* | *Dianthera* | *Dimanisa* | *Drejerella* | *Duvernoia* | *Emularia* | *Ethesia* | *Glosarithys* | *Harnieria* | *Heinzelia* | *Hemichoriste* | *Heteraspidia* | *Ixtlania* | *Jacobinia* | *Kuestera* | *Libonia* | *Lophothecium* | *Lustrinia* | *Nicoteba* | *Orthotactus* | *Parajusticia* | *Petalanthera* | *Plagiacanthus* | *Plegmatolemma* | *Porphyrocoma* | *Psacadocalymma* | *Rhacodiscus* | *Rhiphidosperma* | *Rhyticalymma* | *Rodatia* | *Rostellaria* | *Rostellularia* | *Saglorithys* | *Salviacanthus* | *Sarotheca* | *Sericographis* | **Shrimp Plant** | *Simonisia* | *Solenochasma* | *Stethoma* | *Tabascina* | *Thalestris* | *Thamnojusticia* | *Tyloglossa* | **Water-Willow** |

★SYMBOLIC MEANINGS:

Freedom; The perfection of female loveliness;

intellectual beauty

482
Kalanchoe thyrsiflora

| Desert Cabbage | Flapjacks | Geelplakkie | Kalanchoe | Meelplakkie | Paddle Plant | Plakkie | White Lady |

★ SYMBOLIC MEANINGS:

Endurance; Lasting affection; Your temper is too hasty;

483
Kalmia latifolia ☠

| Calico Bush | Clamoun | Ivybush | Lambkill | Mountain Laurel | Sheep Laurel | Spoonwood |

★ SYMBOLIC MEANINGS:

Ambition; Ambition of a hero; Glory; Treachery; Victory; Words though sweet may deceive;

484
Kennedia

| Kennedya | Kennedia coccinea |

★ SYMBOLIC MEANINGS:

Intellectual beauty; Mental beauty;

485
Koelreuteria paniculata

| China Tree | Goldenrain Tree | Golden Rain Tree | Pride of China | Pride-of-China | Pride of India | Pride-of-India | Varnish Tree |

★ SYMBOLIC MEANINGS:

Dissension;

chivalry

486
Laburnum anagyroides

| **Common Laburnum** | *Cytisus laburnum* | **Golden Chain** | **Golden Rain** | *Laburnum vulgare* |

★**SYMBOLIC MEANINGS:**
Blackness; Forsaken; Pensive beauty;

487
Lactuca sativa

| **Garden Lettuce** | **Lattouce** | **Lettuce** | **Sleep Wort** |

★**SYMBOLIC MEANINGS:**
Chastity; Cold-hearted; Cold-heartedness; Coldness;

★**POTENTIAL POWERS:**
Aphrodisiac; Childbearing; Contraception; Divination; Love; Love divination; Protection; Sleep;

★**FOLKLORE AND FACTS:**
Lactuca sativa is native to the Mediterranean area and is one of the oldest known vegetables on Earth. • It was once believed in England that if "too much" *Lactuca sativa* was growing in the garden it would cause sterility in the household, thus providing an overly effective form of contraceptive. • A love divination using *Lactuca sativa* is to write your love interest's name in the soil then plant the name with *Lactuca sativa* seeds. If they seeds spout then love will grow between you and your love interest.

488
Lagenaria ☠

| *Adenopus* | **Gourd** | *Sphaerosicyos* |

★**SYMBOLIC MEANINGS:**
Bulk; Bulkiness; Extend; Extent; Unrequited affection;

★**POTENTIAL POWERS:**
Protection;

★**FOLKLORE AND FACTS:**
If hung at the front door of the home, *Lagenaria* will offer some protection against

magical fascination. • Carry a piece of *Lagenaria* to fend off evil. • A *Lagenaria* rattle scares off evil spirits. • A bowl made from *Lagenaria* then filled with clean water can be used for scrying.

✎⤙➤

489
Lagerstroemia

| Common Crape Myrtle | Crape Myrtle | Crepe Myrtle | Flower of The Gods | Indian Lagerstroemia | *Laberstroemia indica* | Queen's Crape Myrtle |

★ **SYMBOLIC MEANINGS:**
Eloquence;

★ **POTENTIAL POWERS:**
Chastity;

★ **FOLKLORE AND FACTS:**
Lagerstroemia was greatly favored by China's emperors for many centuries. • In areas where it easily grows *Lagerstroemia* is used as a tree to line streets. • In Medieval times *Lagerstromemia* was often used in bridal garlands. • There is a legend that if *Lagerstromemia* appears in a dream that it signifies a long life with good fortune. • Bring peace and love into a home by growing *Lagerstromemia* on each side of the front door.

✎⤙➤

490
Lagunaria patersonii

| Cow Itch Tree | *Lagunaria* | Norfolk Island Hibiscus | Primrose Tree | Pyramid Tree |

★ **SYMBOLIC MEANINGS:**
Inconstancy;

✎⤙➤

491
Lamprocapnos spectabilis

| Bachelor | Bleeding Heart | Boys and Girls | Butterfly Banners | *Dicentra spectabilis* | *Diclytra spectabilis* | Dutchman's Britches | Dutchman's Trousers | Eardrops | *Fumaria spectabilis* | Kitten | Lady In A Bath | Little Boy's Breeches | Lyre Flower | Lyre-flower | Monk's Head | Old-fashioned Bleeding-heart | Old Fashioned Bleeding Heart | Soldier's Cap | Squirrel Corn | Turkey Corn | Venus's Car | White Hearts |

★ **SYMBOLIC MEANINGS:**
Fly with me; Love;

★POTENTIAL POWERS:
Love;

★FOLKLORE AND FACTS:
If you crush a *Lamprocapnos spectabilis* flower and the juice is red, your love is recip-rocated. if the juice is white, he or she who you love does not love you in return. • If *Lamprocapnos spectabilis* is grown indoors, put a copper penny in the soil to repel negative energy.

492
Lantana camara ☠

| Baho-Baho | Coronet | Coronitas | Fart Flower | *Lantana* | *Lantana aculeata* | *Lantana armata* | Red Sage | Smelly Flower | Spanish Flag | Yellow Sage | Utot-Utot | West Indian Lantana | Wild Sage |

★SYMBOLIC MEANINGS:
Severity; Rigor;

493
Lapageria rosea

| Chilean Bellflower | Copihue | *Lapageria* |

★SYMBOLIC MEANINGS:
There is no complete and unreserved good; There is no unalloyed good;

494
Larix

| Larch |

★SYMBOLIC MEANINGS:
Audacity; Boldness;

★POTENTIAL POWERS:
Anti-fire; Anti-theft; Protection;

★FOLKLORE AND FACTS:
Larix wood is tough, durable and rot resistant enough to be a choice used in yacht building. • *Larix* is a often selected for use in creating a bonsai tree because of its short needles.

495
Lathyrus latifolius

| Everlasting Pea | Perennial Pea | Perennial Peavine |

★ SYMBOLIC MEANINGS:
An appointed meeting; Go not away; Lasting pleasure; Wilt you go with me;

496
Lathyrus odoratus ☠

| Sweetpea | Sweet Pea |

★ SYMBOLIC MEANINGS:
A meeting; Blissful pleasure; Chastity; Delicacy; Departure; Goodbye; I think of you; Meeting; Thank you for a lovely time;

★ POTENTIAL POWERS:
Chastity; Courage; Friendship; Strength;

★ FOLKLORE AND FACTS:
Wear *Lathyrus odoratus* for strength. • To keep someone chaste, place a nosegay of *Lathyrus odoratus* flowers in a vase in their bedroom. • Fresh *Lathyrus odoratus* flowers forge friendships. • Hold a *Lathyrus odoratus* flower in your hand to encourage the truth to be told to you.

497
Laurus nobilis

| Bai | Bay | Bay Laurel | Bay Tree | Grecian Laurel | Laurel | Laurel Tree | Laurus | Moon Laurel | Roman Laurel | Sweet Bay | True Laurel |

★ SYMBOLIC MEANINGS:
Fadeless affection; Fame; Glory; I change but in death; I change but in dying; Immortality; Love; No change till death; Notability; Praise; Prosperity; Renown; Resurrection of Christ; Strength; Success; Symbol of Glory; Symbol of Poets; Victory;

★ POTENTIAL POWERS:
Abundance; Advancement; Clairvoyance; Conscious will; Energy; Friendship; Growth; Healing; Induces prophetic dreams; Joy; Leadership; Life; Light; Natural power; Physical and moral cleansing; Protection against evil spirits; Protection during electrical storms; Protection; Psychic powers; Purification; Strength; Success; Wards off lightning; Wards off evil; Wards off evil magic; Ward off negativity; Wisdom;

★ FOLKLORE AND FACTS:
In ancient Greece poets, heroes, winning athletes, and esteemed leaders were crowed with wreaths made from *Laurus nobilis* leaves. • The term "Poet Laureate" is a result of the custom of crowning an honored poet. • In ancient Rome, *Laurus nobi-*

lis garlands were hung over the doors of the sick to protect them. As a result the university degree of "baccalaureate" began when new qualified doctors were garlanded with *Laurus nobilis.* • Prophets use to hold *Laurus nobilis* boughs when foretelling the future. • It was especially used to protect emperors and warriors going off into battle. • A *Laurus nobilis* Tree planted near a home will protect it's inhabitants against sickness. • To ensure lasting love, a couple will break off a twig of *Laurus nobilis* and then break it in half, each retaining a piece. • Wishes are written on *Laurus nobilis* leaves then buried in a sunny spot to make them come true. • *Laurus nobilis* leaves placed under a pillow will induce prophetic dreams. • According to legend, if you stood by a *Laurus nobilis* Tree you could not be struck by lightning or be affected by the evil of witches. • Write a wish on a *Laurus nobilis* leaf then burn it to make it come true. • Carry a *Laurus nobilis* leaf as an amulet to ward off evil and negativity of any kind.• Place a *Laurus nobilis* amulet in the windows of the house as protection from lightning.

▸ *Laurus nobilis Leaf:*
I change but in death;

▸ *Laurus nobilis Wreath:*
Fame; Glory; Merit reward; Reward of merit;

498
Lavandula angustifolia

| **Common Lavender** | **Elf** | **Elf Leaf** | **English Lavender** | *Lavandula* | *Lavandula officinalis* | *Lavandula pyrenaica* | *Lavandula spica* | *Lavandula vera* | **Lavendula** | **Nard** | **Nardus** | **Narrow-leaved Lavender** | **Official Lavender** | **Spike** | **True Lavender** |

★**SYMBOLIC MEANINGS:**
Constancy; Devotion; Distrust; Faith; Faithful; Humility; Love; Mistrust;

★**POTENTIAL POWERS:**
A Charm against The Evil Eye; Business transactions; Business; Call in Good Spirits; Caution; Chastity; Cleverness; Communication; Creativity; Expansion; Faith; Happiness; Healing; Honor; Illumination; Induces sleep; Initiation; Inner sight; Intelligence; Leadership; Learning; Longevity; Love; Magic; Memory; Peace; Politics; Power; Protection; Prudence; Public acclaim; Purification; Responsibility; Royalty; Science; Self-preservation; Sleep; Sound judgment; Success; Thievery; Wealth; Wisdom;

★**FOLKLORE AND FACTS:**
Since ancient times, *Lavandula officinalis* has been used to freshen rooms, linens, and one's self. • Sprigs of *Lavandula officinalis* were once given to women in labor to hold as squeezing their hands upon it would release the calming scent of Lavender to

ease their travail. • *Lavandula officinalis* in the the home is considered to bring peacefulness into it. • *Lavandula officinalis* sprigs given to newlyweds is thought to bring them good luck. • It is thought that sniffing *Lavandula officinalis* fragrance will enable one to see ghosts. • Wearing clothes that have scented with *Lavandula angustifolia* flowers will attract love. • Writing a love note on paper that has been scented with with the scent of *Lavandula angustifolia* flowers will attract love. • Scatter *Lavandula angustifolia* flowers around the home to induce peacefulness and lift a sense of depression from your environment.

▶ ***Lavandula angustifolia* with *Rosmarinus officinalis*:**
Chastity; Promotes chastity;

499
Lavatera

| **Annual Mallow** | *Anthema* | *Axolopha* | *Navaea* | *Olbia* | **Rose Mallow** | **Royal Mallow** | *Saviniona* | *Steegia* | *Stegia* | **Tree Mallow** |

★ **SYMBOLIC MEANINGS:**
Sweet disposition;

500
Lawsonia inermis ☠

| **Camphire** | **Henna** | **Hina** | **Hinna** | **Mignonette Tree** |

★ **SYMBOLIC MEANINGS:**
Artifice; Fragrance; You are better than handsome;

★ **POTENTIAL POWERS:**
Emotions; Fertility; Generation; Headache relief; Healing; Health; Inspiration; Intuition; Love; Protection from illness; Protection from The Evil Eye; Psychic ability; Sea; Subconscious mind; Tides; Travel by water;

★ **FOLKLORE AND FACTS:**
Wear a sprig of *Lawsonia inermis* near your heart to attract love to come to you.

501
Leaves (Dead)

★ **SYMBOLIC MEANINGS:**
My love has ended; Sadness; Melancholy;

502

Leontodon
| **Hawkbit** | **Hawkbits** | *Scorzoneroides* |
★**SYMBOLIC MEANINGS:**
Hawk-like vision;

503
Leontopodium alpinum
| **Edelweiss** | **Floare de Colt** | **Floarea Reginei** | **Gol-e-yax** | **Ice Flower** | **Queen of Alpine Flowers** |
★**SYMBOLIC MEANINGS:**
Daring; Noble Courage; Noble purity; Nobility;
★**POTENTIAL POWERS:**
Bulletproofing; Courage; Daring; Invisibility; Power;
★**FOLKLORE AND FACTS:**
Leontopodium alpinum is a protected flower, therefore picking the *Leontopodium alpinum* flowers is strictly forbidden. • It was believed that if *Leontopodium alpinum* was fashioned into a wreath and then worn it would make the wearer invisible. • To have your hearts desire grow and care for a *Leontopodium alpinum* plant.

504
Leonurus cardiaca
| **Lion's Ear** | **Lion's Tail** | **Motherwort** | **Throw-wort** |
★**SYMBOLIC MEANINGS:**
Concealed love; Creativity; Imagination; Secret love;

505
Lepidium sativum
| **Chandrashoor** | **Cress** | **Garden Cress** | **Garden Pepper Cress** | **Mustard and Cress** | **Pepper Cress** | **Pepper Grass** | **Pepperwort** | **Poor Man's Pepper** |
★**SYMBOLIC MEANINGS:**
Always reliable; Power; Roving; Stability;

506
Leschenaultia splendens
| *Leschenaultia* | *Lechenaultia splendens* | **Splendid Scarlet Flowered Lechenaul-**

tia |

★SYMBOLIC MEANINGS:
Your are charming;

507
Leucanthemum vulgare

| Bull Daisy | Butter Daisy | Button Daisy | *Chrysanthemum leucanthemum* | Dog Blow | Dog Daisy | Dun Daisy | Dutch Morgan | Field Daisy | Golden Marguertes | Herb Margaret | Horse Daisy | Horse Gowan | Marguerite | Maudlinwort | Midsummer Daisy | Moon Daisy | Moon Flower | Moon Penny | Ox Eye | Ox-Eye Daisy | Oxeye Daisy | Poorland Daisy | Poverty Weed | White Man's Weed |

★SYMBOLIC MEANINGS:
A token; Cheer; Disappointment; Faith; Innocence; Loyal love; Patience; Purity; Simplicity;

★POTENTIAL POWERS:
Divination; Divination for love;

★FOLKLORE AND FACTS:
Leucanthemum vulgare has been used for Divination of love for many generations, with the plucking of the petals to the chant of "he (she) loves me, he (she) loves me not", with the last petal being the answer to the question. • Daisies have been found depicted on many ancient ornaments, decorations, paintings, and ceramics throughout the Middle East. • The ancient Celts believed that Daisies were of the spirits of babies who died at birth. • If one is to dream of Daisies in the spring, it is good luck; in the autumn or winter it is bad luck.

508
Levisticum officinale

| Chinese Lovage | Deveseel | Italian Lovage | Italian Parsley | Lavose | Lestyán | Leustean | Levistico | Libbsticka | Libecek | Liebstöckel | Liebstöckel | Livèche | Lovage | Love Herb | Love Herbs | Love Parsley | Love Rod | Love Root | Love Sticklet | Loving Herbs | Lubczyk | Lubestico | Lyubistok | Maggikraut | Maggiplant | Sea Parsley |

★SYMBOLIC MEANINGS:
Bring love; Love;

★POTENTIAL POWERS:
Attraction; Love;

★FOLKLORE AND FACTS:
It is believed that adding *Levisticum officinale* to the bath water before going out to meet new people will increase your attractiveness.

509
Liatris

| Blazing Star | Blazing-Star | Button Snakeroot | Deerstongue | Gayfeather | Gay-Feather | Hound's Tongue | Kansas Gay Feather | Purple Poker | Spire | Spike | Vanilla Leaf | Wild Vanilla |

★POTENTIAL POWERS:
Lust; Psychic powers;

★FOLKLORE AND FACTS:
Either carried or worn *Liatris* attracts men. • When worn *Liatris* aids psychic powers. • Place *Liatris* under the bed to attract a man to come to it.

510
Ligustrum

| Privet |

★SYMBOLIC MEANINGS:
Invasion; Mildness; Prohibition;

511
Ligustrum vulgare

| European Privet | Common Privet | Wild Privet |

★SYMBOLIC MEANINGS:
Prohibition;

512
Lilium ☠

| Hleri | Hreri | Hrrt | Hrry | Krinon | Leírion | Lily |

★SYMBOLIC MEANINGS:
Beauty; Birth; Devotion; Divinity; Exalted and unapproachable; Honor; Humility; Magnificence; Majesty; Modesty; Religious; Pride; Purity; Purity of Heart; Supreme; Sweetness and humility; Unity of heart;

★POTENTIAL POWERS:
Breaking love spells; Exorcism; Fends off ghosts; Keeps unwanted visitors away;

Protection; Purification; Repel negativity; Truth;

★**FOLKLORE AND FACTS:**

Plant *Lilium* in the garden to fend off ghosts. • Plant *Lilium* in the garden to fend off evil. • Wear or carry *Lilium* to break a love spell which has been cast upon you by a specific person. • Bury an old piece of leather in a bed of *Lilium* to bring forth clues from a crime committed in the past year.

◉ **SPECIFIC COLOR MEANING > Orange:**

Dislike; Hatred; Revenge; Desire; Passion;

◉ **SPECIFIC COLOR MEANING > Scarlet:**

High bred; High souled; High souled aspirations;

◉ **SPECIFIC COLOR MEANING > White:**

Celebration; It's Heavenly to be with you; Majesty; Modesty; Purity; Sociability; Sweetness; Virginity; Youth;

◉ **SPECIFIC COLOR MEANING > Yellow:**

False; Falsehood; Gaiety; Gay; Gratitude; Happiness; I'm walking on air; Lies; Playful beauty;

513

Lilium auratum ☠

| Goldband Lily | Golden Rayed Lily of Japan | Mountain Lily | Oriental Lily | Yamayuri |

★**SYMBOLIC MEANINGS:**

Pure of heart;

514

Lilium canadense ☠

| Canada Lily | Field Lily | Meadow Lily | Wild Yellow Lily | Wild Yellow-Lily |

★**SYMBOLIC MEANINGS:**

Humility;

515

Lilium candidum ☠

| Madonna Lily |

★**SYMBOLIC MEANINGS:**

Purity;

★**FOLKLORE AND FACTS:**
Medieval images of the Blessed Virgin Mary very often show her holding *Lilium candidum*, hence the name "Madonna Lily". • In King Solomon's Temple there were images of *Lilium candidum* on the columns and also upon the Laver.

516
Lilium columbianum ☠

| Columbia Lily | Tiger Lily |

★**SYMBOLIC MEANINGS:**
Wealth; Pride; Prosperity;

517
Lilium longiflorum ☠

| Bermuda Lily | Easter Lily | Jacob's Tears | Japanese Easter Lily | Ladder To Heaven | Longtubed White Lily | Mary's Tears | November Lily | Snow Queen | Teppouyuri | Trumpet Lily | White Trumpet Lily |

★**SYMBOLIC MEANINGS:**
Purity;

★**POTENTIAL POWERS:**
Employment; Gambling; Luck; Power; Protection;

★**FOLKLORE AND FACTS:**
Lilium longiflorum was in the oldest gardening book in Japan that dates back to 1681. • Legend tells that *Lilium longiflorum* grew wherever Eve's repentant tears fell as she left The Garden of Eden. • Ancient Minoan culture disappeared 3,500 years ago and the *Lilium longiflorum* frequently appeared on their ceramics. Older than the Minoan culture, itself, is the Hebrew word for lily, "shusan".

518
Lilium regale ☠

| Regal Lily |

★**SYMBOLIC MEANINGS:**
Regal beauty;

519
Lilium speciosum ☠

| Japanese Lily |

★SYMBOLIC MEANINGS:
You cannot deceive me;

520
Lilium superbum ☠

| **American Tiger Lily | Swamp Lily | Turban Lily | Turk's Cap Lily |**
★SYMBOLIC MEANINGS:
Chivalry; Knight; Misanthropy; Pride; Wealth;

521
Limonium

| **Marsh-Rosemary | Sea Lavender | Statice |**
★SYMBOLIC MEANINGS:
I miss you; Joyous; Lasting Beauty; Remembrance; Success; Sympathy;

522
Limonium caspia

| **Caspia | German Statice | Limonium | Misty | Seafoam | Sea-lavender | Sea Lavender | Statice |**
★SYMBOLIC MEANINGS:
Joyous;

523
Limosella

| **Mudwort |**
★SYMBOLIC MEANINGS:
Tranquility;

524
Linum usitatissimum

| **Aazhi Vidhai | Agasi | Akshi | Alashi | Avisalu | Common Flax | Flax | Javas | Jawas | Linaza | Linseed | Tisi | Sib Muma |**
★SYMBOLIC MEANINGS:
Beauty; Benefactor; Domestic industry; Fate; Genius; Healing; I feel your benefits; I feel your kindness; Kindness; Money;

★**POTENTIAL POWERS:**
Beauty; Healing; Health; Luck; Money; Protection; Psychic powers; Purification;

★**FOLKLORE AND FACTS:**
Linum usitatissimum are one of the oldest fibers plants in history, being grown and processed since the times of ancient Egypt, although dyed prehistoric flax fibers were found in a prehistoric Georgia cave then scientifically determined to be at least 30,000 years old. • Using *Linum usitatissimum* fiber to create cloth in northern Europe is as far back as during Neolithic times. • *Linum usitatissimum* in the pocket with a few coins will draw money to it. • Wear a *Linum usitatissimum* flower as protection against sorcery.

▶ *Linum usitatissimum Dried:*
Utility;

525
Liquidambar

| **American Storax** | **Liquidamber** | **Redgum** | **Satin-walnut** | **Sweetgum** | **Voodoo Witch Burr** | **Witch Burr** |

★**POTENTIAL POWERS:**
Protection;

526
Liriodendron

| **Canoewood** | **Ko-Yen-Ta-Ka-Ah-Tas** | *Liriodendron tulipifera* | **Saddle Leaf Tree** | **Tulip Poplar** | **Tulip Tree** | **White Wood** | **Yellow Poplar** |

★**SYMBOLIC MEANINGS:**
Fame; Rural happiness;

527
Lobelia ☠

| **Asthma Weed** | **Bladderpod** | *Enchysia* | **Gagroot** | *Haynaldia* | **Indian Tobacco** | *Isolobus* | *Laurentia* | *Mezleria* | *Neowimmeria* | *Parastranthus* | **Pukeweed** | *Rapuntium* | *Tupa* | **Vomitwort** |

★**SYMBOLIC MEANINGS:**
Ill will; Malevolence;

★**POTENTIAL POWERS:**
Halting storms; Healing; Love;

★FOLKLORE AND FACTS:
It is believed that a oncoming storming can be stopped by throwing powdered *Lobelia* towards it.

528
Lobelia cardinalis

| Cardinal Flower | Indian Pink | *Lobelia fulgens* | Scarlet Lobelia |

★SYMBOLIC MEANINGS:
Always lovely; Aversion; Dislike; Distinction; Preferment; Splendor;

529
Lolium

| Ryegrass | Rye Grass | Tares |

★SYMBOLIC MEANINGS:
Changeable disposition; Vice;

530
Lolium temulentum ☠

| Cockle | Darnel | Ivraie | *Lolium annuum* | *Lolium berteronianum* | *Lolium cuneatum* | *Lolium gracile* | Poison Darnel | Ray Grass |

★SYMBOLIC MEANINGS:
Absence; Vain is beauty without merit; Vice;

531
Lonicera caprifolium

| Coral Honeysuckle | Dutch Honeysuckle | Goat's Leaf | Italian Woodbine | Perfoliate Honeysuckle | Woodbine |

★SYMBOLIC MEANINGS:
I love you; The color of my fate; Sweetness of disposition;

★POTENTIAL POWERS:
Enhances the understanding of psychic impressions; Money; Protection; Psychic powers;

★FOLKLORE AND FACTS:
Place *Lonicera caprifolium* in a vase in the home to attract money. • *Lonicera caprifolium* flowers worn at the forehead to heightens psychic powers. • It brings good luck if a *Lonicera caprifolium* plant grows near your home.

532
Lonicera japonica

| Er Hua | Geumeunhwa | Japanese Honeysuckle | Jinyinhua | Jin Yín Hua | Ren Dong Téng | Shuang Hua | Suikazura |

★**SYMBOLIC MEANINGS:**
Bonds of Love; Generous; Devoted; Affection;

★**POTENTIAL POWERS:**
Money; Protection; Psychic powers;

533
Lonicera periclymenum

| Common Honeysuckle | European Honeysuckle | Honeysuckle |

★**SYMBOLIC MEANINGS:**
Affection; Bonds of love; Devoted affection; Devoted love; Domestic happiness; Inconstancy; I will not answer hastily; Generous affection; Generous and devoted affection; Lasting pleasure; Permanence and steadfastness; Permanence; Steadfastness;

★**POTENTIAL POWERS:**
Fidelity; Generosity; Happiness; Money; Protection; Psychic powers; Spirit vision;

534
Lonicera xylosteum

| European Fly Honeysuckle | Dwarf Honeysuckle | Fly Honeysuckle | Fly Woodbine | *Lonicera* | Wild Honeysuckle |

★**SYMBOLIC MEANINGS:**
Bonds of love; Devoted affection; Domestic happiness; Inconstancy; Lasting pleasure; Permanence and steadfastness;

★**POTENTIAL POWERS:**
Money; Protection; Psychic powers;

535
Lotus corniculatus

| Butter and Eggs | Eggs and Bacon | Birdfoot Deervetch | Bird's-Foot Trefoil | Deer Vetch |

★**SYMBOLIC MEANINGS:**
Recantation; Retribution; Revenge;

536
Lotus maritimus

| Dragon's Teeth | Dragon's Tooth | Pea Lotus | Sea Dragon | *Tetragonolobus maritimus* |

★POTENTIAL POWER:
Protection;

537
Lunaria

| Honesty | Lunary | Money Plant | Satin Flower | Silver Dollar Plant |

★SYMBOLIC MEANINGS:
Am I forgotten; Fascination; Forgetfulness; Honesty; Repelling monsters; Secret love; Sincerity;

★POTENTIAL POWERS:
Money; Protection;

★FOLKLORE AND FACTS:
One way to pull money towards you is to place one *Lunaria* seed in the socket of a candlestick then top it with a green candle then burn the candle down to the socket.
• Another way to pull money towards you is to carry one *Lunaria* seed in the purse or a pocket.

538
Lupinus ☠

| Altramuz | Blue Pea | Lupin | Lupine | Lupini | Old Maid's Bonnet | Quaker Bonne | Sundial | Wild Bean | Wild Pea | Wolf's Tale |

★SYMBOLIC MEANINGS:
Dejection; Imagination; Voraciousness;

539
Lupinus texensis

| Bluebonnet | Buffalo Clover | Texas Bluebonnet | Wolf Flower |

★SYMBOLIC MEANINGS:
Forgiveness; Self sacrifice; Survival;

⊙ SPECIFIC COLOR MEANING > Pink:
 Struggle to survive; Memories of those who died;

540
Lychnis chalcedonica

| Burning Love | Dusky Salmon | Flower of Bristol | Jerusalem Cross | Maltese Cross | Nonesuch | Scarlet Lychnis |

★SYMBOLIC MEANINGS:
Religious enthusiasm; Sunny beaming eyes;

541
Lychnis flos-cuculi

| Meadow Lychnis | Ragged Robin |

★SYMBOLIC MEANINGS:
Wit;

542
Lycopodiopsida

| Club Moss | Foxtail | Lycopod | Moririr-Wa-Mafika | Selago | Vegetable Sulfur | Wolf Claw |

★POTENTIAL POWERS:
Business Transactions; Cleverness; Creativity; Communication; Intelligence; Memory; Power; Protection; Science; Thievery;

543
Lycoris radiata ☠

| Mañjusaka | Manjushage | Red Spider Lily |

★SYMBOLIC MEANINGS:
Abandonment; Flower of the Afterlife; Hopeful but tragic fate of Lovers; Lost memory; Never to meet again;

★POTENTIAL POWERS:
Guiding the dead into their next reincarnation;

544
Lysimachia nummularia

| Creeping Jenny | Goldilocks | Goldylocks | Herb Twopence | *Lysimachia zawadzkii* | Moneywort | Twopenny Grass |

★ **SYMBOLIC MEANINGS:**
Languishing; Release from strife; Peacemaking;

545
Lythrum

| **Blooming Sally** | **Loosestrife** | **Lythrum** | **Partyke** | *Peplis* | **Purple Willow Herb** | **Rainbow Weed** | **Sage Willow** | *Salicaria* | **Salicaire** |

★ **SYMBOLIC MEANINGS:**
Pretension;

★ **POTENTIAL POWERS:**
Peace; Protection;

★ **FOLKLORE AND FACTS:**
Give *Lythrum* to a friend to settle any argument that you have had. • *Lythrum* strewn around the home will provide vibrations of peacefulness and hold back evil.

546
Lythrum salicaria

| **Purple Loosestrife** | **Purple Lythrum** | **Salicaire** | **Qian Qu Cai** | **Spiked Loosestrife** |

★ **SYMBOLIC MEANINGS:**
Pretension;

calm repose

547

Macadamia tetraphylla

| Bauple Nut | Boombera | Bush Nut | Gyndl | Jindilli | Macadamia | Macadamia Nut | Mac Nut | Maroochi Nut | Queen of Nuts | Queensland Nut | Cucumber Tree |

★**POTENTIAL POWERS:**
Aphrodisiac; Fertility;

★**FOLKLORE AND FACTS:**
Macadamia tetraphylla nut has such an extremely hard shell that it must be cracked opened with a blunt device, such as a hammer. The Hyacinth Macaw is one of the very few animals that are capable of shelling the nut, using only it's powerful beak.

548

Magnolia acuminata

| Blue Magnolia | Cucumber Magnolia | Cucumbertree | Cucumber Tree |

★**SYMBOLIC MEANINGS:**
Determination; Dignity;

★**POTENTIAL POWERS:**
Endurance;

★**FOLKLORE AND FACTS:**
Magnolia acuminata is the cold-hardiest of the magnolias and one of the largest. • With fossils proving that they were around during the time of the dinosaurs, Magnolias are considered among the oldest flowering plants in the world. • Place *Magnolia acuminata* under the bed to assure faithfulness.

549

Magnolia grandiflora

| Big Laurel | Bull Bay | Evergreen Magnolia | Large-flower Magnolia | Laurel Magnolia | Southern Magnolia |

★**SYMBOLIC MEANINGS:**
Beauty; Determination; Dignified; Dignity; Love of nature; Magnificence; Nobility; Peerless and proud; Perseverance; Splendid Beauty; Sweetness; You are a lover of nature;

★**POTENTIAL POWERS:**
Fidelity;

★**FOLKLORE AND FACTS:**
With fossils proving that they were around during the time of the dinosaurs, *Magnolia grandiflora* are considered among the oldest flowering plants in the world. • Place *Magnolia grandiflora* under the bed to assure faithfulness.

550
Magnolia splendens

| **Laurel-Leaved Magnolia** | **Laurel Magnolia** | **Laurel Sabino** | **Shining Magnolia** |

★**SYMBOLIC MEANINGS:**
Dignity;

★**POTENTIAL POWERS:**
Fidelity;

★**FOLKLORE AND FACTS:**
With fossils proving that there were around during the time of the dinosaurs, *Magnolia splendens* is considered among the oldest flowering plants in the world. • Place *Magnolia splendens* under the bed to assure faithfulness.

551
Magnolia virginiana

| **Beaver Tree** | **Swampbay** | **Swamp Magnolia** | **Sweetbay** | **Sweetbay Magnolia** | **Whitebay** |

★**SYMBOLIC MEANINGS:**
Perseverance; Love of nature;

★**FOLKLORE AND FACTS:**
Place *Magnolia virginiana* under the bed to assure faithfulness.

552
Magnolia x soulangeana

| **Chinese Magnolia** | **Saucer Magnolia** |

★**SYMBOLIC MEANINGS:**
Love of nature; Natural;

★**FOLKLORE AND FACTS:**
Place *Magnolia x soulangeana* under the bed to assure faithfulness.

553
Mahonia aquifolium

| California Barberry | *Berberis aquifolium* | Oregongrape | Oregon Grape | Oregon-Grape | Oregan Grape-holly | Oregon Grape-holly | Oregan Holly-grape | Oregon Holly-Grape | Oregon Grape Root | Rocky Mountain Grape | Tall Oregon-grape | Trailing Grape | Wild Oregon Grape |

★**POTENTIAL POWERS:**
Money; Prosperity

★**FOLKLORE AND FACTS:**
Carry a piece of *Mahonia aquifolium* root to attract money and assure financial security. • Carry a piece of *Mahonia aquifolium* root to gain popularity.

554
Malus domestica

| Apple | Apple Tree | Orchard Apple Tree |

★**SYMBOLIC MEANINGS:**
Art; Art and Poetry; Love; Perpetual Concord; Perpetual Peaceful Agreement; Poetry; Temptation; Transformation;

★**POTENTIAL POWERS:**
Garden blessing; Garden magic; Healing; Immortality; Love; Transformation;

★**FOLKLORE AND FACTS:**
Malus domestica appears in the writings of many religions, most often as a forbidden fruit. • A concern about *Malus domestica* in religion, folk stories, and mythology is that the word "apple" was actually a generic term used to describe fruits and even nuts up until, at least, the 17th century. Therefore, it is not possible to know whether any particular "apple" was, in fact, a *Malus domestica* or something altogether different. • A simple divination using *Malus domestica* fruit involves cutting the fruit in half then examining and counting what seeds are visible. If an odd number, the inquirer will remain unmarried in the near future. If the total is an even number, soon there will be marriage. If one of the seeds has been cut, the relationship will be volitle. If two seeds have been cut, widowhood is the foretelling. • For a healing, during the waning of the moon take a *Malus domestica* fruit, cut it into three pieces and then rub each of the pieces wherever there is illness. Then,bury the pieces. • Before eating *Malus domestica* fruit rub it to remove any evil spirit that might be hiding within it.

▶ *Malus domestica Blossom:*
Amorous; Aphrodisiac; Better things to come; Fame speaks well; Fame speaks him

great and good; Fertility; Good fortune; Heady love; He prefers you; Peace; Preference; Sensuality;

▸ *Malus domestica Fruit:*

Lingering love; Motherhood; Presence of love; Purity; Self-control; Temperance; Temptation; Virtue;

555
Malus floribunda

| Japanese Flowering Crabapple |

★**SYMBOLIC MEANINGS:**
Ill-tempered; Ill nature;

556
Malvaceae

| Mallow | Malva |

★**SYMBOLIC MEANINGS:**
Consumed by love; Cruelty between lovers; Delicate beauty; Good and kind; Mildness; Sweetness;

★**POTENTIAL POWERS:**
Exorcism; Love; Protection;

557
Malva moschata

| Musk Mallow | Musk-mallow |

★**SYMBOLIC MEANINGS:**
Childishness; Immaturity;

558
Malva sylvestris

| Almindelig Katost | Amarutza | Apotekerkattost | Blue Mallow | Cheese-cake | Cheeses | Common Mallow | Country-mallow | Crni Slez | Ebegümeci | | Erdei Mályva | Gozdni Slezenovec | Grande Mauve | Groot | Groot Kaasjeskruid | High Mallow | Hobbejza Tar-Raba | Hocysen Gyffredin | Kaasjeskruid | Kiiltomalva | Kultur-Käsepappel | Malba | *Malva* | *Malva ambigua* | Malva Común | Malva de Cementiri | *Malva erecta* | *Malva gymnocarpa* | *Malva mauritiana* | Malva silvestre | Malva silvestre | Malvo granda | Mamarutza | Marmaredda |

Marva | Mauve des Bois | Mauve Sylvestre | Mets-kassinaeris | Méiba | Mályva | Nalba | Nalba de Culturä | Nalba de Padure | Narbedda | Papsajt | Pick-Cheese | Riondella | Round Dock | Rödmalva | Slaz dziki | Slez Lesny | Sljez Crni | Sljez Divlji | Sléz Lesní | Sotsal | Tall Mallow | Vauma | Wild Mallow | Wood Mallow | Ziga | Zigiña |

★**SYMBOLIC MEANINGS:**
Consumed by love; Persuasion;

★**POTENTIAL POWERS:**
Exorcism; Love; Protection;

★**FOLKLORE AND FACTS:**
Since Medevial times *Malva sylvestris* flowers were woven into garlands and wreaths for celebrating May Day (May 1st).

559
Mandevilla

| *Amblyanthera* | *Dipladenia* | *Eriadenia* | *Laseguea* | *Mitozus* | *Salpinctes* |

★**SYMBOLIC MEANINGS:**
You are too bold;

560
Mandragora ☠

| **Herb of Circe** | **Mandrake** | **Mandrake Root** | **Sorcerer's Root** | **Witch's Mannikin** | **Witches Mannikin** | **Wild Lemon** |

★**SYMBOLIC MEANINGS:**
An uncommon thing; Horror; Rarity; Scarcity; Screaming; Uncommon thing; Wickedness replacing love;

★**POTENTIAL POWERS:**
Aphrodisiac; Black Magic; Caution; Conception by way of spell casting; Death; Exorcism; Faith; Fertility; Health; Illumination; Initiation; Learning; Love; Lust; Magical power; Money; Potency; Promote conception; Promote passion; Promote sterility; Protection; Prudence; Self-preservation; Sorcery; Sound judgment; Sudden death; Wisdom; Witchcraft; Witchery;

★**FOLKLORE AND FACTS:**
The likeness of the *Mandragora* root to a human figure is why it was once feared as embodying a demon. It was said that when the *Mandragora* plant was pulled out of the ground a terrible shriek could be heard, and whoever heard it would die. • Witches often used the *Mandragora* root in spell casting. • Many superstitions sur-

round the possession of a *Mandragora* root: if you had one it was fortunate, but it had to be sold before dying at a lower price than what was paid for it. And also a person who received one for free would never be free, for the person would be in the grip of the devil.

꧁꧂

561
Maranta arundinacea

| Araru | Ararao | Arrowroot | Bermuda Arrowroot | Obedience Plant |

★SYMBOLIC MEANINGS:
Obedience;

★POTENTIAL POWERS:
Thicken;

꧁꧂

562
Marantaceae

| Prayer Plant | Prayer-Plant |

★SYMBOLIC MEANINGS:
Prayer;

★POTENTIAL POWERS:
Petition;

꧁꧂

563
Marrubium vulgare

| Bull's Blood | Common Horehound | Even Of The Star | Haran | Hoarhound | Horehound | Huran | Llwyd y cwn | Marrubium | Maruil | Seed of Horns | Soldier's Tea | White Horehound |

★SYMBOLIC MEANINGS:
Fire; Healing; Imitation;

★POTENTIAL POWERS:
Balance; Exorcism; Mental clarity; Mental powers; Protection; Purification;

★FOLKLORE AND FACTS:
Carry *Marrubium vulgare* to protect yourself against magical fascination and sorcery.

꧁꧂

564
Matthiola

| *Mathiola* | Stock |

★SYMBOLIC MEANINGS:

Bonds of affection; Lasting beauty; Promptitude; Promptness; You'll always be beautiful to me;

565
Matthiola incana

| Hoary Stock | Ten Week Stock | Tenweeks Stock |

★SYMBOLIC MEANINGS:

Bonds of affection; Lasting beauty; Promptness; You'll always be beautiful to me;

566
Maurandya barclayana ☠

| Angel's Trumpet Vine | *Asarina barclayana* | *Maurandya barclaiana* |

★SYMBOLIC MEANINGS:

Deathly intoxicating;

567
Medicago sativa

| Alfalfa | Buffalo Herb | Burclover | Jat | Lucerne | Lucerne Grass | Medick | Purple Medic | Qadb |

★SYMBOLIC MEANINGS:

Existence; Life;

★POTENTIAL POWERS:

Abundance; Anti-hunger; Brings in money; Money; Prosperity; Protects against financial misfortune;

★FOLKLORE AND FACTS:

When ashes of *Medicago sativa* are scattered around a house, those who reside within the house are protected from poverty and hunger. • Place a small jar filled with *Medicago sativa* in the food pantry to keep the pantry from being empty.

568
Melianthus major

| Giant Honey Flower | Honey Flower | Kruidjie-roer-my-nie |

★SYMBOLIC MEANINGS:

Generous Affection; Love sweet and secret; Secret love; Sweet and secret love; Sweetness of Disposition;

569
Melissa officinalis

| Balm | Balm Mint | Bee Balm | Blue Balm | Citronelle | Cure-All | Dropsy Plant | Elixir of Life | Garden Balm | Gentle Balm | Harden Balm | Heart's Delight | Honey Leaf | Lemon Balm | Lemon Balsam | *Melissa* | Oghoul | Sweet Balm | Sweet Mary | Sweet Mary Balm | Sweet Melissa | Tourengane | Zitron-melisse |

★ SYMBOLIC MEANINGS:
Brings love; Cure; Joke; Pleasantry; Regeneration; Social intercourse; Sympathy; Wishes will be fulfilled;

★ POTENTIAL POWERS:
Healing; Love; Success;

★ FOLKLORE AND FACTS:
Elizabethan Londoners would often carry posies of Melissa officinalis to sniff throughout the day to mask the odor of the stench of unsanitary filth in the streets. • Carry *Melissa officinalis* to find love. • Rubbed on a new hive *Melissa officinalis* will keep the old bees and attract new bees to it. • Carry *Melissa officinalis* to promote healing.

570
Mentha

| Good Herb | Hierbabuena | Hortel | Hortelã | Mint | Pudina | Yerba Buena |

★ SYMBOLIC MEANINGS:
Love; Refreshment; Suspicion; Virtue; Virtue and wisdom; Warmth; Warmth of feeling; Wisdom;

★ POTENTIAL POWERS:
Binding; Building; Death; Exorcism; Healing; History; Knowledge; Limitations; Lust; Money; Obstacles; Protection; Protection from illness; Time; Travel;

571
Mentha pulegium ☠

| European Pennyroyal | Lurk-In-The-Ditch | Mosquito Plant | Organ Broth | Organs | Organ Tea | Pennyroyal | Piliolerian | Pudding Grass | Run-By-The-Ground | Squaw Mint | Tickweed |

★ SYMBOLIC MEANINGS:

Flee away; Go away;

★ POTENTIAL POWERS:

Banishing; Consecration; Exorcism; Strength; Peace; Protection;

★ FOLKLORE AND FACTS:

A *Menta pulegium* leaf in the shoe is believed to alleviate a traveler's weariness. • Wear a sprig of *Menta pulegium* to guard against The Evil Eye. • Wear a sprig of *Menta pulegium* to help when in the process of making a business deal.

572
Mentha piperita

| **Brandy Mint | Lammint | Menta balsamea | Mentha x piperita | Peppermint |**

★ SYMBOLIC MEANINGS:

Affability; Cordiality; Love; Warmth of feeling;

★ POTENTIAL POWERS:

Healing; Psychic powers; Purification; Sleep; Love;

★ FOLKLORE AND FACTS:

Sniff fresh *Mentha piperita* leaves to help you sleep. • Put *Mentha piperita* leaves under the pillow to perhaps have a prophetic dreams. • Rub *Mentha piperita* leaves on the walls, furniture and etc. around the home to rid the home of negative energies. • Keep a *Mentha piperita* leaf in the handbag or wallet to encourage money to come to it.

573
Mentha spicata

| **Brown Mint | Garden Mint | Green Mint | Green Spine | Lamb Mint | Mackerel Mint | Mismin | Our Lady's Mint | Spearmint | Spear Mint | Spire Mint | Yerba Buena |**

★ SYMBOLIC MEANINGS:

Burning love; Warm feelings; Warm Sentiment; Warmth of sentiment;

★ POTENTIAL POWERS:

Aphrodisiac; Enhances sexuality; Healing; Humble virtue; Love; Mental clarity; Mental powers; Passion; Virtue;

★ FOLKLORE AND FACTS:

In ancient Rome and Greece, *Mentha spicata* was thought to increase the desire for lovemaking. • In ancient Rome and Greece *Mentha spicata* was rubbed on banquet tables as a symbol of hospitality. • In ancient Rome scholars were encourage to wear crowns of *Mentha spicata* to stimulate thinking. • Smelling *Mentha spicata* is supposed to sharpen your mental powers.

574
Menyanthes trifoliata

| Bitterklee | Bog-Bean | Buckbean | Fieberkless |

★ SYMBOLIC MEANINGS:
Calmness; Calm repose; Quiet; Repose;

575
Mercurialis

| Mercury |

★ SYMBOLIC MEANINGS:
Goodness;

576
Mesembryanthemum

| Fig Marigold | Ice Plant | Icicle Plant | *Mesembrianthemum* | Pebble Plant |

★ SYMBOLIC MEANINGS:
Addresses rejected; Coldness of heart; Frigidity; Idleness; Your looks freeze me;

577
Mimosa pudica

| Ant Plant | Ant-Plant | Chuimui | Chui-Mui | Dormilona | Hti Ka Yoan | Humble Plant | Laza Lu | Lojjaboti | Makahiya | Mateloi | Moriviví | Morí-viví | Moving Plant | Pokok Semalu | Putri Malu | Sensitive Plant | Shameful Plant | Sleeping Grass | Thotta-siningi | Thottavaadi | Touch-Me-Not |

★ SYMBOLIC MEANINGS:
Bashful love; Bashfulness; Delicate feelings; Despondency; Humility; Modesty; Sensibility; Sensitiveness; Sensitivity; Shyness; Timidity;

★ POTENTIAL POWERS:
Agitation;

578
Mirabilis jalapa

| Anthi Mandhaarai | Chandrakantha | Evening Flower | Four O'Clock Flower | Godhuli Gopal | Gulabaskhi | Marvel of Peru | Naalu mani poovu | Purple Jasmine | Rice Boiling Flower | Sandhyamaloti | Shower Flower | Xizao hua | Zhufàn hu |

★SYMBOLIC MEANINGS:
Flame of Love; Timidity;

579
Mitraria

| Chilean Mitre Flower | *Mitraria coccinea* |

★SYMBOLIC MEANINGS:
Dullness; Indolence;

580
Moluccella laevis

| Shellflower | Shell Flower | Bells of Ireland | Bells-of-Ireland | Molucca Balmis |

★SYMBOLIC MEANINGS:
Good fortune; Good luck; Gratitude; Luck; Whimsy;

581
Monarda didyma

| American Bee Balm | Bee Balm | Beebalm | Bergamot Herb | Crimson Bee-balm | Crimson Bee Balm | Gold Melissa | Horsemint | Indian Nettle | *Monarda* | Oswego | Oswego Tea | Red Bee Balm | Red Bergamot | Scarlet Beebalm | Scarlet Bee Balm | Scarlet Monarda |

★SYMBOLIC MEANINGS:
You change your mind too much; Your whims are unbearable; Your whims are quite unbearable;

★FOLKLORE AND FACTS:
After the Boston Tea Party, *Monarda didyma* tea was a popular patriotic substitute for imported teas. • *Monarda didyma* is believed to be able to bring clarity to unclear situations and working order to those situations with are disorderly.

582
Monotoca scoparia

| **Prickly Broom Heath** | *Styphelia scoparia* |

★**SYMBOLIC MEANINGS:**
Misanthropy;

583
Morus alba

| **China Mulberry** | **Russian Mulberry** | **Silkworm Mulberry** | **Tuta** | **Tuti** | **Sang Shen Tzu** | **White Mulberry** |

★**SYMBOLIC MEANINGS:**
Kindness; Prudence; Strength; Wisdom;

★**POTENTIAL POWERS:**
Protection;

★**FOLKLORE AND FACTS:**
In ancient times a *Morus alba* forest was the most sacred of places. • Carefully cultivating *Morus alba* began in China well over 4,000 years ago with the intention of using the leaves as the preferred food for raising silkworms.

584
Morus nigra

| **Black Mulberry** | **Gelso** | **Morera** | **Shahtoot** | **Toot** | **Tut** |

★**SYMBOLIC MEANINGS:**
Devotedness; I shall not survive you; I will not survive you; Wisdom;

★**POTENTIAL POWERS:**
Protection; Strength;

★**FOLKLORE AND FACTS:**
Morus nigra will supposedly protect your property from lightning. • Since *Morus nigra* wood is powerfully protective against evil, it makes an excellent wood for a wand.

585
Musa

| **Bacove** | **Banana** | **Maia** | *Musa acuminata* | *Musa acuminata x balbisiana* | *Musa balbisiana* | *Musa cliffortiana* | *Musa dacca* | *Musa paradisiac*a | *Musa x paradisiaca* | *Musa rosacea* | *Musa sapientum* | *Musa x sapientum* | *Musa violacea* | **Plantain** | **Sanging** |

★**SYMBOLIC MEANINGS:**

Goodness;

★**POTENTIAL POWERS:**
Fertility; Money; Potency; Prosperity;

★**FOLKLORE AND FACTS:**
To be married beneath a *Musa* tree is lucky. • Until 1819, in Hawaii, certain kinds of *Musa* were so strictly forbidden to women that the punishment for violating this taboo was death. • The leaves, flowers, and fruit of the *Musa* are used in money and prosperity spells because the *Musa* is such a fruitful plant.

586
Muscari

| **Common Grape Hyacinth** | **Grape Hyacinth** | **Starch Hyacinth** |

★**SYMBOLIC MEANINGS:**
Encourages romance; I am looking for romance;

587
Myosotis

| **Forget-Me-Not** | **Mouse-Eared Scorpion-Grass** | **Scorpion-Grass** |

★**SYMBOLIC MEANINGS:**
Clinging to the past; Do not forget me; Faithful Love; Faithfulness; Forget me not; Humility; Links to the past; Memories; Remembering; Remembrances; True Love;

★**POTENTIAL POWERS:**
Healing; Secrecy;

★**FOLKLORE AND FACTS:**
Myosotis is a symbol of the human desire for loyalty. • *Myosotis* is also a symbol that signals shared secrets.

588
Myrica

| **Bayberry** | **Bay-Rum Tree** | **Candleberry** | **Sweet Gale** | **Wax Myrtle** | **Wax-Myrtle** |

★**SYMBOLIC MEANINGS:**
Discipline; Instruction;

589

Myristica fragrans

| Mace | Nutmeg | Qoust | Sadhika | Wohpala | Bicuiba Acu |

★SYMBOLIC MEANINGS:
Amulet to increase clarity of thought;

★POTENTIAL POWERS:
Aphrodisiac; Breaks hexes; Fidelity; Health; Luck; Mental powers; Money; Protection; Psychic powers;

★FOLKLORE AND FACTS:
Carry the outer covering of *Myristica fragrans* to boost the intellect. • Carry a *Myristica fragrans* as a good luck charm.

590
Myroxylon

| Balsamo | Balsam of Peru | Balsam of Tolu | Quina | Tolu | *Xylosma* |

★SYMBOLIC MEANINGS:
Cure;

★POTENTIAL POWERS:
Aromatic; Healing;

591
Myrrhis odorata

| Cicely | Myrrh Plant | Sweet Cicely |

★SYMBOLIC MEANINGS:
Gladness;

★POTENTIAL POWERS:
Abundance; Advancement; Binding; Building; Conscious will; Death; Energy; Exorcism; Friendship; Growth; Healing; History; Joy; Knowledge; Leadership; Life; Light; Limitations; Natural power; Obstacles; Protection; Purification; Spirituality; Success; Time;

592
Myrtus communis

| Common Myrtle | Myrtle | *Myrtus* | True Myrtle |

★SYMBOLIC MEANINGS:
Good deeds; Heartfelt love; Immortality; Joy; Love; Marriage; Memory of The Garden of Eden; Mirth; Modest worth; Money; Peace; Sacred love; Scent of The Garden

of Eden; Souvenir of The Garden of Eden; Symbol of The Garden of Eden; Weddings; Youth;

★ **POTENTIAL POWERS:**

Assistance; Fertility; Fond memories; Harmony; Independence; Love; Material gain; Money; Peace; Persistence; Stability; Strength; Tenacity; Youth;

★ **FOLKLORE AND FACTS:**

Myrtus communis is considered to be a sacred plant and is both the symbol and the scent of The Garden of Eden. • A sprig of *Myrtus communis* that was in Queen Victoria's bridal bouquet was planted and since then, sprigs of that same plant have been included in royal bridal bouquets. • Carry *Myrtus communis* wood to preserve youthfulness. • Carry *Myrtus communis* to preserve love. • Grow *Myrtus communis* on each side of a house to promote that peace and love will be within the home. • If a woman plants *Myrtus communis* in a window box, it will become lucky.

faith

593
Narcissus ☠

| **Daffadown Dilly** | **Daffydowndilly** | **Daffodil** | **Great Daffodil** | *Narcissus major* |

★**SYMBOLIC MEANINGS:**
Annunciation; Appreciation of honesty; Beauty; Chivalry; Clarity of thought; Contentment; Deceitful hopes; Egotism; Energy that comes from being in love; Excessive self-love; Faith; Forgiveness; Formality; Forthrightness; High regards; Honesty; Hope; Inner beauty; Love; New beginnings; Promise of Eternal Life; Regard; Rebirth; Renewal; Respect; Resurrection and Rebirth; Self-esteem; Self concept; Self-love; Simple pleasures; Singular love and chivalry; Stay as sweet as you are; Sunlight; Sunshine; The sun shines when I'm with you; Truth; Uncertainty; Unrequited love; Unreturned love; Vanity; You're the only one; Vanity and Death; Vanity and egoism;

★**POTENTIAL POWERS:**
Aphrodisiac; Fertility; Love; Luck;

★**FOLKLORE AND FACTS:**
The *Narcissus* is the flower of The Underworld. • Animals do not eat the *Narcissus* flower because the sap contains sharp crystals. • Wear a *Narcissus* flower over your heart for good luck. • During Medieval times in Europe it was thought that if a *Narcissus* drooped while it was being looked at, it was an omen of death. • Chicken farmers were superstitious and would not allow *Narcissus* into their homes as they believed they were unlucky and would stop their hens from laying eggs or keep the eggs from hatching. • In Maine there is a superstition that if you point at a *Narcissus* with your index finger it will not bloom. • The Chinese believe that the *Narcissus* is lucky and will bring good luck for an entire year if forced to bloom during the Chinese New Year. • Fresh *Narcissus* flowers in a vase in the bedroom bodes well for fertility.

594
Narcissus jonquilla ☠

| **Jonquil** | **Jonquille** |

★**SYMBOLIC MEANINGS:**
Affection returned; Desire; Desires fulfilled; Longings; Love me; Return my affection; Sympathy; I desire a return of affection; Have pity on my passion; Return my

affection; Violent Sympathy and Desire;

★FOLKLORE AND FACTS:

The favorite flower of England's Queen Anne, who loved the *Narcissus jonquilla* so dearly that it inspired her to create Kensington Palace Gardens (the first public botanical garden in England).

595

Narcissus papyraceus ☠

| **Paperwhite** | **Paperwhite Narcissus** |

★SYMBOLIC MEANINGS:

Aphrodisiac;

596

Narcissus poeticus ☠

| **Findern Flower** | **Nargis** | **Pheasant's Eye** | **Pinkster Lily** | **Poets' Narcissus** | **Poet's Daffodil** | **Poet's Narcissus** | **White Narcissus** |

★SYMBOLIC MEANINGS:

Egotism; Painful remembrance; Remembrance; Selfishness; Self-love; Sorrowful memories;

597

Nardostachys grandiflora

| **Muskroot** | **Nard** | **Nardin** | *Nardostachys jatamansi* | **Pikenard** | **Spikenard** |

★POTENTIAL POWERS:

Fidelity; Health;

★FOLKLORE AND FACTS:

Pure *Nardostachys grandiflora* is believed to be the perfume ointment that Mary, the sister of Lazarus, used to anoint Jesus's feet six days before the Passover that preceded his crucifixion. Also, two days before that fateful death, an unnamed woman anointed Jesus' head with the same type of perfume taken from an alabaster jar. The use of this exceptionally expensive perfume on Jesus, rather than being sold for three hundred denarii (which would have been about a year's wages) is what incited Judas Iscariot to his betrayal of Jesus, which led to Jesus's arrest and subsequent crucifixion.

598

Nelumbo nucifera

| Ambuja | Aravind | Arvind | Baino | Bean of India | Egyptian Lotus | Flower of Hindus and Buddhists | Indian Lotus | Kamal | Kamala | Kunala | Lotus Flower | Lotus | Lotus-Flower | Nalin | Nalini | Neeraj | *Nelumbium speciosum* | *Nymphaea nelumbo* | Padma | Pankaj | Pankaja | Sacred Lotus | Saroja |

★ **SYMBOLIC MEANINGS:**
Beauty; Chastity; Divine Female Fertility; Eloquence; Enlightened One In A World Of Ignorant Beings; Estranged love; Estrangement; Evolution; Forgetful of the Past; Far from the one who is loved; Mere display; Mystery; Potential; Purity; Resurrection; Spiritual promises; The Enlightened One In A World Of Ignorant Beings; Truth; Virtuous;

★ **POTENTIAL POWERS:**
Lock-opening; Protection; Spirituality;

★ **FOLKLORE AND FACTS:**
The *Nelumbo nucifera* is highly regarded as a meaningful sacred plant in Egypt, India, Greece, and Japan being the mystical symbol of Life, Spirituality, and The Center of The Universe. • The viability of *Nelumbo nucifera* is quite incredible, and if conditions are ideal, the seeds that are viable can last a very long time. Currently, 1,300 years is the oldest germination of ancient *Nelumbo nucifera* seeds that were found in a dry Chinese lake bed. • Most deities of Asian religions are shown sitting upon a *Nelumbo nucifera* flower. • It is believed that anyone who breathes in the fragrance of a *Nelumbo nucifera* flower will benefit from the flower's inherent protection. • Carry or wear any part of the *Nelumbo nucifera* plant to receive good luck and blessings.

599
Nepeta cataria

| Cat | Catnip | Catmint | Catnep | Catrup | Cat's Wort | Catswort | Cat's Wort | Field Balm | Nepeta | Nip |

★ **SYMBOLIC MEANINGS:**
Courage; Happiness;

★ **POTENTIAL POWERS:**
Attraction; Beauty; Cat magic; Friendship; Gifts; Harmony; Joy; Love; Pleasure; Power; Sensuality; The Arts;

★ **FOLKLORE AND FACTS:**
Make a little pouch and fill it with *Nepeta cataria* then give it to your cat to create a psychic bond. • *Nepeta cataria* supposedly attracts good spirits and good luck. • It is believed that if you are to hold *Nepeta cataria* in your hand until it becomes warm

then hold another person's hand, that person will be your friend...but only for as long as you retain the *Nepeta cataria* that you used in the friendship spell in a safe place. • *Nepeta cataria* leaves are supposedly a favorite bookmark for magical books.

600
Nerium oleander ☠

| Adelfa | Ceylon Tree | Dog Bane | *Nerium indicum* | *Nerium odorum* | Oleander | Rose Bay |

★**SYMBOLIC MEANINGS:**
Beauty; Beware; Caution; Danger; Distrust; Grace; I am dangerous;

★**POTENTIAL POWERS:**
Death; Love;

★**FOLKLORE AND FACTS:**
In Italy it is believed that bringing any part of the *Nerium oleander* into the home will surely bring disgrace, misfortune of all types, and also sickness.

601
Nicotiana rustica ☠

| Makhorka | Mapacho | Taaba | Tabacca | Taback | Thuoc Lao | Wild Tobacco |

★**POTENTIAL POWERS:**
Healing; Offerings; Purification; Strength;

★**FOLKLORE AND FACTS:**
Nicotiana rustica has long been regarded as a sacred plant by many Native American and South American Indian tribes. • South American Indians believe that smoking *Nicotiana rustica* makes it possible to speak with spirits. • *Nicotiana rustica* thrown into the water at the beginning of a water journey is to appease the Water Spirit.

602
Nigella damascena

| Devil in the Bush | Jack in Prison | Love In A Mist | Love In A Snarl | Love-Entangle | Love-in-a-mist | Love-in-a-Puzzle |

★**SYMBOLIC MEANINGS:**
Delicacy; Embarrassment; Perplexity; You puzzle me;

603

Nolina lindheimeriana

| Beargrass | Devil's-shoestring | Devil's Shoestring | Lindheimer Nolina | Ribbon Grass |

★ POTENTIAL POWERS:
Employment; Gambling; Luck; Power; Protection;

★ FOLKLORE AND FACTS:
A piece of *Nolina lindheimeriana* in your pocket when gambling, job seeking, having difficulties at work or requesting a pay raise will be a good luck charm.

604
Nosegay

★ SYMBOLIC MEANINGS:
Gallantry;

605
Nuts

★ SYMBOLIC MEANINGS:
Stupidity;

★ POTENTIAL POWERS:
Fertility; Love; Luck; Prosperity;

★ FOLKLORE AND FACTS:
Carry a nut of any kind to aid fertility. • Any nut that grows together with another to create a co-joined double nut is a *very* luck charm.

606
Nymphaea alba

| European White Waterlily | Nenuphar | White Lotus |

★ SYMBOLIC MEANINGS:
Eloquence; Persuasian;

607
Nymphaea lutea

| American Lotus | Yellow Lotus | Yellow Water Lotus |

★ SYMBOLIC MEANINGS:
Growing indifference;

★**POTENTIAL POWERS:**
Protection; Spirituality;

608
Nymphaeaceae
| **Water Lily** |
★**SYMBOLIC MEANINGS:**
Eloquence; Harmony; Modesty; Purity; Purity of heart; Soothing;

peace

609
Ocimum basilicum

| Albahaca| American Dittany | Arjaka | Balanoi | Basil | Brenhinllys | Busuioc | Common Basil | Feslien | Garden Basil | Herb of Kings | Holy Basil | Kiss Me Nicholas | L'herbe Royale | Luole | Njilika | Our Herb | Saint Josephwort | St. Joseph's Wort | Sweet Basil | The Devil's Plant | Tulsi | Witches Herb |

★**SYMBOLIC MEANINGS:**
Best Wishes; Give me your good wishes; Good Luck; Good wishes; Hatred; Hatred of the other; Kingly; Romance; Sacred; Wealth;

★**POTENTIAL POWERS:**
Accidents; Aggression; Anger; Carnal desires; Conflict; Exorcism; Flying; Love; Lust; Machinery; Prosperity; Protection; Rock music; Strength; Struggle; War; Wealth; Witch Flight;

★**FOLKLORE AND FACTS:**
Carry an *Ocimum basilicum* leaf in your pocket to bring you money. • A *Ocimum basilicum* leaf placed on a deceased Hindu is assurance that he or she will reach Paradise. • The ancient Greeks considered *Ocimum basilicum* to be a strong symbol of hate, misfortune and poverty. • In the West Indies, *Ocimum basilicum* is placed around shops to attract customers. In other parts of the world, a *Ocimum basilicum* leaf is placed in cash registers and on the entry doors into shops to not only attract customers but to ensure continued financial success. • In Italy, *Ocimum basilicum* is a symbol for Love and is widely used as a token of Love. • Giving a sprig of *Ocimum basilicum* to a man means, "Be wary, for someone is plotting against you." • According to Jewish legend, if you hold a sprig of *Ocimum basilicum* while fasting it will help you maintain your strength and resolve to proceed. • In Spain, a pot of *Ocimum basilicum* on a windowsill indicated that it was a house of ill repute. • The fragrance of *Ocimum basilicum* is said to provoke sympathy between two unsympathetic people. • *Ocimum basilicum* given as a gift will bring Good Luck into a new home. • A married couple can share one *Ocimum basilicum* leaf between them to rub over their hearts as a request that fidelity will bless their relationship. • In India, the *Ocimum basilicum* plant is considered to be sacred.

610
Oemleria cerasiformis

| Indian Plum | *Nuttallia* | *Oemleria* | *Osmaronia* | Osoberry |

★**SYMBOLIC MEANINGS:**
Privation; Suffering;

611
Oenothera

| **Evening Primrose** | **Evening-Primrose** | *Oenothera biennis* | **Suncups** | **Sundrops** |

★**SYMBOLIC MEANINGS:**
Happy love; Inconstancy; Silent love;

612
Oenothera flava

| **Evening Primrose** | **Long-tube Evening Primrose** | **Tree Primrose** | **Yellow Evening Primrose** | **Yellow Evening-primrose** | **Yellow Evening Primrose** | **War Poison** |

★**POTENTIAL POWERS:**
Hunting;

613
Olea europaea

| **Itm** | **Mitan** | **Olive Tree** | **Olivier** |

★**SYMBOLIC MEANINGS:**
Peace;

★**POTENTIAL POWERS:**
Fertility; Healing; Lust; Peace; Potency; Protection;

★**FOLKLORE AND FACTS:**
Scatter *Olea europaea* leaves in a room to create a vibration of peace. • In ancient times *Olea europaea* oil was commonly used as fuel for lamps. • *Olea europaea* oil is used for healing and for blessings by anointing the recipient. • Brides in ancient Greece would traditionally wear *Olea europaea* crowns as their visible wish for fertility. • Hang an *Olea europaea* branch over the front door to fend evil away from entering into the home. • Wear a *Olea europaea* leaf as a good luck charm.

▸ *Olea europaea Branch:*
Peace;

▸ *Olea europaea Leaf :*
Peace;

614
Onobrychis

| *Dendrobychis* | **Esparceta** | **Esparcette** | **Esparsette** | **Espartset** | **Esparsett** | **Luzerne** | **Sainfoin** | **Sain-foin** | **Saintfoin** | **Sparceta** | *Xanthobrychis* |

★**SYMBOLIC MEANINGS:**
Agitation; Trust in God;

615
Ononis

| *Anonis* | *Bonaga* | *Bugranopsis* | *Natrix* | *Passaea* | **Restharrow** | **Rest-Harrow** |

★**SYMBOLIC MEANINGS:**
Obstacles;

616
Ononis spinosa

| *Ononis vulgaris* | **Restharrow** | **Spiny Restharrow** |

★**SYMBOLIC MEANINGS:**
Obstacles;

617
Onopordum acanthium

| **Cotton Thistle** | **Scotch Thistle** | **Scots Thistle** | **Scottish Thistle** |

★**SYMBOLIC MEANINGS:**
Alerting; Christ's deliverance; Hard work; Retaliation; Suffering; Christ's deliverance;

★**POTENTIAL POWERS:**
Assistance; Dispels melancholy; Fertility; Harmony; Independence; Material gain; Persistence; Protection; Revelation; Stability; Strength; Tenacity;

618
Ophrys apifera

| *Arachnites apifera* | **Bee Orchid** | **Bee Orphrys** | *Orchis apifera* | *Ophrys chlorantha* | *Ophrys insectifera* |

★**SYMBOLIC MEANINGS:**
Error; Industry;

619
Ophrys bombyliflora

| **Bumblebee Flower Eyebrow** | **Bumblebee Orchid** | **Bumblebee Ophrys** |

★**SYMBOLIC MEANINGS:**
Hard work; Industry; Persistence;

620
Ophrys insectifera

| **Fly Orchid** | **Fly Ophrys** | *Orchis insectifera* | *Ophrys myodes* | *Epipactis myodes* | *Orchis myodes* | *Malaxis myodes* |

★**SYMBOLIC MEANINGS:**
Error; Mistake;

621
Opuntia

| *Airampoa* | *Cactodendron* | *Cactus* | *Chaffeyopuntia* | *Clavarioidia* | *Ficindica* | **Indian Fig Opuntia** | **Nochtli** | **Nopal** | *Nopalea* | **Nopales** | **Nopalli** | **Nostle** | **Paddle Cactus** | *Parviopuntia* | *Phyllarthus* | **Prickly Pear** | *Salmiopuntia* | *Subulatopuntia* | **Tuna** | *Tunas* | *Weberiopuntia* |

★**SYMBOLIC MEANINGS:**
Did not forget; I burn; Satire;

622
Orchidaceae

| **Ballockwor** | **Orchid** | **Orchis** | **Ophrys** | **Satyrion** |

★**SYMBOLIC MEANINGS:**
A belle; Beauty; Belle; Refinement; Chinese Symbol for Many Children; Consideration; Thoughtfulness; Beautiful lady; Fertility; Pure affection; Magnificence; Mature charm; Love; Wisdom; Thoughtfulness; Thoughtful Recollection; Refined beauty; Refinement; Understanding;

★**POTENTIAL POWERS:**
Love; Psychic powers; Romance;

⊙ **SPECIFIC COLOR MEANING > Pink:**

Pure affection;

623
Orchis mascula ☠

| Adam and Eve Root Plant | Early Purple Orchid | Hand of Power | Hand Root | Helping Hand | Lucky Hand | Salap |

★POTENTIAL POWERS:
Employment; Luck; Money; Travel; Protection;

★FOLKLORE AND FACTS:
It is believed that witches have used *Orchis mascula* roots in the creation of love potions. • It is believed that to attract love, carry two *Orchis mascula* roots that have been sewn into a small pouch. • Two *Orchis mascula* roots is a good gift to a newly-wed couple to ensure their future happiness.

624
Origanum dictamnus

| Cretan Dittany | Diktamo | Dittany of Crete | Erontas | Fraxinella | Hop Marjoram |

★SYMBOLIC MEANINGS:
Birth; Love;

★POTENTIAL POWERS:
Aphrodisiac; Astral projection; Business transactions; Calling spirits; Cleverness; Creativity; Communication; Divination; Intelligence; Love potions; Manifestations; Memory; Science; Spirit summoning; Thievery;

★FOLKLORE AND FACTS:
Due to the immense danger of collecting the wild *Origanum dictamnus* on the rocky mountainsides and gorges of Crete, a great many deaths of *Origanum dictamnus* collectors have been reported over the centuries.

625
Origanum majorana

| Knotted Marjoram | Marjoram | *Majorana hortensis* | Sweet Majoram |

★SYMBOLIC MEANINGS:
Blushes; Comfort; Consolation; Joy; Love;

★POTENTIAL POWERS:
Happiness; Health; Longevity; Love; Money; Protection; Soothes anxiety; Soothes

grief;

★**FOLKLORE AND FACTS:**
It is thought that if someone rubs *Origanum majorana* on their self before sleeping he or she will dream of their future spouse. • Ancient Greeks believed *Origanum majorana* grew over the grave of a dead person who was happy. • Ancient Greeks and Romans, both, would make crowns of *Origanum majorana* for bridal couples to wear as symbols of love, happiness and honor.

626
Origanum vulgare

| Herb of Magic | Oregano | Wild Marjaram |

★**SYMBOLIC MEANINGS:**
Will banish sadness; Soothing;

★**POTENTIAL POWERS:**
Good luck; Protection against poison; Reveals the mystical secrets for using Black Magic;

★**FOLKLORE AND FACTS:**
Origanum vulgare was virtually unknown in the United States until the end of World War II, when American soldiers who had been stationed in the Mediterranean made a point to bring seeds home with them.

627
Orobanche

| Broomrape | Broom-rape |

★**SYMBOLIC MEANINGS:**
Union;

628
Oryza sativa

| Asian rice | Bras | Dhan | Nirvara | *Oryza glaberrima* | Paddy | Rice |

★**POTENTIAL POWERS:**
Fertility; Fidelity; Money; Protection; Rain;

★**FOLKLORE AND FACTS:**
Put *Oryza sativa* on the roof to protect a house against misfortune. • Put a container filled with *Oryza sativa* near the entry doors of the house to protect the home against evil. • It is believed by some that if you throw *Oryza sativa* up into the air it will

bring rain. • *Oryza sativa* has long been tossed at a newly married couple to increase their fertility (A curious note: It seems mighty strange that after this practice was halted for a variety of reasons, all of a sudden there was a sudden plague of serious infertility problems among married couples. Is there a mystical connection with this? Hmm...it sure makes me wonder.)

629
Osmunda regalis

| Fern | Flowering Fern | Old World Royal Fern | Royal Fern |

★SYMBOLIC MEANINGS:
Confidence; Dreams; Fascination; I dream of thee; I dream of you; Magic; Reverie; Shelter; Sincerity; Wisdom;

★POTENTIAL POWERS:
Exorcism; Health; Luck; Magic; Riches; Protection;

630
Oxalis acetosella

| Common Wood Sorrel | Common Wood-Sorrel | Cuckowe's Meat | Fairy Bells | Shamrock | Sours | Sourgrass | Sour Trefoil | Stickwort | Stubwort | Surelle | Three-Leaved Grass | Wood Sorrel | Wood-sorrel | Wood Sour |

★SYMBOLIC MEANINGS:
Joy; Maternal tenderness;

★POTENTIAL POWERS:
Good luck; Healing; Health;

★FOLKLORE AND FACTS:
Oxalis acetosella is sometimes referred to as a "Shamrock" (all *Trifolium*, but which is actually, *Trifolium repens*) because it has a three-leafed clover look, and so it is widely available and often kept or given as a potted plant gift on St. Patrick's Day. • Put a live plant or nosegay of fresh *Oxalis acetosella* in a sickroom to speed recuperation from wounds or illness.

631
Oxalis tetraphylla

| Lucky Clover | Four-Leaf Clover | Four Leaved Clover | Four-Leaf Sorrel | Four-Leave Pink-Sorrel | Lucky Leaf | Iron Cross |

★SYMBOLIC MEANINGS:
Be mine; Good Luck; Hope, Faith, Love and Luck;

★POTENTIAL POWERS:

Avoids military service; Ability to recognize witches; Ability to see invisible demons; Charm against snakes; Charm against witches; Charm against The Devil; Charm against dangerous creatures, both real and imagined; Enables one to see fairies; Exceptionally Good Luck; Gives the gift of second sight; Luck finding money and treasure; Protection against madness;

★FOLKLORE AND FACTS:

There is a legend that it was Eve who carried an *Oxalis tetraphylla's* Four-Leaf Clover out of Eden to hold onto Luck, Hope, Love, and Faith.• If you want to avoid being inducted into the military, wear an *Oxalis tetraphylla's* Four-Leaf Clover Lucky Leaf. • An *Oxalis tetraphylla's* Four-Leaf Clover Lucky Leaf will also strengthen your psychic powers and enables you to detect the presence other spirits if you are wearing it. • An *Oxalis tetraphylla's* Four-Leaf Clover Lucky Leaf can lead you to money and other riches, most especially treasure and gold. • An *Oxalis tetraphylla's* Four-Leaf Clover Lucky Leaf will offer protection against madness. • If you want to see fairies put seven grains of *Tricum* (wheat) atop an *Oxalis tetraphylla's* Four-Leaf Clover Lucky Leaf. • One *Oxalis tetraphylla's* Four-Leaf Clover Lucky Leaf in your shoe will help you meet a lover who is rich.

courage

632
Paeonia officinalis

| European Peony | Common Peony | Paeonly | Peony | Piney | Sho-Yo |

★SYMBOLIC MEANINGS:

Anger; Aphrodisiac; Bashfulness; Beauty; Bravery; Compassion; Diffidence; Gay Life; Healing; Happy marriage; Life; Loyalty; Omen of good fortune and a happy marriage; Honor; Masculinity; Ostentation; Prosperity; Riches and honor; Romance; Shame; Shyness; Unrealized desires; Wealth;

★POTENTIAL POWERS:

Exorcism; Happy life; Healing; Prosperity; Protection; Purification;

★FOLKLORE AND FACTS:

The earliest record of *Paeonia officinalis* was found in a Chinese tomb dated back to the first century. • Wear *Paeonia officinalis* to protect the body, mind, spirit, and soul. • A *Paeonia officinalis* flower within the home will fend off evil spirits. • Grow *Paeonia officinalis* in the garden to protect the home against storms and evil. • Wear a necklace that you have made from *Paeonia* officinalis root and coral beads to chase away an incubus. • Carry *Paeonia officinalis* as a cure for lunacy.

633
Paeonia suffruticosa

| Beauty of The Empire | King of Flowers | Tree Peony |

★SYMBOLIC MEANINGS:

Beauty; Most beautiful;

634
Panax ☠

| All-Heal | Ginnsuu | Ginseng | Ginseng | Jên Shên | Jîn-Sim | Man Root | Rénshen | Wonder of The World Root |

★POTENTIAL POWERS:

Beauty; Healing; Longevity; Love; Lust; Protection; Sexual potency; Wishes;

★FOLKLORE AND FACTS:

Panax will bring beauty, love, money, sexuality, and health to all who carry it. • An interesting way to make a wish is to carve your wish into a *Panax* root and then throw it into running water.

635
Panicum capillare ☠

| Hairy Panic | Witchgrass | Witch Grass |

★POTENTIAL POWERS:
Exorcism; Happiness; Love; Lust;

636
Papaver orientale ☠

| Blind Buff | Blindeyes | Headaches | Head Waak | Oriental Poppy | Poppy | Scarlet Poppy | White Poppy |

★SYMBOLIC MEANINGS:
Dreaminess; Eternal sleep; Fantastic extravagance; Imagination; Oblivion;

★POTENTIAL POWERS:
Fertility; Fruitfulness; Invisibility; Love; Luck; Magic; Money; Sleep;

★FOLKLORE AND FACTS:
At one time *Papaver orientale* seed pods were gilded and worn to attract wealth. • An interesting divination that could be used to answer a perplexing question is to write the question on a piece of paper using blue ink then folding it up and tucking it within a *Papaver orientale* seed pod. Put the pod under your pillow before sleeping to facilitate a dream that will answer the question.

◉ SPECIFIC COLOR MEANING > Red:
Pleasure;

◉ SPECIFIC COLOR MEANING > White:
Consolation; Dreams; Peace;

637
Papaver rhoeas

| Common Poppy | Corn Poppy | Corn Rose | Field Poppy | Flanders Poppy | Red Poppy | Red Weed |

★SYMBOLIC MEANINGS:
Avoidance of problems; Consolation; Ephemeral charms; Eternal rest; Eternal Sleep; Fun-loving; Good and Evil; Imagination; Life and Death; Light and Darkness; Love; Oblivion; Pleasure; Remembrance;

★POTENTIAL POWERS:
Attitude; Ambition; Clear thinking; Fertility; Fruitfulness; Harmony; Higher under-

standing; Invisibility; Logic; Love; Luck; Magic; Manifestation in material form; Money; Sleep; Spiritual concepts; Thought processes;

★ **FOLKLORE AND FACTS:**

The Romans believed that *Papaver rhoeas* could heal wounds inflicted by love. • Evidence of *Papaver rhoeas* flowers were found in 3,000 year old Egyptian tombs. • The ancient Greeks believed that corn would not grow without the presence of *Papaver rhoeas* growing nearby. • After WWI the battle torn holes in the fields in Flanders, later filled up with *Papaver rhoeas*. A legend began that the flowers had come from the spilt blood of war, making the red *Papaver rhoeas* flower the official remembrance symbol of the war dead.

638
Paronychia

| Chickweed | Nailwort | Whitlow-Wort |

★ **SYMBOLIC MEANINGS:**

I cling to thee; Love; Rendezvous; Will you meet me;

★ **POTENTIAL POWERS:**

Fertility; Fidelity; Love;

639
Parthenocissus quinquefolia

| Engelmann's Ivy | Five-finger | Five-Leaved Ivy | Virginia Creeper |

★ **SYMBOLIC MEANINGS:**

I cling to you for better or worse; I cling to you both in sunshine and shade;

640
Passiflora caerulea

| Blue Passion Flower | Christ's Story Flower | Common Passion Flower | Grandilla | Jesus Flower | Maracoc | Maypops | Mburucuyá | Passionflower | Passion Flower | Passion Vine |

★ **SYMBOLIC MEANINGS:**

Faith; Faith and Piety; Faith and suffering; I have no claims; Piety; Primeval nature; Unpretentious; Yearning for a long-lost Paradise; You have no claims;

★ **POTENTIAL POWERS:**

Friendships' prosperity; Increase libido; Peace; Slep;

★ **FOLKLORE AND FACTS:**

231

Passiflora caerulea is a powerful symbol of the suffering of Christ that has it's own legend and was often used as an early visual teaching aid to explain the Christian Gospel before there were any printed materials. • A *Passiflora caerulea* flower in the home is believed to promote peacefulness by calming trouble and resolving problems. • Carry a *Passiflora caerulea* flower to attract friends. • Put *Passiflora caerulea* leaf under the pillow to help you have restful sleep.

641
Pausinystalia yohimbe ☠

| *Corynanthe yohimbe* | Yohimbe |

★ **POTENTIAL POWERS:**
Aphrodisiac; Love; Lust;

642
Peganum harmala

| African Rue | Esphand | Harmal | Harmal Peganum | Harmal Shrub | Isband | Luotuo-pe | Ozallaik | Peganum | Steppenraute | Syrian Rue | Üzerlik | Wild Rue | Yüzerlik |

★ **SYMBOLIC MEANINGS:**
Changeable disposition; Docility; Regret;

★ **POTENTIAL POWERS:**
Protects against The Evil Eye; Protects against the gazing eyes of strangers;

★ **FOLKLORE AND FACTS:**
In Turkey, it is common that dried seed capsules from the *Peganum harmala* plant are hung in homes and vehicles as protection against The Evil Eye. • In the Middle East, with ancient prayers and the dried seed capsules from the *Peganum harmala* plant are mixed with other ingredients and then put on hot charcoal until they burst with smoke that moves around the head of a person who believes was gazed upon by strangers or directly exposed to The Evil Eye.

643
Pelargonium crispum

| Lemon Geranium | Lemon-Scented Geranium |

★ **SYMBOLIC MEANINGS:**
Gentility; Unexpected meeting;

★ **FOLKLORE AND FACTS:**
Pelargonium of all types are protective when grown or brought into the house as cut

flowers and put into fresh water. • Pots of red *Pelargonium crispum* offer a lot of protection for the home and health.

644
Pelargonium fragrans variegatum

| Nutmeg Geranium | Sweet Leaved Geranium |

★ SYMBOLIC MEANINGS:
Expected meeting; I expect a meeting; I shall never see him;

★ FOLKLORE AND FACTS:
Pelargonium of all types are protective when grown or brought into the house as cut flowers and put into fresh water. • Pots of red *Pelargonium fragrans variegatum* offer a lot of protection for the home and health.

645
Pelargonium graveolens

| Old Fashion Rose Geranium | *Geranium terebinthinaceum* | *Pelargonium* | *Pelargonium incrassatum* | *Pelargonium roseum* | *Pelargonium terebinthinaceum* | Rose Geranium | Rose-scent Geranium | Rose-Scented Geranium | Storksbill | Scented Geranium |

★ SYMBOLIC MEANINGS:
Calm; Happiness; Gentility; I prefer you; Preference; Spiritual happiness;

★ POTENTIAL POWERS:
Happiness; Health; Fertility; Love; Prosperity; Protection;

★ FOLKLORE AND FACTS:
Some *Pelargonium* varieties are said to be able to effectively repel mosquitoes. • *Pelargonium* of all types are protective when grown or brought into the house as cut flowers and put into fresh water. • Pots of red *Pelargonium graveolens* offer a lot of protection for the home and health.

646
Pelargonium inquinans

| Scarlet Geranium | Wild Malva | Wilde Malva |

★ SYMBOLIC MEANINGS:
Comforting; Consolation; Gaiety; Gentility; Melancholy; Silliness; Silly;

★ POTENTIAL POWERS:
Fertility; Health; Love; Protection;

★**FOLKLORE AND FACTS:**

Pelargonium of all types are protective when grown or brought into the house as cut flowers and put into fresh water. • Pots of red *Pelargonium inquinans* offer a lot of protection for the home and health.

647

Pelargonium nubilum

| Clouded Geranium | Clouded Stork's-bill | *Geranium nubilum* |

★**SYMBOLIC MEANINGS:**

Melancholy;

★**POTENTIAL POWERS:**

Gentility; Love; Purification;

★**FOLKLORE AND FACTS:**

Pelargonium of all types are protective when grown or brought into the house as cut flowers and put into fresh water. • Pots of red *Pelargonium nubilum* offer a lot of protection for the home and health.

648

Pelargonium odoratissimum

| Apple Geranium |

★**SYMBOLIC MEANINGS:**

Facility; Gentility; Present preference;

★**POTENTIAL POWERS:**

Fertility; Health; Love; Purification;

★**FOLKLORE AND FACTS:**

Pelargonium of all types are protective when grown or brought into the house as cut flowers and put into fresh water. • Pots of red *Pelargonium odoratissimum* offer a lot of protection for the home and health.

649

Pelargonium peltatum

| Cascading Geranium | Ivy Geranium | Ivy-Leaf Geranium |

★**SYMBOLIC MEANINGS:**

Bridal favor; Gentility; I engage you for the next dance; Your hand for next dance; Your next dance is with me;

★**POTENTIAL POWERS:**

Fertility; Health; Love; Purification;

★**FOLKLORE AND FACTS:**

Pelargonium of all types are protective when grown or brought into the house as cut flowers and put into fresh water. • Pots of red *Pelargonium peltatum* offer a lot of protection for the home and health.

650
Pelargonium quercifolium

| Oak Geranium | Oakleaf Geranium | Oak-Leaf Geranium |

★**SYMBOLIC MEANINGS:**

A melancholy mind; Friendship; Deign to smile; Gentility; Lady; True friendship;

★**POTENTIAL POWERS:**

Fertility; Health; Love; Purification;

★**FOLKLORE AND FACTS:**

Pelargonium of all types are protective when grown or brought into the house as cut flowers and put into fresh water. • Pots of red *Pelargonium quercifolium* offer a lot of protection for the home and health.

651
Pelargonium sidoides

| Kalwerbossie Geranium | Silverleaf Geranium | Silver Leaf Geranium | Silver-Leaved Geranium | South African Geranium | Umca | Umcka | Umckalo-abo |

★**SYMBOLIC MEANINGS:**

Recall; Gentility;

★**FOLKLORE AND FACTS:**

Pelargonium of all types are protective when grown or brought into the house as cut flowers and put into fresh water. • Pots of red *Pelargonium sidoides* offer a lot of protection for the home and health.

652
Pelargonium zonale

| Horsehoe Geranium | *Pelargonium x hortorum* |

★**SYMBOLIC MEANINGS:**

Gentility; Stupidity;

★**POTENTIAL POWERS:**

235

Fertility; Health; Love; Protection;

★**FOLKLORE AND FACTS:**

Pelargonium of all types are protective when grown or brought into the house as cut flowers and put into fresh water. • Pots of red *Pelargonium zonale* offer a lot of protection for the home and health.

653
Persea americana ☠

| **Abacate** | **Aguacate** | **Ahuacotl** | **Alligator Pear** | **Avocado** | **Butter Fruit** | **Butter Pear** | **Nahuatl Ahuacatl** | **Palta** | *Persea* | *Persea gratissima* | **Testicle Tree** | **Zaboca** |

★**POTENTIAL POWERS:**

Aphrodisiac; Beauty; Love; Lust;

★**FOLKLORE AND FACTS:**

To grow a Persea americana plant in the home from the pit of a fruit that you have consumed will bring love into the home.• Carry a Persea americana pit to promote beauty. • A magic wand made from *Persea americana* is believed to be very powerful.

654
Persea borbonia

| **Redbay** | **Red Bay** | **Shorebay** |

★**SYMBOLIC MEANINGS:**

Memory;

655
Persicaria

| **Pinkweed** | **Smartweed** |

★**SYMBOLIC MEANINGS:**

Restoration;

656
Persicaria bistorta

| **Adderwort** | **Bistort** | **Bistora** | **Common Bistort** | **Dragonwort** | **Easter Giant** | **Easter Ledger** | **Easter Ledges** | **Easter Magiant** | **Easter Man-Giant** | **Gentle Dock** | **Great Bistort** | **Osterick** | **Oysterloit** | **Passion Dock** | **Patience Dock** | **Patient Dock** | **Pink Pokers** | **Pudding Dock** | **Pudding Grass** | **Red Legs** |

Snakeweed | Twice-Writhen | Water Ledges |

★**POTENTIAL POWERS:**

Binding; Building; Death; Fertility; History; Knowledge; Limitations; Obstacles; Psychic powers; Time;

★**FOLKLORE AND FACTS:**

If you desire to conceive carry or wear *Persicaria bistorta*. • If a poltergeist has become a pest sprinkle an infusion of *Persicaria bistorta* all around to drive it away.

657
Petasites fragrans

| Sweet-Scented Tussilage | *Tussilago fragrans* **| Winter Heliotrope |**

★**SYMBOLIC MEANINGS:**

Justice shall be done you;

658
Petroselinum crispum

| *Apium crispum* **|** *Apium petroselinum* **| Devil's Oatmeal | Hamburg Parsley | Italian Parsley | Parsley | Percely | Persil | Petersilie |** *Petroselinum* **|** *Petroselinum crispum crispum* **|** *Petroselinum crispum neapolitanum* **|** *Petroselinum crispum tuberosum* **| Petroselinon | Rock Parsley | Selinon | Turnip-rooted Parsley |**

★**SYMBOLIC MEANINGS:**

Festivity; Fickleness; Love;

★**POTENTIAL POWERS:**

Business transactions; Caution; Cleverness; Communication; Creativity; Faith; Illumination; Initiation; Intelligence; Learning; Lust; Memory; Protection; Prudence; Purification; Science; Self-preservation; Sound judgment; Thievery; Wisdom;

★**FOLKLORE AND FACTS:**

Petroselinum crispum has been cultivated since 300BC. • *Petroselinum crispum* was valuable to witches because it was believed that *Petroselinum crispum* went to the Underworld nine times and back again before sprouting. • If one dreams about cutting *Petroselinum crispum* it is a bad omen for love, indicating that the dreamer will be double-crossed by a lover. • It is believed that to transplant *Petroselinum crispum* will bring bad luck for a year. • In Medieval times, it was believed that to pluck a sprig of *Petroselinum crispum* while speaking an enemy's name had the power to kill. • Ancient Romans and Greeks both place *Petroselinum crispum* on the dinner plates to both protect the food and keep away misfortune during mealtime.

659
Petunia

★**SYMBOLIC MEANINGS:**
Anger; Disdain; I'm not proud; Not as proud as you are; Resentment; Your presence soothes me;

660
Phalaris canariensis

| Canary Grass |

★**SYMBOLIC MEANINGS:**
Determination; Perseverance;

661
Phaseolus vulgaris ☠

| Alavese Pinto Bean | Alubia Pinta Alavesa Bean | Anasazi Bean | Black Bean | Black Turtle Bean | Borlotti Bean | Canary Bean | Cannellini Bean | Caparrones Bean | Caraota o Habichuela Negra Bean | Chili Bean | Common Bean | Cranberry Bean | Eléfantes Bean | Enola Bean | Feijão Preto Bean | Frijol Negro Bean | Frijol Pinto | Gígantes Bean | Habichuelas Rosada Bean | Haricot Bean | Kidney Bean | Mayocoba Bean | Mottled Bean | Pea Bean | Peruano Bean | Pink Bean | Pinquito Bean | Pinto Bean | Poor Man's Meat |Poroto Negro Bean | Rajmah Bean | Red Bean | Roman Bean | Romano Bean | Sinaloa Azufrado Bean | Speckled Bean | Sulphur Bean | White Bean | White Navy Bean | Yellow Bean | Zaragoza Bean |

★**POTENTIAL POWERS:**
Deter evil; Divination; Exorcism; Love; Potency; Protection; Reconciliation; Wart Charming;

★**FOLKLORE AND FACTS:**
Particularly in the Far East, scattered *Phaseolus vulgaris* flowers is thought to appease demons. • English tradition associates *Phaseolus vulgaris* with death if one *Phaseolus vulgaris* in a pod is white instead of green. • A common European Divination that is done with *Phaseolus vulgaris* is to hide three pods: one untouched (wealth), one half-peeled (comfort), and one fully peeled (poverty). Whichever *Phaseolus vulgaris* the inquirer found first, foretold the future. • Red *Phaseolus vulgaris* (Red Beans), which are indigenous to the Americas (each tribe having their own names and folk stories for the beans) were used by the Native American Indians as goods worthy of meaningful trade. • In the Middle Ages, a witch's powers

were nullified if one were to spit a mouthful of *Phaseolus vulgaris* at the witch's face. • Put a bean in your mouth then spit it out at an evil sorcerer. • Carry dried beans as an amulet against evil magic and negativity.

662
Philadelphus

| Mock Orange | Mock-Orange |

★**SYMBOLIC MEANINGS:**
Deceit; Counterfeit; Fraternal regard; Memory; Uncertainty;

663
Philodendron ☠

★**SYMBOLIC MEANINGS:**
Love of nature; Tree loving;

★**POTENTIAL POWERS:**
Appreciation of nature;

664
Phlox

★**SYMBOLIC MEANINGS:**
Our souls are united; Sweet Dreams; Unanimity; United hearts; United souls;

665
Phoenix dactylifera

| Date Palm |

★**POTENTIAL POWERS:**
Fertility; Potency;

★**FOLKLORE AND FACTS:**
It is believed by some that if a piece of the *Phoenix dactylifera* frond is carried it will increase fertility. • A *Phoenix dactylifera* frond placed near the door of the home will keep evil from all sources from entering into it.

666
Phragmites australis

| *Arundo phragmites* | **Common Reed** | *Phragmites altissimus* | *Phragmites ber-*

landieri | *Phragmites communis* | *Phragmites dioicus* | *Phragmites maximus* | *Phragmites vulgaris* | **Tambo** |

★**SYMBOLIC MEANINGS:**

Folly; Indiscretion; Music; Musical voice; Single blessedness;

▶ *Phragmites australis Single:*

Music;

▶ *Phragmites australis Split:*

Folly; Indiscretion;

▶ *Phragmites australis Bundle with panicles:*

Music;

667
Phytolacca ☠

| **Coakum** | **Cocan** | **Crowberry** | **Garget** | **Inkberry** | **Ombú** | **Pigeon Berry** | *Pircunia* | **Pocan** | **Poke** | **Pokeberry** | **Pokeberry Root** | **Pokebush** | **Pokeroot** | **Poke Root** | **Polk Root** | **Polk Salad** | **Polk Salat** | **Poke Sallet** | **Pokeweed** | **Polk Sallet** | **Scoke** | **Virginian Poke** |

★**POTENTIAL POWERS:**

Breaks hexes; Courage; Hex Breaking;

★**FOLKLORE AND FACTS:**

Carry a sprig of *Phytolacca* to give you courage.

668
Picea

| **Spruce** |

★**SYMBOLIC MEANINGS:**

Farewell; Hope in adversity;

★**FOLKLORE AND FACTS:**

One specimen of one species of *Picea*, known as "*Picea abies*" or Norway Spruce, has been found on Fulufjället Mountain in Sweden and is nicknamed "Old Tjikko", Old Tjikko is 9,550 years old and considered the oldest known living tree on Earth.

669
Pimenta dioica

| **Allspice** | **Clove Pepper** | **Jamaica Pepper** | **Jamaican Pepper** | **Kurundu** | **Myrtle Pepper** | **Newspice** | **Pepper** | *Pimenta* | **Pimento** |

★SYMBOLIC MEANINGS:

Compassion; Languishing; Love; Luck;

★POTENTIAL POWERS:

Accidents; Aggression; Anger; Carnal desires; Conflict; Healing; Love; Luck; Lust; Machinery; Money; Rock music; Strength; Struggle; War;

★FOLKLORE AND FACTS:

Pimenta dioica is often added to herbal mixtures to attract money or luck.

670
Pimpinella anisum

| Anise | Aniseed | Anneys | *Pimpinella* | Sweet Cumin | Yanisin |

★POTENTIAL POWERS:

Aphrodisiac; Business transactions; Business; Call in Good Spirits; Caution; Cleverness; Communication; Creativity; Expansion; Faith; Honor; Illumination; Initiation; Intelligence; Leadership; Learning; Memory; Politics; Power; Protection; Prudence; Public acclaim; Purification; Repel evil; Responsibility; Royalty; Science; Self-preservation; Sleep; Sound judgment; Success; Thievery; Wards off The Evil Eye; Wealth; Wisdom;

★FOLKLORE AND FACTS:

Place *Pimpinella anisum* seeds in the pillow to fend off unpleasant dreams. • Fresh *Pimpinella anisum* leaves will push away evil and are often used around a magic circle to keep evil spirits away from the magician within the circle.• Hang a spring of fresh or dried *Pimpinella anisum* over the bed to restore your lost youth.

▶ *Pimpinella anisum Seed:*
Restoration of youth;

671
Pinus

| Pine |

★SYMBOLIC MEANINGS:

Boldness; Courage; Daring; Endurance; Hope; Longevity; Loyalty; Pity; Time;

★POTENTIAL POWERS:

Accidents; Aggression; Anger; Carnal desires; Conflict; Exorcism; Fertility; Healing; Lust; Machinery; Money; Rock music; Protection; Spiritual energy; Strength; Struggle; War;

★FOLKLORE AND FACTS:

Cones from *Pinus* trees are carried to have vigor in old age. • Cones from *Pinus* trees are carried to increase fertility. • Because *Pinus* is an evergreen, in Japan it was once the custom to place a *Pinus* branch over the entrance door to the home to provide joy within the home. • Make a cross using *Pinus* needles and place it near the fireplace to prevent evil from entering the home via the chimney.

▶ *Pinus Cone:*
Conviviality;

672
Pinus nigra
| **European Black Pine** |

★ **SYMBOLIC MEANINGS:**
Pity;

673
Pinus rigida
| **Pitch Pine** |

★ **SYMBOLIC MEANINGS:**
Faith; Philosophy; Time; Time and faith;

674
Pinus sylvestris
| **Scotch Fir** | **Scots Pine** |

★ **SYMBOLIC MEANINGS:**
Elevation;

675
Piper

| *Anderssoniopiper* | *Arctottonia* | *Artanthe* | *Chavica* | *Discipiper* | *Lepianthes* | *Lindeniopiper* | *Macropiper* | *Ottonia* | **Pepper Plant** | **Pepper Vine** | *Pleiostachyopiper* | *Pleistachyopiper* | *Pothomorphe* | *Trianaeopiper* |

★ **POTENTIAL POWERS:**
Accidents; Aggression; Anger; Carnal desires; Conflict; Lust; Machinery; Rock music; Strength; Struggle; War;

676

Piper cubeba
| Cubeb | Java Pepper | Tailed Pepper | Vidanga | Vilenga |

★POTENTIAL POWERS:
Aphrodisiac; Exorcism; Love; Repel evil; Repulse demons; Ward off incubi;

677
Piper methysticum ☠
| Ava | Ava Pepper | Ava Root | *Awa* | Awa Root | Intoxicating Pepper | Kava | Kava-kava | Sakau | Yaqona |

★POTENTIAL POWERS:
Astral projection; Luck; Lust; Protection while traveling; Visions;

678
Piper nigrum
| Black Pepper | Pepper | Marica | Pepe | Peper | Pfeffer | Pipor | Pippali | Poivre |

★POTENTIAL POWERS:
Energy; Exorcism; Protection;

★FOLKLORE AND FACTS:
Carry a pouch with a bit of *Piper nigrum* within it to protect yourself against The Evil Eye. • Carry a pouch with a bit of *Piper nigrum* within it to protect yourself from having persistant envious thoughts. • Mix equal amounts of *Piper nigrum* with natural sea salt then scatter around your property to rid it of evil and protect it from returning.

679
Piscidia erythrina
| Fish Poison Tree | Fishfuddle | Florida Fishpoison Tree | Jamaica Dogwood | Jamaican Dogwood | *Piscidia* | *Piscidia piscipula* |

★SYMBOLIC MEANINGS:
Keeps secrets;

★POTENTIAL POWERS:
Protection; Wishes;

680

Pistacia lentiscus

| Mastic Tree |

★POTENTIAL POWERS:

Abundance; Advancement; Conscious will; Energy; Friendship; Growth; Healing; Joy; Leadership; Life; Light; Lust; Natural power; Psychic powers; Success;

681
Pistacia vera ☠

| Pista | Pistacchio | Pistacia | Pistachio | Pistáke | Pistákion |

★POTENTIAL POWERS:

Breaking love spells;

★FOLKLORE AND FACTS:

To bring a zombie out of it's trance and allow it to pass into death give it *Pistacia vera* nuts that have been dyed red.

682
Pisum sativum

| Pea | Field Pea | Garden Pea |

★SYMBOLIC MEANINGS:

An appointed meeting; Appointed meeting; Respect;

★POTENTIAL POWERS:

Love; Money;

★FOLKLORE AND FACTS:

Bring fortune and profit to business by shelling *Pisum sativum*. • One interesting love divination is for a unmarried woman to find a *Pisum sativum* pod with exactly nine seeds within it. When this is done, if she hangs the pod over a door, the first single man that walks beneath it will be her future husband.

683
Plantago

| Mother of Herbs | Plantain | *Psyllium* | Wegbrade |

★POTENTIAL POWERS:

Healing; Ingredient in the ancient Nine Herbs Charm; Protection; Strength; Wards off The Evil Eye;

684
Plantago major

| Broad-Leaved Plantain | Broadleaf Plantain | Cart Track Plant | Common Plantain | Cuckoo's Bread | Dooryard Plantain | Englishman's Foot | Greater Plantago | Greater Plantain | Healing Blade | Hen Plant | Lambs Foot | Leaf of Patrick | Patrick's Dock | Plantain | Ripple Grass | Roadweed | Roundleaf Plantain | Saint Patrick's Leaf | Slan-lus | Snakebite | Snakeweed | Soldier's Herb | St. Patrick's Leaf | The Leaf of Patrick | Watcher by the Wayside | Watcher-by-the-Wayside | Waybread | Wayside Plantain | Weybroed | White Man's Foot | White Man's Footprint |

★SYMBOLIC MEANINGS:
Never despair;

★FOLKLORE AND FACTS:
After North America was first colonized the Native American Indians began referring to *Plantago major* as "White Man's Footprint" and "Englishman's Foot" because to them, it seemed as if *Plantago major* would grow wherever white men went. This "phenomena" occurred because colonists would bring cereal crop seeds with them to The New World and *Plantago major* seeds were commonly mixed into the seed bags. So, where settlers would plant cereal crops...which would be near to where they lived...*Plantago major* would grow and ultimately naturalize. • Hang *Plantago major* in the car to keep evil from entering into it.

685
Platanus

| Plane| Plane Tree | Sycamore |

★SYMBOLIC MEANINGS:
Genius; Grace;

686
Platanus occidentalis

| American Plane | American Sycamore | Buttonwood Tree | Occidental Plane |

★SYMBOLIC MEANINGS:
Matrimony;

★FOLKLORE AND FACTS:
The New York Stock Exchange terms of formation are called *The Buttonwood Agreement* because it was signed under a *Platanus occidentalis* tree located at 68 Wall Street, New York City, NY back in 1792.

687
Platycodon grandiflorus

| Balloon Flower | Chinese Bellflower | Common Balloon Flower | Japanese Bellflower | Jie Geng | *Platycodon* | Turkish Balloon Flower |

★SYMBOLIC MEANINGS:
Honesty; Obedience; Unchanging love;

688
Plumeria ☠

| Araliya | Calachuchi | Champa | Egg Yolk Flower Tree | Frangipani | Gaai Daan Fa | Graveyard Flowers | Melia | Temple Tree |

★SYMBOLIC MEANINGS:
Perfection; New; Springtime;

★POTENTIAL POWERS:
Emotions; Fertility; Generation; Inspiration; Intuition; Love; Psychic ability; Sea; Subconscious mind; Tides; Travel by water; Worship;

★FOLKLORE AND FACTS:
Asians have thought that the *Plumeria* provides shelter for demons and ghosts. • Malaysian folklore makes mention of the scent of *Plumeria* in association with the Pontianak (a type of vampire) which is supposedly the "undead" women who have died in childbirth and are seeking revenge. • *Plumeria* flowers, in the Pacific Islands, are worn over an ear by the women: over the right ear if available, and over the left if not. • *Plumeria* flowers are frequently used to make exquisite leis. • *Plumeria* is often associated with cemeteries and graves.

689
Poaceae

| *Gramineae* | Grass | Grasses | True Grasses |

★SYMBOLIC MEANINGS:
Homosexual love; Submission; Utility; Usefulness;

★POTENTIAL POWERS:
Protection; Psychic powers;

★FOLKLORE AND FACTS:
A ball of green *Poaceae* hanging in your front window or knots of *Poaceae* tied around your home will drive out evil and protect your home from evil entering back into it. • Carry blades of *Poaceae* are helpful to your psychic powers. • To make a

wish using *Poaceae*, rub some on a stone to create a green mark upon it, make your wish upon that green spot, then either bury the stone or throw it into running water.

690
Podophyllum peltatum ☠

| American Mandrake | Devil's Apple | Duck's Foot | False Mandrake | Mayapple | May Apple | Hogapple | Hog Apple | Indian Apple | Mayflower | Racoon Berry | Umbrella Plant | Wild Lemon | Wild Mandrake |

★POTENTIAL POWERS:
Money;

691
Pogostemon cablin

| Ellai | Kablin | Patchai | Pachouli | Patchouli | Patchouly | Pucha-Pot | Xukloti |

★POTENTIAL POWERS:
Abundance; Accidents; Advancement; Aggression; Anger; Binding; Breaks hexes; Building; Carnal desires; Conflict; Conscious will; Death; Energy; Fertility; Friendship; Growth; Healing; History; Joy; Knowledge; Leadership; Life; Light; Limitations; Lust; Machinery; Money; Natural power; Obstacles; Rock music; Strength; Struggle; Success; Time; War;

★FOLKLORE AND FACTS:
A touch of *Pogostemon cablin* oil on money, handbags, and wallets is believed to increase prosperity.

692
Polemonium caeruleum

| Blue-flowered Greek Valerian | Greek Valerian | Jacob's Ladder |

★SYMBOLIC MEANINGS:
Come down; Rupture;

693
Polianthes tuberosa

| Azucena | Bone Flower | Bunga Sedap Malam | Gole Maryam | King of Fragrance | Nilasambangi | Nishi Ghanda | Mary Flower | Mixochitl | Raat ki Rani | Rajnigandha | Rojoni-Gondha | Sambangi | Sampangi | Scent of the Night |

Sugandaraja | Tuberose | Wan Xiang Yu | Ye Lai Xiang | Yue Xia Xiang |

★ **SYMBOLIC MEANINGS:**

Dangerous pleasures; Funerary; Pleasures that inevitably cause pain; Sweet voice; Voluptuousness;

694

Polygala

| Milkwort | Mountain Flax | Seneca Snakeroot | Seneca Snake Root | Seneka | Seneka Snakeroot | Snakeroot |

★ **SYMBOLIC MEANINGS:**

Hermitage;

★ **POTENTIAL POWERS:**

Money; Protection;

695

Polygonatum

| Dropberry | King Solomon's-Seal | Lady's Seal | Lady's Seals | Saint Mary's Seal | Sealroot | Sealwort | Solomon Seal | Solomon's Seal | St. Mary's Seal |

★ **SYMBOLIC MEANINGS:**

Be my support;

★ **POTENTIAL POWERS:**

Exorcism; Love; Protection;

★ **FOLKLORE AND FACTS:**

Polygonatum root placed in all four corners of your home to protect it.

696

Polygonatum multiflorum

| Common Solomon's Seal | David's-Harp | David's Harp | Ladder-to-Heaven | Solomon's-seal |

★ **SYMBOLIC MEANINGS:**

Be my support;

★ **POTENTIAL POWERS:**

Aphrodisiac; Consecration; Binding magical works; Binding sacred oaths;

★ **FOLKLORE AND FACTS:**

There is a legend that the scars on the roots of *Polygonatum multiflorum* were placed there by King Solomon to testify to it's powerful virtues. • The age of the *Polygona-*

tum multiflorum plant can be determined by the number of scars along the root, as each year produces a new stem that dies at the end of each summer to leave a new scar. • One can tell True Solomon's Seal (*Polygonatum multiflorum*) from False Solomon's Seal(*Maianthemum racemosum*) by the fact that *Polygonatum multiflorum* has bell shaped flowers dangling down along the stem. On the other hand, *Maianthemum racemosum* has flowering plumes at the end of the plant's stems.

697
Polygonum

| Armstrong | Ars-Smerte | Bistort | Buckwheat | Centinode | Cowgrass | Hogweed | Knotgrass | Knotweed | Mile-A-Minute | Nine Joints | Ninety Knot | Pigrush | Pigweed | Red Robin | Sparrow's Tongue | Swynel Grass | Tear-Thumb |

★SYMBOLIC MEANINGS:
Horror;

★POTENTIAL POWERS:
Binding; Binding spells; Divination; Fertility; Health; Protection; Psychic powers; Trances;

★FOLKLORE AND FACTS:
If you want to conceive, carry a *Polygonum* amulet. • If carried close to the breast *Polygonum* is considered to be a good charm to help those suffering from frenzy. • *Polygonum* is also thought to heal one of their desires. • Another power of *Polygonum* is that when a person touches it, *Polygonum* is believed to give that person the special powers offered by their astrological sun sign. • *Polygonum* is good for attracting money.

698
Polytrichum

| Bird Wheat | Haircap Moss | Hair Moss | Pigeon Wheat |

★SYMBOLIC MEANINGS:
Secret;

699
Populus

| Aspen | Cottonwood | Poplar |

★SYMBOLIC MEANINGS:
Eloquence; Flying; Lamentation; Money; Wealth;

★POTENTIAL POWERS:
Anti-theft; Astral projection; Money; Protection;

700
Populus alba

| Abeel | Abele | Albellus | Aubel | Silver Poplar | Silver-Leaf Poplar | White Poplar |

★SYMBOLIC MEANINGS:
Courage; Time;

701
Populus nigra

| Black Poplar |

★SYMBOLIC MEANINGS:
Affliction; Courage;

702
Populus tremula

| Aspen | Common Aspen | Eurasian Aspen | European Aspen | Poplar | Quaking Aspen |

★SYMBOLIC MEANINGS:
Advantage; Alteration; Awareness; Connectivity; Eloquence; Fear; Focus; Groan; Lamentation; Manipulation; Opportunity; Purity; Sighing; Transformation; Transition;

★POTENTIAL POWERS:
Anti-theft; Astral projection; Binding; Building; Death; Eloquence; Flying; History; Knowledge; Limitations; Obstacles; Time;

★FOLKLORE AND FACTS:
Carry a *Populus tremula* bud or leaf to attract money to you. • Place a *Populus tremula* bud or leaf to attract facilitate an attempt at astral projection.

▶ *Populus tremula Leaf:*
Lamentation; Sighing;

703
Portulaca grandiflora

| Garden Purslane | Golden Purslane | Hoa muoi gio | Moss Rose | Moss-Rose

| Moss-Rose Purslane | Pigweed | Purslane | Sun Rose | Ten O'Clock Flower | Time Flower | Time Fuul |

★SYMBOLIC MEANINGS:
Superior merit; Voluptuous love; Voluptuousness;

★POTENTIAL POWERS:
Happiness; Love; Luck; Sleep; Protection;

★FOLKLORE AND FACTS:
Prepare a sachet with *Portulaca grandiflora* within it and give it to a soldier to carry as a protection when in battle. • Grow *Portulaca grandiflora* to protect the home and bring happiness to it.

▶ *Portulaca grandiflora Bud:*
Confessions of love;

704
Potentilla

| Cinquefoil | Crampweed | *Duchesnea* | Five Fingers | Five Finger Blossom | Five Finger Grass | Goosegrass | Goose Tansy | Moor Grass | Silver Cinquefoil | Silverweed | Sunkfield | Synkefoyle |

★SYMBOLIC MEANINGS:
Beloved child; Beloved daughter; Care of the young; Maternal affection; Parental love; The dead;

★POTENTIAL POWERS:
Business; Expansion; Honor; Leadership; Money; Politics; Power; Promote an abundant harvest; Prophetic dreams; Protection; Public acclaim; Responsibility; Royalty; Sleep; Success; Wealth;

★FOLKLORE AND FACTS:
There is a legend that the five points of the *Potentilla* leaves represent love, money, health, power, and wisdom. So, if carried about, these powers will be granted unto you. • If you happen to find a *Potentilla* leaf with seven points, if you put it under your pillow you will dream of your future lover. • Worn or carried *Potentilla* will give you the ability to ask favors with a positive outcome. • Wear a *Potentilla* leaf to court for a positive outcome.

705
Potentilla erecta

| Biscuits | Bloodroot | Common Tormentil | Earthbank | Ewe Daisy | Five Fingers | Flesh and Blood | *Potentilla tormentilla* | Septfoil | Shepherd's Knot |

Thormantle | Tormentil | Tormentilla erecta |

★ POTENTIAL POWERS:

Love; Protection;

★ FOLKLORE AND FACTS:

To drive away evil hang *Potentilla erecta* in the home. • To attract love carry a sprig of *Potentilla erecta.*

706
Potentilla indica

| *Duchesnea indica* | False Strawberry | Gurbir | Indian Strawberry | Mock Strawberry |

★ SYMBOLIC MEANINGS:

Deceitful appearances;

707
Prenanthes

| Rattlesnake Root |

★ POTENTIAL POWERS:

Money; Protection;

708
Primula

| Primrose | Polyanthus |

★ SYMBOLIC MEANINGS:

Confidence; Contentment; Desperate; Early youth; Eternal love; Feminine energy; Frivolity; Happiness; I cannot be without you; I can't live without you; Inconstancy; Modest worth; Obsessive love; Pleasure; Pride of riches; Satisfaction; Silent love; Thoughtlessness; Woman; Young Love; Youth;

★ POTENTIAL POWERS:

Love; Protection;

◉ SPECIFIC COLOR MEANING > Crimson:

Confidence; Heart's mystery; Pride of riches;

◉ SPECIFIC COLOR MEANING > Lilac:

Confidence;

◉ SPECIFIC COLOR MEANING > Red:

Merit; Unsupported merit; Unsolicited recognition;

⊙ SPECIFIC COLOR MEANING > Rose:
Neglected genius;

709
Primula auricula

| Auricula | Bear's Ear | Mountain Cowslip | *Primula balbisii* | *Primula ciliata* |

★ **SYMBOLIC MEANINGS:**
Painting;

⊙ SPECIFIC COLOR MEANING > Scarlet:
Avarice;

710
Primula sinensis

| *Auganthus praenitens* | Chinese Primrose | *Oscaria chinensis* | *Primula mandarina* | *Primula praenitens* | *Primula semperflorens* | *Primula sertulosa* | *Primulidium sinese* | Zang Bao Chun |

★ **SYMBOLIC MEANINGS:**
Lasting love;

711
Primula veris

| Artetyke | Arthritica | Buckles | Cowslip | Crewel | Cuslyppe | Cuy | Cuy Lippe | Drelip | Fairy Cup | Frauenschlussel | Herb Peter | Key of Heaven | Keyflower | Key Flower | Lady's Key | Lady's Keys | Lippe | Our Lady's Keys | Paigle | Palsywort | Paralysio | Password | Peggle | Petty Mulleins | Plumrocks | *Primula officinalis* |

★ **SYMBOLIC MEANINGS:**
Birth; Consummation; Death; Women;

★ **POTENTIAL POWERS:**
Healing; Love spells; Find treasure; Youth;

★ **FOLKLORE AND FACTS:**
Fairies love and protect *Primula veris*. • *Primula veris* flowers are considered fairy flowers in Ireland and Wales. • It is thought to be that touching a fairy rock with a *Primula veris* nosegay will open an invisible door into fairyland. However, if there are not the proper number of flowers in the nosegay there will be certain doom. The problem is that no one knows for sure what the proper number of flowers actually is! • It is also believed that *Primula veris* help children find hidden treasures ... par-

ticularly fairy gold. • If you do not want visitors put a sprig of *Primula veris* under or on the front porch. • Wear or carry *Primula veris* to preserve or restore your youth.

712
Primula vulgaris

| Butter Rose | Common Primrose | English Cowslip | English Primrose | Password | Primrose | Primerose | *Primula acaulis* |

★ **SYMBOLIC MEANINGS:**
Contentment; Eternal love; Frivolity; Happiness; Modest worth; Pleasure; Satisfaction; Thoughtlessness; Wantonness;

★ **POTENTIAL POWERS:**
Finding treasures; Healing; Love; Protection;

★ **FOLKLORE AND FACTS:**
Grow red and blue *Primula vulgaris* in the garden to attract fairies to it and to protect it from all adversities. • Carry a *Primula vulgaris* flower to attract love. • Carry a *Primula vulgaris* flower to cure madness.

713
Prosopis

| Mesquite |

★ **POTENTIAL POWERS:**
Healing;

714
Protea cynaroides

| Giant Protea | Honeypot | King Protea | King Sugar Bush |

★ **SYMBOLIC MEANINGS:**
Courage;

★ **FOLKLORE AND FACTS:**
Protea cynaroides is one of the oldest flowers on Earth.

715
Prunus americana

| American Plum | Common Wild Plum | Marshall's Large Yellow Sweet Plum | Wild Plum |

★**SYMBOLIC MEANINGS:**

Independence; Independent;

★**POTENTIAL POWERS:**

Healing;

★**FOLKLORE AND FACTS:**

The Native American Dakota Indians have used *Prunus americana* tree sprouts to create prayer sticks.

▸ *Prunus americana Blossom:*

Beauty; Longevity;

716

Prunus armeniaca ☠

| **Abrecock** | **Abricot** | **Abrecoc** | **Albaricoque** | **Alperce** | **Apricot Tree** | **Armenian plum** | *Armeniaca vulgaris* | **Damasco** | **Umublinkosi** | **Xing Ren** | **Zard-alu** |

★**SYMBOLIC MEANINGS:**

Timid love;

★**POTENTIAL POWERS:**

Aphrodisiac; Love;

★**FOLKLORE AND FACTS:**

It is supposedly lucky for *Prunus armeniaca* to appear in a dream. • *Prunus armeniaca* has been cultivated in Armenia since prehistoric times indicated by seeds found at an Eneolithic-era (Eneolithic being the transitional period between the Neolithic period and the Bronze Age) excavation site at Garni, Armenia. • However, the Vavilov Center of Origin indicates that *Prunus armeniaca* was domesticated in the Chinese region; whereas others believe that *Prunus armeniaca* was first cultivated in India around 3000 BC. • Carry a *Prunus armeniaca* pit to attract love.

▸ *Prunus armeniaca Blossom:*

Distrust; Doubt; Timid Love;

717

Prunus avium ☠

| **Bird Cherry** | **Cherry** | **Gean** | **Mazzard** | **Sweet Cherry** | **Wild Cherry** |

★**SYMBOLIC MEANINGS:**

A good education; Education; Faith; Good education; Intelligence; Love;

★**POTENTIAL POWERS:**

Attraction; Beauty; Divination; Friendship; Gifts; Harmony; Joy; Love; Pleasure;

Sensuality; The Arts;

★FOLKLORE AND FACTS:

To find love tie one strand of your hair to a *Prunus avium* tree.

▶ *Prunus avium Blossom:*

A good education; Ascetic beauty; Education; Feminine beauty; Gentle; Good education; Honor of graceful resignation; Insincerity; Kind; Peace; Spiritual beauty; Transience of life; Transience melancholy;

718
Prunus cerasifera

| Cherry Plum | Myrobalan Plum | *Prunus divaricata* |

★SYMBOLIC MEANINGS:

Privation;

719
Prunus domestica

| Plum Tree | *Prunus x domestica* | Zwetschge |

★SYMBOLIC MEANINGS:

Fidelity; Beauty; Genius; Keep promises; Keep your promises; Longevity; Promise;

★POTENTIAL POWERS:

Love; Protection;

★FOLKLORE AND FACTS:

Hang a *Prunus domestica* branch over the home's doors and windows to protect it from evil entering into it.

720
Prunus dulcis

| Almond Tree | *Amygdalus communis* | *Prunus amygdalus* |

★SYMBOLIC MEANINGS:

Fruitfulness; Giddiness; Heedlessness; Hope; Indiscretion; Promise; Prosperity; Stupidity; Thoughtlessness; Union; Virginity; Wisdom;

★POTENTIAL POWERS:

Attitude; Ambition; Clear thinking; Harmony; Higher understanding; Logic; Manifestation in material form; Money; Overcoming alcohol dependency; Prosperity; Spiritual concepts; Success in business ventures; Thought processes; Wisdom;

★FOLKLORE AND FACTS:

It is believed by some that *Prunus dulcis* nuts carried about in a pocket could lead you to treasures. • The nuts on a wild *Prunus dulcis* tree can be bitter and are not ever to be eaten as they are poisonous. Domesticated *Prunus dulcis* trees are not toxic. • It is believed that one can guarantee a successful business venture by climbing a *Prunus dulcis* tree. • Magic wands made of *Prunus dulcis* wood are highly valued.

▶ *Prunes dulcis Blossom:*
Hope; Watchfulness;

721
Prunus japonica

| *Cerasus japonica* | **Flowering Almond** | **Korean Cherry** | **Oriental Bush Cherry** |

★**SYMBOLIC MEANINGS:**
Hope;

722
Prunus laurocerasus

| **Almond Laurel** | **Cherry Laurel** | **Common Laurel** | **English Laurel** | *Prunus* |

★**SYMBOLIC MEANINGS:**
Perfidy;

▶ *Prunes laurocerasus Flower:*
Perfidy;

723
Prunus padus

| **Asian Bird Cherry** | **Bird Cherry** | *Cerasus padus* | **European Bird Cherry** | **Hackberry** | *Prunus racemosa* |

★**SYMBOLIC MEANINGS:**
Perfidy;

★**POTENTIAL POWERS:**
Ward off plague; Witchcraft;

★**FOLKLORE AND FACTS:**
During Medevial times, *Prunus padus* bark was placed at the door to ward off plague. • In some parts of northern Scotland *Prunus padus* wood is particularly avoided as being considered a wood from a "witches tree".

724
Prunus persica

| Peach Tree (velvety skinned fruit) | Nectarine Tree (smooth skinned fruit) |

★SYMBOLIC MEANINGS:
Bridal Hope; Generosity; Gentleness; Happiness; Honors; Peace; Riches; Young brides; Your qualities and charms are unequaled;

★POTENTIAL POWERS:
Exorcism; Fertility; Longevity; Love; Repels spirits; Wishes;

★FOLKLORE AND FACTS:
In China *Prunus persica* branches are used to drive off evil spirits. • Chinese children once wore a *Prunus persica* pit as a pendent to keep demons away from them. • It is believed that to carry a small piece of *Prunus persica* wood will lengthen your life and might even make you immortal. • In Japan *Prunus persica* branches have been used as divining rods.

▶ *Prunus persica Blossom:*
Captive; I am yours; I am your captive; Longevity; Long life; My heart is yours; Unequaled qualities;

725
Prunus rainier

| Rainier Cherry | White Cherry |

★SYMBOLIC MEANINGS:
Deception; Good education;

726
Prunus spinosa

| Blackthorn | Mother of The Wood | Sloe | Wishing Thorn |

★SYMBOLIC MEANINGS:
Austerity; Blessing to come after a challenge; Challenges ahead; Constraint; Difficulty; Inevitability; Preparation; Strife;

★POTENTIAL POWERS:
Banish negative energies and entities; Exorcism; Protection;

★FOLKLORE AND FACTS:
Hang *Prunus spinosa* over doorways to ward off evil, calamity, negative vibrations, and banish demons from the home. • A fork branch of *Prunus spinosa* will make a useful divining rod. • *Prunus spinosa* wood will make a good magical wand.

727
Pteridium aquilinum ☠

| Bracken | Bracken Fern | Common Bracken | Fernbrake | Fern | Huckleberry's Blanket |

★POTENTIAL POWERS:
Fertility; Healing; Prophetic dreams; Protection; Rain magic;

★FOLKLORE AND FACTS:
It was once believed that a traveler would become disoriented, to the point of losing his direction, if he were to step upon Pteridium aquilinum. • To make it rain, burn some Pteridium aquilinum. • Place a frond of Pteridium aquilinum under the pillow to dream of the solution to a perplexing problem. • Add *Pteridium aquilinum* fronds to flower arrangements to increase protection.

▶ *Pteridium aquilinum Seed:*
Provides magical qualities; Invisibility;

728
Pteridophyta

| Devil Brushes | Ferns |

★POTENTIAL POWERS:
Health; Luck; Magical powers; Protection; Riches;

★FOLKLORE AND FACTS:
In England it was once believed that hanging dried *Pteridophyta* in the house would protect everyone who dwelled there from thunder and lightning. • In England it was also once believed that cutting or burning *Pteridophyta* would bring on rain. • It was believed that the *Pteridophyta* seed would provide magic powers, such as invisibility, if carried in a pocket. • It was once believed that walking upon *Pteridophyta* would cause the traveler to become so confused that he would lose his way.

729
Pterocarpus santalinus

| Chandan | Ciwappuccantanam | Raktachandana | *Rakta chandana* | Red Sanders | Red Sandalwood | Tzu-t'an Wood Tree | Zitan Wood Tree |

★POTENTIAL POWERS:
Accidents; Aggression; Anger; Attraction; Beauty; Carnal desires; Conflict; Friendship Gifts; Harmony; Joy; Love; Lust; Machinery; Pleasures; Rock music; The Arts; Sensuality; Strength; Struggle; War;

730
Pulmonaria

| Bethlehem Sage | Jerusalem Cowslip | Joseph and Mary | Lungenkraut | Lungwort | Medunitza | Miodunka | Soldiers and Sailors | Spotted Dog |

★SYMBOLIC MEANINGS:
Thou art my life; You are my life;

731
Pulsatilla

| *Anemone pulsatilla* | Easter Flower | Meadow Anemone | Pasque Flower | Pasqueflower | Passe Flower | Prairie Crocus | Shamefaced Maiden | Wind Flower |

★SYMBOLIC MEANINGS:
I have no claims; Unpretentious; You have no claims;

★POTENTIAL POWERS:
Healing; Health; Protection;

★FOLKLORE AND FACTS:
At one time, *Pulsatilla* sepals were used to color eggs for use in various spring festivals, as they will create an impermanent green stain. Since these spring events took place near Easter, the custom of coloring eggs was adopted by Christians celebrating Easter. • Growing red *Pulsatilla* flowers in the home garden with protect both the garden and the home. • It is believed that in the Spring if you wrap the first *Pulsatilla* flowers that are seen in a red cloth, then wear or carry it with you, it will prevent disease.

732
Pulsatilla montana

| Mountain Pasque |

★SYMBOLIC MEANINGS:
Endurance;

733
Punica granatum

| Anaar | Apple of Granada | Carthage Apple | Daalim | Garnet Apple | Granatapfel | Grenadier | Malicorio | Malum Granatum | Malum Punicum | Mela-

grana | Melograno | Pomegranate | Pomme-grenade | Pound Garnet | *Punica malus* **|**

★**SYMBOLIC MEANINGS:**

Abundance; A first housewarming gift; Compassion; Conceit; Conceited; Elegance; Foolishness; Foppery; Fullness; Good luck; Good things; Marriage; Mysteriousness; Paradise; Prosperity; Resurrection; Righteousness; Suffering; Summer; Sweetness of the Heavenly Kingdom;

★**POTENTIAL POWERS:**

Aphrodisiac; Creative power; Divination; Fertility; Intellectual ability; Immortality; Love; Luck; Passion; Sensuous love; Wealth; Wishes;

★**FOLKLORE AND FACTS:**

Carry a piece of *Punica granatum* husk to increase fertility. • Use a forked branch of *Punica granatum* as a divining rod to find hidden wealth. • A fun divination for a girl to try to find how many children she might have is to throw a *Punica granatum* fruit onto the ground hard enough to break it open. However many seeds fall out of the fruit are the number of children she will someday have. • Hang a *Punica granatum* branch over a doorway to fend off evil.

▶ *Punica granatum Blossom:*

Binding; Divination; Elegance; Fertility; Incarceration; Mature elegance; Unreciprocated love magic; Wealth;

▶ *Punica granatum Seeds:*

Love;

734

Pyrus

| Pear Tree |

★**SYMBOLIC MEANINGS:**

Affection; Health; Hope;

★**POTENTIAL POWERS:**

Love; Lust;

★**FOLKLORE AND FACTS:**

Pyrus wood is desirable for constructing a wand.

▶ *Pyrus Blossom:*

Comfort; Long life;

love

735
Quassia amara
| **Bitter Ash** | *Quassia* |
★**POTENTIAL POWERS:**
Love;

736
Quercus
| **Evergreen Oak** | *Lepidobalanua* | *Leucobalanus* | **Live Oak** | **Oak Tree** |

★**SYMBOLIC MEANINGS:**
Endurance; Hospitality; Liberty; Noble presence; Personal Finances; Regal Power; Wealth;

★**POTENTIAL POWERS:**
Abundance; Advancement; Business; Conscious will; Energy; Expansion; Friendship; Growth; Healing; Health; Honor; Joy; Leadership; Life; Light; Luck; Money; Natural power; Politics; Potency; Power; Protection; Public acclaim; Responsibility; Royalty; Success; Success; Wealth;

★**FOLKLORE AND FACTS:**
Quercus has been revered, even worshipped, since prehistoric times. • The Druids would only perform rituals under a *Quercus* tree. • A powerful protector against evil is a cross of *Quercus* wood made from equal lengths that is tied together in the center with red thread and hung in the house. • Carry a small piece of *Quercus* wood as protection from harm and as a good luck charm. • If you happen to catch a falling autumn *Quercus* leaf you will not have a cold for all of winter. • Carry a *Quercus* acorn for protection against aches and pains and illness. • Carry a *Quercus* acorn to promote youthfulness, and for longevity and even immortality. It will also increase fertility and improve sexual powers.

▶ *Quercus Leaves:*
Bravery; Strength; Welcome;

▶ *Quercus Sprig:*
Hospitality;

▶ *Quercus Nut (Acorn):*
Fruition of long hard labor; Good luck; Immortality; Life; Patience;

737
Quercus alba

| Duir | Jove's Nuts | Juglans | White Oak |

★**SYMBOLIC MEANINGS:**
Independence;

★**POTENTIAL POWERS:**
Fertility; Healing; Health; Luck; Money; Potency; Protection;

★**FOLKLORE AND FACTS:**
Quercus alba has been revered, even worshipped, since prehistoric times. • The Druids would only perform rituals under a *Quercus alba* tree. • A powerful protector against evil is a cross of *Quercus alba* wood made from equal lengths that is tied together in the center with red thread and hung in the house. • Carry a small piece of *Quercus alba* wood as protection from harm and as a good luck charm. • If you happen to catch a falling autumn *Quercus alba* leaf you will not have a cold for all of winter. • Carry an *Quercus alba* acorn for protection against aches and pains and illness. • Carry an *Quercus alba* acorn to promote youthfulness, and for longevity and even immortality. It will also increase fertility and improve sexual powers.

▶ *Quercus alba Leaves:*
Bravery; Strength; Welcome;

▶ *Quercus alba Sprig:*
Hospitality;

▶ *Quercus alba Nut (Acorn):*
Fruition of long hard labor; Good luck; Immortality; Life; Patience;

B

graces

738
Ranunculus acris ☠

| Meadow Buttercup | *Ranunculus acer* | *Ranunculus stevenii* | Tall Buttercup |
Tall Field Buttercup |

★SYMBOLIC MEANINGS:
Ambition; Childhood reminiscence; Childishness; Ingratitude; Memories of childhood; Perfidy; Riches; Self-esteem; Social matters; Verbal communication; Wealth;

★FOLKLORE AND FACTS:
In Medieval times, manipulative beggars would deliberately rub the irritating *Ranunculus acris* sap on their skin to make open blistered sores to create sympathy in passerbys who might then give them money out of pity for the beggars painful appearing condition.

739
Ranunculus asiatucus ☠

| Garden Ranunculus | Persian Buttercup | Ranunculus |

★SYMBOLIC MEANINGS:
Ambition; Attractive; Beautiful; Childhood reminiscence; Childishness; Fascination; Ingratitude; Memories of childhood; Perfidy; Riches; Self-esteem; Social matters; You are radiant with charm; Riches; You are rich in attractions; Verbal communication; Wealth;

740
Ranunculus ficaria ☠

| Celandine | Chistotel | *Fiscaria grandiflora* | *Fiscaria verna* | Lesser Celandine | Pilewort | Scharbockskraut | Scurvyherb |

★SYMBOLIC MEANINGS:
Escape; Future joy; Happiness; Joys to come; Legal matters; Protection;

★POTENTIAL POWERS:
Escape; Happiness; Joy; Legal Matters; Protection;

741
Ranunculus sardous ☠

| Hairy Buttercup | *Ranunculus parvulus* | Sardane | Sardonia | Sardonion | Sardony |

★SYMBOLIC MEANINGS:
Invitation; Irony; Scorn; Scornful laughter; Death;

742
Ranunculus sceleratus ☠

| Celery-leaved Buttercup | Cursed Buttercup | Biting Crowfoot | Blisterwort |

★SYMBOLIC MEANINGS:
Brilliancy; Ingratitude;

743
Raphanus sativus

| Radish | Rapuns |

★POTENTIAL POWERS:
Lust; Protection;

★FOLKLORE AND FACTS:
Carry a *Raphanus sativus* to offer protection against The Evil Eye. • There was a time in Germany when *Raphanus sativus* was carried to seek out the location of sorcerers.

744
Rauvolfia tetraphylla ☠

| Be-Still | Be Still Tree | Devil-pepper | Devil Pepper | *Rauwolfia tetraphylla* |

★POTENTIAL POWERS:
Luck;

745
Reseda

| Bastard Rocket | Dyer's Rocket | Weld | Mignonette | Sweet Reseda |

★SYMBOLIC MEANINGS:
Mental beauty; Moral beauty; Moral and mental beauty; Worth; Worth and loveliness; You are better than handsome; Your qualities surpass your charms;

★POTENTIAL POWERS:
Health; Beautification;

746
Rhamnus cathartica

| Common Buckthorn | Buckthorn | Hart's Thorn | Purging Buckthorn |

★**POTENTIAL POWERS:**
Exorcism; Legal matters; Protection; Wishes;

★**FOLKLORE AND FACTS:**
To drive away all sorceries and enchantments from the home and occupants place branches of *Rhamnus cathartica* near the windows and doors. • Carry or wear *Rhamnus cathartica* to undertake legal matters, including being in court. • Carry or wear *Rhamnus cathartica* to create good luck.

747
Rhamnus purshiana

| **Bearberry** | **Bitter Bark** | **Cascara** | **Cascara Buckthorn** | **Cascara Sagrada** | **Chittam** | **Chitticum** | **Cittim Bark** | **Ecorce Sacree** | *Frangula purshiana* | *Rhamnus purshianus* | **Sacred Bark** | **Yellow Bark** |

★**POTENTIAL POWERS:**
Legal matters; Money; Protection;

★**FOLKLORE AND FACTS:**
To help win a court case, before going to court sprinkle bits of *Rhamnus purshiana* around the home. • Wear *Rhamnus purshiana* to fend off hexes and evil.

748
Rheum rhabarbarum

| Pie Plant | Rhubarb |

★**SYMBOLIC MEANINGS:**
Advice;

★**POTENTIAL POWERS:**
Fidelity; Health; Protection;

★**FOLKLORE AND FACTS:**
Wear a piece of *Rheum rhabarbarum* around the neck on a string as protection against stomach pain.

749
Rhododendron maximum

| American Rhododendron | Bay | Bayis | Bigleaf Laurel | Big Rhododendron | Deertongue Laurel | Great Laurel | Great Rhododendron | Late Rhododendron | Mountain Laurel | *Rhododendron* | Rose Bay | Summer Rhododendron |

★SYMBOLIC MEANINGS:
Agitation; Ambition; Ambitious; Beware; Danger;

★POTENTIAL POWERS:
Banishing; Learning who is against you; Power; Power to overcome enemies; Stirring up agitation;

750
Rhodymenia palmata

| Creathnach | Dillisk | Dilsk | Dulse | Red Dulse | Sea Lettuce Flakes |

★POTENTIAL POWERS:
Harmony; Lust;

751
Rhus ☠

| Sumach | Sumac |

★SYMBOLIC MEANINGS:
Intellectual greatness; Misery; Splendid; Splendor;

752
Ribes nigrum

| Blackcurrant | Black Currant | Flasa | Phalsa | *Ribes cyathiforme* | *Ribes olidum* | *Ribes nigrum chlorocarpum* | *Ribes nigrum sibiricum* |

★SYMBOLIC MEANINGS:
Thankfulness; Thy frown will kill me; You please me; Your frown will kill me; Your unhappiness will kill me; Your disapproval will kill me;

▶ *Ribes nigrum Branch:*
You please all;

753
Ribes rubrum

| Redcurrant | Red Currant |

★SYMBOLIC MEANINGS:

Thankfulness; Thy frown will kill me; You please me; Your frown will kill me; Your unhappiness will kill me; Your disapproval will kill me;

▶ *Ribes rubrum Branch:*
You please all;

754
Ribes uva-crispa

| Fea Berry | Fea-berry | Gooseberry | Grozet | Hairy Amber | Old Rough Red | Prickly Berry | Ribes | Stikkelsbaer |

★SYMBOLIC MEANINGS:
Anticipation; Regret;

755
Robinia

| Locust Rose | Acacia |

★SYMBOLIC MEANINGS:
Concealed Love; Elegance; Friendship; Platonic;

756
Roots

★POTENTIAL POWERS:
Divination; Power; Protection;

757
Rosa

| *Hulthemia* | *Hulthemia x Rosa* | Rhodon | Rose | Vareda | Vard | Wâr | Ward | Wrodon |

★SYMBOLIC MEANINGS:
Balance; Beauty; Carrier of secrets and understanding; Divination; Equilibrium; Healing; Hope and passion; Love; Luck; Magic; Messenger of love; Passion; Perfection; Protection; Psychic powers; Strength through silence; Ultimate beauty;

★POTENTIAL POWERS:
Beauty; Divination; Healing; Love; Peace; Protection; Psychic powers; Purification;

★FOLKLORE AND FACTS:
In 1840 there was a *Rosa* collection of over one thousand different cultivars, varieties

and species planted at a Victorian arboretum and non-denominational cemetary in England called Abney Park Cemetary, which operated from 1840 to around 1978 and is now a public park. • In Roman times a wild *Rosa* would be put on the door of a room where confidential matters were being discussed. Hence, the term *sub rosa* which meant "under the rose" meant, and still means, to keep a secret. • Plant *Rosa* in the garden to attract fairies to it. • Scatter *Rosa* petals around the home to alleviate stress and household problems that have surfaced and are upsetting.

⊙ **SPECIFIC COLOR MEANING > Black:**
Beauty; Death; Farewell; Hatred; Impending Death; Rebirth; Rejuvenation;

⊙ **SPECIFIC COLOR MEANING > Blue:**
Attaining the impossible; Mystery;

⊙ **SPECIFIC COLOR MEANING > Blush:**
If you love me you will discover it; If you love me you will find me out;

⊙ **SPECIFIC COLOR MEANING > Bridal:**
Bliss; Happiness; Happy Love;

⊙ **SPECIFIC COLOR MEANING > Burgundy:**
Implicitly; Unconscious beauty;

⊙ **SPECIFIC COLOR MEANING > Coral:**
Desire; Enthusiasm; Happiness; Passion;

⊙ **SPECIFIC COLOR MEANING > Dark crimson:**
Mourning;

⊙ **SPECIFIC COLOR MEANING > Dark Pink:**
Thank You;

⊙ **SPECIFIC COLOR MEANING > Deep Red:**
Bashful; Mourning;

⊙ **SPECIFIC COLOR MEANING > Dried white:**
Death before loss of innocence;

⊙ **SPECIFIC COLOR MEANING > Green:**
Masculine energy;

⊙ **SPECIFIC COLOR MEANING > Lavender:**
Enchantment; Love at first sight; Magic;

⊙ **SPECIFIC COLOR MEANING > Light Pink:**
Admiration;

⊙ **SPECIFIC COLOR MEANING > Orange:**
Desire; Enthusiasm; Fascination; Passion; Pride; Wonder;

⊙ **SPECIFIC COLOR MEANING > Pale:**
Friendship;

⊙ **SPECIFIC COLOR MEANING > Peach:**
Appreciation; Closing of the deal; Gratitude; Immortality; Let's Get Together; Modesty; Sincerity;

⊙ **SPECIFIC COLOR MEANING > Pink:**
Confidence; Desire; Elegance; Energy; Everlasting joy; Gentility; Grace; Grace and sweetness; Gratitude; Happiness; Indecision; Joy; Joy of life; Love; Passion; Perfect happiness; Perfection; Please believe Me; Romance; Romantic love; Secret love; Sweetness; Thankfulness; Thank you; Trust; You're So Lovely; Youth

⊙ **SPECIFIC COLOR MEANING > Red:**
Beauty; Congratulations; Courage; Desire; Healing; I Love You; Job Well Done; Love; Passion; Protection; Respect; Well done;

⊙ **SPECIFIC COLOR MEANING > Striped or Variegated:**
Warmth of heart; Immediate affection; Love at first sight;

⊙ **SPECIFIC COLOR MEANING > Unique color:**
Uniquely beautiful;

⊙ **SPECIFIC COLOR MEANING > Violet:**
Admiration; Deepest love; Enchantment; Love at first sight; Magic; Majestic; Opulent; Special;

⊙ **SPECIFIC COLOR MEANING > White:**
Charm; Eternal love; Exorcism; Heavenly; Humility; I am worthy of you; Innocence; I would be single; Purity; Reverence; Secrecy; Silence; Virtue; Wistfulness; Worthiness; You're Heavenly; Youthfulness;

⊙ **SPECIFIC COLOR MEANING > Yellow:**
Apology; Caring; Dying Gladness; Love; Friendship; Gladness; Infidelity; Jealousy; Joy; Love; Platonic Love; Remember Me; Welcome; Welcome back;

⊙ **SPECIFIC COLOR MEANING > Pink and White together:**
I Love You Still And I Always Will;

⊙ **SPECIFIC COLOR MEANING > Red and White together:**
Together; Unity;

⊙ **SPECIFIC COLOR MEANING > Full bloom single stem any color:**
I Love You; Simplicity;

⊙ **SPECIFIC COLOR MEANING > Yellow single and eleven Red:**
Love and Passion;

⊙ **SPECIFIC COLOR MEANING > Orange and Yellow together:**
Passionate Thoughts;

⊙ **SPECIFIC COLOR MEANING > Red and Yellow together:**
Congratulations; Excitement; Happiness; Joy;

▶ *Rosa Bud:: see> Rosa (Bud) / Rose Bud*

▶ *Rosa Bouquet in full-bloom:*
Gratitude;

▶ *Rosa Full-blown:*
You are beautiful

▶ *Rosa Garland:*
Beware of virtue; Reward of merit; Reward of virtue; Symbol of superior merit;

▶ *Rosa Crown:*
Beware of virtue; Reward of merit; Reward of virtue; Superior merit; Virtue;

▶ *Rosa Wreath:*
Beware of virtue; Reward of merit; Reward of virtue; Symbol of superior merit;

▶ *Rosa Leaf:*
I never trouble; You may hope;

▶ *Rosa One full-blown rose placed over two rosebuds:*
Secrecy;

▶ *Rosa Thornless:*
Affection; Early attachment;

▶ *Rosa Withered:*
Departed loveliness;

758
Rosa acicularis

| **Artic Rose** | **Bristly Rose** | **Prickly Rose** | **Prickly *Rosa baicalensis*** | ***Rosa carelica*** | ***Rosa gmelinii*** | ***Rosa nipponensis*** | **Wild Rose** |

★**SYMBOLIC MEANINGS:**
A poetical person;

★**FOLKLORE AND FACTS:**
It is believed that a fairy is supposedly able to render itself invisible by eating a *Rosa acicularis* hip then turning counterclockwise three times. To become visible again, the fairy would need to eat another *Rosa acicularis* hip then turn clockwise three times.

759
Rosa (Bud)

| **Rose Bud** |

★**SYMBOLIC MEANINGS:**
A heart innocent of love; Beauty; Confessed love; Confession of love; Innocence;

Virginity; Young girl; Youth;

⊙ **SPECIFIC COLOR MEANING > Pink:**
Pure; Pure and lovely; You are young and beautiful;

⊙ **SPECIFIC COLOR MEANING > White:**
A heart ignorant of love; Girlhood; The heart that knows not love; Too young to love; Too young to marry;

⊙ **SPECIFIC COLOR MEANING > Red:**
Romance;

760
Rosa canina

| **Dog Rose** | **Itburunu** | **Kusburnu** | **Stenros** | **Steinnype** |

★ **SYMBOLIC MEANINGS:**
Ferocity; Honesty; Pain and pleasure; Simplicity;

761
Rosa carolina

| **Carolina Rose** | **Low Rose** | **Pasture Rose** |

★ **SYMBOLIC MEANINGS:**
Love is dangerous;

762
Rosa centifolia

| **Cabbage Rose** | **Hundred-Leaved Rose** | **Hundred-Petaled Rose** | **Provence Rose** | **Rose de Mai** |

★ **SYMBOLIC MEANINGS:**
Ambassador of love; Dignity of mind; Gentleness; Graces; Love's ambassador; Pride;

763
Rosa chinensis

| **China Rose** | **Chinese Hibiscus** | **Chinese Rose** | **Daily Rose** | **Monthly Rose** | *Rosa indica vulgaris* | **Old Blush Rose** | **Rose Old Blush China Rose** |

★ **SYMBOLIC MEANINGS:**
Beauty always new; Beauty ever new; Grace; I want to smile like you; Relieve my

anxiety; That smile I would aspire to; Thy smile I aspire to;

★POTENTIAL POWERS:
Protection; Relief; Smiles;

764
Rosa foetida

| Austrian Copper | Austrian Rose | Capucine | Capucine Briar | Copper | Corn Poppy Rose | *Rosa cerea* | *Rosa eglanteria* | *Rosa harisonii* | *Rosa lutea* | *Rosa sulphurea* | Rose Comtesse | Rosier Eglantier | Vermilion Rose of Austria | The Yellow Rose of Texas |

★SYMBOLIC MEANINGS:
Decrease of love; Friendship; Infidelity; Jealousy; Joy; Loveliness; Platonic love; Thou art all that is lovely; Try to care; Unfaithfulness; Very lovely; You are all that is lovely;

765
Rosa gallica versicolor

| Fair Rosamond's Rose | Garnet Stripe Rose | Gemengte Rose | Monday Rose | Mundi Rose | Mundy Rose | *Rosa versicolor*| *Rosa praenestina versicolor* | *Rosa praenestina versicolor plena* | Rosemonde | Rosemondi | Rosemunde | Rose Mundi | Striped Rose of France |

★SYMBOLIC MEANINGS:
Variety; You are merry;

766
Rosa gymnocarpa

| Baldhip Rose | Dwarf Rose | Wood Rose |

★SYMBOLIC MEANINGS:
Luck;

767
Rosa majalis

| Cinnamon Rose | Double Cinnamon Rose | *Rosa cinnamomea* |

★SYMBOLIC MEANINGS:
Without pretension;

768
Rosa moschata

| Musk Rose |

★SYMBOLIC MEANINGS:
Capricious beauty;

▶ *Rosa moschata Cluster:*
Charming;

769
Rosa multiflora

| Baby Rose | Inermis Rose | Multiflora Rose | Rambler Rose |

★SYMBOLIC MEANINGS:
Grace; Ingratitude;

770
Rosa rubiginosa

| Eglantine Rose | Sweetbriar | Sweet Briar | Sweet-Briar |

★SYMBOLIC MEANINGS:
A Wound to heal; Healing a wound; Poetry; Simplicity; Spring; Sympathy; Wound to heal;

771
Rosa rugosa

| Rugosa Rose | Japanese Rose | Ramanas Rose | Japan Rose | Hamanashi | Hamanasu | Haedanghwa | Rugged Rose |

★SYMBOLIC MEANINGS:
Beauty is not your only attraction;

772
Rosa x damascena

| Damascus Rose | Damask | Damask Rose | *Rosa damascena* | *Rosa damascena trigintipetela* | *Rosa gallica trigintipetala* | *Rosa trigintipetala* | Rose of Castile |

★SYMBOLIC MEANINGS:

Bashful love; Brilliant complexion; Freshness; Inspiration for love; Refreshing love;

773
Rosmarinus officinalis

| Compass Weed | Dew of the Sea | Elf Leaf | Guardrobe | Herb of Remembrance | Incensier | Libanotis | Old Man | Polar Plant | Romarin | Romero | Rose of Mary | Rosemarie | Rosemary | Rosmarin | Rosmarine | Rosmarino | Ros Maris | Sea Dew |

★**SYMBOLIC MEANINGS:**

Affectionate remembrance; Attraction of love; Constancy; Death; Fidelity; Friendship; Love; Loyalty; Memory; Remembrance; Restore balance of domestic power; Vitality; Wedding herb;

★**POTENTIAL POWERS:**

Abundance; Advancement; Conscious will; Divination; Emotions; Energy; Exorcism; Fertility; Friendship; Generation; Growth; Healing; Inspiration; Intuition; Joy; Leadership; Life; Light; Love; Love charm; Lust; Mental clarity; Mental powers; Natural power; Protection; Protection from illness; Psychic ability; Purification; Repelling nightmares; Repelling witches; Sea; Sleep; Subconscious mind; Success; Tides; Travel by water; Youth;

★**FOLKLORE AND FACTS:**

To fragrance the house during the holidays, *Rosmarinus officinalis* was commonly spread upon the floor at Christmas time during the Middle Ages. • It is believed that anyone who smells the aroma of *Rosmarinus officinalis* on Christmas Eve will have happiness throughout the coming year. • Since ancient times, when the practice was started in Greece, *Rosmarinus officinalis* has been used in both funeral and marriage rituals. • Students in ancient Greece would tuck sprigs of *Rosmarinus officinalis* behind an ear or in their hair to enhance their memories during academic exams. • *Rosmarinus officinalis* has been liberally used in wedding flowers as the plant was thought to encourage the bridal couple to remember and stay true to their marriage vows. • It was believed that one would fall in love if touched on the finger by a sprig of *Rosmarinus officinalis*. • *Rosmarinus officinalis* was often included in specific magic spells. • A sprig of *Rosmarinus officinalis* under the pillow is supposed to be a remedy for nightmares. • Since back in the time of ancient Egypt *Rosmarinus officinalis* was part of funeral rituals, also being used in the embalming process. • In Medieval times it was thought that one must be righteous to grow *Rosmarinus officinalis* in their own garden. • In Australia, a sprig of *Rosmarinus officinalis* is worn on Anzac Day to remember the war dead of WWI. • *Rosmarinus officinalis* is supposedly grossly offensive to evil spirits. • In the Middle Ages a newlywed couple would plant a branch of *Rosmarinus officinalis*. If the branch did not thrive, it was a bad omen for the marriage and the family. • *Rosmarinus officinalis* is a common stuffing in the making of poppets used specifically to attract a lover. • *Rosmarinus officinalis* plant on each side of an entry door to a home is said to repel witches.

774
Rubia

| Madder |

★SYMBOLIC MEANINGS:
Calumny; Talkative;

775
Rubus

| *Batidaea* | Blackberry | Blessed Bramble | Bly | Bokbunja | Bramble | Bramble Allegheny Blackberry | Bramble-Kite | Brambleberry | Brameberry | Brameberry | Brummel | Bumble-Kite | Cloudberrry | *Comarobatia* | Common Blackberry | Dewberry | European Blackberry | European Raspberry | Goutberry | High Blackberry | Piao | Rasperry | Red Raspberry | Salmonberry | Scaldhead | Scaldhead | Thimbleberry | Wild Western Thimbleberries | Wineberry |

★SYMBOLIC MEANINGS:
Envy; Lowliness; Remorse;

★POTENTIAL POWERS:
Happiness; Healing; Love; Money; Prosperity; Protection; Visions;

★FOLKLORE AND FACTS:
Rubus wreaths mixed with *Sorbus* (Rowan) and *Hedera helix* (Ivy) can be used on a door front to keep away evil spirits. • In England it was considered bad luck to pick the *Rubus* fruit after October 11th. • *Rubus* was planted on graves to keep the dead from leaving their resting places as ghosts. • There was a time when after a death had occurred that *Rubus* branches were placed at all the windows and exterior doors to prevent the spirit of the dead individual from re-entering the home and taking up permanent resident there again in the form of a haunting.

776
Rubus idaeus

| European Raspberry | Framboise | Raspberry | Red Raspeberry |

★SYMBOLIC MEANINGS:
Scornful beauty; Temptation;

★POTENTIAL POWERS:

Happiness; Healing; Love; Money; Prosperity; Protection; Visions;

777
Rubus odoratus

| Flowering Raspberry | Purple-flowering Raspberry | Virginia Raspberry |

★POTENTIAL POWERS:
Happiness; Healing; Love; Money; Prosperity; Protection; Visions;

778
Rudbeckia hirta

| Black-Eyed Susan | Blackeyed Susan | Blackihead | Brown Betty | Brown-Eyed Susan | Coneflower | Gloriosa Daisy | Golden Jerusalem | Poorland Daisy | *Rudbeckia* | Yellow Daisy | Yellow Ox-eye Daisy |

★SYMBOLIC MEANINGS:
Justice; Pure-minded;

★POTENTIAL POWERS:
Healing;

779
Ruellia

| *Aphragmia* | *Arrhostoxylum* | *Brunoniella* | *Copioglossa* | *Cryphiacanthus* | *Dinteracanthus* | *Dipteracanthus* | *Endosiphon* | *Dipteracanthus spectabilis* | *Gymnacanthus* | *Leptosiphonium* | *Nothoruellia* | *Pararuellia* | *Pattersonia* | *Sclerocalyx* | *Stenoschista* | *Stephanophysum* | *Tacoanthus* | Wild Petunia |

★SYMBOLIC MEANINGS:
Glory; Immortality;

780
Rumex acetosa ☠

| Common Sorrel | Garden Sorrel | Juopmu | Kuzu Kulagı | Macris | Narrow-Leaved Dock | Rugstyne | *Rumex stenophyllus* | Shchavel | Sóska | Spinach Dock | Sorrel | Stevie | Szczaw | Wild Sorrel |

★SYMBOLIC MEANINGS:
Affection; Parental affection; Refreshes the spirit; Wit; Ill-timed wit;

★POTENTIAL POWERS:
Health; Healing;

781
Rumex crispus ☠

| Curled Dock | Curly Dock | Narrow Dock | Sour Dock | Yellow Dock |

★POTENTIAL POWERS:
Fertility; Healing; Money;

★FOLKLORE AND FACTS:
Supposedly, to help a woman conceive a child place a small amount of *Rumex crispus* seeds in a small cotton pouch and tie it to her left arm.

782
Rumex patientia

| Dock| Garden Patience| Herb Patience| Monk's Rhubarb |Patience Dock |

★SYMBOLIC MEANINGS:
Patience; Religious superstition; Shrewdness;

★POTENTIAL POWERS:
Fertility; Healing; Money;

783
Ruta graveolens ☠

| Bashoush | Common Rue | Garden Rue | German Rue | Herb-of-grace | Herb of Grace | Herb of Repentance | Herbygrass | Hreow | Mother Of The Herbs | Rewe | Rue | Ruta | Witches Bane |

★SYMBOLIC MEANINGS:
Regret;

★POTENTIAL POWERS:
Breaks hexes; Endurance; Exorcism; Healing; Health; Love; Mental clarity; Mental Patience; Powers; Protection; Purification; Repels cats; Repels witches; Virginity;

★FOLKLORE AND FACTS:
Catholic priests use to sprinkle holy water off the branch of *Ruta graveolens*. • A *Ruta graveolens* plant can live for hundreds of years. • There was once a time when Lithuanian brides would wear *Ruta graveolens* wreaths at their wedding. • In Medieval times, *Ruta graveolens* was hung in the windows to keep any evil entity from coming into the house. • Also, in Medieval times, *Ruta graveolens* was worn in a bunch at the waist to repel witches. • A *Ruta graveolens* leaf on the forehead is believed to relieve a headache. • Rub fresh *Ruta graveolens* leaves on the floor to revert any negative spells back to whoever cast them upon you. • It is believed that you can fend off werewolves by carrying a sprig of *Ruta graveolens*.

dignity

784
Saccharum

| Ko | Sugar Cane | Sugarcane |

★**POTENTIAL POWERS:**
Celebration; Love; Lust;

785
Sagina subulata

| Heath Pearlwort | *Sagina pilifera* | Scotch Moss |

★**POTENTIAL POWERS:**
Luck; Money; Protection;

786
Saintpaulia

| African Violet | *Saintpaulia ionantha* | *Saintpaulia kewensis* |

★**SYMBOLIC MEANINGS:**
Such worth is rare;

★**POTENTIAL POWERS:**
Spirituality; Protection;

★**FOLKLORE AND FACTS:**
Grow *Saintpaulia* in the home to promote spirituality.

787
Salix

| Osier | Pussy Willow | Rods of Life | Sallow | Willow |

★**SYMBOLIC MEANINGS:**
Receiving a blessing; Illness recovery; Motherhood; Spring;

★**FOLKLORE AND FACTS:**
In ancient Rome, women were initiated into the role of motherhood by being flogged with *Salix* branches in a ritual that wished fertility upon them. • *Salix* is often the plant of choice to create living scupltures that are shaped to form figures and garden features such as domes and seating. • In Christian churches in Northwestern

Europe *Salix* branches are often used as a substitute for palm on Palm Sunday ceremonies. • In China, *Salix* branches are often placed on gates and front doors to ward off evil spirts that wander about during the Qingming (Tomb Sweeping) Festival. • Taoist witches will often use a carving made of *Salix* wood to communicate with spirits of the dead by sending the image into the nether world where a spirit is to enter it, provide the information requested, and then given to relatives upon its return. • In old English folklore, a *Salix* tree can be malicious because it has the ability to uproot and move about stalking travellers.

788
Salix alba

| Osier | Pussy Willow | Saille | Salicyn Willow | Saugh Tree | Tree of Enchantment | White Willow | Witches' Aspirin | Withe | Withy |

★**POTENTIAL POWERS:**
Blessing; Bindings; Healing; Love; Love divination; Protection;

★**FOLKLORE AND FACTS:**
Salix alba leaves attract love. • *Salix alba* is often used in wands that are particularly used for Moon Magic. • *Salix alba* in the home will offer protection against evil. • If you absolutely *need* to "knock on wood", do it on a *Salix alba* tree.

789
Salix babylonica

| Babylon Willow | Napoleon Willow | Peking Willow | *Salix matsundana* | Weeping Willow |

★**SYMBOLIC MEANINGS:**
Forsaken; Melancholy; Metaphysics; Mourning; Sadness; Tenacity;

★**POTENTIAL POWERS:**
Divination; Healing;

790
Salix repens

| Creeping Willow |

★**SYMBOLIC MEANINGS:**
Forsaken love; Love forsaken;

791

Salvia apiana

| Bee Sage | Sacred Sage | Sage | White Sage |

★POTENTIAL POWERS:

Artistic ability; Banishes evil; Banishes negativity; Business; Cleanses the aura; Consecration; Expansion; Female fidelity; Great Respect; Healing; Honor; Immortality; Leadership; Longevity; Memory; Politics; Power; Prosperity; Protection; Public acclaim; Purification; Responsibility; Royalty; Success; Wealth; Wisdom; Wishes;

★FOLKLORE AND FACTS:

For healing and/or prosperity, *Salvia apiana* is burned as an incense, worn as an amulet, and/or used as an ingredient in a sachet. • Burning *Salvia apiana* will purify an area by removing negativity, spiritual impurities, and banishing evil, thus consecrating the area and providing protection.

792
Salvia cacaliifolia

| Blue Salvia | Blue Vine Sage | *Salvia cacaliaefolia* |

★SYMBOLIC MEANINGS:

I think of you;

793
Salvia officinalis

| Broadleaf Sage | Common Sage | Culinary Sage | Dalmatian Sage | Garden Sage | Kitchen Sage | Purple Sage | Red Sage |Sage | Sage The Savior | Sawge |

★SYMBOLIC MEANINGS:

Agelessness; Alleviate grief; Domestic virtue; Esteem; Good health; Immortality; Long life; Wisdom;

★POTENTIAL POWERS:

Business; Cleanses the aura; Expansion; Female fidelity; Honor; Immortality; Leadership; Longevity; Politics; Power; Protection; Public acclaim; Purification; Responsibility; Royalty; Snakebites; Success; Wealth; Wisdom; Wishes;

★FOLKLORE AND FACTS:

The ancient Romans believed that *Salvia officinalis* was powerful enough to create immortal life. • It was once believed that *Salvia officinalis* would thrive only in gardens of homes controlled by a woman. • *Salvia officinalis* was often planted in cemeteries because it was believed that it would easily thrive on neglect and therefore live and grow forever. • Since ancient times, *Salvia officinalis* has been used to ward off evil and more. It was an major ingredient in a Medieval medicinal/magical concoction called *Four Thieves Vinegar* which was supposedly used to ward off the plague. • If you write a wish on a *Salvia officinalis* leaf, put it under your pillow and then sleep upon it for three consecutive days, and you dream of it coming true, it will come true. If you do not dream of that wish coming true you must take that leaf and bury it immediately so that it brings you no harm.

794
Salvia sclarea

| Clary | Clary Sage |

★ **POTENTIAL POWERS:**

Emotions; Fertility; Generation; Inspiration; Intuition; Psychic ability; Subconscious mind; Travel by water; Sea; Tides;

795
Sambucus

| Elder | Elderberry |

★ **SYMBOLIC MEANINGS:**

Compassion; Creativity; Cycles; Death; Endings; Kindness; Rebirth; Regeneration; Renewal; Transformation; Zeal; Zealousness;

★ **POTENTIAL POWERS:**

Exorcism; Healing; Protection; Prosperity; Sleep;

▶ *Sambucus Flower:*

Compassion; Humility; Kindness; Zeal;

796
Sambucus nigra ☠

| Absolute | Alhuren | Battree | Black Elder | Bore Tree | Bour Tree | Boure Tree | Common Elder | Elder | Elderberry | Elder Bush | Elder Flower | Eldrum | Ellhorn | European Black Elderberry | European Elder | European Elderberry | Frau Holle | Hildemoer | Hollunder | Hylan Tree | Hylder | Lady Ellhorn | Old Gal | Old Lady | Pipe Tree | Rob Elder | *Sambucus canadensis* | Sureau | Sweet Elder | Tree of Doom | Yakori Bengeskro |

★ **POTENTIAL POWERS:**

Death; Exorcism; Good luck; Healing; Magic; Prosperity; Protection; Protection against evil spirits; Protection against witches; Kill serpents; Send away thieves; Sleep;

★**FOLKLORE AND FACTS:**
Sambucus nigra is associated with witches. • When the dead were once buried, branches of *Sambucus nigra* were planted with the body to protect them from evil spirits. • Stone Age arrowheads were shaped to look like elder leaves. • A cross made of *Sambucus nigra* wood then attached to the stables is supposed to keep evil away from the animals. • Cradles were not to be made of *Sambucus nigra* wood because the baby would either fall out of it, not be able to sleep, or be pinched by fairies. • The English believe that burning logs of *Sambucus nigra* will bring the devil into the house. • Before pruning an *Sambucus nigra* Tree, one must ask the tree's permission then spit three times before making the first cut. • *Sambucus nigra* leaves gathered on the last day of April can be attached to the doors and windows to keep witches from entering the home. • *Sambucus nigra* Trees or *Sambucus nigra* hedges grown near a home's entrance will keep evil from entering. • An amulet of a piece of *Sambucus nigra* wood on which the sun never has shone is tied between two knots then worn around the neck as protection against evil.

797
Sanguinaria ☠

| Bloodroot | Bloodwort | Coon Root | Indian Paint | Indian Plant | Indian Red Paint | Paucon | Pauson | Pauson | Red Paint Root | Red Puccoon Root | Red Pucoon | Red Root | *Sanguinaria canadensis* | Snakebite | Sweet Slumber | Tetterwort |

★**POTENTIAL POWERS:**
Love; Protection; Purification;

★**FOLKLORE AND FACTS:**
Sanguinaria worn in an amulet will attract love, repel evil spells and all types of negativity. • Place *Sanguinaria* near windows and doors to protect the home.

798
Sanguisorba

| Burnet |

★**SYMBOLIC MEANINGS:**
A merry heart;

799
Sansevieria

| Bow String Hemp | Devil's Tongue | Jinn's Tongue | Mother-In-Law's Tongue

| Sanseveria | Snake's Lounge | Snake Plant |

★**SYMBOLIC MEANINGS:**

Slander;

★**POTENTIAL POWERS:**

Reducing coarseness in children; Counters vibrations that drain down;

800

Santalum album

| Indian Sandalwood Tree | Sandal | Sandalwood | Santal | *Santalum* | White Sandalwood | White Saunders | Yellow Sandalwood |

★**POTENTIAL POWERS:**

Against dog bites; Against ghosts; Against snake bites; Against sorcery; Business; Caution; Cleverness; Communication; Creativity; Emotions; Exorcism; Faith; Fertility; Generation; Healing; Illumination; Initiation; Inspiration; Intelligence; Intuition; Learning; Love; Memory; Protection; Protection Against drunkenness; Protection; Prudence; Psychic ability; Purification; Science; Self-preservation; Spirituality; Sound judgment; Subconscious mind; Thievery; Transactions; Travel by water; Sea; Tides; Wisdom; Wishes;

★**FOLKLORE AND FACTS:**

Beads made of *Santalum album* are protective and facilitate spiritual awareness whenever they are worn.

801

Santolina

★**SYMBOLIC MEANINGS:**

Virtue;

802

Sassafras ☠

| Ague Tree | Cinnamon Wood | *Pseudosassafras* | Sassafras Tree | Saxifrax |

★**POTENTIAL POWERS:**

Healing; Health; Money;

★**FOLKLORE AND FACTS:**

Carry a piece of *Sassafras* in the purse or wallet to attract money to it.

803

Satureja

| Garden Savory | Herbe de St. Julien | Savory |

★ SYMBOLIC MEANINGS:
Interest;

★ POTENTIAL POWERS:
Arts; Attraction; Beauty; Friendship; Gifts; Harmony; Joy; Love charm; Love; Mental clarity; Mental powers; Pleasure; Sensuality; Strength;

★ FOLKLORE AND FACTS:
Carry or wear a sprig of *Satureja* to strengthen your mind.

804
Saxifraga hypnoides

| Dovetail Moss | Mossy Saxifrages |

★ SYMBOLIC MEANINGS:
Affection;

805
Saxifraga x urbium

| London Pride | London Pride Saxifrages | Look Up And Kiss Me | Prattling Parnell | Saint Patrick's Cabbage | True London Pride | Whimsey |

★ SYMBOLIC MEANINGS:
Fortitude; Frivolity; Refusal to submit; Resistance;

★ FOLKLORE AND FACTS:
Saxifraga x urbium grew quickly at the bombed locations following the London Blitz of WWII, to become the symbol of Londoners to represent resistance, fortitude, and the refusal to submit to being bombed into submission by an enemy.

806
Scabiosa atropurpurea

| Egyptian Rose | Pincushion Flower | Mourning Bride | Mournful Widow | *Scabiosa* | Sweet Scabious |

★ SYMBOLIC MEANINGS:
I have lost all; Unfortunate attachment; Unfortunate love; Widowhood;

807

Schinus

| Brazilian Pepper Tree | California Pepper Tree | Christmasberry | *Duvaua* | Jesuit's Balsam | Pepper Tree | Peruvian Mastic Tree | Peruvian Pepper Tree | Piru |

★SYMBOLIC MEANINGS:
Marriage; Religious enthusiasm;

★POTENTIAL POWERS:
Healing; Protection; Purification;

★FOLKLORE AND FACTS:
Mexican traditional healers have used *Schinus* branches in healing by brushing the branch over the sick individual with the expectation that the branch will absorb the sickness before burning the branch to destroy the disease.

808
Schlumbergera russelliana

| *Cereus russellianus* | Crab Cactus | Christmas Cactus | *Epiphyllum russellianum* | Holiday Cactus | Orchid Cactus | *Phyllocactus russellianus* | *Schulumbergera epiphylloides* | Thanksgiving Cactus | Winterflowering Cactus | *Zygocactus* |

★POTENTIAL POWERS:
Endurance;

809
Scilla ☠

| Red Squill | Sea Onion | Squill | White Squill |

★POTENTIAL POWERS:
Accidents; Aggression; Anger; Break hexes; Carnal desires; Conflict; Lust; Machinery; Money; Protection; Rock music; Strength; Struggle; War;

★FOLKLORE AND FACTS:
Scilla has been used in Greek magic since the 5th century. • A method of attracting money is to put *Scilla* in a jar then add silver coins to the jar. • To break a hex, wear or carry *Scilla*.

810
Scrophularia

| Figwort |

★POTENTIAL POWERS:
Health; Protection; Protection against The Evil Eye;

811
Scutellaria

| *Anaspis* | *Cruzia* | **Greater Scullcap** | *Harlanlewisia* | **Helmet Flower** | **Hoodwort** | **Madweed** | *Perilomia* | **Quaker Bonnet** | *Salazaria* | **Skullcap** | *Theresa* |

★POTENTIAL POWERS:
Assistance; Fertility; Fidelity; Harmony; Independence; Love; Material gain; Peace; Persistence; Stability; Strength; Tenacity;

★FOLKLORE AND FACTS:
When a woman wears or carries a sprig of *Scutellaria* she protects her husband against the enticing charms of another woman.

812
Secale cereale

| **Rye** | *Secale fragile* |

★SYMBOLIC MEANINGS:
Apostasy; Condemnation; Dealings with The Devil; Disgust; Mockery; Sardonicism; Trickery;

★POTENTIAL POWERS:
Bondage; Black magick; Devilry;

813
Securigera varia ☠

| *Coronilla* | **Crown Vetch** | **Purple Crown Vetch** |

★SYMBOLIC MEANINGS:
Success to you;

814
Sedum

| *Aithales* | *Aizopsis* | *Amerosedum* | *Anacampseros* | *Asterosedum* | *Breitungia* | *Cepaea* | *Chetyson* | *Clausenellia* | *Cockerellia* | *Congdonia* | *Corynephyllum* | *Diamorpha* | *Etiosedum* | *Gormania* | *Helladia* | *Hjaltalinia* | *Hylotelephium* | *Keratolepis* | *Lenophyllum* | *Leucosedum* | *Macrosepalum* | *Meterostachys* | *Mucizonia* | *Ohbaea* | *Oreosedum* | *Parvisedum* | *Petrosedum* | *Phedimus* | *Pis-*

torinia | *Poenosedum* | *Procrassula* | *Prometheum* | *Pseudorosularia* | *Sedastrum* | *Sedella* | *Sedella* | *Spathulata* | **Stonecrop** | *Telmissa* | *Tetrorum* | *Triactina* |

★**SYMBOLIC MEANINGS:**
Tranquility;

815
Sempervivum

| **Hens and Chicks** | **Hen-and-chickens** | **Hen and Chickens** | **Houseleek** | **Live-forever** | **Sengren** | **Welcome-Home-Husband-Though-Never-So-Drunk** | **Welcome-Home-Husband-Though-Never-So-Late** |

★**SYMBOLIC MEANINGS:**
Domestic economy; Domestic industry; Liveliness; Vivacity; Welcome home husband;

★**POTENTIAL POWERS:**
Love; Luck; Protection; Wards off fire; Wards off lightning; Wards off witchery;

★**FOLKLORE AND FACTS:**
Sempervivum once commonly grown on rooftops to ward off fire, lightning strikes, and witches. • If worn fresh and replaced every third day, *Sempervivum* is believed to bring love.

816
Senecio cambrensis

| **Cankerwort** | **Dog Standard** | **Fairies' Horses** | **Groundsel** | **Groundeswelge** | **Ground Glutton** | **Ground-Swallower** | **Grundy Swallow** | **Ragweed** | **Saint James' Wort** | **Sention** | **Simson** | **St. James' Wort** | **Staggerwort** | **Stammerwort** | **Stinking Nanny** | **Stinking Willie** | **Welsh Groundsel** | **Welsh Ragwort** |

★**POTENTIAL POWERS:**
Healing; Health; Teeth;

★**FOLKLORE AND FACTS:**
Wearing a *Senecio cambrensis* amulet is believed to prevent toothaches. • The ancient Greeks used *Senecio cambrenis* as a amulet of choice against spells and charms used against the wearer. • During the dark days of persecution of witches, it was claimed that the witches rode out at midnight, not upon broomsticks, but on stalks of *Senecio cambrenis*.

817
Senna ☠

| *Cathartocarpus* | *Chamaefistula* | *Diallobus* | *Earleocassia* | *Herpetica* | *Isandrina* | **Jué Míng Zi** | **Ketsumei-shi** | **Locust Plant** | *Palmerocassia* | **Wild Senna** |

★**SYMBOLIC MEANINGS:**
Purging;

★**POTENTIAL POWERS:**
Love; Purgative;

818
Sesamum indicum

| **Ajonjoli** | **Benne** | **Bonin** | | **Gergelim** | **Gingli** | **Hoholi** | **Jaljala** | **Kunjid** | **Kunzhut** | **Logowe** | **Sesame** | **Shaman shammi** | **Shamash-shammu** | **Shawash-shammu** | **Shumshema** | **Simsim** | **Sumsum** | **Til** | **Ufuta** | **Ziele** |

★**POTENTIAL POWERS:**
Conception; Finds hidden treasure; Lust; Money; Opens locked doors; Protection; Reveals secret paths; Success in business;

★**FOLKLORE AND FACTS:**
Every month, put fresh *Sesamum indicum* seeds in a jar in the house and leave the lid off of it to draw money to it.

819
Sida fallax

| **Flower of Oahu** | **Ilima** |

★**SYMBOLIC MEANINGS:**
Royalty; Hello; Welcome;

★**FOLKLORE AND FACTS:**
Sida fallax is a flower often used in the construction of Hawaiian leis. • In ancient Hawaii *Sida fallax* flowers and leaves were reserved for royalty.

820
Silene
| **Campion** | **Catchfly** |

★**SYMBOLIC MEANINGS:**
Caught at last; Snare;

821

Silene coronaria

| *Agrostemma coronaria* | **Bloody William** | **Dusty Miller** | *Lychnis coronaria* | **Mullein-Pink** | **Rose Campion** |

★**SYMBOLIC MEANINGS:**
Gentleness; Only deserve my love;

822
Silene dioica

| **Red Campion** | **Red Catchfly** |

★**SYMBOLIC MEANINGS:**
I fall victim; Youthful love;

823
Silene noctiflora

| **Nightflowering Catchfly** | **Nightflowering Silene** |

★**SYMBOLIC MEANINGS:**
Night;

824
Silene nutans

| **Nottingham Catchfly** | *Silene dubia* | *Silene glabra* | *Silene grecescui* | *Silene infracta* | *Silene insurbrica* | *Silene livida* | *Silene brachypoda* | **White Catchfly** |

★**SYMBOLIC MEANINGS:**
Betrayed; I fall a victim;

825
Silphium laciniatum

| **Compass Flower** | **Compass Plant** | **Rosinweed** |

★**SYMBOLIC MEANINGS:**
Faith;

★**POTENTIAL POWERS:**
Finding North;

★**FOLKLORE AND FACTS:**
Amazingly, like a magnet, the living *Silphium laciniatum* flower's head and leaves align north and south. • Legend tells that God created the *Silphium laciniatum* to aid

travelers.

826
Silphium perfoliatum

| Carpenter's Weed | Compass Plant | Cup Plant | Cup Rosinweed | Indian-cup | Pilot Weed | Squareweed |

★POTENTIAL POWERS:
Protection;

827
Silybum marianum

| Blessed Milk Thistle | Marian Thistle | Mary Thistle | Mediterranean Milk Thistle | Milk Thistle | Our Lady's Thistle | Saint Mary's Thistle | Sow Thistle | St. Mary's Milk Thistle | Varigated Thistle | Wild Artichoke |

★POTENTIAL POWERS:
Assistance; Fertility; Harmony; Independence; Material gain; Persistence; Snake enraging; Stability; Strength; Tenacity;

★FOLKLORE AND FACTS:
There is an old Anglo-Saxon belief that if a man were to wear *Silybum marianum* around his neck any snakes anywhere within his presence will become enraged and begin to fight.

828
Sinacalia tangutica

| Acalia | *Cacalia* | Chinese Groundsel | Chinese Ragwort | *Senecio tanguticus* |

★SYMBOLIC MEANINGS:
Adulation; Temperance;

★POTENTIAL POWERS:
Health; Healing; Protection;

829
Smilax

| Bamboo Briar | Catbrier | Greenbrier | *Nemexia* | Prickly-Ivy | Sarsaparilla | Zarzaparrila |

★SYMBOLIC MEANINGS:

Lovely; Loveliness; Mythology;

★**POTENTIAL POWERS:**
Love; Money;

➤⬥

830
Solanum dulcamara ☠

| Amara Dulcis | Bitter Nightshade | Bittersweet | Bittersweet Nightshade | Blue Bindweed | Climbing Nightshade | Fellenwort | Felonwood | Poisonberry | Poisonflower | Scarlet Berry | Snakeberry | Trailing Bittersweet | Trailing Nightshade | Violet Bloom | Woody Nightshade |

★**SYMBOLIC MEANINGS:**
Truth;

★**POTENTIAL POWERS:**
Death; Healing; Lunar activity; Protection; Rebirth; Truth;

★**FOLKLORE AND FACTS:**
Put a small piece of *Solanum dulcamara* in a little pouch and tie it to somewhere on the body to remove evil.

➤⬥

831
Solanum lycopersicum ☠

| Armani Badenjan | Gojeh Farangi | Golden Apple | Guzungu | Kamatis | Love Apples | *Lycopersicon esculentum* | *Lycopersicon lycopersicum* | Pomo d'Oro | Tomatl | Tomato | Wolf Peach | Xitomatl |

★**POTENTIAL POWERS:**
Love; Protection; Prosperity;

★**FOLKLORE AND FACTS:**
It is believed by some that a large fruit of the *Solanum lycopersicum* placed on the mantle in a home will bring prosperity. • The fruit of the *Solanum lycopersicum* placed at any entrance to the home will repel evil from entering. • *Solanum lycopersicum* growing in the garden will scare away evil.

➤⬥

832
Solanum tuberosum ☠

| Blue Eyes | Flukes | Irish Potato | Lapstones | Leather Jackets | Murphies | No Eyes | Pinks | Potato | Potatta | Red Eyes | Rocks | Spud | Tatta | Taters | Tatties | White Potato |

★**SYMBOLIC MEANINGS:**
Beneficence; Benevolence;

★**POTENTIAL POWERS:**
Healing;

★**FOLKLORE AND FACTS:**
It is believed by some that if you carry a very small *Solanum tuberosum* in your pocket it will protect you against gout, warts, rheumatism, cure a toothache, and cure a cold if you have one and protect you from contracting one if you carry the tuber all winter long.

▶ *Solanum tuberosum Blossom:*
Benevolence;

833
Solidago

| Anise-scented Goldenrod | Blue Mountain Tea | European Goldenrod | Gizi-somukiki | Golden Rod | Goldenrod | Missouri Goldenrod | Sweet Goldenrod | Sweet-scented Goldenrod | True Goldenrod | Virgaureae Herba | Verg d'Or | Wound Weed | Woundwort |

★**SYMBOLIC MEANINGS:**
Be cautious; Encouragement; Good fortune; Good luck; Precaution; Strength; Success;

★**POTENTIAL POWERS:**
Divination; Luck; Money; Prosperity;

★**FOLKLORE AND FACTS:**
Solidago gets the primary blame for hay fever. • Witches frequently used *Solidago* in their potions. • It is believed that if you wear a sprig of *Solidago* one day, your future love will apear to you on the next day. • It is believed by some that *Solidago* can be utilized as a simple divining device, citing that if you hold *Solidago* in your hand, the flower will nod in the direction of the lost or hidden object...perhaps even treasure. • If *Solidago* suddenly grows near a door at your house in a place where it did not once grow before, expect an abundance of good fortune for the entire household.

834
Sorbus

| Delight of The Eye | European Mountain Ash | Mountain Ash | Quickbane | Ran Tree | Roden-Quicken | Roynetree | Rowan | Rowan Tree | Sorb Apple | Thor's Helper | Whitty | Wicken-Tree | Wiggin | Wiggy | Wiky | Wild Ash |

Witchbane | Witch Bane | Witchen | Witchwood |

★**SYMBOLIC MEANINGS:**

Balance; Connection; Mystery; Transformation;

★**POTENTIAL POWERS:**

Divination; Healing; Power; Protection; Psychic powers; Success; Visions;

★**FOLKLORE AND FACTS:**

Sorbus that is growing near a stone circle is the most potent of all. • Carry *Sorbus* wood to increase your psychic powers. • *Sorbus* wood is often a preferred choice in the making of a magical wand. • An effective diving rod can be made using a forked *Sorbus* branch. • Carry *Sorbus* berries to help recuperate from an illness. • Carry a piece of *Sorbus* bark to help recuperate from an illness. • In Europe, for hundreds of years, protective crosses have been made from *Sorbus* twigs that have been tied together with red thread and then carried. • *Sorbus* walking sticks help those who do a lot of walking at night. • Plant *Sorbus* on a grave to keep the deceased's ghost from haunting.

835
Sorbus americana

| American Mountain Ash | American Mountain-ash | *Pyrus americana* |

★**SYMBOLIC MEANINGS:**

Prudence; With me you are safe;

★**POTENTIAL POWERS:**

Healing; Love; Prosperity;
Protection;

836
Sorbus domestica

| Service Tree | Sorb | Sorb Tree | True Service Tree | Whitty Pear |

★**SYMBOLIC MEANINGS:**

Harmony; Prudence;

★**FOLKLORE AND FACTS:**

There is a huge *Sorbus domestica* tree in Moravia, Czech Republic that is estimated to be approximately 400 years old.

837
Spartium junceum

| *Genista juncea* | Retama | Spanish Broom | Weaver's Broom |

★SYMBOLIC MEANINGS:
Cleanliness;

838
Spathiphyllum

| Peace Lily | White Flag | Nana-honau' | Spath |

★POTENTIAL POWERS:
Peacefulness;

839
Specularia speculum

| European Venus' Looking Glass | *Githopsis latifolia* | *Legousia speculum-veneris* | *Specularia speculum-veneris* | Venus' Looking Glass | Venus' Looking-Glass | Venus's Looking-glass |

★SYMBOLIC MEANINGS:
Flattery;

840
Spiranthes

| Ladies'-tresses | Lady's Tresses |

★SYMBOLIC MEANINGS:
Bewitching grace;

841
Spondias purpurea

| Hog Plum | Jocote | Purple Mombin | Red Mombin | Sineguela | Siriguela | Siwèl |

★SYMBOLIC MEANINGS:
Privation;

842
Stachys

| *Betonica* | Betony | Heal-All | Hedgenettle | Lamb's Ears | Self-Heal | Woundwort |

★SYMBOLIC MEANINGS:
Love; Surprise;

★POTENTIAL POWERS:
Guards against harm; Healing of body and soul; Love; Protection; Protection against witchcraft and sorcery; Purification; Wards off evil spirits;

843
Stachys byzantina

| Lamb's Ear | Lamb's-Ear | *Stachys lanata* | *Stachys olympica* |

★POTENTIAL POWERS:
Guards against harm; Wards off evil spirits;

844
Stachys officinalis

| Betaine | Betonie | *Betonica officinalis* | Betony | Bishopwort | Lousewort | Purple Betony | *Stachys betonica* | Wild Hop | Wood Betony |

★SYMBOLIC MEANINGS:
Love; Surprise;

★POTENTIAL POWERS:
Business; Expansion; Honor; Leadership; Love; Politics; Power; Protection; Protection against dog bites; Protection against drunkenness; Protection against ghosts; Protection against snake bites; Protection against sorcery; Protection against witchcraft; Public acclaim; Purification; Responsibility; Royalty; Success; Wards off evil spirits; Wealth; Effective against sorcery;

★FOLKLORE AND FACTS:
Stachys officinalis is the original magical herb. • One superstition regarding *Stachys officinalis* is that a pair of serpents would kill each other if placed in a circle made of *Stachys officinalis*. • Wear an amulet of *Stachys officinalis* to be cured of a psychosomatic illness. • During the Middle Ages, *Stachys officinalis* was grown in monastery gardens to fend off many different types of evil. • *Stachys officinalis* is used in magic to purify one's body and soul before performing serious healing rituals. • The Druids believed that *Stachys officinalis* was magical enough to use it to be rid of evil spirits, bad dreams, and overwhelming sadness. • *Stachys officinalis* can be rubbed on all door and window frames to create a protection barrier that is impervious to evil . • A small pillow filled with *Stachys officinalis* and placed under the bed pillow will help end nightmares. • Plant *Stachys officinalis* in a cemetery to deter ghostly activity. • *Stachys officinalis* is believed to protect the body and the soul.• Place *Stachys officinalis* under a pillow to block visions and dreams that plague the

sleeper. • When *Stachys officinalis* is grown in the garden it will protect the home. • Carry *Stachys officinalis* when ready to approach a potential love.

845
Staphylea

| Bladdernut | Bladder Nut Tree | Jonjoli |

★ SYMBOLIC MEANINGS:
Amusement; Frivolity;

846
Stellaria americana

| American Starwort |

★ SYMBOLIC MEANINGS:
Cheerfulness in old age; Welcome to a stranger;

847
Stenocereus eruca

| Creeping Cereus | Creeping Devil |

★ SYMBOLIC MEANINGS:
Horror; Modest gain; Modest genius;

848
Stephanotis

★ SYMBOLIC MEANINGS:
Desire to travel; Marital happiness;

849
Sternbergia lutea

| Autumn Daffodil | Fall Daffodil | Lily-of-the-field | Lily of The Field | *Sternbergia aurantiaca* | *Sternbergia sicula* | *Sternbergia greuteriana* | Winter Daffodil | Yellow Autumn Crocus |

★ SYMBOLIC MEANINGS:
Pride;

850
Stillingia sylvatica

| Cockup hat | Marcory | Queen's Delight | Queen's Root | Silver Leaf | Stillingia | Yaw Root |

★POTENTIAL POWERS:
Psychic powers;

851
Straw

★SYMBOLIC MEANINGS:
Agreement; Constancy; United;

★POTENTIAL POWERS:
Image magic; Luck;

★FOLKLORE AND FACTS:
Carry Straw in a little bag for good luck. • Some people believe that a tiny fairy lives in the hollow center within a piece of Straw.

852
Straw (broken)

| Broken Straw |

★SYMBOLIC MEANINGS:
Broken agreement; Broken contract; Contention; Quarrel; Rupture of a contract; Trouble;

853
Strelitzia reginae

|Bird of Paradise | Crane's Bill | Crane Flower | Crane's Flower | *Strelitzia* |

★SYMBOLIC MEANINGS:
Faithfulness; Joyfulness; Magnificence; Romance's surprises; Splendor;

★FOLKLORE AND FACTS:
If given from a woman to a man *Strelitzia* is a symbol of her faithfulness to him.

854
Streptosolen jamesonii

| *Browallia jamesonii* | Fire Bush | Marmalade Bush |

★**SYMBOLIC MEANINGS:**
Could you bear poverty; Can you cope with being poor;

855
Stylophorum diphyllum

| Celandine Poppy | Poppywort | *Stylophorum* | Wood Poppy | Yellow Poppy |

★**SYMBOLIC MEANINGS:**
Joys to come;

★**POTENTIAL POWERS:**
Money; Success; Wealth;

856
Styrax benzoin

| Ben| Benjamen | Benzoin | Gum Benjamin | Gum Benzoin | Kemenyan | Loban | Onycha | Siam Benzoin | Siamese Benzoin | Sumatra | Storax |

★**POTENTIAL POWERS:**
Abundance; Advancement; Astral travel; Binding; Building; Business transactions; Caution; Cleverness; Communication; Conscious will; Creativity; Death; Energy; Enhances concentration; Faith; Friendship; Growth; Healing; History; Illumination; Intelligence; Initiation; Joy; Knowledge Leadership; Learning; Life; Light; Limitations; Memory; Natural power; Obstacles; Promotes generosity; Prosperity; Protects spirit during during astral Prudence; Purification; Travel; Provides focus; Self-preservation; Science; Sound judgment; Success; Thievery; Time; Wisdom;

★**FOLKLORE AND FACTS:**
A combination of *Styrax benzoin* (Benzoin), *Cinnamomum verum* (Cinnamon), and *Ocimum basilicum* (Basil) incense could attract customers to your place of business.

857
Succisa pratensis

| Devil's Bit | Devil's Bit Scabious |

★**SYMBOLIC MEANINGS:**
Scratch my itch;

★**POTENTIAL POWERS:**
Exorcism; Love; Luck; Protection;

★**FOLKLORE AND FACTS:**
In folk tales, the short black roots of the *Succisa pratensis* plant are the result of the

devil biting off the roots in anger after hearing a rumor that the plant may have had curative powers against the Bubonic Plague.

858
Symphyotrichum novae-angliae

| **American Starwort** | *Aster novae-angliae* | **New England Aster** |

★**SYMBOLIC MEANINGS:**
Afterthought; Cheerfulness in old age; Welcome; Welcome to a stranger;

859
Symphytum officinale

| **Assear** | **Black Wort** | **Boneset** | **Bruisewort** | **Comfrey** | **Comphrey** | **Conso-hada** | *Consolida majoris* | **Consound** | **Gavez** | **Gum Plant** | **Healing Herb** | **Karakaffes** | **Knit Back** | **Knitbone** | **Knit Bone** | **Miracle Herb** | **Slipperyroot** | **Slippery-root** | **Slippery Root** | **Smeerwartel** | **Wallwort** | **Yalluc** | **Ztworkost** |

★**POTENTIAL POWERS:**
Ensures safety during travel; Heals broken bones; Healing; Money; Restoration of virginity;

★**FOLKLORE AND FACTS:**
Symphytum officinale worn or tucked in a pocket will provide safe travel. • A piece of *Symphytum officinale* root in each suitcase will protect luggage while traveling.

860
Symplocarpus foetidus ☠

| **Clumpfoot Cabbage** | *Dracontium foetidum* | **Eastern Skunk Cabbage** | **Foetid Pothos** | **Meadow Cabbage** | **Pole Cat Weed** | **Polecat Weed** | **Skunk Cabbage** | **Skunk Weed** | *Spathyema foetida* | **Suntull** | **Swamp Cabbage** |

★**POTENTIAL POWERS:**
Good fortune; Legal matters;

861
Syngonium podophyllum ☠

| **American Evergreen** | **Arrowhead Philodendron** | **Arrowhead Plant** | **Arrow-head Vine** | **Goosefoot** |

★**POTENTIAL POWERS:**
Direction;

862

Syringa

| Common Lilac | Field Lilac | French Lilac | Lilac | Lilak | Nila | Nilak | Paschalia | *Syringa vulgaris* |

★**SYMBOLIC MEANINGS:**

Disappointment; Do You Still Love Me?; First emotion of love; Fraternal love; Fraternal sympathy; Humility; Love; Love's first emotions; Memory; Remember me; Reminder of young love;Youthful innocence;

★**POTENTIAL POWERS:**

Exorcism; Protection; Purification;

★**FOLKLORE AND FACTS:**

Plant or strew *Syringa* where you wish to drive away evil. • In New England, the *Syringa* bushes were originally plant to fend evil from the properties. • Fresh *Syringa* flowers can help clear out a haunted house of ghosts and haunting energies.

⊙ **SPECIFIC COLOR MEANING > Pink:**

Acceptance; Youth;

⊙ **SPECIFIC COLOR MEANING > Purple:**

First emotions of love; First love; Infatuation; Obsession;

⊙ **SPECIFIC COLOR MEANING > White:**

Candor; Children; First Dream of Love; Youth; Youthful innocence; Youthful looks;

863

Syzygium aromaticum

| Bol del Dlavo | Carenfil | *Caryophyllus aromaticus* | Cengkeh | Cengkih | Clavo de Olor | Clou de Girofle | Clove | Cravo-da-India | Cravo-das-Molucas | Cravo-de-Doce | Dlavero Giroflé | *Eugenia aromatica* | *Eugenia caryophyllat* | *Eugenia caryophyllus* | Gewürznelkenbaum | Giroflier | Grampoo | Karabu Nati | Kirambu | Kruidnagel | Laong | Laung | Lavang | Lavanga | Lavangam | Lawang | Mykhet |

★**SYMBOLIC MEANINGS:**

Dignity; Lasting friendship; Love; Money; Restraint;

★**POTENTIAL POWERS:**

Abundance; Advancement; Conscious will; Energy; Exorcism; Friendship; Growth; Healing; Joy; Leadership; Life; Light; Love; Mental clarity; Money; Natural power; Protection; Purification; Success;

★**FOLKLORE AND FACTS:**

Worn or carried in a pocket *Syzygium aromaticum* will attract the opposite sex.• Worn or carried *Syzygium aromaticum* will comfort someone who suffered an emotional loss and is bereaved.• If *Syzygium aromaticum* is burned as an incense it will do the following: stop people gossiping about you, attract riches, drive away hostility; turn away negative energies and produce positive spiritual energy all the while that it is also purifying wherever the scent goes to.

wishing for love

864
Tagetes

| *Adenopappus* | **African Marigold** | **African Marygold** | **American Marigold** | **Common Marigold** | *Diglossus* | **Drunkards** | *Enalcida* | **Herb of The Sun** | **Marigold** | **Mary's Gold** | *Solenotheca* | *Vilobia* |

★**SYMBOLIC MEANINGS:**
Creativity; Grief; Jealousy; Pain; Passion; Vulgar minded; Vulgar minds;

★**POTENTIAL POWERS:**
Legal matters; Love charms; Prophetic dreams; Protection; Psychic powers;

★**FOLKLORE AND FACTS:**
Early Christians would offer *Tagetes* blossoms around statues of The Virgin Mary, in place of coins. • The Welsh believed that *Tagetes* could be used to predict the stormy weather if the flowers did not open in the morning.

▸ *Tagetes with Cupressus:*
Despair;

865
Tagetes erecta

| **Aztec Marigold** | **Cempasúchil** | **Cempazúchil** | **DaoRung** | **Flor de Muertos** | **Flower of the Dead** | **Mexican Marigold** | **Twenty Flower** | **Zempoalxochitl** |

★**SYMBOLIC MEANINGS:**
Chagrin; Cruelty; Grief; Sacred affection;

866
Tagetes patula

| **Dao Ruang Lek** | **French Marigold** | **French Marygold** | **Garden Marigold** | **Marygold** | **Rainy Marigold** | *Tagetes corymbosa* | *Tagetes lunulata* | *Tagetes remotiflora* | *Tagetes signata* | *Tagetes tenuifolia* |

★**SYMBOLIC MEANINGS:**
A storm; Creativity; Grief; Jealousy; Passion; Storm; Uneasiness;

★**POTENTIAL POWERS:**
Legal matters; Prophetic dreams; Protection; Psychic powers;

867
Tamarindus indica

| Aamli | Amli | Asam | Asem | Bwemba | Chinch | Chintapandu | Chintachettu | Dawadawa | Demir Hindi | Hunase | Imli | Indian Date | Javanese Asam | Javanese Sour | Jawa | Kaam | Kily | Loan-tz | Maak-Kham | Magee-bin | Magee-thee | Ma-Kham | Me | Mkwayu | Puli | Sambag | Sambaya | Sambalog | Sampaloc | Sampalok | Siyambala | Tamarene | Tamar hind | Tamarind | Tamarindo | Tambran | Tamón | Tchwa | Teteli | Tetul | Tintidi | Tsamiya | Vaalanpuli | Voamadilo |

★**POTENTIAL POWERS:**
Love;

★**FOLKLORE AND FACTS:**
Carry or wear *Tamarindus indica* seeds to attract love.

868
Tamarix

| Salt Cedar | Tamarisk |

★**SYMBOLIC MEANINGS:**
Crime;

★**POTENTIAL POWERS:**
Exorcism; Protection;

★**FOLKLORE AND FACTS:**
The use of *Tamarix* in exorcism rituals to drive away evil and demons date back to over 4,000 years. • In the Bible's Genesis 21:33, it is written that Abraham planted *Tamarix* in Beer-sheda.

869
Tanacetum balsamita

| Alecost | Balsam Herb | *Balsamita vulgaris* | Bible Leaf | Costmary | Mint Geranium | Patagonian Mint |

★**SYMBOLIC MEANINGS:**
Gentility; Virtue;

★**FOLKLORE AND FACTS:**
A sprig of *Tanacetum balsamita* was used in Medieval times as a place marker in bibles.

870

Tanacetum parthenium

| Altamisa | Amargosa | Bachelor's Button | Bride's Button | *Chrysanthemum parthenium* | Featherfew | Featherfew | Featherfoil | Featherfoil | Febrifuge Plant | Febrifuge Plant | Feverfew | Flirtwort | Manzanilla | Mum | Mutter-kraut | *Pyrethrum* | *Pyrethrum parthenium* | *Tanacetum* | Wild Chamomile | Wild Chamomile | Wild Quinine |

★SYMBOLIC MEANINGS:
Good health;

★POTENTIAL POWERS:
Protection;

★FOLKLORE AND FACTS:
It is believed by some that bees do not like the scent of *Tanacetum parthenium*, so one might choose to carry *Tanacetum parthenium* around to fend off bees. • *Tanacetum parthenium* is good at keeping insects away from plants, so it is often planted around gardens for pest control.• A woman can attract a man by wearing *Tanacetum parthenium* flower. • Carry a sprig of *Tanacetum parthenium* for protection against fevers and accidents.

871
Tanacetum vulgare

| Bitter Buttons | Buttons | Common Tansy | Cow Bitter | Golden Buttons | Mugwort | Tansy | Wild Tansy |

★SYMBOLIC MEANINGS:
Courage; Declaration against you; Declaration of war; Happiness; Hostility; I declare against you; I declare war against you; War;

★POTENTIAL POWERS:
Attraction; Beauty; Friendship; Gifts; Harmony; Healing; Health; Joy; Longevity; Love; Pleasure; Sensuality; The Arts;

★FOLKLORE AND FACTS:
Carry *Tanacetum vulgare* to extend the length of your life.

872
Taraxacum officinale

| Blowball | Cankerwort | Canker-wort | Common Dandelion | Dandelion | Dent de Lion | Faceclock | Irish Daisy | *Leontodon taraxacum* | Lion's-Tooth | Milk-witch | Monks-head | Pee-A-Bed | Piss-a-Bed | Priest's-Crown | Priest's Crown | Puff-ball | Puffball | Swine Snout |Swine's Snout | *Taraxacum dens-*

311

leonis | *Taraxacum retroflexum* | **Tharakhchakon** | **Wet-A-Bed** | **Wild Endive** | **White Endive** | **Yellow-gowan** |

★ **SYMBOLIC MEANINGS:**

Coquetry; Faithfulness; Happiness; Prosperity; Wishes; Wishing For Love;

★ **POTENTIAL POWERS:**

Calling Spirits; Divination; Oracle; Purification; Rustic oracle; Wishes;

★ **FOLKLORE AND FACTS:**

Bury a *Taraxacum officinale* seed ball in the northwest corner of your house to bring desirable winds. • A curious divination is that if you blow the seeds off a *Taraxacum officinale* seed ball you will supposedly live for as many years as there are seeds that remain on the stem head. • Also, for every *Taraxacum officinale* seed ball that you blow the seeds off of you will be granted a wish. • To send a message to your loved one, visualize the message then blow on the *Taraxacum officinale* seed ball in his or her direction.

▶ ***Taraxacum officinale Seed Ball:***

Depart; Love's oracle; Oracle; Rustic oracle; Spirit magic; Wish magic; Wishes come true;

873

Taxus ☠

| **Yew** |

★ **SYMBOLIC MEANINGS:**

Honor; Illusion; Immortality; Introspection; Leadership; Longevity; Mortality; Mystery; Penitence; Power; Repentance; Sadness; Sanctity; Silence; Sorrow; Strength; Victory; Worship;

★ **POTENTIAL POWERS:**

Raising the dead;

★ **FOLKLORE AND FACTS:**

In Medieval times, *Taxus* was planted in churchyards because it was believed that the roots would grow down and through the eyes of the dead so that they would stop seeing into the world of the living, and prevent them from trying to return as spirits.

874

Tendrils of all Plants

★ **SYMBOLIC MEANINGS:**

Ties;

875
Thalictrum

| Meadow Rue |

★POTENTIAL POWERS:
Divination; Love;

876
Theobroma cacao

| **Cacahuatl** | **Cocoa** | *Cacao* | **Cocoa Tree** | **Kakaw** |

★POTENTIAL POWERS:
Arts; Attraction; Beauty; Friendship Gifts; Harmony; Joy; Love; Pleasures; The Arts; Sensuality;

★FOLKLORE AND FACTS:
In some areas of Mexico, such as Yucatan, *Theobroma cacao* beans were used as currency until as late as the late 1800's.

877
Thevetia peruviana ☠

Be-Still | **Flor Del Peru** | **Lucky Nut** | **Trumpet Flower** | **Yellow Oleander** |

★POTENTIAL POWERS:
Luck;

★FOLKLORE AND FACTS:
All parts of the *Thevetia peruviana* are extremely poisonous, most especially the seeds and many accidental poisonings of humans are well documented. • The deadly poisonous seeds of *Thevetia peruviana* are worn as talismans in Sri Lanka to attract luck.

878
Thorn (Branch)

★SYMBOLIC MEANINGS:
Severity; Sincerity; Rigor;

879
Thorn (Evergreen)

★SYMBOLIC MEANINGS:

Solace in adversity;

880
Thuja

| Arborvitae | Arbor vitae | Tree of Life |

★ SYMBOLIC MEANINGS:

Everlasting friendship; Friendship; Live for me; Unchanging; Unchanging affection; True Friendship; Unchanging friendship;

881
Thymus vulgaris

| Common Thyme | English Wild Thyme| Garden Thyme | Thyme |

★ SYMBOLIC MEANINGS:

Action; Activity; Affection; Bravery; Courage; Daring; Death; Elegance; Energy; Ensures restful sleep; Happiness; Healing; Health; Love; Psychic powers; Purification; Restful sleep; Sleep; Strength; Swift movement; Thriftiness;

★ POTENTIAL POWERS:

Ability to see fairies; Aphrodisiac; Attraction; Beauty; Courage; Friendship; Gifts; Harmony; Healing; Health; Irresistibility; Joy; Love; Pleasure; Psychic powers; Purification; Sensuality; Sleep; The Arts;

★ FOLKLORE AND FACTS:

Because *Thymus vulgaris* was a symbol of bravery and courage in Medieval times it was common for knights on their way to the Crusades to be carrying scarves or wearing tunics that had the image of a sprig of *Thymus vulgaris* embroidered upon them by their fair ladies. • In ancient Greece *Thymus vulgaris* was burned as an incense to purify their temples. • It was once thought that if a woman were to tuck a sprig of *Thymus vulgaris* in her hair, it would render her irresistible. • *Thymus vulgaris* was once used in nosegays to ward off disease and to also help mask any encountered bad odors. • *Thymus vulgaris* placed under the pillow is supposedly intended to repel nightmares. • *Thymus vulgaris* was once commonly worn by both men and women to ward off negativity and evil as they went about their daily business. • *Thymus vulgaris* is thought to provide a home for fairies and a place for them to dance. • Wear a sprig of *Thymus vulgaris* to attract good health. • Wear a sprig of *Thymus vulgaris* to be able to see fairies. • When a member of The Order of Oddfellows is buried, *Thymus vulgaris* is tossed into his grave. • It is believed that it is possible to cleanse yourself of all the ills and sorrows of the past, each Spring, by taking a purifying bath that has had crushed *Thymus vulgaris* and *Origanum majorana* (Sweet Marjaram) leaves added to the water until it is fragrant.

882
Tibouchina semidecandra

| Glory Bush | Lasiandra | Princess Flower |

★SYMBOLIC MEANINGS:
Glorious beauty; Glory;

883
Tilia

| Basswood | Lime | Lime-Tree | Lime Tree | Linden | Linnflowers | *Tilia* |

★SYMBOLIC MEANINGS:
Conjugal affection; Conjugal love; Love; Luck; Marriage; Matrimony;

★POTENTIAL POWERS:
Immortality; Love; Luck; Prevents intoxication; Protection; Sleep;

★ FOLKLORE AND FACTS:
It is believed that one can prevent intoxication by having a few *Tilia* leaves in the pocket. • Good luck charms can be carved from *Tilia* wood.

▸ *Tilia Sprig:*
Conjugal love;

884
Tillandsia usneoides

| Air Plant | Spanish Moss |

★POTENTIAL POWERS:
Protection;

885
Tradescantia ohiensis

| Common Spiderwort | Spider Lily | Spiderwort | Spider Wort |

★SYMBOLIC MEANINGS:
Esteem but not love; Esteem not love; Love;

★POTENTIAL POWERS:
Love;

★ FOLKLORE AND FACTS:
The Native American Dakota Indians would carry *Tradescantia ohiensis* to attract

love.

886
Tradescantia virginiana

| Virginia Spiderwort | Virginian Spiderwort |

★ **SYMBOLIC MEANINGS:**
Momentary happiness; Transient felicity;

★ **POTENTIAL POWERS:**
Love;

887
Trifolium

| Clover | Honey | Honeystalks | Shamrock | Three-Leaved Grass | Trefoil | Trifoil |

★ **SYMBOLIC MEANINGS:**
Domestic Virtue; Fertility; Revenge;

★ **POTENTIAL POWERS:**
Consecration; Exorcism; Fidelity; Love; Good luck; Money; Protection; Success;

★ **FOLKLORE AND FACTS:**
If love has broken your heart, wear *Trifolium* over your heart on a piece of blue silk to help get you through it. Otherwise, always wear it over the right breast. • Brides and Grooms should enter into marriage with any other three-leaf *Trifolium* (better yet, a four-leaf *Trifolium*!) tucked into each shoe. • The Druids considered all *Trifolium* to be sacred and magical plants. To them, the three-leaf *Trifolium* are symbolic of The Earth, The Sea, and The Sky; which is why all spells are repeated three times. • Put a *Trifolium* in your left shoe and leave it there to keep evil from you.

888
Trifolium pratense

| Beebread | Broadleafed Clover | Cleaver Grass | Clover | Cow Grass | Honey-suckle Clover | Marl Grass | Meadow Clover | Peavine Clover | Purple Clover | Red Clover | Trefoil | Wild Clover |

★ **SYMBOLIC MEANINGS:**
Industry; I promise; Provident; Revenge;

★ **POTENTIAL POWERS:**
Consecration; Exorcism; Fidelity; Love; Money; Protection; Success;

★FOLKLORE AND FACTS:

If love has broken your heart, wear *Trifolium pratense* over your heart on a piece of blue silk to help get you through it. Otherwise, always wear it over the right breast. • Brides and Grooms should enter into marriage with any three-leaf *Trifolium pratense* (better yet, a four-leaf *Trifolium pratense*!) tucked into each shoe. • The Druids considered all *Trifolium pratense* to be sacred and magical plants. To them, the three-leaf *Trifolium pratense* are symbolic of The Earth, The Sea, and The Sky; which is why all spells are repeated three times. • Wear *Trifolium pratense* before signing a financial contract of any kind.

889
Trifolium repens

| Dutch White Clover | Saint Patrick's Herb | Seamroq | Seamroy | Shamrock | Three-Leaved Grass | White Clover | White Shamrock |

★SYMBOLIC MEANINGS:

I promise; Lightheartedness; Promise; Think of me;

★POTENTIAL POWERS:

Happy marriage with good luck; Joyfulness; Good luck; Marital longevity with happiness and good fortune; Prosperity; Protection; Virility;

★FOLKLORE AND FACTS:

If love has broken your heart, wear *Trifolium repens* over your heart on a piece of blue silk to help get you through it. Otherwise, always wear it over the right breast. • The legend is that in the 5th Century, Saint Patrick used *Trifolium repens* to teach about the Christian belief in The Holy Trinity. • From the Middle Ages onward, *rifolium repens* has been considered a symbol of The Trinity. • Shamrocks are also used as symbols of Love in weddings. • Brides and Grooms should enter into marriage with *Trifolium repens* (or any other three-leaf clover...better yet, a four-leaf clover!) tucked into each shoe. • The Druids considered all clovers to be sacred and magical plants. To them, *Trifolium repens* (and any other three-leaf Clover) is symbolic of The Earth, The Sea, and The Sky; which is why all spells are repeated three times. • Scatter *Trifolium repens* around an area of magical negativity to break a hex. • If you have a hex upon you wear *Trifolium repens* to break it.

890
Trigonella goenum-graecum

| Abesh | Bockhornsklöver | Bockshornklee | Fenugreek | Halba | Hilbeh | Holba | Methi | Menthya | Methya | Menti | Ram's Horn Clover | Shanbalîleh | Uluhaal | Uluva | Vendayam |

★**POTENTIAL POWERS:**
Money; Prosperity; Wealth;

★**FOLKLORE AND FACTS:**
One easy way to bring money into the house fund is to add *Trigonella goenum-graecum* seeds to the water you mop the floors with.

891
Trillium

| Beth | Beth Root | Indian Root | Painted Lady | Painted Trillium | *Trillium erectum* | *Trillium pictum* | *Trillium undulatum* | Trille Ondulé | True Love |

★**SYMBOLIC MEANINGS:**
Modest beauty;

★**POTENTIAL POWERS:**
Love; Luck; Money;

892
Triodanis perfoliata

| Clasping Venus's Looking Glass | *Legousia perfoliata* | *Specularia perfoliata* |

★**SYMBOLIC MEANINGS:**
Love lost;

893
Triosteum

| Fever Root | Feverwort | Horse Gentian | Tinker's Root |

★**SYMBOLIC MEANINGS:**
Delay;

894
Triptilion spinosum

| Chilean Siempreviva |

★**SYMBOLIC MEANINGS:**
Be prudent;

895
Triticum

| Wheat |

★**SYMBOLIC MEANINGS:**
Friendliness; Prosperity; Riches; Wealth and prosperity; Wealth; You will be rich;

★**POTENTIAL POWERS:**
Fertility; Money;

★**FOLKLORE AND FACTS:**
Carry or wear *Triticum* to encourage fertility. • A bundle of *Triticum* placed in the home attracts money.

896
Tropaeolum

| Indian Cress | Nasties | *Nasturtium* **|**

★**SYMBOLIC MEANINGS:**
Charity; Conquest; Maternal love; Paternal love; Patriotism; Resignation; Splendor; Victory in battle; Warlike trophy;

897
Tulipa

| Lale | Lâleh | Pot Of Gold | Tulip | Tulipan | Tulipant |

★**SYMBOLIC MEANINGS:**
Absolute romance; A declaration of love; A lover's heart darkened by the heart of passion; Adjustment; Advancement; Aloof; Arrogant; Aspiration; Charity; Declaration of Love; Determination; Dreaminess; Elegance and grace; Fame; Imagination; Importance; Lust; Notoriety; Opportunity; Perfect Lover; Resurrection; Romance; Sensuality; Spiritual awareness; Spring; Wild speculation; Vanity; Wealth;

★**POTENTIAL POWERS:**
Love; Prosperity; Protection;

★**FOLKLORE AND FACTS:**
Wear a *Tulipa* as protection against bad luck and poverty.

⊙ **SPECIFIC COLOR MEANING > Orange:**
I am fascinated by you;

⊙ **SPECIFIC COLOR MEANING > Pink:**
My perfect lover;

⊙ **SPECIFIC COLOR MEANING > Purple:**
Eternal love;

⊙ **SPECIFIC COLOR MEANING > Red:**

Believe; Believe Me; Charity; Declaration of love; Fame; Trust; Undying love; Irresistible love;

⊙ **SPECIFIC COLOR MEANING > White:**
Virgin; Forgiveness; Literary debut; Sincerity;

⊙ **SPECIFIC COLOR MEANING > Yellow:**
Hopeless love; There is sunshine in my smile; No chance of reconciliation;

⊙ **SPECIFIC COLOR MEANING > Variegated:**
Beautiful eyes; Image magic; Splendid eyes; You have beautiful eyes;

898
Tulipa gesneriana

| **Didier's Tulip** | *Tulipa didieri* | *Tulipa suaveolens* |

★ **SYMBOLIC MEANINGS:**
Declaration of love;

899
Turnera diffusa ☠

| **Damiana** | **Mexican Damiana** |

★ **POTENTIAL POWERS:**
Aphrodisiac; Divination; Dreams; Love; Lust; Psychic powers; Sex magic; Visions;

★ **FOLKLORE AND FACTS:**
All or any part or its derivatives of *Turner diffusa* plants are strictly prohibited and illegal in Louisian, USA to grow, possess, or distribute.

900
Tussilago farfara

| **Ass's Foot** | **British Tobacco** | **Bull's Foot** | **Butterbur** | **Coltsfoot** | **Coughwort** | **Farfara** | **Foalswort** | **Foal's Foot** | **Horse Foot** | **Pas d'ane** | **Sponnc** | **Tash Plant** | *Tussilago* | *Tussilago farfara* | **Winter Heliotrope** |

★ **SYMBOLIC MEANINGS:**
Justice; Justice shall be done you; Justice shall be done; Love; Maternal Love; Political power;

★ **POTENTIAL POWERS:**
Healing; Love; Prosperity; Psychic visions; Visions; Wealth;

★ **FOLKLORE AND FACTS:**
Tussilago farfara can be carried in a small pouch to induce tranquility and a peace-

fulness.

901
Typha latifolia

| Balangot | Broadleaf Cattail | Bullrush | Bulrush | Cat Tail | Cat-O'-Nine-Tails | Cats Tail | Cattail | Cat's Tail | Common Bulrush | Common Cattail | Cooper's Reed | Cumbungi | Espadaña común | Great Reedmace | Ibhuma | Piriope | Roseau des étangs | Punk | Tabua | Tabua-larga | Totora | Tule espidilla | Tule-reed | *Typha* |

★SYMBOLIC MEANINGS:
Docility; Independence; Indiscretion; Peace; Prosperity;

★POTENTIAL POWERS:
Lust;

★FOLKLORE AND FACTS:
A woman who wants to enjoy sex but does not already like it at all, she should carry *Typha latifolia* with her at all times as a charm to help promote her future enjoyment.

a magic spell

902
Ulex

| Broom | Common Gorse | Frey | Furse | Furze | Fyrs | Gorse | Gorst | Goss | Prickly Broom | Ruffet | Whin |

★SYMBOLIC MEANINGS:
Anger; Endearing affection; Independence; Industry; Intelligence; Love for all occasions; Love for all seasons; Love in all seasons; Light; Vibrancy;

★POTENTIAL POWERS:
Money; Protection;

★FOLKLORE AND FACTS:
Ulex hedges in Wales were originally planted as a preventative against fairies because they cannot get through the prickly row of bushes.

903
Ulmus

| American Elm | Elm | Elven | English Elm | European Elm | *Planera aquatica* | *Ulmus americana* | Water Elm | White Elm | *Zelkova* |

★SYMBOLIC MEANINGS:
Dignity; Dignity and grace; Patriotism;

★POTENTIAL POWERS:
Love; Protection;

★FOLKLORE AND FACTS:
Ulmus is know to be a favorite tree of elves. • Carry bits of *Ulmus* bark or leaves to attract love.

904
Ulmus rubra

| Gray Elm | Indian Elm | Moose Elm | Red Elm | Slippery Elm | Soft Elm | *Ulmus americana rubra* | *Ulmus crispa* | *Ulmus dimidiata* | *Ulmus fulva* | *Ulmus pinguis* | *Ulmus pubescens* |

★POTENTIAL POWERS:
Halts gossip;

905
Urtica dioica

| Bull Nettle | Burning Nettle | Burning Weed | California Nettle | Common Nettle | Fire Weed | Jaggy Nettle | Nettle | Ortiga Ancha | Slender Nettle | Stinging Nettle | Tall Nettle | *Urtica dioica* | *Urtica breweri* | *Urtica californica* | *Urtica cardiophylla* | *Urtica lyalli* | *Urtica major* | *Urtica procera* | *Urtica serra* | *Urtica strigosissima* | *Urtica trachycarpa* | *Urtica viridis* |

★ **SYMBOLIC MEANINGS:**
Cruelty; Slander;

★ **POTENTIAL POWERS:**
Ambition; Attitude; Attraction; Beauty; Clear thinking; Exorcism; Friendship Gifts; Harmony; Healing; Higher understanding; Joy; Logic; Love; Lust; Manifestation in material form; Pleasures; Protection; The Arts; Sensuality; Spiritual concepts; Thought processes;

★ **FOLKLORE AND FACTS:**
Carry *Urtica doica* in a pouch to remove a curse and send it back to whoever created it.

a token

906
Vaccinium corymbosum

| Bilberry | Blueberry |

★**SYMBOLIC MEANINGS:**
Prayer;

★**POTENTIAL POWERS:**
Applying knowledge; Astral plane; Controlling lower principles; Finding lost objects; Overcoming evil; Protection; Protection against psychic attack; Regeneration; Removing depression; Sensuality; Uncovering secrets; Victory;

★**FOLKLORE AND FACTS:**
A few *Vaccinium corymbosum* berries under the front doormat will keep evil, unpleasant people, and negative entities from entering into the house.

907
Vaccinium myrtillus

| Bilberry | Black-Hearts | Blaeberry | Blaeberry | Blue Whortleberry | Common Bilberry | Fraughan | Fraughan | Ground Hurts | Hurtleberry | Hurts | Myrtle Blueberry | Whinberry | Whortleberry | Wimberry | Winberry | Windberry |

★**SYMBOLIC MEANINGS:**
Treachery; Treason;

★**POTENTIAL POWERS:**
Luck; Protection; Curse breaking; Dream Magic; Hex breaking;

★**FOLKLORE AND FACTS:**
Vaccinium myrtillus leaves will bring luck, fend off evil, and break curses and hexes if carried.

908
Vaccinium oxycoccus

| Common Cranberry | Cranberry | Cranberry Plant |

★**POTENTIAL POWERS:**
Cure for heartache; Heartache cure;

909
Vaccinium parvifolium

| **Huckleberry** | **Red Huckleberry** |

★ **SYMBOLIC MEANINGS:**
Faith; Simple leisures;

★ **POTENTIAL POWERS:**
Break hexes; Dream magic; Luck; Protection;

910
Vaccinium reticulatum

| **Ohelo `ai** | *Vaccinium berberidifolium* | *Vaccinium pahalae* | *Vaccinium peleanum* |

★ **POTENTIAL POWERS:**
Healing;

★ **FOLKLORE AND FACTS:**
Hawaiians consider the berries of the *Vaccinium reticulatum* plant so sacred that they would toss some berries into a volcano, as an offering to the Goddess Pele, before eating any of them.

911
Vachellia farnesiana

| *Acacia acicularis* | *Acacia farnesiana* | *Acacia indica* | *Acacia lenticellata* | *Acacia minuta* | **Aroma** | **Cascalotte** | **Casha** | **Casha Tree** | **Cashaw** | **Cashia** | **Cassia** | **Cassic** | **Cassie** | **Cassie Flower** | **Cassie-Flower** | **Cuntich** | **Cushuh** | **Dead Finish** | **Ellington's Curse** | **Farnese Wattle** | *Farnesia odora* | *Farnesiana odora* | **Honey-ball** | **Huisache** | **Iron Wood** | **Mealy Wattle** | *Mimosa acicularis* | **Mimosa Bush** | *Mimosa farnesiana* | *Mimosa indica* | *Mimosa suaveolens* | **Mimosa Wattle** | **Needle Bush** | **Needle Bush** | **North-West Curara** | **Opoponax** | *Pithecellobium acuminatum* | *Pithecellobium minutum* | *Popanax farnesiana* | **Popinac** | *Poponax farnesiana* | **Prickly Mimosa Bush** | **Prickly Moses** | **Sheep's Briar** | **Sponge Wattle** | **Sweet Acacia** | **Sweet Briar** | **Texas Huisache** | **Thorny Acacia** | **Thorny Feather Wattle** | **Wild Briar** |

★ **SYMBOLIC MEANINGS:**
Decrease of love; Let us forget; Poetry;

★ **POTENTIAL POWERS:**
Abundance; Advancement; Business transactions; Caution; Cleverness; Communication; Conscious will; Creativity; Energy; Faith; Friendship; Growth; Healing; Illumination; Initiation; Intelligence; Joy; Leadership; Learning; Life; Light; Love; Mem-

ory; Natural power; Prophetic dreams; Protection; Prudence; Purification; Science; Self-preservation; Sound judgment; Success; Thievery; Wisdom;

912
Valeriana officinalis

| All-Heal | Amantilla | Bloody Butcher | Capon's Trailer | Cat's Valerian | Common Valerian | English Valerian | Fragrant Valerian | Garden Heliotrope | Garden Valerian | Phu | Red Valerian | Saint George's Herb | St. George's Herb | Set Well | Valerian | Vandal Root |

★**SYMBOLIC MEANINGS:**
An accommodating disposition; Facility; Good disposition;

★**POTENTIAL POWERS:**
Applying knowledge; Astral plane; Controlling lower principles; Finding lost objects; Love; Overcoming evil; Protection; Purification; Regeneration; Removing depression; Sensuality; Sleep; Uncovering secrets; Victory;

★**FOLKLORE AND FACTS:**
Valeriana officianalis has been used for protection against lightning by hanging it in the home. • Place a sprig *Valeriana officianalis* under the pillow to use as a sleep aid. • If a woman wears a sprig of *Valeriana officianalis* men will follow her. • *Valeriana officianalis* placed in the room of a quarreling couple will calm their disagreements. • *Valeriana officianalis* placed under a window will repel evil.

913
Vanilla planifolia

| Banilje | Bourbon Vanilla | Flat-leaved Vanilla | Madagascar Vanilla | Tlilxochitl | *Vanilla aromatica* | Vanilla Orchid | *Vanilla fragrans* |

★**POTENTIAL POWERS:**
Energy; Love; Lust; Mental clarity; Mental powers;

★**FOLKLORE AND FACTS:**
Vanilla plantifolia flowers bloom after the flowers are fully grown, opening in the morning and closing late that same afternoon...never to reopen. If the *Vanilla plantifolia* flower was not pollinated by a certain type of bee or hummingbird, or by hand the flower will fall off. • A *Vanilla plantifolia* fruit, erroneously called a "bean" will take eight to nine months to ripen. • The fragrance of *Vanilla plantifolia* is believed to be able to induce lust. • Carry a *Vanilla plantifolia* bean for mental clarity and improved energy.

914
Verbascum

| Aaron's Rod | Blanket Leaf | Candlewick Plant | Clot | Doffle | Feltwort | Flannel Plant | Hag's Tapers | Hedge Taper | Jupiter's Staff | Lady's Foxglove | Mullein | Old Man's Fennel | Peter's Staff | Shepherd's Club | Shepherd's Herb | Torches | Velvetback | Velvet Plant | White Mullein |

★SYMBOLIC MEANINGS:
Good-nature; Good-natured;

★POTENTIAL POWERS:
Calling Spirits; Courage; Divination; Exorcism; Health; Love; Protection;

★FOLKLORE AND FACTS:
If worn, *Verbascum* is believed to give courage and attract love. • Sleep on a pillow stuffed with *Verbascum* to fend off nightmares. • In India *Verbascum* is considered to be the most powerful protection against magic and evil spirits and effective in banishing negativity and demons, so it is often worn, carried, and hung over doors and in windows. • A love divination used at one time by the young men of the Ozark mountain area was to find a live *Verbascum* plant and then bend it towards the object of his love. If the girl loved him back then the *Verbascum* would grow back upright again. If she loved someone else, it would die.

915
Verbascum arcturus

| *Celsia cretica* | Cretan Mullein | Great Flowered Celsia |

★SYMBOLIC MEANINGS:
Immortality;

916
Verbena officinalis

| Bijozakura | Blue Vervain | Brittanica | Common Verbena | Common Vervain | Devil's Bane | Echtes Eisenkraut | Enchanter's Plant | Herb of Grace | Herb of The Cross | Holy Herb | IJzerhard | Juno's Tears | Laege-Jernurt | Mosquito Plant | Pigeon's Grass | Pigeonwood | Rohtorautayrtti | Simpler's Joy | The Vervain | Tears of Isis | Traveler's Joy | Traveller's Joy | Van-Van | Verbena | *Verbena domingensis* | *Verbena macrostachya* | Vervan | Vervain | Wild Hyssop | Zelezník Lekársky |

★SYMBOLIC MEANINGS:
Abilities; Beauty; Chastity; Cooperativeness; Enchantment; Healing; Hope in darkness; Inspires artistry; Inspires creativity; Instills a love of and for learning; Love;

Money; Peace; Pray for me; Problems; Rest; Safety; Security; Sensibility; Sensitiveness; You enchant me; Youth;

★POTENTIAL POWERS:

Divine forces; Divine offering; Enchantment; Feminine power; Love; Money; Peace; Healing; Protection; Protection from vampires; Protection from witchcraft; Protects from negative emotions; Protects against depression; Purification; Repels negativity; Remedy for over-enthusiasm; Repels witches; Repels vampires; Repels evil intentions; Sorcery; Sleep; Supernatural forces; Women's power; Youth;

★FOLKLORE AND FACTS:

There is a legend that *Verbena officinalis* was used to stop the bleeding of Jesus' crucifixion wounds after he was taken down from the cross. • In ancient Rome *Verbena officianalis* would be bundled together as whisk brooms then used to sweep the alters. • Carry a piece of *Verbena officianalis* as an amulet. • Use *Verbena officianalis* in the home as protection against destructive storms and lightning. • Scatter *Verbena officianalis* around the home to bring peace inside. • Grow *Verbena officianalis* to encourage the other plants to produce abundantly. • Carry a sprig of *Verbena officianalis* to encourage everlasting youth. • *Verbena officianalis* placed under the bed or pillow offers protection from harmful dreams. • To determine if someone has stolen something from you, wear a sprig of *Verbena officianalis* then ask them if they did what you suspect.

⊙ SPECIFIC COLOR MEANING > Pink:

Family union;

⊙ SPECIFIC COLOR MEANING > Purple:

I weep for you; Regret; I am so sorry;

⊙ SPECIFIC COLOR MEANING > Scarlet:

Church unity; Unite against evil;

⊙ SPECIFIC COLOR MEANING > White:

Pray for me;

917
Veronica chamaedrys

| Bird's Eye Speedwell | Bird's-eye Speedwell | Germander Speedwell | Männertreu |

★SYMBOLIC MEANINGS:

Facility; Fidelity;

918
Veronica spicata

| Spiked Speedwell |

★SYMBOLIC MEANINGS:
Semblance;

919
Viburnum opulus

| Cramp Bark | European Cranberrybush | Guelder Rose | Snowball Tree | Water Elder |

★SYMBOLIC MEANINGS:
Age; Bound; Ennui; Goodness; Good news; Heavenly journeys; Thoughts of Heaven; Tuesday's Flower; Winter; Young when old;

920
Viburnum tinus

| Laurestine | Laurustinus | Laurustinus Viburnum | *Viburnum rigidum* | *Viburnum rugosum* | *Viburnum strictum* | *Tinus lucidus* | *Tinus lauriformis* | *Tinus laurifolius* | *Viburnum lauriforme* | *Viburnum hyemale* |

★SYMBOLIC MEANINGS:
A token; Delicate attentions; I die if neglected; Token;

921
Vicia

| *Faba* | Giant Vetch | Vetch |

★SYMBOLIC MEANINGS:
I cling to thee; Shyness; Vice;

922
Vicia nigricans gigantea

| Black Vetch | Giant Vetch |

★POTENTIAL POWERS:
Fidelity;

923
Vinca major ☠

| Bigleaf Periwinkle | Big Leaf Periwinkle | Blue Periwinkle | Great Blue Peri-

winkle | Greater Periwinkle | Large Periwinkle | *Vinca major variegata* **|**

★SYMBOLIC MEANINGS:

Early attachment; Early friendship; Early love; Early recollections; Education; Memories; Money; Pleasures of memories; Protection; Recollections; Sweet memories; Sweet remembrance; Tender recollections;

★POTENTIAL POWERS:

Love; Lust; Mental clarity; Mental powers; Protection;

924

Vinca minor ☠

| Blue Buttons | Centocchiio | Common Periwinkle | Creeping Myrtle | Devil's Eye | Hundred Eyes | Joy On The Ground | Lesser Periwinkle | Myrtle | Periwinkle | Sorcerer's Violet | Small Periwinkle |

★SYMBOLIC MEANINGS:

Desirability; Early recollections; Education; Memories; Money; Pleasures of memories; Recollections; Sweet memories; Sweet remembrance; Tender recollections;

★POTENTIAL POWERS:

Banishes negative energy; Love; Lust; Mental clarity; Protection;

★FOLKLORE AND FACTS:

It is believed that if you gaze upon *Vinca minor* flowers your lost memories will return to you.

⊙ SPECIFIC COLOR MEANING > Blue:

Early attachment; Early friendship;

⊙ SPECIFIC COLOR MEANING > White:

Pleasant recollections; Pleasures of memory;

925

Vine

★SYMBOLIC MEANINGS:

Connection; Drunkenness; Friendship; Flowing state of mind; Growth; Intoxicating; Intoxication; Opportunity; Renewal;

926

Viola

| Heartsease | Violet | Pansy |

★SYMBOLIC MEANINGS:

Affection; Artistic ability; Faithfulness; Fidelity; Honesty; Loyalty; Modesty; Simiplicity; Think of me; Thoughtful Recollection; Thoughts; Virtue;

★POTENTIAL POWERS:
Calms tempers; Divination; Induces sleep; Love; Psychic sensitivity;

927
Viola alba

| **White Violet** |

★SYMBOLIC MEANINGS:
Candor; Impulsive acts of love; Innocence; Let's take a chance on happiness; Modesty; Purity;

★POTENTIAL POWERS:
Healing; Love; Luck; Lust; Peace; Protection; Wishes;

928
Viola odorata

| **Banafsa** | **Banafsha** | **Banaksa** | **Blue Violet** | **Common Violet** | **English Violet** | **Garden Violet** | **Sweet Violet** |

★SYMBOLIC MEANINGS:
Modesty;

★POTENTIAL POWERS:
Attraction; Beauty; Friendship; Gifts; Harmony; Healing; Joy; Love; Luck; Lust; Peace; Pleasure; Protection; Sensuality; The Arts; Wishes;

★FOLKLORE AND FACTS:
Carry *Viola odorata* to provide protection against wicked spirits. • Carry *Viola odorata* for good luck. • It is believed that if you pick the very first *Viola odorata* that you find in the Spring, you can make a wish on it and the wish will come true.

929
Viola pubescens

| **Downy Yellow Violet** | **Yellow Violet** |

★SYMBOLIC MEANINGS:
Modest worth; Rare Worth; Rural happiness;

★POTENTIAL POWERS:
Healing; Love; Luck; Lust; Peace; Protection; Wishes;

930
Viola sororia

| Blue Violet | Common Blue Violet | Common Meadow Violet | Hooded Violet | Purple Violet | *Viola papillionacea* | Wood Violet | Woolly Blue Violet |

★**SYMBOLIC MEANINGS:**
Faithfulness;

★**POTENTIAL POWERS:**
Attraction; Beauty; Friendship; Gifts; Harmony; Healing; Joy; Love; Luck; Lust; Peace; Pleasure; Protection; Sensuality; The Arts; Wishes;

931
Viola tricolor

| Banwort | Banewort | Bird's Eye | Bonewort | Bouncing Bet | Bouncing Betty | Dolly Flower | Field Pansy | Garden Violet | Heart's Ease | Horse Violet | Johnny Jumper | Johnny Jump Up | Kiss-Me-At-The-Garden-Gate | Lady's Delight | Little Stepmother | Love Idol | Love-In-Idleness | Loving Idol | Meet-Me-In-The-Entry | Monkeyflower | Pansy | Pansy Violet | Pensee | Pied Heart's-Ease | Stepmother | Tickle-My-Fancy | Tittle-My-Fancy | *Viola arvensis* | Wild Pansy |

★**SYMBOLIC MEANINGS:**
Caring; Cheerfulness; Fond memories of the love and kindness of those who have passed; Forget me not; Memory; Merriment; Reflection; Remembrance; Romantic thoughts; Think of me; Thoughtful; Thought; Thoughts; Togetherness; Union; You are in my thoughts; You occupy my thoughts;

★**POTENTIAL POWERS:**
Divination; Love; Love charm; Love divination; Rain magic;

★**FOLKLORE AND FACTS:**
The *Viola tricolor* was a common ingredient in Celtic love potions because the individual petals are heart-shaped and were thought to be able to cure a broken heart. • In many parts of the world it is the *Viola tricolor* that is most closely associated with love on Valentine's Day, and is often exchanged between lovers. • There is a superstition that if a *Viola tricolor* is picked while still wet with dew there will be death of a loved one, and there would be continuous weeping until the next full moon. • Wear or carry the *Viola tricolor* flower to attract love. • To bring love into your life, plant *Viola tricolor* plants in the garden in the shape of a heart. If they grow, so will love.

932

Viscaria oculata

| Catchfly | German Catchfly | *Lychnis viscaria* |

★SYMBOLIC MEANINGS:
Invitation; Will you dance with me?;

933
Viscum album ☠

| All-heal | Common Mistletoe | European Mistletoe | Golden Bough | Holy Wood | Mistletoe | Thunderbesom |

★SYMBOLIC MEANINGS:
Affection; Difficulties; Give me a kiss; Hunting; I surmount everything; I surmount difficulties; Kiss me; Looking; Love; Obstacles to be overcome; To surmount difficulties;

★POTENTIAL POWERS:
Exorcism; Fertility; Healing; Health; Love; Protection; Hunting;

★FOLKLORE AND FACTS:
The ancient Greeks believed that *Viscum album* had mystical powers. • *Viscum album* is one of the most magical plants of all European folk beliefs as it was thought to be able to cure diseases, make poisons harmless, reproduce animals to enormous herds and flocks, protect one against witchcraft, protect houses from ghosts...even making them speak when so desired. • *Viscum album* was believed to bring good luck to anyone who possessed it. • The ancient Celts hung *Viscum album* to ward off evil and to welcome the New year. • The ancient Celts would hang *Viscum album* over a baby's cradle to protect the child from being stolen away by fairies. • During Christmas time, if a girl is standing under *Viscum album* she cannot be refused to be kissed. If she is refused, she cannot expect to be married the coming year.

934
Vitex agnus-castus

| Abraham's Balm | Chasteberry | Chaste Berry | Chaste Tree | Monk's Pepper | *Vitex* |

★SYMBOLIC MEANINGS:
Coldness; Indifference; Life without love;

935
Vitis vinifera

| **Common Grape Vine** | **Grape** | *Vitis sylvestris* |

★**SYMBOLIC MEANINGS:**

Charity; Fertility; Initiation; Intemperance; Kindness; Meekness; Mental powers; Money; Rural felicity;

★**POTENTIAL POWERS:**

Fertility; Garden Magic; Mental clarity; Mental powers; Money;

★**FOLKLORE AND FACTS:**

Paint pictures of *Vitis vinifera* on your garden walls to promote fertility.

936

Volkameria

| **Volkamenia** |

★**SYMBOLIC MEANINGS:**

May you be happy;

welcome

937
Warszewiczia coccinea

| Chaconia | Pride of Trinidad and Tobago | Wild Poinsettia |

★ SYMBOLIC MEANINGS:
The imperishability of Life;

938
Winged Seed (all)

★ SYMBOLIC MEANINGS:
Messengers;

939
Wisteria

★ SYMBOLIC MEANINGS:
Love; Poetry; Protection; Welcome; Youth;

940
Wisteria sinensis

| Chinese Wisteria | Wistaria | *Wisteria* |

★ SYMBOLIC MEANINGS:

Your friendship is agreeable to me; Let's be friends; Welcome fair stranger;

941
Withania somnifera ☠

| Ajagandha | Amukkuram | Ashwagandha | Ashwagandha Root | Indian Ginseng | Kanaje Hindi | *Physalis somnifera* | Samm Al Ferakh | Winter Cherry | Winter Cherry Herb |

★ SYMBOLIC MEANINGS:
Deception;

942
Withered Flowers Bouquet
| Bouquet of Withered Flowers |
★**SYMBOLIC MEANINGS:**
Rejected love;

immortality

943
Xanthium strumarium

| Clotbur | Common Cocklebur | Large Cocklebur | Rough Cocklebur | Woolgarie Bur | *Xanthium canadense* | *Xanthium chinese* | *Xanthium glabratum* | *Xanthium strumarium canadense* | *Xanthium strumarium glabratum* | *Xanthium strumarium strumarium* |

★SYMBOLIC MEANINGS:
Pertinacity; Rudeness;

944
Xeranthemum annum

| Immortal Flower | *Xeranthemum* |

★SYMBOLIC MEANINGS:
Cheerfulness under adverse conditions; Cheerfulness under adversity; Eternity; Immortality; Immortal remembrance;

★POTENTIAL POWERS:
Eternity; Immortality;

best friends

945
Yucca

| *Clistoyucca* | **Ghosts In The Graveyard** | *Samuela* | *Sarcoyuccca* | **Yuca** | **Yucca** |

★**POTENTIAL POWERS:**
Protection; Purification; Transmutation;

★**FOLKLORE AND FACTS:**
Yucca is commonly found in Midwestern USA rural graveyards and when they are blooming the flowers appear to be floating apparitions, or "ghosts". • *Yucca* fibers twisted into a cross then placed in the center of the home will protect the house from evil. • It is believed that if a person jumps through a loop of twisted *Yucca* he will magically transmute into an animal.

946
Yucca gloriosa

| **Adam's Needle** | **Moundlily** | **Sea Islands Yucca** | **Soft-tipped Yucca** | **Spanish Bayonet** | **Spanish Dagger** | **Yucca** |

★**SYMBOLIC MEANINGS:**
A Friend In Need; Best friends;

i miss you

947

Zantedeschia aethiopica ☠

| Arum Lily | *Calla aethiopica* | Calla Lily | *Colocasia aethiopica* | Easter Lily | Lily of the Nile | *Richardia africana* | *Richardia aethiopica* | Trumpet Lily | Varkoor |

★**SYMBOLIC MEANINGS:**
Beauty; Beauty and the price gained from shared wisdom over time; Delicacy; Feminine beauty; Magnificent beauty; Majestic Beauty; Modesty; Panache; Religion; Transition and growth;

★**POTENTIAL POWERS:**
Declaration of religiousness; Repentance; Spirituality;

★**FOLKLORE AND FACTS:**
Zantedeschia aethiopica one of the oldest known flowers. • According to a legend, *Zantedeschia aethiopica* grew wherever Eve's tears of sorrow and repentance fell as she and Adam were leaving The Garden of Eden.

948

Zantedeschia albomaculata

| Spotted Arum Lily |

★**SYMBOLIC MEANINGS:**
Ardor; Great warmth;

949

Zanthoxylum

| *Fagara* | Hercules' Club | *Ochroxylum* | Prickly Ash | Prickly-Ash | *Xanthoxylum* |

★**POTENTIAL POWERS:**
Love;

950

Zea mays

| Corn | Giver of Life | Maize | Mealie | Mielie | Milho | Sacred Mother | Seed of Seeds |

★**SYMBOLIC MEANINGS:**
Abundance; Quarrel; Riches;

★**POTENTIAL POWERS:**
Divination; Luck; Protection;

★**FOLKLORE AND FACTS:**
Some believe that to place an ear of *Zea mays* in an infant's cradle will protect the baby from negative energies and forces. • A bundle of *Zea mays* husks over a mirror will bring good luck into the house.

▸ *Zea mays Broken:*
Quarrel;

▸ *Zea mays Ear:*
Delicacy;

▸ *Zea mays Straw:*
Agreement;

951
Zeltnera beyrichii

| Mountain Pink | Quinine Weed | Rock Centaury |

★**SYMBOLIC MEANINGS:**
Aspiring;

952
Zephyranthes

| Andromeda | Atamasco Lily | August Rain Lily | Autumn Zephyr Lily | Fairy Lily | Magic Lily | Peruvian Swamp-Lily | Rain Lily | Rainflower | White Zephyr Lily |Zephyr Flower | Zephyr Lily |

★**SYMBOLIC MEANINGS:**
Expectation; Fond caresses; Healing; Love; Self-sacrifice; Sickness; Sincerity; Sorrow; Will you help me;

★**POTENTIAL POWERS:**
Healing; Help; Love;

953
Zigadenus ☠

| Deathcamas | Sandbog Deathcamas | Star Lily |

★**SYMBOLIC MEANINGS:**

Deadly; Death; Poison; Suffering death;

954
Zinnia

| *Crassina* | *Diplothrix* | *Mendezia* | *Tragoceros* |

★**SYMBOLIC MEANINGS:**
Absent friends; I miss you; I mourn your absence; Loyalty; Thoughts of absent friends; Thoughts of friends;

◉ **SPECIFIC COLOR MEANING > Magenta:**
Affection; Lasting affection;

◉ **SPECIFIC COLOR MEANING > Pink:**
Lasting Affection;

◉ **SPECIFIC COLOR MEANING > Scarlet:**
Constancy;

◉ **SPECIFIC COLOR MEANING > White:**
Goodness;

◉ **SPECIFIC COLOR MEANING > Yellow:**
Daily Remembrance; Haunting memories; Memories;

◉ **SPECIFIC COLOR MEANING > Mixed colors:**
Memories beyond reach; Remembering an absent friend; Memories beyond your reach;

Indexes

- Akshi 524
- Al-karawYa 174
- Alanaasi 059
- Alashi 524
- Alavese Pinto Bean 661
- Albahaca 609
- Albaricoque 716
- Albellus 700
- Alcaravea 174
- Alcea rosea 028
- Alchemilla 029
- Alchimilla 029
- Alder 040
- Aldinia 270
- Alecost 869
- Alehoof 398
- Aletris 030
- Aletris farinosa 030
- Aleurites javanicus 031
- Aleurites moluccana 031
- Aleurites pentaphyllus 031
- Aleurites remyi 031
- Aleurites trilobus 031
- Alfalfa 567
- Alfarrobeira 194
- Algarrobo 194
- Alho Bravo 034
- Alho Inglês 034
- Alison 048
- Alkanet 061
- All-Heal 634
- All-Heal 912
- All-heal 933
- Allamanda 032
- Alligator Pear 653
- Alligator Pepper 020
- Allium 033
- Allium ampeloprasum 034
- Allium ascalonicum 036
- Allium cepa 035

- Allium oschaninii 036
- Allium porrum 034
- Allium sativum 037
- Allium schoenoprasum 038
- Allium tuberosum 039
- Allspice 669
- Almindelig Katost 558
- Almond 720
- Almond Laurel 722
- Almond Tree 720
- Alnus 040
- Aloe 023
- Aloe 041
- Aloe barbadensis 041
- Aloe vera 041
- Aloeroot 030
- Alopecurus 042
- Alopecurus pratensis 042
- Aloysia citriodora 043
- Aloysia citrodora 043
- Alperce 716
- Alpine Strawberry 367
- Alpinia 044
- Alpinia galanga 045
- Alstroemeria 046
- Altamisa 870
- Althaea 047
- Althaea frutex 433
- Althaea officinalis 047
- Althea 047
- Altramuz 538
- Alubia Pinta Alavesa Bean 661
- Alum Bloom 391
- Alum Root 391
- Alyssum 048
- Alyxia oliviformis 049
- Alyxia stellata 049

- Amantilla 912
- Amara Aromatica 066
- Amara Dulcis 830
- Amarant 050
- Amaranth 050
- Amaranthus 050
- Amaranthus caudatus 051
- Amaranthus hypochondriacus 052
- Amargosa 870
- Amarillo 053
- Amarutza 558
- Amaryllis 053
- Amaryllis belladona 053
- Amber 450
- Amblyanthera 559
- Ambrosia artemisiifolia 054
- Ambrosiaceae 105
- Ambuja 598
- Amellus officinalis 106
- Amellus vulgaris 106
- American Adder's Tongue 338
- American Agave 023
- American Aloe 023
- American Bee Balm 581
- American Bittersweet 184
- American Blue Flag 471
- American Century 023
- American Cowslip 312
- American Cudweed 402
- American Dittany 609
- American Dogwood 258
- American Elm 903

- American Evergreen 861
- American Lotus 607
- American Mandrake 690
- American Marigold 864
- American Mountain Ash 835
- American Mountainash 835
- American Plane 686
- American Plum 715
- American Rhododendron 749
- American Starwort 846
- American Starwort 858
- American Storax 525
- American Sycamore 686
- American Tiger Lily 520
- American Trout Lily 338
- American Wintergreen 384
- Amerosedum 814
- Amethyst Flower 137
- Amli 867
- Amorphophallus titanum 055
- Amphiscopia 481
- Amukkuram 941
- Amygdalus communis 720
- Anaar 733
- Anaasa 059
- Anacampseros 814
- Anacamptis papilionacea 056
- Anacardium curatellifolium 057

- Anacardium occidentale 057
- Anagallis arvensis 058
- Anagallis phoenicea 058
- Ananas 059
- Ananas comosus 059
- Ananá 059
- Anarosh 059
- Anasazi Bean 661
- Anaspis 811
- Anastatica 060
- Anastatica hierochuntica 060
- Anchusa officinalis 061
- Anderssoniopiper 675
- Andromeda 952
- Anemone 062
- Anemone 063
- Anemone coronaria 063
- Anemone nemorosa 064
- Anemone pulsatilla 731
- Anethum 065
- Anethum graveolens 065
- Aneton 065
- Angcm 067
- Angel Hair 277
- Angel Plant 066
- Angel Wings 145
- Angelandra 270
- Angelica 066
- Angelica archangelica 066
- Angelica officinalis 066
- Angelica officinalis himalaica 066
- Angel's Trumpet 138
- Angel's Trumpet 292

- Baldhip Rose 766
- Balfae 151
- Bali 242
- Ballockwor 622
- Balloon Flower 687
- Balm 569
- Balm Mint 569
- Balm of Gilead Tree 246
- Balm of Mecca Tree 246
- Balsam 458
- Balsam 459
- Balsam Herb 869
- Balsam of Gilead Tree 246
- Balsam of Mecca Tree 246
- Balsam of Peru 590
- Balsam of Tolu 590
- Balsamine 458
- Balsamita vulgaris 869
- Balsamo 590
- Bamboo 116
- Bamboo Briar 829
- Bambou de Chine 116
- Bambu Ampel 116
- Bambu Vulgar 116
- Bambusa vulgaris 116
- Bambuseae 116
- Banafsa 928
- Banafsha 928
- Banaksa 928
- Banal 286
- Banalia 270
- Banana 585
- Banewort 110
- Banewort 931
- Bang Seed 458
- Banilje 913
- Banksia laricina 117
- Banwort 931
- Banyan 360
- Barbados 041
- Barbados Aloe 041

- Barbed Wire Grass 282
- Barberry 122
- Barberton Daisy 394
- Bardana 084
- Bargad 360
- Barhamia 270
- Bark of Barks Tree 215
- Barley 437
- Basam 286
- Bashoush 783
- Basil 609
- Basket of Gold 111
- Bassia scoparia 118
- Basswood 883
- Bastard Ipe-cacuanha 099
- Bastard Rocket 745
- Batatas 461
- Batidaea 775
- Bauple Nut 547
- Bay 497
- Bay 749
- Bay Laurel 497
- Bay Tree 497
- Bay-Rum Tree 588
- Bayberry 588
- Bayis 749
- Be Still Tree 744
- Be-Still 744
- Be-Still 877
- Bean of India 598
- Bear Weed 335
- Bearberry 085
- Bearberry 747
- Bearded Crepis 267
- Bearded Iris 469
- Beargrass 603
- Bearss Lime 227
- Bear's Breach 005
- Bear's Breeches 005
- Bear's Ear 709
- Bear's Foot 010
- Bear's Foot 425

- Bear's Grape 085
- Beauty of The Empire 633
- Beaver Poison 247
- Beaver Tree 551
- Bedstraw 382
- Bee Balm 569
- Bee Balm 581
- Bee Orchid 618
- Bee Orphrys 618
- Bee Plant 233
- Bee Sage 791
- Bee's-nest 293
- Bee's-nest Plant 293
- Beebalm 581
- Beebread 888
- Beech 356
- Beech Tree 356
- Beechwheat 354
- Beechwood 356
- Beeplant 233
- Beet 124
- Beetroot 124
- Beggarweed 277
- Beggar's Buttons 084
- Begonia 119
- Beharki 336
- Beijo de Frade 458
- Beithe 125
- Belgian Evergreen 317
- Belia 287
- Bell Chillie 167
- Bell Flower 158
- Bell Peppers 167
- Belladonna 110
- Belladonna Lily 053
- Belle of the Night 448
- Bellflower 157
- Bellis alpina 120
- Bellis armena 120
- Bellis croatica 120
- Bellis hortensis 120
- Bellis hybrida 120
- Bellis integrifolia 120

- Bellis margaritifolia 120
- Bellis minor 120
- Bellis perennis 120
- Bellis perennis caulescens 120
- Bellis perennis discoidea 120
- Bellis perennis fagetorum 120
- Bellis perennis flore plen 121
- Bellis perennis hybrida 120
- Bellis perennis margaritifolia 120
- Bellis perennis microcephala 120
- Bellis perennis plena 120
- Bellis perennis pumila 120
- Bellis perennis pusilla 120
- Bellis perennis rhodoglossa 120
- Bellis perennis strobliana 120
- Bellis perennis subcaulescens 120
- Bellis perennis tubulosa 120
- Bellis pumila 120
- Bellis pusilla 120
- Bellis scaposa 120
- Bellis validula 120
- Bells of Ireland 580
- Bells-of-Ireland 580
- Bellyache Root 066
- Beloperone 481
- Belvedere 118
- Bemgsag 191
- Ben 856
- Bengal Fig 360
- Benjamen 856
- Benne 818
- Bennet 395
- Bent El Consu 348
- Benzoin 856

- Berberis 122
- Berberis aquifolium 553
- Bereza 125
- Bergamot 224
- Bergamot Herb 581
- Bergamot Orange 224
- Berke 125
- Bermuda Arrowroot 561
- Bermuda Lily 517
- Bertholletia excelsa 123
- Besom 286
- Beta vulgaris 124
- Betaine 844
- Beth 125
- Beth 891
- Beth Root 891
- Bethlehem Sage 730
- Betonica 842
- Betonica officinalis 844
- Betonie 844
- Betony 842
- Betony 844
- Bettie Grass 030
- Betula 125
- Bevu 114
- Bhutanashini 011
- Bible Leaf 869
- Bibo Tree 057
- Bicuiba Acu 589
- Big Laurel 549
- Big Leaf Periwinkle 923
- Big Rhododendron 749
- Bigarade Orange 226
- Bigleaf Laurel 749
- Bigleaf Periwinkle 923
- Bignonia radicans 162
- Bijozakura 916
- Bilberry 906

- Bilberry 907
- Billardiera 126
- Bindweed 461
- Bindwood 412
- Birch 125
- Birch Tree 125
- Bird Cherry 717
- Bird Cherry 723
- Bird Wheat 698
- Bird of Paradise 853
- Bird's-nest 293
- Bird's-nest Plant 293
- Bird's-nest Root 293
- Birdfoot Deervetch 535
- Bird's Eye 931
- Bird's Eye Speed-well 917
- Bird's-Foot Trefoil 535
- Bird's-eye Speed-well 917
- Biscuits 705
- Bishop of Llandaff 287
- Bishopwort 844
- Bishop's Flower 293
- Bisom 286
- Bison Grass 070
- Bistora 656
- Bistort 656
- Bistort 697
- Biting Crowfoot 742
- Bitter Almond 720
- Bitter Ash 735
- Bitter Bark 747
- Bitter Buckwheat 354
- Bitter Buttons 871
- Bitter Grass 030
- Bitter Nightshade 830
- Bitter Orange 224
- Bitter Orange 226

- Bitter-Cress 168
- Bittercress 168
- Bitterklee 574
- Bittersweet 184
- Bittersweet 830
- Bittersweet Night-shade 830
- Bitterweed 054
- Bizzon 286
- Black Arum 318
- Black Bean 661
- Black Bryony 306
- Black Bugbane 012
- Black Cherry 110
- Black Cohosh 012
- Black Currant 752
- Black Dragon 318
- Black Elder 796
- Black Hellebore 426
- Black Mulberry 584
- Black Nightshade 449
- Black Pepper 678
- Black Poplar 701
- Black Root 030
- Black Sampson 326
- Black Snakeroot 012
- Black Tang 375
- Black Tany 375
- Black Tea 161
- Black Turtle Bean 661
- Black Vetch 922
- Black Widow 392
- Black Wort 859
- Black-Eyed Susan 778
- Black-Hearts 907
- Blackberry 775
- Blackcurrant 752
- Blackeyed Susan 778
- Blackihead 778
- Blackthorn 726
- Bladder Fucus 375

- Bladder Hibiscus 434
- Bladder Ketmia 434
- Bladder Nut Tree 845
- Bladder Senna 245
- Bladder Weed 434
- Bladder Wrack 375
- Bladder-Senna 245
- Bladdernut 845
- Bladderwrack 375
- Blaeberry 907
- Blaeberry 907
- Blanket Leaf 914
- Blazing Star 030
- Blazing Star 509
- Blazing-Star 509
- Bleeding Heart 491
- Blero 052
- Blessed Bramble 775
- Blessed Herb 395
- Blessed Milk Thistle 827
- Blessed Thistle 236
- Bletia pumila 181
- Blind Buff 636
- Blindeyes 636
- Blisterwort 742
- Blood Drops 015
- Blood Flower 099
- Blood Root 099
- Blood Turnip 124
- Blood-flower 099
- Blooddrops 015
- Bloodflower 099
- Bloodroot 099
- Bloodroot 705
- Bloodroot 797
- Bloodweed 054
- Bloodwort 797
- Bloody Butcher 912
- Bloody William 821
- Blowball 872
- Blue African Lily 021
- Blue Balm 569
- Blue Bindweed 830

- Camphire 217
- Camphire 500
- Camphor Laurel 217
- Camphor Tree 217
- Camphorwood 217
- Campion 820
- Campsis radicans 162
- Canada Lily 514
- Canada Root 100
- Canada Tea 384
- Canary Bean 661
- Canary Grass 660
- Candleberry 031
- Candleberry 588
- Candlemas Bells 377
- Candlenut 031
- Candlewick Plant 914
- Candytuft 453
- Cane Apple 081
- Cane Cholla 281
- Canelo 319
- Canker-wort 872
- Cankerwort 816
- Cankerwort 872
- Cannabis sativa 163
- Cannellini Bean 661
- Canoe Plant 463
- Canoewood 526
- Canterbury Bells 158
- Caparrones Bean 661
- Cape Dandelion 082
- Cape Gum 004
- Cape Jasmine 383
- Cape Jessamine 383
- Cape Marigold 082
- Cape Weed 082
- Caper Berry Bush 164
- Caper Bush 164
- Caperberry Bush 164
- Capon's Trailer 912
- Capparis spinosa 164
- Caprifolium 165
- Capsella bursa-pastoris 166
- Capsicum 167
- Capucine 764
- Capucine Briar 764
- Caraota o Habichu-ela Negra Bean 661
- Caraway 174
- Cardamine 168
- Cardamine praten-sis 169
- Cardamom 327
- Cardamon 327
- Cardinal Creeper 467
- Cardinal Flower 528
- Cardinal Vine 467
- Cardo-ananaz 448
- Carduaceae 105
- Carduus 170
- Carenfil 863
- Carica papaya 171
- Carnation 300
- Caro 174
- Carob Tree 194
- Caroba 194
- Carobinha 194
- Carolina Jasmine 386
- Carolina Jessamine 386
- Carolina Rose 761
- Carota 293
- Carotte 293
- Caroube 194
- Caroubier 194
- Carpathian Walnut 478
- Carpenter's Weed 008
- Carpenter's Weed 826
- Carpet Bugle 027
- Carphephorus odo-ratissimus 172
- Carpinus 173
- Carrizo 097
- Carrot 293
- Carrubba 194
- Cart Track Plant 684
- Carthage Apple 733
- Carum 174
- Carum carvi 174
- Carya 478
- Carya illinoinensis 175
- Carya oliviformis 175
- Carya ovata 176
- Carya pecan 175
- Caryophyllus aro-maticus 863
- Cascading Gera-nium 649
- Cascalotte 911
- Cascara 747
- Cascara Buckthorn 747
- Cascara Sagrada 747
- Cascarilla 270
- Casha 911
- Casha Tree 911
- Cashaw 911
- Cashew Apple Tree 057
- Cashew Nut Tree 057
- Cashew Tree 057
- Cashia 911
- Caspia 522
- Cassia 911
- Cassic 911
- Cassie 911
- Cassie Flower 911
- Cassie-Flower 911
- Cassiniaceae 105
- Castan-wydden 177
- Castanea 177
- Cat 599
- Cat Tail 901
- Cat-O'-Nine-Tails 901
- Catalonian Jasmine 476
- Catalpa 178
- Catananche caeru-lea 179
- Catawba 178
- Catbrier 829
- Catchfly 820
- Catchfly 932
- Catchweed 379
- Cathartocarpus 817
- Cathedral Bells 237
- Catmint 599
- Catnep 599
- Catnip 599
- Cato-barse 448
- Catrup 599
- Cats Tail 901
- Catsfoot 398
- Catshair 347
- Catspaw 068
- Catswort 599
- Cattail 901
- Cattleya 180
- Cattleya Orchid 180
- Cattleya deckeri 408
- Cattleya laelioides 408
- Cattleya marginata 181
- Cattleya pachecoi 408
- Cattleya pinelli 181
- Cattleya pumila 181
- Cattleya pumila ma-jor 181
- Cattleya skinneri 408
- Cattleya spectabilis 181

- Chinese Hibiscus 432
- Chinese Hibiscus 763
- Chinese Lantern Mallow 002
- Chinese Leek 039
- Chinese Magnolia 552
- Chinese Parsley 255
- Chinese Pearl Barley 242
- Chinese Primrose 710
- Chinese Ragwort 828
- Chinese Rose 763
- Chinese Star Anise 457
- Chinese Wisteria 940
- Chinkapin 177
- Chinquapin 177
- Chintachettu 867
- Chintapandu 867
- Chiranthodendron pentadactylon 206
- Chistotel 740
- Chittam 747
- Chittarattai 045
- Chitticum 747
- Chives 038
- Chlorophytum comosum 207
- Chorizema varium 208
- Chornobylnik 095
- Christmas Aconite 424
- Christmas Cactus 808
- Christmas Eve Flower 348
- Christmas Flower 348
- Christmas Holly 455

- Christmas Orchid 067
- Christmas Rose 424
- Christmasberry 807
- Christ's Story Flower 640
- Christ's Tears 242
- Chrysanth 209
- Chrysanthemum 209
- Chrysanthemum Weed 095
- Chrysanthemum leucanthemum 507
- Chrysanthemum morifolium 210
- Chrysanthemum parthenium 870
- Chrysocoma linosyris 211
- Chrysopogon zizanioides 212
- Chuan Gu 242
- Chui-Mui 577
- Chuimui 577
- Church Flower 377
- Church Steeples 025
- Cháhua 155
- Châtaigne 177
- Cicely 591
- Cichoriaceae 105
- Cichorium endivia 213
- Cichorium intybus 214
- Cieca 270
- Cierge-Lézard 448
- Cigar Tree 178
- Cilantro 255
- Cilentro 255
- Cimicifuga racemosa 012
- Cinchona 215
- Cineraria 216
- Cinnamomum camphora 217

- Cinnamomum verum 218
- Cinnamomum zeylanicum 218
- Cinnamon 218
- Cinnamon Rose 767
- Cinnamon Tree 218
- Cinnamon Wood 802
- Cinquefoil 704
- Circaea 219
- Circaea lutetiana 219
- Cirsium 220
- Cistaceae 221
- Cistus ladanifer 222
- Citron 225
- Citronella Grass 282
- Citronelle 569
- Citrullus lanatus 223
- Citrus aurantium bergamia 224
- Citrus bergamia 224
- Citrus limon 228
- Citrus medica 225
- Citrus sinensis 229
- Citrus tangerina 230
- Citrus x aurantium 226
- Citrus x latifolia 227
- Citrus x limon 228
- Cittim Bark 747
- Civet 038
- Ciwappuccantanam 729
- Clamoun 483
- Clarkia amoena 231
- Clary 794
- Clary Sage 794
- Clasping Venus's Looking Glass 892
- Clausenellia 814
- Clavarioidia 621

- Clavo de Olor 863
- Cleaver Grass 888
- Cleavers 379
- Clematis 232
- Clementine 230
- Cleodora 270
- Cleome 233
- Clianthus puniceus 234
- Climbing Nightshade 830
- Clinging Woodbine 386
- Clistoyucca 945
- Clitoria 235
- Clivers 379
- Closed Bottle Gentian 388
- Closed Gentian 388
- Clot 914
- Clotbur 084
- Clotbur 943
- Cloth of Gold Yarrow 007
- Cloth-Of-Gold 007
- Clou de Girofle 863
- Cloudberrry 775
- Clouded Geranium 647
- Clouded Stork's-bill 647
- Clove 863
- Clove Pepper 669
- Clove Pink 300
- Clove Root 395
- Clover 887
- Clover 888
- Cloveroot 395
- Club Moss 542
- Clumpfoot Cabbage 860
- Cnicus 236
- Cnicus benedictus 236
- Coachweed 379
- Coakum 667
- Cobaea scandens 237
- Coca Plant 339

- Cocan 667
- Cochlearia armoracia 091
- Cockerellia 814
- Cockle 530
- Cocklebur 025
- Cockleburr 084
- Cockscomb 185
- Cockscomb Amaranth 185
- Cockup hat 850
- Cock's Head 413
- Coco 238
- Cocoa 876
- Cocoa Tree 876
- Cocoanut 238
- Coconut 238
- Coconut Palm 238
- Cocos nucifera 238
- Cocoxochitl 287
- Codariocalyx motorius 239
- Codonocalyx 270
- Coeloglossum viride 240
- Coffea 241
- Coffee 241
- Coffee Tree 241
- Coffeeweed 214
- Coix 242
- Coix Seed 242
- Coix lacryma-jobi 242
- Coixseed 242
- Colchicum autumnale 243
- Coleonema 244
- Colewort 395
- Colic Root 030
- Colicroot 030
- Colicweed 030
- Colocasia aethiopica 947
- Coltsfoot 900
- Columbia Lily 516
- Columbine 078
- Colutea 245
- Colutea arborescens 245

- Comarobatia 775
- Comatocroton 270
- Comet Orchid 067
- Comfrey 859
- Commiphora gileadensis 246
- Commiphora opobalsamum 246
- Common Agrimony 025
- Common Ash 370
- Common Aspen 702
- Common Balloon Flower 687
- Common Bamboo 116
- Common Basil 609
- Common Bean 661
- Common Bearberry 085
- Common Bilberry 907
- Common Bistort 656
- Common Blackberry 775
- Common Blue Violet 930
- Common Bluebell 442
- Common Bracken 727
- Common Broom 286
- Common Buckthorn 746
- Common Buckwheat 354
- Common Bugloss 061
- Common Bulrush 901
- Common Carrot 293
- Common Cattail 901
- Common Chickory 214

- Common Cocklebur 943
- Common Corn Cockle 026
- Common Corncockle 026
- Common Cornflower 187
- Common Cranberry 908
- Common Crape Myrtle 489
- Common Daisy 120
- Common Dandelion 872
- Common Daylily 427
- Common Elder 796
- Common Fig 361
- Common Flax 524
- Common Foxglove 304
- Common Gardenia 383
- Common Gorse 902
- Common Grape Hyacinth 586
- Common Grape Vine 935
- Common Hazel 260
- Common Heather 149
- Common Hollyhock 028
- Common Honeysuckle 533
- Common Hop 441
- Common Horehound 563
- Common Horse Chestnut 018
- Common Hyacinth 443
- Common Ivy 412
- Common Jasmine 477
- Common Laburnum 486

- Common Laurel 722
- Common Lavender 498
- Common Lilac 862
- Common Male Fern 322
- Common Mallow 558
- Common Marigold 147
- Common Marigold 864
- Common Marshmallow 047
- Common Meadow Violet 930
- Common Mistletoe 933
- Common Monkshood 010
- Common Moonwort 129
- Common Myrtle 592
- Common Nettle 905
- Common Onion 035
- Common Passion Flower 640
- Common Peony 632
- Common Periwinkle 924
- Common Plantain 684
- Common Poppy 637
- Common Primrose 712
- Common Privet 511
- Common Reed 666
- Common Rue 783
- Common Sage 793
- Common Saint John's Wort 450

- Damasco 716
- Damascus Rose 772
- Damask 772
- Damask Rose 772
- Damask Violet 431
- Dames-Wort 431
- Dame's Gilliflower 431
- Dame's Rocket 431
- Dame's Violet 431
- Damiana 899
- Dandelion 872
- DaoRung 865
- Dao Ruang Lek 866
- Daphne 288
- Daphne cneorum 289
- Daphne mezereum 290
- Daphne odora 291
- Dark Geranium 392
- Darnel 530
- Darwin's Orchid 067
- Date Palm 665
- Date-Plum 309
- Datura 292
- Daucon 293
- Daucus carota 293
- David's Harp 696
- David's Tears 242
- David's-Harp 696
- Dawadawa 867
- Dawke 293
- Day Lily 427
- Day Lily 438
- Daylily 427
- Dead Finish 911
- Dead Man's Bells 304
- Dead Nettle 066
- Deadly Nightshade 110
- Death Cherries 110
- Death Flower 008
- Deathcamas 953
- Death's Herb 110
- Decarinium 270

- Deer Vetch 535
- Deerberry 384
- Deerstongue 509
- Deertongue Laurel 749
- Deer's Tongue 172
- Delight of The Eye 834
- Delonix regia 294
- Delphinium 295
- Demir Hindi 867
- Dendrobium 296
- Dendrobium Orchid 296
- Dendrobium tetra-gonum 297
- Dendrobychis 614
- Dendrocoryne te-tragonum 297
- Dent de Lion 872
- Dentaria 168
- Deri 287
- Desert Cabbage 482
- Desert Candles 333
- Desert-Rose 013
- Deveseel 508
- Devil Brushes 728
- Devil Pepper 744
- Devil in the Bush 602
- Devil's-plague 293
- Devil-pepper 744
- Devils and Angels 096
- Devil's Apple 292
- Devil's Apple 690
- Devil's Bane 916
- Devil's Berries 110
- Devil's Bit 030
- Devil's Bit 857
- Devil's Bit Scabious 857
- Devil's Cherries 110
- Devil's Cucumber 292
- Devil's Dung 357
- Devil's Eye 449
- Devil's Eye 924

- Devil's Flower 187
- Devil's Guts 277
- Devil's Hair 277
- Devil's Hand Tree 206
- Devil's Ivy 331
- Devil's Milk 201
- Devil's Nettle 008
- Devil's Oatmeal 658
- Devil's Porridge 247
- Devil's Ringlet 277
- Devil's Shoestring 603
- Devil's Tongue 799
- Devil's Trumpet 292
- Devil's Turnip 140
- Devil's Weed 292
- Devil's-shoestring 603
- Dew Plant 076
- Dew of the Sea 773
- Dew-cup 029
- Dewberry 775
- Dewcup 029
- Dhan 628
- Dhania 255
- Diallobus 817 818
- Diamorpha 814
- Dianthera 481
- Dianthus 298
- Dianthus barbatus 299
- Dianthus caryophyl-lus 300
- Dianthus chinensis 301
- Diatremis 461
- Dicentra spectabilis 491
- Diclytra spectabilis 491
- Dictamnus 302
- Dictamnus albus 302
- Didier's Tulip 898
- Dierama 303
- Digitalis purpurea 304

- Diglossus 864
- Diktamo 624
- Dill 065
- Dill Weed 065
- Dillisk 750
- Dilly 065
- Dilsk 750
- Dimanisa 481
- Dimerodisus 461
- Dingle-Dangle 377
- Dinosaur Plant 060
- Dinteracanthus 779
- Dionaea muscipula 305
- Dios Pyros 309
- Dioscorea commu-nis 306
- Diosma 022
- Diosma 244
- Diosphaera 157
- Diospyros 307
- Diospyros ebenum 308
- Diospyros lotus 309
- Dipladenia 559
- Diplopappus asper-rimus 106
- Diplopappus laxus 106
- Diplothrix 954
- Dipsacus fullonum 310
- Dipteracanthus 779
- Dipteracanthus spectabilis 779
- Dipteryx odorata 311
- Dipteryx tetraphylla 311
- Discipiper 675
- Distelbirne 448
- Ditch Lily 428
- Dittany of Crete 624
- Divale 110
- Divine Flower 300
- Divine Tree 114
- Divya 191
- Dlavero Giroflé 863

- Dock 782
- Dodder 277
- Dodecatheon 312
- Doffle 914
- Dog Bane 600
- Dog Blow 507
- Dog Daisy 507
- Dog Rose 760
- Dog Standard 816
- Dog-Strangling Vine 283
- Dogbane 075
- Dogon Yaro 114
- Dogtooth Violet 338
- Dogtree 258
- Dogwood 257
- Dog's Finger 304
- Dog's Mouth 072
- Dog's Tooth Violet 338
- Dog's-Tooth Violet 338
- Dok Ratree 196
- Dollar Plant 265
- Dollof 364
- Dolly Flower 931
- Dongbaek-kkot 155
- Doomoor 361
- Dooryard Plantain 684
- Dormilona 577
- Double Cinnamon Rose 767
- Double Daisy 121
- Dovetail Moss 804
- Downy Yellow Violet 929
- Dracaena 313
- Dracaena arborea 314
- Dracaena cinnabari 315
- Dracaena reflexa 316
- Dracaena sanderi-ana 317
- Dracaena terminalis 252
- Drachenfrucht 448

- Dracontium foeti-dum 860
- Dracunculus vul-garis 318
- Dragon Arum 318
- Dragon Blood Tree 315
- Dragon Herb 094
- Dragon Plant 313
- Dragon Root 088
- Dragon's Teeth 536
- Dragon's-Teeth 536
- Dragon's-Tooth 536
- Dragon Tree 314
- Dragon Wort 094
- Dragonfruit 448
- Dragonwort 318
- Dragonwort 656
- Dragon's Blood Tree 315
- Dragon's Herb 094
- Dragon's Wort 094
- Dragon's-wort 094
- Drakondia 318
- Drejerella 481
- Drelip 711
- Drepadenium 270
- Drimys 319
- Drimys winteri 319
- Dropberry 695
- Dropsy Plant 569
- Drosera rotundifolia 320
- Drunkard 147
- Drunkards 864
- Dryas 321
- Dryopteris filix-mas 322
- Drypetes australa-sica 323
- Drypetes de-planchei 323
- Duchesnea 704
- Duchesnea indica 706
- Duck's Foot 690
- Duir 737
- Dulse 750
- Dumur 361

- Dun Daisy 507
- Dungwort 425
- Duranta erecta 324
- Duranta repens 324
- Durian Tree 325
- Durio 325
- Dusky Cranesbill 392
- Dusky Salmon 540
- Dusty Miller 821
- Dutch Amaryllis 053
- Dutch Hyacinth 443
- Dutch Morgan 507
- Dutch White Clover 889
- Dutchman's Britches 491
- Dutchman's Trou-sers 491
- Duvaua 807
- Duvernoia 481
- Dwale 110
- Dwaleberry 110
- Dwarf Honeysuckle 534
- Dwarf Rose 766
- Dwarf Sophronitis 181
- Dway Berry 110
- Dwayberry 110
- Dyers Fucus 375
- Dyer's Rocket 745
- Dysphania botrys 204

E
- Eardrops 491
- Earleocassia 817, 818
- Early Purple Orchid 623
- Earth Apple 418
- Earth Star 271
- Earthbank 705
- Easter Flower 348
- Easter Flower 731
- Easter Giant 656
- Easter Ledger 656

- Easter Ledges 656
- Easter Lily 517
- Easter Lily 947
- Easter Magiant 656
- Easter Man-Giant 656
- Eastern Skunk Cabbage 860
- Eastern Teaberry 384
- Eastern Wahoo 345
- Ebegümeci 558
- Ebony 307
- Ebony 308
- Echinacea 326
- Echtes Eisenkraut 916
- Ecorce Sacree 747
- Edelweiss 503
- Edible Burdock 084
- Eerie 008
- Egg Yolk Flower Tree 688
- Eggs and Bacon 535
- Eglantine Rose 770
- Egyptian Rose 806
- Egyptian Thorn 004
- Eight-Horn 407
- Ekpanni 191
- Ela 327
- Elachi 327
- Elaichi 327
- Elakkaai 327
- Elam 327
- Elder 795
- Elder 796
- Elder Bush 796
- Elder Flower 796
- Elderberry 795
- Elderberry 796
- Elecampane 460
- Elephant Ear 145
- Elephant Garlic 034
- Elettaria carda-momum 327
- Elettaria repens 327
- Elf 498

- Elf Leaf 773
- Elfwort 460
- Elijah's Chariot 295
- Elixir of Life 569
- Ellai 691
- Ellington's Curse 911
- Elm 903
- Eluteria 270
- Eléfantes Bean 661
- Emularia 481
- Enalcida 864
- Enchanter's Nightshade 219
- Enchanter's Plant 916
- Enchysia 527
- Endive 213
- Endosiphon 779
- Endro 065
- Enebro 480
- Engelmannia 270
- Engelmann's Ivy 639
- English Bluebell 442
- English Broom 286
- English Chamomile 069
- English Cowslip 712
- English Daisy 120
- English Hawthorn 266
- English Holly 455
- English Ivy 412
- English Laurel 722
- English Lavender 498
- English Mandrake 140
- English Marigold 147
- English Monkshood 010
- English Primrose 712
- English Valerian 912
- English Violet 928
- English Walnut 478
- English Wild Thyme 881
- Englishman's Foot 684
- Enola Bean 661
- Epidendrum huegelianum 408
- Epigaea repens 328
- Epilepis 253
- Epilobium 329
- Epilobium angustifolium 330
- Epipactis myodes 620
- Epiphyllum russellianum 808
- Epipremnum aureum 331
- Equisetum hyemale 332
- Er Hua 532
- Erdei Mályva 558
- Eremocarpus 270
- Eremurus 333
- Erhonghua 432
- Eriadenia 559
- Erica 149
- Erigeron 334
- Erigeron perennis 120
- Eriodictyon californicum 335
- Erioxylum 405
- Erontas 624
- Eruca 336
- Eruca sativa 336
- Erva Mate 456
- Erva-Mate 456
- Eryngium 337
- Eryngo 337
- Erysimum cheiri 200
- Erythraea 190
- Erythronium 338
- Erythronium denscanis 338
- Erythroxylum coca 339
- Eschalot 036
- Eschscholzia 340
- Espadaña común 901
- Esparceta 614
- Esparcette 614
- Esparsett 614
- Esparsette 614
- Espartset 614
- Esphand 642
- Espárrago 102
- Ethesia 481
- Etiosedum 814
- Etrog 225
- Eucalyptus 341
- Eucalyptus regnans 342
- Eucharis 343
- Eucharis Lily 343
- Eugenia aromatica 863
- Eugenia caryophyllat 863
- Eugenia caryophyllus 863
- Eukkie 341
- Euonymus 344
- Euonymus atropurpureus 345
- Eupatoriaceae 105
- Eupatorium 346
- Euphorbia 347
- Euphorbia pulcherrima 348
- Euphrasia 349
- Euphrasiae herba 349
- Eurasian Aspen 702
- Eurasian Smoketree 263
- European Ash 370
- European Aspen 702
- European Bird Cherry 723
- European Black Elderberry 796
- European Black Pine 672
- European Blackberry 775
- European Cornel 259
- European Cranberrybush 919
- European Elder 796
- European Elderberry 796
- European Fly Honeysuckle 534
- European Goldenrod 833
- European Holly 455
- European Honeysuckle 533
- European Michaelmas Daisy 106
- European Mistletoe 933
- European Mountain Ash 834
- European Pennyroyal 571
- European Peony 632
- European Privet 511
- European Raspberry 775
- European Raspberry 776
- European Sage 092
- European Strawberry 367
- European Venus' Looking Glass 839
- European White Waterlily 606
- European Wild Angelica 066
- Euryangium Ferula sumbul 358
- Eustoma 350
- Euthrochium 351

- Holy Wood 933
- Homoeos 461
- Honesty 537
- Honey 887
- Honey Flower 568
- Honey Leaf 569
- Honey Locust 399
- Honey-ball 911
- Honeypot 714
- Honeystalks 887
- Honeysuckle 533
- Honeysuckle Clover 888
- Hongfusang 432
- Hongmujin 432
- Hooded Violet 930
- Hoodwort 811
- Hop 441
- Hop Marjoram 624
- Hordeum vulgare 437
- Horehound 563
- Hornbeam 173
- Horse Blob 151
- Horse Daisy 507
- Horse Foot 900
- Horse Gentian 893
- Horse Gowan 507
- Horse Violet 931
- Horse-Heal 460
- Horse-Radish 091
- Horsehoe Geranium 652
- Horsemint 581
- Horseradish 091
- Horseradish Root 091
- Horsetail Rush 332
- Hortel 570
- Hortelã 570
- Hortensia 446
- Hosen-ka 458
- Hosta 438
- Hostaceae 438
- Hot Bo Bo 242
- Hot Capsicum 167
- Hot Peppers 167
- Hot Water Plant 009

- Hound's Tongue 509
- Houseleek 815
- Houstonia 439
- Houstonia caerulea 439
- Hoya 440
- Hreow 783
- Hreri 512
- Hrrt 512
- Hrry 512
- Hti Ka Yoan 577
- Hu-Sui 255
- Huauhtli 052
- Huautli 050
- Huckleberry 909
- Huckleberry's Blanket 727
- Huisache 911
- Hulthemia 757
- Hulthemia x Rosa 757
- Hulwa 065
- Humble Plant 577
- Hummingbird Vine 162
- Hummingbird Vine 467
- Humulus lupulus 441
- Hunase 867
- Hundred Eyes 924
- Hundred Leaved Grass 008
- Hundred-Leaved Rose 762
- Hundred-Petaled Rose 762
- Huohonghua 432
- Huolóngguo 448
- Hurrburr 084
- Hurtleberry 907
- Hurts 907
- Hurtsickle 187
- Husan t'sao 429
- Husbandman's Dial 147
- Hvonn 066
- Hvönn 066

- Hyacinth 443
- Hyacinthoides non-scripta 442
- Hyacinthus orientalis 443
- Hybrid Perpetual Rose 444
- Hybrid Tea 445
- Hybrid Tea Rose 445
- Hybrides remontants 444
- Hydrangea 446
- Hydrastis canadensis 447
- Hydrocotyle asiatica 191
- Hylan Tree 796
- Hylder 796
- Hylocereus tricostatus 448
- Hylocereus undatus 448
- Hylotelephium 814
- Hyoscyamus niger 449
- Hypericum perforatum 450
- Hypocalymma angustifolium 451
- Hyssop 452
- Hyssopus 452
- Hyssopus decumbens 452
- Hyssopus officinalis 452

I

- IJzerhard 916
- Iberis 453
- Iberis sempervirens 454
- Ice Flower 503
- Ice Plant 576
- Iceland Moss 197
- Icho 396
- Icicle Plant 576
- Ilex 455
- Ilex aquifolium 455

- Ilex paraguariensis 456
- Ilima 819
- Illicium verum 457
- Imli 867
- Immortal Flower 944
- Immortality Plant 041
- Immortelles 419
- Impatiens 458
- Impatiens 459
- Impatiens balsamina 458
- Impatiens sultanii 459
- Impatiens walleriana 459
- Impatient 458
- Imperial Lily 372
- In Xìng 396
- Inca Lily 046
- Incensier 773
- India Ebony 308
- India Fig 360
- Indian Apple 292
- Indian Apple 690
- Indian Arrow Wood 345
- Indian Arrowwood 258
- Indian Bean Tree 178
- Indian Cress 896
- Indian Date 867
- Indian Elm 904
- Indian Fig Opuntia 621
- Indian Fig Tree 360
- Indian Ginseng 941
- Indian God Tree 360
- Indian Hemp 075
- Indian Hyacinth 154
- Indian Jasmine 461
- Indian Lagerstroemia 489
- Indian Lilac 114

- Indian Lotus 598
- Indian Mallow 002
- Indian Nettle 581
- Indian Nut 238
- Indian Paint 797
- Indian Paint Brush 100
- Indian Paintbrush 100
- Indian Pennywort 191
- Indian Pink 528
- Indian Plant 797
- Indian Plum 610
- Indian Posy 100
- Indian Red Paint 797
- Indian Root 891
- Indian Saffron 276
- Indian Sandalwood Tree 800
- Indian Strawberry 706
- Indian Tobacco 527
- Indian Turnip 096
- Indian Walnut 031
- Indian Whiskey 292
- Indian-cup 826
- Industrial Hemp Plant 163
- Inermis Rose 769
- Ingenhouzia 405
- Ingu 357
- Ingua 357
- Inkberry 667
- Intybus 214
- Inula helenium 460
- Inulaceae 105
- Ipomoea 461
- Ipomoea alba 462
- Ipomoea batatas 463
- Ipomoea coccinea 464
- Ipomoea cordatotri-loba 465
- Ipomoea jalapa 466
- Ipomoea quamoclit 467

- Iraakuuccittam 034
- Iridorchis 279
- Iris 468
- Iris germanica 469
- Iris pseudacorus 470
- Iris versicolor 471
- Irish Broom 286
- Irish Daisy 872
- Irish Moss 086
- Irish Potato 832
- Irish Strawberry Tree 081
- Irish Tops 286
- Iron Cross 631
- Iron Wood 911
- Isandrina 817
- Isatis indigotica 472
- Isatis tinctoria 472
- Isband 642
- Isolobus 527
- Italian Fitch 378
- Italian Parsley 658
- Italian Woodbine 531
- Itburunu 760
- Itm 613
- Ivraie 530
- Ivy 412
- Ivy Geranium 649
- Ivy Vine 412
- Ivy-Leaf Geranium 649
- Ivybush 483
- Ixia 473
- Ixora 474
- Ixora coccinea 474
- Ixtlania 481

J
- Jaba 432
- Jacaranda 475
- Jacaranda acutifolia 475
- Jacaranda mimosi-folia 475
- Jack in Prison 602

- Jack in the Pulpit 096
- Jack-in-the-Pulpit 096
- Jacobinia 481
- Jacob's Ladder 692
- Jacob's Tears 249
- Jacob's Tears 517
- Jade Plant 265
- Jaggy Nettle 905
- Jali 242
- Jaljala 818
- Jamaica Dogwood 679
- Jamaica Pepper 669
- Jamaican Dogwood 679
- Jamaican Pepper 669
- Jambu Monyet 057
- Jamestown Weed 292
- Japan Rose 156
- Japan Rose 771
- Japanese Bellflower 687
- Japanese Camellia 156
- Japanese Easter Lily 517
- Japanese Flowering Crabapple 555
- Japanese Honey-suckle 532
- Japanese Lily 519
- Japanese Quince 198
- Japanese Rose 771
- Japonica 198
- Jara Pringosa 222
- Jarjeer 336
- Jarum-Jarum 474
- Jasmine 477
- Jasminum grandi-florum 476
- Jasminum officinale 477
- Jaswand 432

- Jat 567
- Jatamansi 358
- Jatil 011
- Jatropha moluccana
- Java Pepper 676
- Javanese Asam 867
- Javanese Sour 867
- Javas 524
- Jawa 867
- Jawas 524
- Jawz Hindi 238
- Jensoa 279
- Jeongguji 039
- Jericho Rose 060
- Jerusalem Artichoke 418
- Jerusalem Cowslip 730
- Jerusalem Cross 540
- Jerusalem Oak 204
- Jerusalem Oak Goosefoot 204
- Jessamine 386
- Jessamine 477
- Jesuit's Balsam 807
- Jesuit's Bark Tree 215
- Jesus Flower 640
- Jewelweed 458
- Ji Xing 458
- Jiamudan 432
- Jie Geng 687
- Jiimsonweed 292
- Jimson Weed 292
- Jin Yín Hua 532
- Jinchoge 291
- Jindilli 547
- Jinn's Tongue 799
- Jinyinhua 532
- Jiu Cai 039
- Jobs Tears 242
- Job's Tears 242
- Jocote 841
- Joe-Pye Weed 351
- Johannisbrotbaum 194

378

- Madagascar Vanilla 913
- Madder 774
- Madderwort 093
- Madherb 292
- Madonna Lily 515
- Madrona 080
- Madrone 080
- Madroño 080
- Madweed 811
- Magee-bin 867
- Magee-thee 867
- Maggikraut 508
- Maggiplant 508
- Magic Flowers 009
- Magic Lily 952
- Magnolia acuminata 548
- Magnolia grandiflora 549
- Magnolia splendens 550
- Magnolia virginiana 551
- Magnolia x soulan-geana 552
- Maguey 023
- Maha Aushadhi 191
- Mahonia aquifolium 553
- Mai-Luang 116
- Maia 585
- Maidenhair Fern 014
- Maidenhair Tree 396
- Maids Of February 377
- Maid's Hair 382
- Maid's Ruin 092
- Maikoa 138
- Maile 049
- Maile Vine 049
- Maize 950
- Majjigegadde 102
- Majorana hortensis 625
- Makahiya 577

- Makhorka 601
- Malabars Temga 238
- Malaxis myodes 620
- Malba 558
- Male Fern 322
- Male Lily 249
- Malicorio 733
- Malinche 294
- Mallow 556
- Malpitte 292
- Maltese Cross 540
- Malum Granatum 733
- Malum Punicum 733
- Malus domestica 554
- Malus floribunda 555
- Malva 556
- Malva 558
- Malva Común 558
- Malva ambigua 558
- Malva de Cementiri 558
- Malva erecta 558
- Malva gymnocarpa 558
- Malva mauritiana 558
- Malva moschata 557
- Malva silvestre 558
- Malva silvestre 558
- Malva sylvestris 558
- Malvaceae 556
- Malvo granda 558
- Mamarutza 558
- Mamdaram 432
- Man Root 634
- Mancanilla 436
- Manchineel Tree 436
- Mancinella 436
- Mandarin Orange 230

- Mandevilla 559
- Mandookaparni 191
- Mandragora 560
- Mandrake 560
- Mandrake Root 560
- Manduckaparni 191
- Manduki 191
- Mandukparni 191
- Mang tây 102
- Mangel 124
- Mangles' Kangaroo Paw 068
- Mangold 124
- Manicon 292
- Manimuni 191
- Manjal 276
- Manjushage 543
- Manna Grass 070
- Manzanilla 069
- Manzanilla 870
- Manzanilla del la muerte 436
- Mapacho 601
- Maple 006
- Maple Tree 006
- Mapou 077
- Maracoc 640
- Maranta arundina-cea 561
- Maranta galanaga 045
- Marantaceae 562
- Marathron 365
- Marañón Tree 057
- Marchalan 460
- Marcory 850
- Margosa 114
- Marguerite 507
- Marian Thistle 827
- Marianthus 126
- Marica 678
- Marigold 147
- Marigold 864
- Marigold of Peru 416
- Marijuana 163

- Marine Heliotrope 422
- Marjoram 625
- Markery 203
- Marl Grass 888
- Marmalade Bush 854
- Marmalade Orange 226
- Marmaredda 558
- Maroochi Nut 547
- Marrubium vulgare 563
- Marsh Everlasting 403
- Marsh Mallow 047
- Marsh Marigold 151
- Marsh-Rosemary 521
- Marshall's Large Yellow Sweet Plum 715
- Marshmallow 047
- Marshmellow 047
- Marshwort 074
- Marva 558
- Marvel of Peru 578
- Mary Flower 693
- Mary Gold 151
- Mary Thistle 827
- Marybud 147
- Marygold 866
- Mary's Flower 060
- Mary's Gold 147
- Mary's Gold 864
- Mary's Grass 070
- Mary's Hand 060
- Mary's Tapers 377
- Mary's Tears 517
- Marzanilla 436
- Master of the Woods 380
- Mastic Tree 680
- Mate 456
- Mateloi 577
- Mathiola 564
- Matthiola 564

- Matthiola incana 565
- Maudlinwort 507
- Maurandya barclaiana 566
- Maurandya barclayana 566
- Mauve Sylvestre 558
- Mauve des Bois 558
- May 266
- May Apple 690
- May Bells 249
- May Blobs 151
- May Blossom 266
- May Bush 266
- May Flower 266
- May Flower 328
- May Lily 249
- May Tree 266
- Mayapple 690
- Mayflower 151
- Mayflower 328
- Mayflower 690
- Mayocoba Bean 661
- Maypops 640
- Maythen 069
- Mazzard 717
- Mañjusaka 543
- Mbiba 057
- Mburucuyá 640
- Me 867
- Meadow Anemone 731
- Meadow Buttercup 738
- Meadow Cabbage 860
- Meadow Clover 888
- Meadow Garlic 037
- Meadow Lily 514
- Meadow Lychnis 541
- Meadow Queen 364
- Meadow Rue 875
- Meadow Saffron 243
- Meadow Sweet 364
- Meadow-Wort 364
- Meadowsweet 364
- Meadsweet 364
- Mealberry 085
- Mealie 950
- Mealy Starwort 030
- Mealy Wattle 911
- Medea 270
- Median 225
- Medicago sativa 567
- Medicinal Aloe 041
- Medicine Plant 041
- Medick 567
- Mediterranean Milk Thistle 827
- Medunitza 730
- Meelplakkie 482
- Meet-Me-In-The-Entry 931
- Melagrana 733
- Melampode 426
- Melegueta Pepper 020
- Melia 688
- Melianthus major 568
- Melissa 569
- Melissa officinalis 569
- Melograno 733
- Mendezia 954
- Menta balsamea 572
- Mente Tree 057
- Mentha 570
- Mentha piperita 572
- Mentha pulegium 571
- Mentha spicata 573
- Mentha x piperita 572
- Menthya 890
- Menti 890
- Menyanthes trifoliata 574
- Mercurialis 575
- Mercury 575
- Meridian Fennel 174
- Merleta 270
- Mesembrianthemum 576
- Mesembryanthemum 576
- Mesembryanthemum cordifolium 076
- Mesk el-leel 196
- Mesquite 713
- Meterostachys 814
- Methi 890
- Methya 890
- Mets-kassinaeris 558
- Mexican Butterfly Weed 099
- Mexican Damiana 899
- Mexican Fireweed 118
- Mexican Georgiana 287
- Mexican Hand Tree 206
- Mexican Holly 455
- Mexican Marigold 865
- Mexican Morning Glory 464
- Mexican Tree of Life and Abundance 023
- Mezereon 290
- Mezleria 527
- Mfungu 185
- Mgunga 004
- Michaelmas Daisy 106
- Midsummer Daisy 507
- Mielie 950
- Mignonette 745
- Mignonette Tree 500
- Mile-A-Minute 697
- Milefolium 008
- Milfoil 008
- Milho 950
- Militaris 008
- Military Herb 008
- Milk Thistle 827
- Milk-Vetch 109
- Milk-witch 872
- Milkvetch 109
- Milkweed 098
- Milkwort 694
- Millefoil 008
- Millefolium 008
- Mimosa 003
- Mimosa Bush 911
- Mimosa Wattle 911
- Mimosa acicularis 911
- Mimosa farnesiana 911
- Mimosa indica 911
- Mimosa pudica 577
- Mimosa suaveolens 911
- Mina 461
- Minart 395
- Minarta 395
- Mini Rainbow 148
- Mint 570
- Mint Geranium 869
- Miodunka 730
- Mirabilis jalapa 578
- Miracle Herb 859
- Miracle Plant 041
- Miracle of Nature 023
- Mirodjija 065
- Mirrot 293
- Mismin 573
- Missouri Goldenrod 833
- Mistletoe 933
- Misty 522
- Mitan 613
- Mitozus 559
- Mitraria 579
- Mitraria coccinea 579

- Mixochitl 693
- Mkanju 057
- Mkwatia 004
- Mkwayu 867
- Moccasin Flower 285
- Mock Orange 662
- Mock Strawberry 706
- Mock-Orange 662
- Modesty 434
- Mokala 004
- Mollyblobs 151
- Molokhia 251
- Molucca Balmis 580
- Moluccella laevis 580
- Monarda 581
- Monarda didyma 581
- Mondaro 432
- Monday Rose 765
- Money Plant 265
- Money Plant 331
- Money Plant 537
- Moneywort 544
- Monguia 270
- Monkeyflower 931
- Monkey's Hand Tree 206
- Monks-head 872
- Monkshood 010
- Monk's Blood 010
- Monk's Head 491
- Monk's Pepper 934
- Monk's Rhubarb 782
- Monotoca scoparia 582
- Montane Larkspur 295
- Monthly Honeysuckle 165
- Monthly Rose 763
- Moolee 091
- Moon Daisy 507
- Moon Flower 448
- Moon Flower 507

- Moon Laurel 497
- Moon Penny 507
- Moon Vine 462
- Moonflower 462
- Moonflower Vine 462
- Moonwort 129
- Moose Elm 904
- Moras 212
- Morera 584
- Moririr-Wa-Mafika 542
- Moriviví 577
- Morning Glory 461
- Mortificaton Root 047
- Morus alba 583
- Morus nigra 584
- Morí-viví 577
- Moschatel 016
- Moschuswurzel 358
- Mosquito Bills 312
- Mosquito Plant 571
- Mosquito Plant 916
- Moss 141
- Moss Rose 703
- Moss-Rose 703
- Moss-Rose Purslane 703
- Mossy Saxifrages 804
- Mother Of The Herbs 783
- Mother of Herbs 683
- Mother of The Wood 726
- Mother-In-Law's Tongue 799
- Mother-of-the-Evening 431
- Motherwort 504
- Mottled Bean 661
- Moundlily 946
- Mountain Ash 342
- Mountain Ash 834
- Mountain Balm 335
- Mountain Box 085

- Mountain Cowslip 709
- Mountain Cranberry 085
- Mountain Flax 694
- Mountain Laurel 483
- Mountain Laurel 749
- Mountain Lily 513
- Mountain Pasque 732
- Mountain Pink 951
- Mountain Tea 384
- Mountain Tobacco 085
- Mournful Widow 806
- Mourning Bride 806
- Mourning Widow 392
- Mouse-Ear Chickweed 193
- Mouse-Eared Scorpion-Grass 587
- Moving Plant 577
- Muarubaini 114
- Mucizonia 814
- Mudwort 523
- Muggons 095
- Mugua 171
- Muguet 249
- Mugunghwa 433
- Mugwort 095
- Mugwort 871
- Mulaithi 401
- Mullein 914
- Mullein-Pink 821
- Multi-Colored Blue Flag 471
- Multiflora Rose 769
- Mulukhiyah 251
- Mum 870
- Mums 209
- Mundi Rose 765
- Mundy Rose 765
- Murangi 116
- Murphies 832
- Musa 585

- Musa acuminata 585
- Musa acuminata x balbisiana 585
- Musa balbisiana 585
- Musa cliffortiana 585
- Musa dacca 585
- Musa paradisiaca 585
- Musa rosacea 585
- Musa sapientum 585
- Musa violacea 585
- Musa x paradisiaca 585
- Musa x sapientum 585
- Muscari 586
- Musk Mallow 557
- Musk Root 358
- Musk Rose 768
- Musk-mallow 557
- Muskroot 016
- Muskroot 358
- Muskroot 597
- Musquash Root 247
- Mustard Plant 134
- Mustard and Cress 505
- Mutisiaceae 105
- Mutterkraut 870
- Mwanzi 116
- Mykhet 863
- Myosotis 587
- Myrica 588
- Myriogomphus 270
- Myristica fragrans 589
- Myrobalan Plum 718
- Myroxylon 590
- Myrrh Plant 591
- Myrrhis 071
- Myrrhis odorata 591
- Myrtle 592

- Nymphaeaceae 608

O

- Oak Geranium 650
- Oak Tree 736
- Oak-Leaf Geranium 650
- Oakleaf Geranium 650
- Oat 113
- Obedience Plant 561
- Ocalia 270
- Occidental Plane 686
- Oceanopapaver 251
- Ochroxylum 949
- Ocimum basilicum 609
- Odermenning 025
- Oemleria 610
- Oemleria cerasiformis 610
- Oenothera 611
- Oenothera biennis 611
- Oenothera flava 612
- Official Lavender 498
- Officinal Aconite 010
- Ofnokgi 358
- Oghoul 569
- Ohbaea 814
- Ohe 116
- Ohelo `ai 910
- Oingnum 035
- Olbia 499
- Old Blush Rose 763
- Old Fashion Rose Geranium 645
- Old Fashioned Bleeding Heart 491
- Old Maid's Bonnet 538

- Old Maid's Nightcap 391
- Old Man 092
- Old Man 095
- Old Man 773
- Old Man's Beard 232
- Old Man's Fennel 914
- Old Man's Mustard 008
- Old Man's Pepper 008
- Old Rough Red 754
- Old Uncle Henry 095
- Old Woman 093
- Old World Royal Fern 629
- Old-Maid's-Pink 026
- Old-fashioned Bleeding-heart 491
- Oldman Wormwood 092
- Olea europaea 613
- Oleander 600
- Olive Tree 613
- Olivier 613
- Ombú 667
- Oncosporum 126
- Ondelaga 191
- Onion 035
- Onobrychis 614
- Ononis 615
- Ononis spinosa 616
- Ononis vulgaris 616
- Onopordum acanthium 617
- Onycha 856
- Onyoun 035
- Oodh 077
- Oolong 161
- Ophioscorodon 037
- Ophrys 622
- Ophrys apifera 618
- Ophrys bombyliflora 619

- Ophrys chlorantha 618
- Ophrys insectifera 618
- Ophrys insectifera 620
- Ophrys myodes 620
- Opoponax 911
- Opuntia 621
- Opuntia imbricata 281
- Orange 229
- Orange Bergamot 224
- Orange Daylily 428
- Orange Milkweed 100
- Orange Mint 224
- Orange Root 447
- Orange Swallow-wort 100
- Orange Tree 229
- Orange-Root 447
- Orangeroot 447
- Orchard Apple Tree 554
- Orchid 622
- Orchid Cactus 808
- Orchidaceae 622
- Orchis 622
- Orchis apifera 618
- Orchis insectifera 620
- Orchis mascula 623
- Orchis myodes 620
- Oregan Grape-holly 553
- Oregan Holly-grape 553
- Oregano 626
- Oregon Grape 553
- Oregon Grape Root 553
- Oregon Grape-holly 553
- Oregon Holly-Grape 553
- Oregon-Grape 553

- Oregongrape 553
- Oreosedum 814
- Organ Broth 571
- Organ Tea 571
- Organs 571
- Oriental Bush Cherry 721
- Oriental Garlic Chives 039
- Oriental Lily 513
- Oriental Poppy 636
- Origanum dictamnus 624
- Origanum majorana 625
- Origanum vulgare 626
- Ornithogalum narbonense 067
- Orobanche 627
- Orthotactus 481
- Ortiga Ancha 905
- Oruga 336
- Oryza glaberrima 628
- Oryza sativa 628
- Oscaria chinensis 710
- Osier 787
- Osier 788
- Osmaronia 610
- Osmunda 629
- Osmunda regalis 629
- Osoberry 610
- Osterick 656
- Oswego 581
- Oswego Tea 581
- Ottonia 675
- Ouchi 358
- Our Herb 609
- Our Lady's Bedstraw 382
- Our Lady's Keys 711
- Our Lady's Mint 573
- Our Lady's Tears 249

- Our Lady's Thistle 827
- Our Lord's Wood 092
- Outhouse Lily 428
- Ox Eye 507
- Ox-Eye Daisy 507
- Oxalis acetosella 630
- Oxalis tetraphylla 631
- Oxblood Lily 053
- Oxeye Daisy 507
- Oxydectes 270
- Oyster Plant 005
- Oysterloit 656
- Ozallaik 642

P

- Paccha Karpoora 217
- Paccha Karpoo-ramu 217
- Pacchaik Karpoo-ram 217
- Pachai Karpuram 217
- Pachouli 691
- Pachyrhizanthe 279
- Paddle Cactus 621
- Paddle Plant 482
- Paddy 628
- Padma 598
- Paeonia officinalis 632
- Paeonia suffruticosa 633
- Paeonly 632
- Paigle 711
- Pain de Pourceau 278
- Painted Lady 891
- Painted Tongue 073
- Painted Trillium 891
- Palanostigma 270
- Palestinian Tumbleweed 060
- Palm 083

- Palm Lily 252
- Palm Tree 083
- Palmae 083
- Palmerocassia 817
- Palsywort 711
- Palta 653
- Pan 474
- Pan Porcino 278
- Panacea For All Diseases 114
- Panax 634
- Panicum capillare 635
- Panini o Kapunahou 448
- Panini-O-Ka-Puna-Hou 448
- Pankaj 598
- Pankaja 598
- Pansy 926
- Pansy 931
- Pansy Violet 931
- Papao 171
- Papaver orientale 636
- Papaver rhoeas 637
- Papaw 171
- Papaya 171
- Paper Daisy 419
- Paper Flower 130
- Paper Reed 284
- Paperwhite 595
- Paperwhite Narcissus 595
- Paphiopedilum 285
- Paprica 167
- Paprika 167
- Papryka 167
- Papryka Ostra 167
- Papryka Piman 167
- Papsajt 558
- Papyrus Plant 284
- Papyrus Sedge 284
- Paraguay Tea 456
- Parajusticia 481
- Paralysio 711
- Pararuellia 779

- Parasitipomoea 461
- Parastranthus 527
- Paronychia 638
- Parrot-billed Aloe 234
- Parrot's Beak 234
- Parrot's Bill 234
- Parry's Dwarf-Sunflower 415
- Parsley 658
- Partheniaceae 105
- Parthenocissus quinquefolia 639
- Parti-Colored Daisy 132
- Partridge Berry 384
- Partridgeberry 384
- Party-Colored Daisy 132
- Party-Coloured Daisy 132
- Parviopuntia 621
- Parvisedum 814
- Pas d'ane 900
- Paschalia 862
- Pasque Flower 731
- Pasqueflower 731
- Passaea 615
- Passe Flower 731
- Passiflora caerulea 640
- Passion Dock 656
- Passion Flower 640
- Passionflower 640
- Password 711
- Password 712
- Pasture Rose 761
- Patagonian Mint 869
- Patchai 691
- Patchouli 691
- Patchouly 691
- Path Rush 479
- Patience Dock 656
- Patience Dock 782
- Patient Dock 656
- Patient Lucy 459
- Patrick's Dock 684

- Pattersonia 779
- Paucon 797
- Pausinystalia yohimbe 641
- Pauson 797
- Pauson 797
- Paw-paw 171
- Pawpaw 171
- Pea 682
- Pea Bean 661
- Pea Lotus 536
- Peace Lily 838
- Peach Tree (velvety skinned fruit) 724
- Peacock Tree 294
- Pear Tree 734
- Pearl Onion 034
- Peavine Clover 888
- Pebble Plant 576
- Pecan 175
- Pee-A-Bed 872
- Peepal 362
- Pegaga 191
- Pegagan 191
- Peganum 642
- Peganum harmala 642
- Peggle 711
- Peking Willow 789
- Pelargonium 645
- Pelargonium crispum 643
- Pelargonium graveolens 645
- Pelargonium incrassatum 645
- Pelargonium inquinans 646
- Pelargonium nubilum 647
- Pelargonium odoratissimum 648
- Pelargonium peltatum 649
- Pelargonium quercifolium 650
- Pelargonium roseum 645

- Pimpinella anisum 670
- Pincushion Flower 806
- Pine 671
- Pine Apple 059
- Pineapple 059
- Pinemat manzanita 085
- Piney 632
- Pink 298
- Pink Bean 661
- Pink Pokers 656
- Pinkaou 022
- Pinks 300
- Pinks 832
- Pinkster Lily 596
- Pinkweed 655
- Pinquito Bean 661
- Pinto Bean 661
- Pinus 671
- Pinus nigra 672
- Pinus rigida 673
- Pinus sylvestris 674
- Pinyin 161
- Pinyin 429
- Pipe Tree 796
- Piper 675
- Piper cubeba 676
- Piper methysticum 677
- Piper nigrum 678
- Pipor 678
- Pippali 678
- Pipsissewa 205
- Pipul 362
- Pircunia 667
- Piriope 901
- Piru 807
- Piscaria 270
- Piscidia 679
- Piscidia erythrina 679
- Piscidia piscipula 679
- Piss-a-Bed 872
- Pista 681
- Pistacchio 681
- Pistachio 681

- Pistacia 681
- Pistacia lentiscus 680
- Pistacia vera 681
- Pistorinia 814
- Pistáke 681
- Pistákion 681
- Pisum sativum 682
- Pitahaya Orejona 448
- Pitahaya Roja 448
- Pitajava 448
- Pitch Pine 673
- Pithecellobium acuminatum 911
- Pithecellobium minutum 911
- Piña 059
- Plagiacanthus 481
- Plains Coreopsis 254
- Plakkie 482
- Plane 685
- Plane Tree 685
- Planera aquatica 903
- Plant of Immortality 041
- Plantago 683
- Plantago major 684
- Plantain 585
- Plantain 683
- Plantain 684
- Plantain Lily 438
- Platanus 685
- Platanus occidentalis 686
- Platycodon 687
- Platycodon grandiflorus 687
- Plegmatolemma 481
- Pleiostachyopiper 675
- Pleistachyopiper 675
- Pleomele 316
- Pleopadium 270
- Pleurisy Root 100

- Plum Tree 719
- Plumajillo 008
- Plume Thistle 220
- Plumeria 688
- Plumrocks 711
- Poaceae 689
- Pocan 667
- Pocketbook Flower 146
- Podophyllum peltatum 690
- Podostachys 270
- Poenosedum 814
- Poets' Narcissus 596
- Poet's Daffodil 596
- Poet's Jasmine 477
- Poet's Narcissus 596
- Pogostemon cablin 691
- Poinciana 294
- Poinsettia 348
- Points d'Amour 102
- Poire de Chardon 448
- Poireau 034
- Poison Darnel 530
- Poison Flag 471
- Poison Hemlock 247
- Poison Parsley 019
- Poison Parsley 247
- Poison Tobacco 449
- Poisonberry 830
- Poisonflower 830
- Poivre 678
- Poivron 167
- Poke 667
- Poke Root 667
- Poke Sallet 667
- Pokeberry 667
- Pokeberry Root 667
- Pokebush 667
- Pokeroot 667
- Pokeweed 667
- Pokok Semalu 577

- Polar Plant 773
- Pole Cat Weed 860
- Polecat Weed 860
- Polemonium caeruleum 692
- Polianthes tuberosa 693
- Polk Root 667
- Polk Salad 667
- Polk Salat 667
- Polk Sallet 667
- Pollyblobs 151
- Polyanthus 708
- Polygala 694
- Polygonatum 695
- Polygonatum multiflorum 696
- Polygonum 697
- Polytrichum 698
- Pom-Pom Banksia 117
- Pom-Pom Rose 117
- Pomegranate 733
- Pomme-grenade 733
- Pomo d'Oro 831
- Pompion 273
- Pompom Rose 117
- Ponna 474
- Poor Man's Asparagus 203
- Poor Man's Meat 661
- Poor Man's Pepper 505
- Poor Man's Weather Glass 058
- Poorland Daisy 507
- Poorland Daisy 778
- Poorman's Barometer 058
- Pop Weed 458
- Popanax farnesiana 911
- Popinac 911
- Poplar 699
- Poplar 702

- Poponax farnesiana 911
- Poppy 636
- Poppy Anemone 063
- Poppywort 855
- Populus 699
- Populus alba 700
- Populus nigra 701
- Populus tremula 702
- Porcelain Garlic 037
- Poroto Negro Bean 661
- Porphyrocoma 481
- Portulaca grandiflora 703
- Pot Marigold 147
- Pot Of Gold 897
- Potato 832
- Potatta 832
- Potentilla 704
- Potentilla anserina 087
- Potentilla erecta 705
- Potentilla indica 706
- Potentilla tormentilla 705
- Pothomorphe 675
- Pothos 331
- Pound Garnet 733
- Poverty Weed 507
- Poziomki 367
- Prairie Coreopsis 254
- Prairie Crocus 731
- Prairie Gentian 350
- Prattling Parnell 805
- Prayer Plant 562
- Prayer-Plant 562
- Prenanthes 707
- Price's Pine 205
- Prickly Ash 949
- Prickly Berry 754

- Prickly Broom Heath 582
- Prickly Burr 292
- Prickly Mimosa Bush 911
- Prickly Moses 911
- Prickly Pear 621
- Prickly Rosa baicalensis 758
- Prickly Rose 758
- Prickly-Ash 949
- Prickly-Ivy 829
- Pricklyburr 292
- Pride of China 485
- Pride of India 485
- Pride of Trinidad and Tobago 937
- Pride of the Meadow 364
- Pride-of-China 485
- Pride-of-India 485
- Priest's Crown 872
- Primerose 712
- Primrose 708
- Primrose 712
- Primrose Tree 490
- Primula 708
- Primula acaulis 712
- Primula auricula 709
- Primula balbisii 709
- Primula ciliata 709
- Primula mandarina 710
- Primula officinalis 711
- Primula praenitens 710
- Primula semperflorens 710
- Primula sertulosa 710
- Primula sinensis 710
- Primula veris 711
- Primula vulgaris 712
- Primulidium sinese 710

- Prince-of-Wales-Feather 052
- Princess Feather 052
- Princess Flower 882
- Princess Marina 422
- Princess Pine 205
- Princess of The Night 448
- Prince's Feather 050
- Prince's Feather 052
- Prince's Feathers 050
- Prince's Pine 205
- Privet 510
- Procrassula 814
- Professor-Weed 378
- Prometheum 814
- Pronaya 126
- Prophetic Marigold 147
- Prophetic Marygold 147
- Prosopis 713
- Protea cynaroides 714
- Provence Rose 762
- Prunus 722
- Prunus americana 715
- Prunus amygdalus 720
- Prunus armeniaca 716
- Prunus avium 717
- Prunus cerasifera 718
- Prunus divaricata 718
- Prunus domestica 719
- Prunus dulcis 720
- Prunus japonica 721

- Prunus laurocerasus 722
- Prunus padus 723
- Prunus persica 724
- Prunus racemosa 723
- Prunus rainier 725
- Prunus spinosa 726
- Prunus x domestica 719
- Psacadocalymma 481
- Pseudorosularia 814
- Pseudosassafras 802
- Psyllium 683
- Pteridium aquilinum 727
- Pteridophyta 728
- Pterocarpus draco 315
- Pterocarpus santalinus 729
- Pua Keni Keni 355
- Pua-Lulu 355
- Pua-kenikeni 355
- Puarangi 434
- Publican 151
- Pucha-Pot 691
- Pudding Dock 656
- Pudding Grass 571
- Pudding Grass 656
- Pudina 570
- Puerh Tea 161
- Puff-ball 872
- Puffball 872
- Pugiopappus 253
- Pukeweed 527
- Puli 867
- Pull-Down 277
- Pulmonaria 730
- Pulsatilla 731
- Pulsatilla montana 732
- Pumpkin 273
- Punahou cactus 448

- Red Catchfly 822
- Red Chestnut 017
- Red Chickweed 058
- Red Clover 888
- Red Cockscomb 052
- Red Cock's Comb 050
- Red Currant 753
- Red Daisy 210
- Red Daisy Chrysanthemum 210
- Red Daisy Mum 210
- Red Dulse 750
- Red Elm 904
- Red Eyes 832
- Red Fucus 375
- Red Huckleberry 909
- Red Legs 656
- Red Mombin 841
- Red Morning Glory 464
- Red Paint Root 797
- Red Pepper 167
- Red Pimpernel 058
- Red Pitahaya 448
- Red Pitaya 448
- Red Poppy 637
- Red Puccoon Root 797
- Red Pucoon 797
- Red Raspberry 775
- Red Raspeberry 776
- Red Root 797
- Red Sage 492
- Red Sage |Sage 793
- Red Sandalwood 729
- Red Sanders 729
- Red Spider Lily 543
- Red Squil 809
- Red Sunflower 326
- Red Valerian 192
- Red Valerian 912
- Red Weed 637
- Red-edged Dracaena 316
- Redbay 654
- Redcurrant 753
- Redgum 525
- Redstar 464
- Regal Lily 518
- Reina de la Noche 448
- Ren Dong Téng 532
- Reseda 745
- Rest-Harrow 615
- Restharrow 615
- Restharrow 616
- Resurrection Plant 060
- Retama 837
- Revenelle 200
- Rewe 783
- Rfaudraksh 004
- Rhacodiscus 481
- Rhamnus cathartica 746
- Rhamnus purshiana 747
- Rhamnus purshianus 747
- Rheum rhabarbarum 748
- Rheumatism Root 030
- Rheumatism Weld 075
- Rhiphidosperma 481
- Rhododendron 749
- Rhododendron maximum 749
- Rhodon 757
- Rhodymenia palmata 750
- Rhubarb 748
- Rhus 751
- Rhus cotinus 263
- Rhyticalymma 481
- Ribbon Dracaena 317
- Ribbon Grass 603
- Ribbon Plant 317
- Ribes 754
- Ribes cyathiforme 752
- Ribes nigrum 752
- Ribes nigrum chlorocarpum 752
- Ribes nigrum sibiricum 752
- Ribes olidum 752
- Ribes rubrum 753
- Ribes uva-crispa 754
- Rice 628
- Rice Boiling Flower 578
- Richardia aethiopica 947
- Richardia africana 947
- Riches 155
- Richette 087
- Riondella 558
- Ripple Grass 684
- Rjii 432
- Roadside Daylily 428
- Roadweed 684
- Robin-run-the-hedge 379
- Robinia 755
- Rocambole Garlic 037
- Rock Centaury 951
- Rock Madwort 111
- Rock Parsley 658
- Rock Rose 221
- Rock Wrack 375
- Rock-rose 221
- Rocket 336
- Rocket Leaf 336
- Rocketsalad 336
- Rocks 832
- Rockweed 375
- Rocky Mountain Grape 553
- Rodatia 481
- Roden-Quicken 834
- Rods of Life 787
- Rogac 194
- Rogue's Gilliflower 431
- Rohtorautayrtti 916
- Rojoni-Gondha 693
- Roka 336
- Rokka 336
- Roman Bean 661
- Roman Camomile 069
- Roman Chamomile 069
- Roman Laurel 497
- Romano Bean 661
- Romarin 773
- Romero 773
- Rooster Comb 185
- Roots 756
- Roquette 336
- Ros Maris 773
- Rosa 757
- Rosa (Bud) 759
- Rosa Perpetua 444
- Rosa acicularis 758
- Rosa canina 760
- Rosa carelica 758
- Rosa carolina 761
- Rosa centifolia 762
- Rosa cerea 764
- Rosa chinensis 763
- Rosa cinnamomea 767
- Rosa damascena 772
- Rosa damascena trigintipetela 772
- Rosa eglanteria 764
- Rosa foetida 764
- Rosa gallica trigintipetala 772
- Rosa gallica versicolor 765
- Rosa gmelinii 758
- Rosa gymnocarpa 766

- Spider Flower 407
- Spider Lily 885
- Spider Plant 207
- Spider Plant 233
- Spider Weed 233
- Spider Wort 885
- Spiderflower 233
- Spiderplant 233
- Spiderweed 233
- Spiderwort 885
- Spike 498
- Spike 509
- Spike-Primrose 330
- Spiked Aloe 023
- Spiked Loosestrife 546
- Spiked Speedwell 918
- Spiked Willowherb 330
- Spikenard 597
- Spinach Dock 780
- Spindle 344
- Spindle Tree 344
- Spindle Tree 345
- Spiny Restharrow 616
- Spiranthes 840
- Spire 509
- Spire Mint 573
- Spleen Amaranth 050
- Splendid Scarlet Flowered Lechenaultia 506
- Spondias purpurea 841
- Sponge Wattle 911
- Sponnc 900
- Spoonwood 483
- Spotted Alder 410
- Spotted Arum Lily 948
- Spotted Corobane 247
- Spotted Dog 730
- Spotted Hemlock 247

- Spotted Snapweed 458
- Spotted Spotted Cranesbill 391
- Spotted Thistle 236
- Sprenger's Asparagus 101
- Spring Crocus 269
- Spring Wintergreen 384
- Spruce 668
- Spud 832
- Spur Valerian 192
- Spurge 347
- Spárga 102
- Squareweed 826
- Squash 273
- Squaw Mint 571
- Squaw Root 012
- Squill 809
- Squirrel Corn 491
- Sri Lanka Cinnamon 218
- St John's Wort 450
- St Mary's Milk Thistle 827
- St. Benedict's Herb 395
- St. George's Herb 912
- St. James' Wort 816
- St. Joseph's Wort 609
- St. Mary's Flower 060
- St. Mary's Seal 695
- St. Patrick's Leaf 684
- Stachys 842
- Stachys betonica 844
- Stachys byzantina 843
- Stachys lanata 843
- Stachys officinalis 844
- Stachys olympica 843

- Staggerwort 816
- Stammerwort 816
- Stanch Griss 008
- Stanch Weed 008
- Staphylea 845
- Staphylinos 293
- Star Aniseed 457
- Star Glory 467
- Star Lily 953
- Star Root 030
- Star of Bethlehem 067
- Star of Bethlehem Orchid 067
- Star of The Earth 395
- Starch Hyacinth 586
- Starch-Root 096
- Starflower 127
- Stargrass 030
- Starwort 030
- Starwort 106
- Statice 521
- Statice 522
- Staunch Weed 008
- Steegia 499
- Stegia 499
- Steinnype 760
- Stellaria americana 846
- Stenactis 334
- Stenocereus eruca 847
- Stenoschista 779
- Stenros 760
- Stephanophysum 779
- Stephanotis 848
- Stepmother 931
- Steppenraute 642
- Sternbergia aurantiaca 849
- Sternbergia greuteriana 849
- Sternbergia lutea 849
- Sternbergia sicula 849

- Stethoma 481
- Stevie 780
- Sticklewort 025
- Stickwort 025
- Stickwort 630
- Stickyjack 379
- Stickyleaf 379
- Stickyweed 379
- Stickywilly 379
- Stikkelsbaer 754
- Stillingia 850
- Stillingia sylvatica 850
- Stinging Nettle 905
- Stink Lily 318
- Stink Weed 292
- Stinkdillsamen 255
- Stinking Gum 357
- Stinking Hellebore 425
- Stinking Nanny 816
- Stinking Nightshade 449
- Stinking Willie 816
- Stinkweed 292
- Stinky Fruit Tree 325
- Stock 564
- Stonecrop 814
- Storax 856
- Storksbill 645
- Storm Hat 010
- Strangel Tare 277
- Strangler Fig 360
- Strangleweed 277
- Straw 851
- Straw (broken) 852
- Strawberry 368
- Strawberry Pear 448
- Strawberry Tree 080
- Strawberry Tree 081
- Strawflower 419
- Strelitzia 853
- Strelitzia reginae 853

- Streptosolen jamesonii 854
- Stringy Gum 342
- Striped Rose of France 765
- Stubwort 630
- Stutia 405
- Stylophorum 855
- Stylophorum diphyllum 855
- Styphelia scoparia 582
- Styrax benzoin 856
- Subulatopuntia 621
- Succisa pratensis 857
- Succory 214
- Sugandaraja 693
- Sugar Beet 124
- Sugar Cane 784
- Sugarcane 784
- Suikazura 532
- Sulphur Bean 661
- Sultana 459
- Sumac 751
- Sumach 751
- Sumatra 856
- Sumbul 358
- Sumbul Radix 358
- Sumbulwurzel 358
- Summer Cypress 118
- Summer Lilac 431
- Summer Rhododendron 749
- Summer Starwort 334
- Summer's Bride 147
- Sumsum 818
- Sum'bul 358
- Sun Rose 703
- Sunchoke 418
- Suncups 611
- Sundial 538
- Sundrops 611
- Sunflower 416
- Sunroot 418
- Suntull 860

- Supadi Phool 404
- Surelle 630
- Swallow Herb 201
- Swallow Wort 283
- Swallow-Wort 201, 283
- Swamp Cabbage 860
- Swamp Gum 342
- Swamp Lily 520
- Swamp Magnolia 551
- Swampbay 551
- Sweet Acacia 911
- Sweet Alyssum 048
- Sweet Balm 569
- Sweet Basil 609
- Sweet Bay 497
- Sweet Briar 770
- Sweet Briar 911
- Sweet Cane 011
- Sweet Capsicum 167
- Sweet Cherry 717
- Sweet Chestnut 177
- Sweet Cicely 591
- Sweet Cumin 670
- Sweet Fennel 365
- Sweet Flag 011
- Sweet Gale 588
- Sweet Goldenrod 833
- Sweet Grass 011
- Sweet Grass 070
- Sweet Majoram 625
- Sweet Mary 569
- Sweet Mary Balm 569
- Sweet Melissa 569
- Sweet Orange 229
- Sweet Pea 496
- Sweet Peppers 167
- Sweet Potato 463
- Sweet Reseda 745
- Sweet Rocket 431
- Sweet Root 011
- Sweet Root 401

- Sweet Rush 011
- Sweet Scabious 806
- Sweet Sedge 011
- Sweet Shrub 152
- Sweet Slumber 797
- Sweet Sultan 188
- Sweet Vernal-Grass 070
- Sweet Violet 928
- Sweet Weed 047
- Sweet William 299
- Sweet Wood 218
- Sweet Woodruff 380
- Sweet-Briar 770
- Sweet-Scented Tussilage 657
- Sweet-scented Bedstraw 381
- Sweet-scented Goldenrod 833
- Sweetbay 551
- Sweetbay Magnolia 551
- Sweetbriar 770
- Sweete Williams 299
- Sweetgrass 070
- Sweetgum 525
- Sweetpea 496
- Sweetshrub 152
- Sweth 038
- Swine Snout 872
- Swine's Snout 872
- Sword Flag 468
- Sword Lily 397
- Sycamore 363
- Sycamore 685
- Sycamore Fig 363
- Sycomore 363
- Symphiandra 157
- Symphyotrichum novae-angliae 858
- Symphytum officinale 859
- Symplocarpus foetidus 860

- Syngonium podophyllum 861
- Syrian Ketmia 433
- Syrian Mallow 433
- Syrian Rue 642
- Syringa 862
- Syringa vulgaris 862
- Syzygium aromaticum 863
- Szczaw 780
- Sóska 780

T
- Taaba 601
- Tabacca 601
- Tabachine 294
- Tabaibas 347
- Tabak 601
- Tabascina 481
- Tabua-larga 901
- Tacoanthus 779
- Tagetes 864
- Tagetes corymbosa 866
- Tagetes erecta 865
- Tagetes lunulata 866
- Tagetes patula 866
- Tagetes remotiflora 866
- Tagetes signata 866
- Tagetes tenuifolia 866
- Tahiti Lime 227
- Tailed Pepper 676
- Takip-Kohol 191
- Tall Buttercup 738
- Tall Field Buttercup 738
- Tall Mallow 558
- Tall Nettle 905
- Tall Oregon-grape 553
- Tall Sunflower 417
- Tamar 114
- Tamar hind 867
- Tamarene 867

- Tillandsia usneoides 884
- Timandra 270
- Time Flower 703
- Time Fuul 703
- Ting 357
- Tinker's Root 893
- Tintidi 867
- Tinus laurifolius 920
- Tinus lauriformis 920
- Tinus lucidus 920
- Tipitiwitchet 305
- Tippity Twitchet 305
- Tipton Weed 450
- Tipton's Weed 450
- Tisi 524
- Titan Arum 055
- Tlilxochitl 913
- Toadflax 072
- Toad's Mouth 072
- Togarashi 167
- Tolache 292
- Tolguacha 292
- Tolu 590
- Tomatl 831
- Tomato 831
- Tonka 311
- Tonka Bean Plant 311
- Tonqua 311
- Tonquin Bean 311
- Toot 584
- Toothbrush 407
- Topinambour 418
- Torches 914
- Tormentil 705
- Tormentilla erecta 705
- Totora 901
- Touch-Me-Not 458
- Touch-Me-Not 577
- Tourengane 569
- Townhall Clock 016
- Tracheliopsis 157
- Tradescantia ohiensis 885
- Tradescantia virginiana 886
- Tragoceros 954
- Trailing Arbutus 328
- Trailing Bittersweet 830
- Trailing Grape 553
- Trailing Nightshade 830
- Transvaal Daisy 394
- Traveler's Joy 916
- Traveller's Joy 232
- Traveller's Joy 916
- Tree Cholla 281
- Tree Ivy 412
- Tree Mallow 499
- Tree Peony 633
- Tree Primrose 611
- Tree Spider Orchid 297
- Tree of Death 275
- Tree of Doom 796
- Tree of Enchantment 788
- Tree of Life 396
- Tree of Life 880
- Tree of the Forty 114
- Tree of the Forty Cures 114
- Trees of Kafoor 217
- Trefoil 887
- Trefoil 888
- Triactina 814
- Trianaeopiper 675
- Tricycla 130
- Tridesmis 270
- Trifoil 887
- Trifolium 887
- Trifolium pratense 888
- Trifolium repens 889
- Trigonella goenumgraecum 890
- Trille Ondulé 891
- Trillium 891
- Trillium erectum 891
- Trillium pictum 891
- Trillium undulatum 891
- Triodanis perfoliata 892
- Triosteum 893
- Triplandra 270
- Triptilion spinosum 894
- Trisanthus cochinchinensis 191
- Triticum 895
- Trollius paluster 151
- Tropaeolum 896
- Tropical Milkweed 099
- Tropolis tetragona 297
- Trout Lily 338
- Trout-lily 338
- True Aloe 041
- True Cardamom 327
- True Cinnamon 218
- True Geranium 390
- True Goldenrod 833
- True Grasses 689
- True Laurel 497
- True Lavender 498
- True London Pride 805
- True Love 891
- True Myrtle 592
- True Rose of Jericho 060
- True Service Tree 836
- True Shallot 036
- True Unicorn Root 030
- True Winter's Bark 319
- Trumpet Creeper 162
- Trumpet Flower 877
- Trumpet Lily 517
- Trumpet Lily 947
- Trumpet Vine 162
- Truti 327
- Tsamiya 867
- Tsubaki 155
- Tuber Root 100
- Tuberose 693
- Tuberous Crowfoot 016
- Tuberous Morning Glory 463
- Tuckermannia 253
- Tuhonghua 432
- Tule espidilla 901
- Tule-reed 901
- Tulip 897
- Tulip Gentian 350
- Tulip Poplar 526
- Tulip Tree 526
- Tulipa 897
- Tulipa didieri 898
- Tulipa gesneriana 898
- Tulipa suaveolens 898
- Tulipan 897
- Tulipant 897
- Tulsi 609
- Tumeric 276
- Tuna 621
- Tunas 621
- Tunhoof 398
- Tupa 527
- Turban Lily 520
- Turkey Corn 491
- Turkish Balloon Flower 687
- Turkish Cedar 183
- Turk's Cap Lily 520
- Turnera diffusa 899
- Turnip 134
- Turnip Mustard 134
- Turnip Rape 134
- Turnip-rooted Parsley 658
- Turnsole 422
- Tussilago 900

- White Sage 791
- White Sandalwood 800
- White Saunders 800
- White Shamrock 889
- White Squill 809
- White Tea 161
- White Thorn 266
- White Trumpet Lily 517
- White Violet 927
- White Willow 788
- White Wood 526
- White Zephyr Lily 952
- White-Root 100
- Whitebay 551
- Whiteweed 024
- Whitlow-Wort 638
- Whitty 834
- Whitty Pear 836
- Whortleberry 907
- Wice Hazel 410
- Wiches Bells 304
- Wiches Thimbles 304
- Wicken-Tree 834
- Widow's Tears 009
- Wigandia californica 335
- Wiggin 834
- Wiggy 834
- Wiky 834
- Wild Angelica 066
- Wild Artichoke 827
- Wild Arum 096
- Wild Ash 834
- Wild Baby's Breath 380
- Wild Bean 538
- Wild Briar 911
- Wild Cabbage 133
- Wild Cane 097
- Wild Carrot 293
- Wild Celery 066
- Wild Chamomile 069

- Wild Chamomile 870
- Wild Cherry 214
- Wild Cherry 717
- Wild Clover 888
- Wild Cranesbill 391
- Wild Daisy 120
- Wild Endive 872
- Wild European Strawberry 367
- Wild Fennel 365
- Wild Garlic 037
- Wild Geranium 391
- Wild Honeysuckle 534
- Wild Hop 844
- Wild Hyacinth 154
- Wild Hyssop 916
- Wild Ipecac 075
- Wild Leek 034
- Wild Lemon 560
- Wild Lemon 690
- Wild Licorice 108
- Wild Liquorice 108
- Wild Mallow 558
- Wild Malva 646
- Wild Mandrake 690
- Wild Marjaram 626
- Wild Mustard 134
- Wild Onion 037
- Wild Oregon Grape 553
- Wild Pansy 931
- Wild Pea 538
- Wild Petunia 779
- Wild Plantains 421
- Wild Plum 715
- Wild Poinsettia 937
- Wild Privet 511
- Wild Quinine 870
- Wild Rose 758
- Wild Rue 642
- Wild Sage 492
- Wild Senna 817
- Wild Sorrel 780
- Wild Strawberry 367
- Wild Succory 214
- Wild Tansy 871

- Wild Teasel 310
- Wild Tobacco 601
- Wild Vanilla 509
- Wild Western Thimbleberries 775
- Wild Wormwood 095
- Wild Yellow Lily 514
- Wild Yellow-Lily 514
- Wilde Malva 646
- Willow 787
- Willow Herb 330
- Willowherb 329
- Willowherb 330
- Wimberry 907
- Winberry 907
- Wind Flower 731
- Windberry 907
- Windflower 064
- Windroot 100
- Wineberry 775
- Winged Seeds 938
- Winter Cherry 941
- Winter Cherry Herb 941
- Winter Daffodil 849
- Winter Daphne 291
- Winter Gilliflower 431
- Winter Heliotrope 657
- Winter Heliotrope 900
- Wintera 319
- Wintera Aromatics 319
- Winterbloom 410
- Winterflowering Cactus 808
- Wintergreen 384
- Winter's Bark 319
- Winter's Cinnamon 319
- Wire-Grass 479
- Wiregrass 479
- Wishing Thorn 726
- Wistaria 940
- Wisteria 939

- Wisteria 940
- Wisteria sinensis 940
- Witch Bane 834
- Witch Flower 010
- Witch Grass 635
- Witch Hazel 410
- Witch-Hazel 410
- Witchbane 834
- Witchen 834
- Witches Bane 783
- Witches Herb 609
- Witches Mannikin 560
- Witches' Aspirin 788
- Witches' Berry 110
- Witches' Thimble 292
- Witchgrass 635
- Witchwood 834
- Witch' Bells 304
- Witch's Hair 277
- Witch's Mannikin 560
- Witch's Thimble 304
- Withania somnifera 941
- Withe 788
- Withered Flowers Bouquet 942
- Withy 788
- Woad 472
- Wohpala 589
- Wolf Claw 542
- Wolf Flower 539
- Wolf Peach 831
- Wolfsbane 010
- Wolf's Bane 010
- Wolf's Hat 010
- Wolf's Milk 347
- Wolf's Tale 538
- Wood Aloes 077
- Wood Anemone 064
- Wood Avens 395
- Wood Betony 844
- Wood Mallow 558

- Zig-Zag Camellia 156
- Ziga 558
- Zigadenus 953
- Zigiña 558
- Zinnia 954
- Zitan Wood Tree 729
- Zitronmelisse 569
- Ztworkost 859
- Zwetschge 719
- Zygalchemilla 029
- Zygocactus 808

Symbolic Meanings

A

- A Rainbow 468
- A Wound to heal 770
- A bell 303
- A belle 622
- A boaster 446
- A deadly foe is near 010
- A declaration of love 897
- A fanciful nature 119
- A first housewarming gift 733
- A flirt 290
- A foe is near 010
- A good education 717
- A heart innocent of love 759
- A heart left to desolation 209
- A kiss 359
- A lover's heart darkened by the heart of passion 897
- A magic spell 410
- A meeting 496
- A melancholy mind 650
- A merry heart 798
- A message 468
- A monstrosity 150
- A mother's love 300
- A mother's undying love 300
- A poetical person 758
- A serenade 076
- A spell 410
- A spell is on me 410
- A storm 866
- A token 507, 920
- A treasure 173
- A wish 304
- A woman's love 300
- Abandonment 062, 064, 543
- Abiding love 062
- Abilities 916
- Ability to transcend the bounds of space and time 295
- Abruptness 127
- Absence 092, 093, 530
- Absent friends 954
- Absolute romance 897
- Abundance 073, 209, 733, 950
- Abundance and Wealth 209
- Abundance and loveliness 209
- Abuse not 269
- Acceptance 300, 862
- Acknowledgment 158
- Action 881
- Activity 881
- Adaptability 125
- Addresses rejected 576
- Adhesiveness 435
- Adjustment 897
- Admiration 137, 149, 155, 300, 757
- Admiration from afar 300
- Adoration 073, 156, 415, 423
- Adoration Desire 155
- Adroitness 297
- Adulation 828
- Adultery 093
- Advancement 897
- Advantage 702
- Adversity 200
- Advice 748
- Affability 572
- Affection 011, 147, 185, 300, 412, 461, 532, 533, 734, 757, 780, 804, 881, 926, 933, 954
- Affection beyond the grave 194, 399
- Affection returned 594
- Affectionate remembrance 773
- Affirmative 300
- Affliction 701
- Affluence 265
- Aflutter 011
- A Friend in Need 946
- Afterthought 106, 148, 858
- Against dog bites 800
- Against ghosts 800
- Against snake bites 800
- Against sorcery 800
- Age 396, 919
- Agelessness 793
- Agitation 135, 239, 614, 749
- Agreement 419, 851, 950
- Aid 480
- Airy 295
- Alas for my poor heart 300
- Alerting 617
- All who know you will love you 069
- Alleviate grief 793
- Aloof 897
- Alteration 702
- Always 445
- Always cheerful 253
- Always delightful 216
- Always lovely 445, 528
- Always on my mind 300
- Always reliable 505
- Am I forgotten 455, 537
- Ambassador of love 762
- Ambition 028, 416, 483, 738, 739, 749
- Ambition of a hero 483
- Ambition of a scholar 028
- Ambition of my love thus plagues itself 374
- Ambitious 749
- Amiability 374, 477
- Amorous 554
- Amulet to increase clarity of thought 589
- Amusement 845
- An accommodating disposition 912
- An appointed meeting 495, 682
- An attack against love for love 099
- An open heart 295

- An uncommon thing 560
- Ancient symbol of The Sun 268
- Anger 632, 659, 902
- Animosity 450
- Annunciation 593
- Anti-hunger 079
- Anticipation 062, 366, 754
- Antipathy 300
- Anxiety 424
- Anxious 078
- Anxious and trembling 078
- Anxious to please 412
- Aphrodisiac 011, 092, 554, 595, 632
- Apology 757
- Apostasy 812
- Appointed meeting 682
- Appointmen 058
- Appreciation 757
- Appreciation of honesty 593
- Architecture 453
- Ardent attachment 295
- Ardent love 144, 156, 298, 300, 458
- Ardent love Desire 155
- Ardor 088, 089, 096, 169, 948
- Argument 361
- Arrogance 372, 897
- Art 005, 554
- Art and Poetry 554
- Artfulness 232
- Artifice 005, 232, 299, 305, 500
- Artistic ability 926
- Artistic endeavors 053
- Arts 005
- Ascetic beauty 717
- Aspiration 897

- Aspiring 159, 951
- Assiduous to please 412
- Assignation 058
- Astonishment 318
- Asylum 480
- Atonement 067
- Attachment 269, 461, 463
- Attaining the impossible 757
- Attraction 043, 149
- Attraction of love 773
- Attractive 739
- Attracts the opposite sex 043
- Attracts wealth 069
- Audacity 170, 494, 726
- Austerity 726
- Autumn 243, 389
- Availability 390
- Avarice 709
- Aversion 301, 528
- Avoidance of problems 637
- Awakening 362
- Awareness 702
- Awareness of our spiritual path 095

B
- Bad luck 300
- Balance 119, 757, 834
- Banquet 074
- Bantering 092
- Baseness 277
- Bashful 757
- Bashful love 577, 772
- Bashfulness 577, 632
- Be cautious 833
- Be cordial 119
- Be mine 631
- Be my support 695, 696

- Be of Good Cheer 348
- Be prudent 894
- Beautiful 739
- Beautiful but timid 053
- Beautiful crown 148
- Beautiful eyes 897
- Beautiful lady 622
- Beauty 120, 132, 149, 156, 218, 279, 296, 432, 512, 524, 549, 593, 598, 600, 622, 632, 633, 715, 719, 757, 759, 916, 947
- Beauty Desire 155
- Beauty always new 763
- Beauty and innocence 120
- Beauty and the price gained from shared wisdom over time 947
- Beauty ever new 763
- Beauty is not your only attraction 771
- Beauty under the moon's light 448
- Beauty unknown to possessor 210
- Being forsaken 062
- Believe 897
- Believe me 897
- Bell 303
- Belle 622
- Beloved child 704
- Beloved daughter 704
- Benefactor 524
- Beneficence 832
- Benefit 310
- Benevolence 152, 433, 832
- Best Wishes 609

- Betrayal 195, 436, 824
- Better things to come 554
- Beware 010, 119, 600, 749
- Beware of a false friend 369
- Beware of excess 268
- Beware of false friends 369
- Beware of the coquette 178
- Beware of virtue 757
- Bewitching grace 840
- Big-Hearted 295
- Birth 512, 624, 711
- Bitterness 041, 093
- Blackness 308, 486
- Blemish 449
- Blessing to come after a challenge 726
- Bliss 757
- Blissful pleasure 496
- Bluntness 127
- Blushes 625
- Boaster 446
- Boldness 298, 494, 671
- Bonds 461
- Bonds of Love 532
- Bonds of affection 200, 300, 564, 565
- Bonds of love 165, 533, 534
- Boredom 084
- Bound 919
- Bravery 127, 144, 329, 330, 632, 736, 737, 881
- Bravery and humanity 329
- Bridal favor 649
- Bridal Hope 724

- Heavenly 295, 300, 757
- Heavenly bliss 269
- Heavenly chief 032
- Heavenly journeys 919
- Heedlessness 720
- Height 001
- Hello 819
- Hermitage 694
- Hidden merit 255
- Hidden worth 255
- High bred 512
- High regards 593
- High souled 512
- High souled aspirations 512
- Higher perspective 370
- Hilarity 295
- Holiness 452
- Homage 416
- Homosexual love 689
- Honesty 001, 537, 593, 687, 760, 926
- Honor 512, 632
- Honor of graceful resignation 717
- Honors 724
- Hope 067, 106, 187, 209, 266, 377, 468, 593, 671, 720, 721, 734
- Hope and passion 757
- Hope for better days 126
- Hope in adversity 668
- Hope in darkness 916
- Hope in love 187
- Hope in misery 098
- Hope in sorrow 377
- Hope, Faith, Love and Luck 631
- Hopeful but tragic fate of Lovers 543

- Hopeless 051
- Hopeless love 897
- Hopeless not heartless 051
- Hopelessness 051
- Horror 094, 318, 346, 560, 697, 847
- Horseman's star 053
- Hospitality 073, 736, 737
- Hostility 871
- Humanity 329, 330
- Humble love 374
- Humble Perseverance 250
- Humility 160, 249, 250, 380, 442, 461, 498, 512, 514, 577, 587, 757, 795, 862
- Hunting 933
- Hush 110
- Hypocrisy 308

I

- I Love 209
- I Love You 209, 757
- I Promise to be true 228
- I adore you 422
- I am ambitious only for you 304
- I am burning with love 468
- I am cured 246
- I am dangerous 600
- I am fascinated by you 897
- I am his 269
- I am looking for romance 586
- I am so sorry 916
- I am too happy 383
- I am worthy of you 757
- I am your captive 724
- I am yours 724

- I attach myself to you 461, 463
- I burn 468, 621
- I cannot be without you 708
- I can't live without you 708
- I change but in death 497
- I change but in dying 497
- I cling to thee 638, 921
- I cling to you both in sunshine and shade 639
- I cling to you for better or worse 639
- I dare not 411
- I declare against you 108, 118, 871
- I declare war against you 871
- I desire a return of affection 594
- I desire to please 289
- I die if neglected 920
- I dream of thee 629
- I dream of you 629
- I engage you for the next dance 649
- I expect a meeting 644
- I fall a victim 824
- I fall victim 822
- I feel my obligations 405
- I feel your benefits 524
- I feel your kindness 524
- I have a message for you 468
- I have lost all 806
- I have no claims 640, 731

- I live but for thee 182
- I live for thee 182
- I live for you 182
- I look to Heaven 389
- I love 423
- I love you 531
- I Love You In Secret 383
- I Love You Still And I Always Will 757
- I miss you 521, 954
- I mourn your absence 954
- I never trouble 757
- I offer you financial assistance 146
- I offer you my all 166
- I offer you my fortune 146
- I offer you pecuniary assistance 146
- I partake your sentiments 106, 120, 148
- I prefer you 645
- I promise 888, 889
- I remain true 422
- I shall die tomorrow 222
- I shall never see him 644
- I shall not survive you 584
- I share your sentiments 120
- I surmount difficulties 933
- I surmount everything 933
- I think of thee 402
- I think of you 496, 792
- I turn to thee 423
- I turn to you 423
- I want to be with you 300

- I want to smile like you 763
- I watch over you 342
- I weep for you 916
- I will be ever constant 157
- I will be faithful unto death 104
- I will not answer hastily 165, 533
- I will not survive you 584
- I will think of it 120, 132, 148
- I will think of thee 148
- I will think of you 148
- I wish I was rich 151
- I wish you Sweet Dreams 388
- I would be single 757
- I would not have you otherwise 291
- I'll Never tell 120
- I'll never forget you 300
- I'll pray for you 433
- I'll remember 445
- I'm sincere 397
- I'm walking on air 512
- Idea 468
- Idleness 067, 576
- Idolatry 093
- If you love me you will discover it 757
- If you love me you will find me out 757
- Ill at ease 376
- Ill nature 555
- Ill temper 122
- Ill will 527
- Ill-natured beauty 225
- Ill-tempered 555

- Ill-timed wit 780
- Illness 062
- Illness recovery 787
- Illumination 800
- Illusion 013
- Image magic 897
- Imagination 504, 538, 636, 637, 897
- Imitation 563
- Immature 371
- Immaturity 557
- Immediate affection 757
- Immortal 054
- Immortal beauty 444
- Immortal love 063, 404
- Immortal remembrance 944
- Immortality 003, 050, 288, 404, 497, 592, 736, 737, 757, 779, 793, 915, 944
- Impatience 269, 458
- Impatience of happiness 251, 253
- Impatience resolves 458
- Impatient 459
- Impatient of absence 251, 253
- Impatient resolves 458
- Impending Death 757
- Imperfection 449
- Imperial 209, 475
- Imperishability of Life 937
- Imperishable 114
- Implicitly 757
- Importance 897
- Importunity 084
- Imprudence 097
- Impulsive acts of love 407, 927
- Impulsiveness 433

- In Love 209
- In love 156
- In love Desire 155
- In waiting 052
- Incarceration 305
- Inconstancy 165
- Inconstancy 490, 533, 534, 611, 708
- Incorruptibility 183
- Incorruptible 183
- Increases physical beauty 149
- Indecision 757
- Independence 170, 715, 737, 901, 902
- Independent 715
- Indifference 134, 143, 258, 324, 453, 454, 934
- Indiscretion 072, 157, 666, 720, 901
- Indolence 579
- Industry 618, 619, 888, 902
- Inevitability 726
- Infatuation 397, 423, 862
- Infertility 478, 757, 764
- Ingeniousness 298
- Ingenuity 069, 232
- Ingenuous simplicity 193
- Ingratitude 151, 738, 739, 742, 769
- Initiation 125, 800, 935
- Initiative 069
- Injustice 177, 441
- Inner beauty 593
- Innocence 053, 120, 229, 300, 371, 394, 409, 439, 507, 757, 759, 927
- Insincerity 304, 717
- Insinuation 153
- Inspiration 066, 075, 362, 416, 800

- Inspiration for love 772
- Inspire me 066
- Inspires artistry 916
- Inspires creativity 916
- Instability 287
- Instills a love of and for learning 916
- Instruction 588
- Insult 202
- Integrity 041, 397
- Intellect 478
- Intellectual beauty 484
- Intellectual excellence 263
- Intellectual greatness 419, 751
- Intelligence 717, 800, 902
- Intemperance 935
- Interest 803
- Intoxicating 925
- Intoxication of love 422
- Intrinsic worth 389
- Intuition 800
- Invasion 510
- Invitation 741, 932
- Irony 741
- Irresistibility 224
- Irresistible love 897
- It's Heavenly to be with you 512
- I'll still be waiting 107
- I'm going to get you 313
- I'm not proud 659
- I'm sorry 433

J
- Jealousy 147, 148, 310, 433, 757, 764, 864, 866
- Jest 092
- Jesting 092
- Job well done 757

580, 623, 669, 757, 766, 883
- Lust 011, 144, 218, 307, 897
- Lustful bed partner 092
- Lusty love 073
- Luxury 018, 156, 177

M
- Magic 629, 757
- Magic spell 410
- Magical 148
- Magnificence 512, 549, 622, 853
- Magnificent beauty 947
- Maiden charms 343
- Majestic 757
- Majestic Beauty 947
- Majesty 372, 512
- Make beautiful that which is beautiful 291
- Make haste 298
- Male energy 266
- Malevolence 527
- Manifestation 001, 246
- Manipulation 702
- Manners 320
- Man's symbol 455
- Marital happiness 848
- Marriage 229, 412, 592, 733, 807, 883
- Masculine energy 155, 156, 757
- Masculinity 632
- Material wealth 477
- Maternal affection 704
- Maternal love 141, 144, 896, 900
- Maternal tenderness 630

- Matrimony 412, 686, 883
- Matronly grace 181
- Mature charm 408, 622
- Mature charms 180
- Mature elegance 733
- May you be happy 936
- Meanness 277
- Meditation 002, 362
- Meekness 125, 935
- Meeting 496
- Melancholy 112, 392, 501, 646, 647, 789
- Melancholy mind 650
- Memories 587, 923, 924, 954
- Memories beyond reach 954
- Memories beyond your reach 954
- Memories of childhood 738, 739
- Memories of those who died 539
- Memory 654, 662, 773, 800, 862, 931
- Memory of The Garden of Eden 592
- Mental beauty 232, 484, 745
- Mental powers 935
- Mere display 598
- Merit 708
- Merit reward 497
- Merriment 074, 348, 931
- Merry heart 798
- Message 468
- Messenger of love 757
- Messengers 938
- Metaphysics 789
- Mildness 510, 556

- Mirth 268, 441, 592
- Misanthropy 010, 220, 310, 425, 520, 582
- Misery 005, 419, 751
- Misfortune 200, 300
- Mistake 620
- Mistrust 498
- Mockery 812
- Modest 115
- Modest beauty 891
- Modest gain 847
- Modest genius 847
- Modest merit 472, 592, 708, 712, 929
- Modesty 105, 386, 409, 477, 512, 577, 608, 757, 926, 927, 928, 947
- Momentary happiness 886
- Money 524, 592, 623, 699, 829, 863, 916, 923, 924, 935
- Monstrosity 150
- Moonlit beauty 448
- Moral and mental beauty 745
- Moral beauty 745
- Moral integrity 397
- Most beautiful 633
- Most effective healer 041
- Motherhood 429, 554, 787
- Mother's Day symbol 300
- Mother's love 300
- Mother's undying love 300
- Mourning 189, 275, 757, 789
- Music 097, 113, 666
- Musical 097
- Musical 113
- Musical voice 666

- Mutual love 054
- My Heart Dreams come to fruition 144
- My ambitious love plagues itself 374
- My best days are gone 243
- My best days are past 243
- My best days fled 243
- My compliments 468
- My divinity 312
- My happy days are past 243
- My heart aches for you 300
- My heart is yours 724
- My love has ended 501
- My perfect lover 897
- My regrets follow you to the grave 104
- Mysteriousness 733
- Mystery 304, 598, 757, 834
- Mythology 829

N
- Naiveté 087
- Native grace 312
- Natural 552
- Natural beauty 200
- Neglected genius 708
- Never 072
- Never ceasing memory 403
- Never ceasing remembrance 403
- Never despair 684
- Never fading flower 050
- Never to meet again 543

- Remembering 396, 587
- Remembering an absent friend 954
- Remembrance 001, 362, 397, 521, 596, 637, 773, 931
- Remembrances 587
- Reminder of young loveYouthful inno-cence 862
- Remorse 775
- Rendezvous 058, 097, 116, 638
- Renewal 125, 593, 795, 925
- Repelling monsters 537
- Repose 461, 574
- Renown 497
- Resentment 659
- Reserve 006
- Resignation 278, 896
- Resilience 001
- Resistance 309
- Respect 593, 682, 757
- Rest 916
- Restraint 863
- Restful sleep 881
- Restoration 655
- Restore balance of domestic power 773
- Resurrection 003, 269, 598, 733, 897
- Resurrection and Heavenly bliss 269
- Resurrection and Rebirth 593
- Resurrection of Christ 497
- Retaliation 170, 617
- Retirement 160
- Retribution 535
- Return my affection 594

- Return of happiness 249
- Returning joy 390
- Reveals the inner self 149
- Revenge 512, 535, 887, 888
- Reverence 757
- Reverie 629,
- Reward of merit 497, 757
- Reward of virtue 757
- Riches 155, 156, 724, 738, 739, 895, 950
- Riches and honor 632
- Righteousness 733
- Rigor 492, 878
- Rivalry 336
- Romance 073, 115, 149, 532, 609, 757, 759, 897
- Romance's sur-prises 853
- Romantic love 757
- Romantic thoughts 931
- Roughness 163
- Roving 505
- Royalty 067, 819
- Rudeness 084, 127, 382, 943
- Rupture 692
- Rupture of a con-tract 852
- Rural felicity 935
- Rural happiness 526, 929
- Rustic beauty 413
- Rustic oracle 872
- Rusticity 312
- Ruthlessness 446

S
- Sacred 609
- Sacred affection 147, 865

- Sacred love 592
- Sacred to fairies 169
- Sacred tree 362
- Sacredness 362
- Sad memories 015
- Sadness 392, 433, 501, 789
- Safe 044
- Safety 916
- Sanctuary 293
- Sardonicism 812
- Satire 122, 621
- Satisfaction 708, 712
- Scandal 424
- Scarcity 560
- Scent of The Gar-den of Eden 592
- Scholastic achievement 053
- Science 800
- Scorn 299, 741
- Scorned in love 209
- Scornful beauty 280, 776
- Scornful laughter 741
- Scratch my itch 857
- Screaming 560
- Sculpture 440
- Sea 800
- Secrecy 014, 757
- Secret 698
- Secret bond of love 014
- Secret love 003, 383, 504, 537, 568, 757
- Security 023, 221, 916
- Seduction 092
- Self concept 593
- Self sacrifice 539
- Self-control 554
- Self-esteem 300, 593, 738, 739

- Self-love 593, 596
- Self-preservation 800
- Self-sacrifice 952
- Self-seeking 234
- Self-willed 133
- Selfishness 596
- Semblance 918
- Send a warning 119
- Sensibility 577, 916
- Sensitiveness 003, 577, 916
- Sensitivity 577
- Sensuality 073, 476, 554, 897
- Sentimental love 300
- Separation 093, 138, 161, 386
- Serenade 076
- Serenity 071
- Severity 492, 878
- Sex 073, 144
- Sexual attraction 043
- Sexual attractive-ness 043
- Sexuality 073
- Shame 632
- Sharpness 122
- Sharpness of tem-per 122
- She loves you 461
- Shelter 629
- Shocking occur-rence 094
- Shrewdness 782
- Shy 053
- Shyness 053, 577, 632, 921
- Sickness 062, 063, 064, 952
- Sighing 702
- Sign 082
- Silence 110, 757
- Silent love 611, 708
- Silliness 019, 185, 646

419

- Welcome to a stranger 846, 858
- Well done 757
- Whimsical 300
- Whimsy 580
- Why are you crying? 038
- Wickedness replacing love 560
- Widowhood 188, 806
- Wild speculation 897
- Will banish sadness 626
- Will bring peaceful thoughts 327
- Will you dance with me? 932
- Will you help me 952
- Will you meet me 638
- Will you smile 299
- Willful promises 461
- Wilt you go with me 495
- Win me 285
- Win me and wear me 285
- Winning grace 312
- Winter 919
- Wisdom 041, 069, 078, 106, 362, 455, 468, 570, 583, 584, 622, 629, 720, 793, 800
- Wish 304
- Wish magic 872
- Wishes 116, 800, 872
- Wishes come true 872
- Wishes will be fulfilled 569
- Wishes will come true 149

- Wishing For Love 872
- Wishing for wealth 151
- Wistfulness 757
- Wit 424, 541, 780
- Witching soul of music 113
- With me you are safe 835
- Withered hopes 062, 063, 283
- Without pretension 157, 767
- Woman 708
- Womanhood 115
- Woman's love 300
- Women 711
- Wonder 757
- Woodwind 097
- Words though sweet may deceive 483
- Worldliness 234
- Worth 745
- Worth and loveliness 745
- Worth beyond beauty 048
- Worth sustained by judicious and tender affection 461
- Worthiness 757
- Worthy of all praise 365
- Wound to heal 770
- Writing 053

X

Y

- Yearning for a long-lost Paradise 640
- Yes 300
- You are a lover of nature 549
- You are all that is lovely 764

- You are beautiful 757
- You are better than handsome 500, 745
- You are cold 446
- You are fair 298
- You are in my thoughts 931
- You are lovely 383
- You are merry 765
- You are my divinity 312
- You are my life 730
- You are near a snare 313
- You are perfect 059
- You are radiant with charm 739
- You are rich in attractions 739
- You are the only one I love 080
- You are the queen of coquettes 431
- You are too bold 559
- You are young and beautiful 759
- You cannot deceive me 519
- You change your mind too much 581
- You enchant me 916
- You have a false friend 369
- You have as many virtues as this daisy has petals 120
- You have beautiful eyes 897
- You have disappointed me 300
- You have my love 208
- You have no claims 640, 731
- You left me 144
- You may hope 757

- You occupy my thoughts 931
- You pierce my heart 397
- You please all 752, 753
- You please me 752, 753
- You puzzle me 602
- You weary me 084
- You will be my death 247
- You will be rich 895
- You will cause my death 247
- You will succeed 256
- You'll always be beautiful to me 564, 565
- Your Determination 660
- You're a flame in my heart 156
- You're a flame in my heart Desire 155
- You're a wonderful friend 209
- You're Heavenly 757
- You're lovely 383
- You're so Lovely 757
- Young brides 724
- Young girl 759
- Young Love 708
- Young when old 919
- Your are charming 506
- Your charms are graven on my heart 344
- Your devout admirer 415
- Your disapproval will kill me 752, 753
- Your friendship is agreeable to me 940

420

- Your Friendship means so much to me 468
- Your frown will kill me 752, 753
- Your hand for next dance 649
- Your image is engraved on my heart 344
- Your looks freeze me 576
- Your love is given back 054
- Your love is reciprocated 054, 204
- Your love is returned to you 054
- Your next dance is with me 649
- Your presence soothes me 659
- Your purity equals your loveliness 229
- Your qualities and charms are unequaled 724
- Your qualities surpass your charms 745
- Your simple elegance charms me 244
- Your temper is too hasty 264, 482
- Your unhappiness will kill me 752, 753
- Your whims are quite unbearable 581
- Your whims are unbearable 581
- Youth 304, 512, 592, 708, 757, 759, 862, 916, 939
- Youthful beauty 312
- Youthful gladness 269
- Youthful innocence 862

- Youthful looks 862
- Youthful love 822
- Youthfulness 757
- You're adorable 156
- You're adorable Desire 155
- You're a wonderful friend 209
- You're elegant 033
- You're late 211
- You're perfect 033
- You're perfect and elegant 033
- You're the only one 593
- You've made my life complete 249

Z
- Zeal 096, 795
- Zealousness 795
- Zest 228, 385

Possible Powers

A
- A Charm against The Evil Eye 498
- A sense of well-being 127
- A talisman of Love 106
- Ability to recognize witches 631
- Ability to see fairies 881
- Ability to see invisible demons 631
- Abundance 003, 023, 044, 060, 069, 128, 218, 480, 497, 567, 591, 680, 691,

736, 773, 856, 863, 911
- Abuse 268
- Accidents 044, 315, 609, 669, 671, 675, 691, 729, 809
- Advancement 003, 044, 069, 128, 218, 480, 497, 591, 680, 691, 736, 773, 856, 863, 911
- Adventurousness 053
- Afterlife 104
- Aggression 044, 315, 609, 669, 671, 675, 691, 729, 809
- Agitation 577
- Ambition 432, 637, 720, 905
- Amorousness 147
- Anger 044, 315, 609, 669, 671, 675, 691, 729, 809
- Animal communications 007
- Animal healing 236
- Anti-Lightning 260
- Anti-Lightning 455
- Anti-fire 494
- Anti-hunger 567
- Anti-theft 037, 174, 212, 274, 285, 480, 494, 699, 702
- Antidote for magic potions 092
- Aphrodisiac 037, 074, 164, 226, 255, 268, 325, 396, 487, 547, 560, 573, 589, 593, 624, 641, 653, 670, 676, 696, 716, 733, 881, 899
- Applying knowledge 047, 387, 906, 912
- Appreciation of nature 663
- Aromatic 590
- Artistic ability 791

- Arts 008, 043, 803, 876
- Assistance 075, 170, 220, 236, 592, 617, 811, 827
- Astral plane 047, 387, 906, 912
- Astral projection 095, 110, 426, 624, 677, 699, 702
- Astral travel 125, 856
- Attitude 432, 637, 720, 905
- Attract Good spirits 047
- Attract love 029, 096
- Attract prosperity 061
- Attraction 008, 043, 095, 172, 212, 508, 599, 717, 729, 803, 871, 876, 881, 905, 928, 930
- Attracts and repels energies 455
- Attracts good fortune 077
- Attracts love 077
- Authority 468
- Avoiding spirits 357
- Avoids military service 631

B
- Balance 010, 074, 563
- Banish entities 025
- Banish negative energies and entities 726
- Banish negative energy 025
- Banish negative spirits 054
- Banish negativity 134
- Banishes evil 791

- Banishes negative energy 924
- Banishes negativity 791
- Banishing 003, 571, 749
- Barrier against negative energies 025
- Beautification 745
- Beauty 008, 014, 043, 095, 172, 212, 335, 524, 599, 634, 653, 717, 729, 757, 803, 871, 876, 881, 905, 928, 930
- Beneficence 047
- Best friends 946
- Binding 049, 141, 246, 346, 379, 456, 480, 570, 591, 656, 691, 697, 702, 733, 856
- Binding magical works 696
- Binding sacred oaths 696
- Binding spells 697
- Bindings 788
- Black Magic 560
- Black magick 812
- Blessing 788
- Bondage 812
- Break hexes 045, 072, 116, 167, 170, 212, 236, 345, 346, 387, 446, 809, 909
- Breaking hexes 384
- Breaking love spells 512, 681
- Breaks hexes 025, 030, 389, 466, 589, 667, 691, 783
- Brings good luck 041
- Brings in money 567
- Building 246, 346, 456, 480, 570, 591, 656, 691, 702, 856
- Bulletproofing 503
- Business 335, 477, 498, 670, 704, 736, 791, 793, 844
- Business transactions 174, 401, 498, 542, 624, 658, 670, 856, 911

C

- Call in Good Spirits 498, 670
- Calling Spirits 093, 624, 872, 914
- Calling in good spirits 070, 205
- Calm anger 048
- Calming 069
- Calms tempers 926
- Carnal desires 044, 315, 609, 669, 671, 675, 691, 729, 809
- Cat magic 599
- Caution 174, 401, 498, 560, 658, 670, 856
- Caution 911
- Celebration 049, 784
- Change 141, 241
- Changing sex 307
- Charity 141
- Charm against The Devil 631
- Charm against The Evil Eye 498
- Charm against dangerous creatures, both real and imagined 631
- Charm against snakes 631
- Charm against witches 631
- Chastity 144, 217, 238, 266, 272, 334, 489, 496, 498
- Childbearing 487
- Clairaudience 072
- Clairvoyance 497
- Cleanses the aura 791, 793
- Cleansing 149
- Clear thinking 432, 637, 720, 905
- Cleverness 174, 401, 498, 542, 624, 658, 670, 856, 911
- Comfort 275
- Commitment 379
- Communication 174, 401, 498, 542, 624, 658, 670, 856, 911
- Concentration 074
- Conception 818
- Conception by way of spell casting 560
- Confidence 466
- Conflict 044, 315, 609, 669, 671, 675, 691, 729, 809
- Conscious will 003, 044, 069, 128, 218, 480, 497, 591, 680, 691, 736, 773, 856, 863, 911
- Consecration 571, 696, 791, 887, 888
- Constancy 416
- Contemplation 163
- Continuity 266
- Contraception 487
- Controlling lower principles 047, 387, 906, 912
- Counters vibrations that drain down 799
- Courage 008, 012, 054, 066, 078, 108, 118, 127, 141, 161, 241, 311, 345, 365, 450, 496, 503, 667, 881, 914
- Creative power 733
- Creativity 174, 346, 401, 498, 542, 624, 658, 670, 856, 911
- Cure for heartache 008, 908
- Cure for werewolves 010
- Cures the tendency to have bad dreams 182
- Curse breaking 480, 907
- Curses 357

D

- Daring 503
- Death 104, 184, 207, 246, 266, 292, 346, 449, 456, 480, 560, 570, 591, 600, 656, 691, 702, 796, 830, 856
- Death and Revival 433
- Declaration of religiousness 947
- Deep loyalty 416
- Delays sexual maturity 433
- Destiny 207
- Destroys the libido 247
- Deter evil 661
- Determining guilt 020
- Devilry 812
- Dexterity 297
- Diminish sorrow by causing forgetfulness 429
- Diminishes the libido 247
- Direction 861
- Dispels anger 093
- Dispels melancholy 617

- Spiritual growth 207
- Spirituality 004, 035, 077, 128, 218, 268, 383, 390, 591, 598, 607, 786, 947
- Stability 075, 170, 220, 236, 592, 617, 811, 827
- Stamina 191
- Stimulation 339
- Stirring up agitation 749
- Strength 044, 066, 072, 075, 095, 161, 170, 220, 236, 268, 300, 315, 326, 365, 450, 466, 496, 497, 571, 584, 592, 601, 609, 617, 669, 671, 675, 683, 691, 729, 803, 809, 811, 827, 873
- Strengthening spells 326
- Strong mental powers 478
- Struggle 044, 315, 609, 669, 671, 675, 691, 729, 809
- Subconscious mind 011, 217, 270, 477, 500, 688, 773, 794
- Success 003, 044, 069, 128, 218, 224, 319, 335, 345, 466, 480, 497, 498, 569, 591, 670, 680, 691, 704, 736, 773, 791, 793, 833, 834, 844, 855, 856, 863, 887, 888, 911
- Success in business 471, 818
- Success in business ventures 720
- Sudden death 560
- Supernatural forces 916

- Survival 065
- Sustenance 416, 419
- Swiftness 295

T
- Talisman of Love 106
- Teeth 816
- Tenacity 075, 170, 220, 236, 379, 592, 617, 811, 827
- The Arts 008, 043, 095, 172, 212, 599, 717, 729, 871, 876, 881, 905, 928, 930
- Thicken 561
- Thievery 174, 401, 498, 542, 624, 658, 670, 856, 911
- Thought processes 432, 637, 720, 905
- Tides 011, 217, 270, 477, 500, 688, 773, 794
- Time 246, 346, 456, 480, 570, 591, 656, 691, 702, 856
- Trances 697
- Tranquility 069
- Transformation 554
- Transmutation 945
- Travel 570, 856
- Travel by water 011, 217, 270, 477, 500, 688, 773, 794
- Traveler's luck 337
- Truth 160, 184, 350, 512, 830
- Turns away evil 030

U
- Un-reciprocated love magic 733
- Uncovering secrets 047, 387, 906, 912
- Union 286
- Unrequited love 037

- Uprightness 281

V
- Victory 047, 141, 241, 380, 387, 873, 906
- Virginity 783
- Virility 255, 365, 889
- Virtue 573
- Visions 066, 110, 163, 260, 269, 677, 775, 776, 777, 834, 899, 900
- Vivid exposure of one's own pomposity 150

W
- War 044, 315, 609, 669, 675, 691, 729, 809
- Ward off evil spirits 092
- Ward off incubi 676
- Ward off negativity 497
- Ward off plague 723
- Warding off inappropriate suitors 149
- Wards away evil spirits 452
- Wards off The Evil Eye 037, 167, 320, 670, 683
- Wards off disasters of all types 066
- Wards off evil 004, 037, 065, 497
- Wards off evil magic 497, 066, 087, 167, 346, 842, 843, 844
- Wards off fire 815
- Wards off illness 037
- Wards off lightning 497, 815

- Wards off lightning strikes 066
- Wards off vampires 037
- Wards off werewolves 037
- Wards off witchcraft 025, 087
- Wards off witchery 815
- Warmth 416
- Wart Charming 661
- Wealth 017, 046, 133, 155, 294, 296, 335, 422, 423, 471, 477, 498, 609, 670, 704, 733, 736, 791, 793, 844, 855, 890, 900
- Weather-working 149
- Wind raising 268
- Wisdom 174, 362, 401, 416, 419, 468, 469, 470, 497, 498, 560, 658, 670, 720, 791, 793, 856, 911
- Wish magic 149, 416, 419
- Wish that things had turned out differently 106
- Wishes 020, 116, 171, 242, 257, 258, 259, 260, 311, 346, 416, 419, 478, 634, 679, 724, 733, 746, 791, 793, 872, 927, 928, 929, 930
- Witch Flight 609
- Witchcraft 219, 449, 560, 723
- Witchery 560
- Wolf bait 357
- Women's power 916
- Worldly success 041
- Worship 688, 873

Bibliography

Acamovic, T., Stewart, C.S., Pennycott, T.W.,"Poisonous Plants and Related Toxins", 2004

American Herbal Products Association's botanical safety handbook, By American Herbal Products Association, Michael McGuffin

Australian National Herbarium: Australian national Botanic Gardens, Australian Biological Resources Study Databases, cpbr.gov.au

Bailey, L.H.; Bailey, E.Z.; the staff of the Liberty Hyde Bailey Hortorium. ,. Hortus third: A concise dictionary of plants cultivated in the United States and Canada. Macmillan, New York.1976

Baynes, Thomas Spencer; Kellogg, Day Otis; Smith, William Robertson ,. The Encyclopædia Britannica 1897

Behind The Name: The Etymology and History of First Names, behindthename.com

Beyerl, Paul; A Compendium of Herbal Magick

Biodiversity Hertiage Library, Botony, biodiversitylibrary.org

Blanchan, Neltje,. Wild Flowers Worth Knowing, 2005

Brickell, Christopher,The Royal Horticultural Society A–Z Encyclopedia of Garden Plants,, Dorling Kindersley, London, 1996

Botanical.com, botanical.com

Buhner, Stephen Harrod; Sacred Plant Medicine

Chauncey, Mary, ed. The Floral Gift, from Nature and the Heart. New York: Leavitt & Allen, 1853

Coats, Alice M., Garden Shrubs and Their Histories 1964

Coombes, Allen J., The Collingridge Dictionary of Plant Names, 1985

Connecticut Botanical Society, ct-botanical-society .org

Cullina,William, New England Wildflower Society guide to growing and propagating wildflowers of the United States and Canada, New England Wildflower Society, Houghton Mifflin Harcourt, 2000

Culpeper, The Complete Herbal 1652, bibliomania.com

Cunningham, Scott; Magickal Herbalism

Cunningham, Scott;Cunningham's Encyclopedia of Magical Herbs

Delaware Valley Unit of The Herb Society of America, herbsocietydelawarevalleyunit.org

Dobelis, Inge N.; Magic and Medicine of Plants

eFloras.org, efloras.org

Encycloweedia, California Department of Food and Agriculture, cdfa.ca.gov/plantcommname .htm

Factbites, "Floriography", factbites.com/topics/Floriography

Fairchild Tropical Botanic Garden, fairchildgarden.org

Flora of China, Harvard University. 2007

Francis, Rose,. The Wild Flower Key. Frederick Warne & Co 1981

Greenaway, Kate; "Language of Flowers";1901; London/New York; F. Warne;

Grieve, Maud; A Modern Herbal, Vol 1 & 2

Gualtiero Simonetti,. Stanley Schuler. ed. Simon & Schuster's Guide to Herbs and Spices. Simon & Schuster, Inc,, 1990

Harner, Michael J, . Hallucinogens and Shamanism. Oxford [Oxfordshire]: Oxford University Press. 1973

Hazlitt, William Carew; Brand, John (1905). Faiths and Folklore and Facts: a dictionary of national beliefs. New York: Charles Scribner's Sons

Harvard University Herbaria, kiki.huh.harvard.edu/ databases/botanist_index .html

Hoffman, David; The Complete Illustrated Holistic Herbal

Howard, Michael. Traditional Folk remedies., Century, 1987,

Hutchens, Alma R.; Indian Herbalogy

Huxley, Anthony, Griffiths, Mark, and Levy, Margot,. The New Royal Horticultural Society Dictionary of Gardening. The Macmillan Press,Limited: London. The Stockton Press: New York.1992

Ildrewe, Miss; "The Language of Flowers"; 1865; Boston; De Vries, Ibarra

Ingram, John;"The Language of Flowers; or, Flora Symbolica. Including Floral Poetry, Original and Selecte"; 1897; London/New York; Frederick Warne and Company

James A. Duke, Peggy-Ann K. Duke, Judith L. duCellie, . Duke's Handbook of Medicinal Plants of the Bible 2007

Johnson, A.T. & Smith, H.A., Plant Names Simplified, 1964

Kew Royal Botanic Gardens: World Checklist of Selected Plant Families,

Kilmer,.John, The Perennial Encyclopedia 1989

Kepler, Angela Kay,. Hawaiian Heritage Plants. University of Hawaii Press. 1998

Lad, Dr. Vasant K.; Ayurveda: The Science of Self-Healing

Large List Of Species: Plants, nic.funet.fi/pub/sci/bio/life/plants/index.html

Leighton, Ann, American Gardens in the Eighteenth Century: 'For Use or Delight' , 1976

Llewellyn's Herbal Almanac by Llewellyn 2010

Lust, John, N.D, The Herb Book. Bantam Books 1979

McGuffin, Michael; American Herbal Products Association's botanical safety handbook, By American Herbal Products Association

Mehl-Madrona, Lewis, M.D.; Coyote Medicine

Missouri Botanical Garden, missouribotanicalgarden.org/gardens-gardening

Occult 100 Search Archive, occult100.com/bos/herbsbypower.html

Ody, Penelope; The Complete Medicinal Herbal

Parsons' Hand-Book of Forms: A Compendium of Business and Social Rules and a Complete Work of Reference and Self-Instruction, with Illustrations, 13th ed. Battle Creek, MI: The Central Manufacturing Co., 1899.

Peterson, Roger Tory; Margaret McKenny,. A Field Guide to Wildflowers of Northeastern and North-central North America. Boston: Houghton Mifflin Company. 1968

Phillips, Edward, The New World of Words., 1720

Philips, Roger, Trees of North America and Europe, Random House, Inc., New York, 1979

Pierre Delforge, Orchids of Europe, North Africa And the Middle East - 2006, Timber Press

Plants of Greek Myth, theoi.com/Flora1.html

Plants For A Future: Earth, Plants, People, pfaf.org

Puri, H.S, Neem: The Divine Tree Azadirachta indica. 1999

Robinson, Nugent. Collier's Cyclopedia of Commercial and Social Information and Treasury of Useful and Entertaining Knowledge. New York: P. F. Collier, Publisher, 1892

Rushforth, K.,. Trees of Britain and Europe. Collins , 1999

Simoons, Frederick, Plants of life, plants of death. Univ of Wisconsin Press.1998

Smithsonian Naational Museum of Natural History: Botony, Index Nominum Genericorum (ING), botany.si.edu/ing/

Sunset Western Garden Books

Surburg, Horst; Johannes Panten, . Common Fragrance and Flavor Materials: Preparation, Properties and Uses 2006

Taylor, Gladys,. Saints and their Flowers. London, England: A. R. Mowbray & Co., Oxford,1956

Tyas, Robert; "The Language of Flowers, or, Floral Emblems of Thoughts, Feelings, and Sentiments";1869; London/New York; G. Routledge;

Tutin, T.G., Flora Europaea, second edition - 1993

USDA, United States Department of Aagriculture, Natural Resources Conservation Service,

Waterman, Catharine H.; "Flora's Lexicon: An Interpretation of the Language and Sentiment of Flowers with an outline of botany and a poetical introduction"; 1855; Boston; Philips, Sampson;

Wichtl, Max,Herbal drugs and phytopharmaceuticals: a handbook,2004

Wikipedia: The Free Encyclopedia, wikipedia.org

Wood, John; Hardy Perennials and Old Fashioned Flowers, 2006

Small floral sprig images included in the alphabetical opening illustrations at the beginnings of flower sections A thru Z were originally part a portion of scientific botanical illustrations by the following botanical illustrators/illustrations:

Curtis, William; *born: 1746 died: 1799*; Z - includes part of a botanical illustration of *Zinnia*

Edwards, John; *born: 1742 died: 1815*; F - includes part of a botanical illustration of *Fritillaria imperialis*

Edwards, Sydenham Teast ; *born: 1768 died: 1819*; P - includes part of a botanical illustration of *Protea cynaroides*

Huysum, Jacob van; *born: 1689 died: 1740*; V - includes part of a botanical illustration of *Viburnum tinus*

Lindman, Carl Axel Magnus; *born: 1856 died: 1928*; I - includes part of a botanical illustration of *Iris persica*, U - - part of botanical illustration of *Ulmus glabra*

Köhler, Hermann Adolph; *born: 1834 died: 1879*; A - includes part of a botanical illustration of *Angelica archangelica*, B - includes part of a botanical illustration of *Boswellia sacra*, C - includes part of a botanical illustration of *Citrus x aurantium*, D - includes part of a botanical illustration of *Daphne mezereum*, E - includes part of a botanical illustration of *Erythroxylum coca*, G - includes part of a botanical illustration of *Glycyrrhiza glabra*, O - includes part of a botanical illustration of *Olea europaea*, Q - includes part of a botanical illustration of *Quassia amara*, R - includes part of a botanical illustration of *Rosa centifolia*, S - includes part of a botanical illustration of *Syzygium aromaticum,* T - includes part of a botanical illustration of *Taraxacum officinale;* also, included within the front cover's bouqet image are *Olea europaea* and *Rosa centifolia*

Paxton, Joseph; *born: 1803 died: 1865*; K - includes part of a botanical illustration of *Kennedia coccinea*

Redouté, Pierre Joseph; *born: 1759 died: 1840*; H - includes part of a botanical illustration of Hyacinth, J - includes part of a botanical illustration of *Jasmine* gradiflorum, L -includes part of a botanical illustration of *Lilium superbum*, Y - includes part of a botanical illustration of *Yucca gloriosa*

Rowan, Ellis; *born: 1847 died: 1922*; W - includes part of a botanical illustration of *Wisteria frutescens*

Step, Edward; *born: 1835 died: 1931*; X - includes part of a botanical illustration of *Xeranthemum annum*

Winkler, Eduard; *born: 1799 died: 1862*; N - includes part of a botanical illustration of *Narcissus*

The Magic Flower

THROUGH many days and many days
The seed of love lay hidden close;
We walked the dusty tiresome ways
Where never a leaf or blossom grows.

And in the darkness, all the while,
The little seed its heart uncurled,
And we by many a weary mile
Travelled towards it, round the world.

To the hid centre of the maze
At last we came, and there we found —
O happy day, O day of days!
— Twin seed-leaves breaking holy ground.

We dropped life's joys, a garnered sheaf,
And spell-bound watched, still hour by hour,
Magic on magic, leaf by leaf,
The unfolding of our love's white flower.

Edith Nesbit
1858 – 1924

Made in the USA
Lexington, KY
26 April 2014